Myths, Muses and Mortals

MYTHS, MUSES AND MORTALS

THE WAY OF LIFE IN ANCIENT GREECE

WILLIAM FURLEY

REAKTION BOOKS

ΘΕΟΙΣ

Published by
REAKTION BOOKS LTD
Unit 32, Waterside
44–48 Wharf Road
London N1 7UX, UK
www.reaktionbooks.co.uk

First published 2024

Printed and bound in Great Britain by TJ Books Ltd, Padstow, Cornwall

A catalogue record for this book is available from the British Library

ISBN 978 1 78914 917 3

Contents

INTRODUCTION

There is good reason to be interested in ancient Greece nowadays. Almost everyone has heard of some legendary period of ancient history called 'Classical Greece', and even those who have had no Latin or Greek during their education will have picked up quite a lot of incidental knowledge about ancient Greece from various media sources, whether film, television documentaries, the printed word, holidays, commerce (such as Hermes parcel delivery service or Pegasus Air), art, photography, architecture, possibly even religion. Large abstracts like 'freedom', 'democracy', 'justice', 'philosophy' and 'tragedy' may be associated with ancient Greece in people's imagination. This book is for people who have no more knowledge of 'Classics' than these generalities but feel curiosity about who these Greeks were, what they were thinking about and how their lives may have differed from ours.

What is ancient Greece geographically? It differed from modern Greece in being more widely spread. Taking the modern map of Greece, we need to extend east into Turkey, as the western seaboard of Asia Minor was colonized by Ionian Greeks from the eleventh century BC, and west as far as Sicily and southern Italy, an area that came to be known as Magna Graecia.[1] This area was also Hellenized by Greek city-states sending out colonies from the eighth century BC on. We must also range north into what is now Macedonia and Bulgaria and along the southern coast of the Black Sea, where there were also Greek colonies extending as far as modern Georgia. And Greece positively exploded in the late fourth century BC when Alexander ('the Great', king of Macedon) conquered a vast swathe of territory extending through Persia to India, and round the Mediterranean through Syria, Palestine, Arabia and Egypt (334–323 BC). Following that, there were several centuries when Greek became the common language and culture of the whole Mediterranean area. The Greek spoken then (by foreigners in this sphere of influence as well as Greeks) was called *koinē*, the common language, much as English has now become a *koinē* in many countries of the world, as were French during the eighteenth and nineteenth centuries and Russian throughout the Soviet Union. Then, from the first century BC, the Romans extended their rule from Italy all round the Mediterranean lands. Interestingly, they did not dispel Greek as a language and culture but rather absorbed it into the Roman Empire. Many Romans were bilingual. Roman literature – what used to be painstakingly taught as Latin in schools – is unthinkable without the Greek models, and the Romans were quite happy to acknowledge their vast cultural debt to the urbane Greeks. The word 'urbane' itself, *urbanus*, is a translation of the Greek *asteios*, meaning 'of the town' (*asty*).

So this ancient Greek culture existed over 2,000 years ago. In fact, it began approximately 1,000 years before Europeans begin counting AD (or CE). Greek appears to have been spoken already in Greece in the so-called Bronze Age (when tools were made of bronze: down to *c.* 1200 BC) as baked clay tablets inscribed with signs were deciphered by an architect-linguist in London in the 1950s, Michael Ventris (1922–1956), as being Greek written in a syllabic script (a sign-persyllable, as opposed to a sign-per-letter): so-called Linear B. This Bronze Age culture was called Mycenaean by archaeologists after a main centre, Mycenae, in the Peloponnese. It was from Mycenae under its kings Agamemnon and Menelaos that the Greek fleet set off to reclaim Helen, who in the story had been abducted by a Trojan, Paris, precipitating the Trojan War. Again, this is something that is a concept to many nowadays, even if they have never encountered a word of 'Homer', the Greek poet who composed an epic about it, probably around 800 BC. The famous Greek cities (*poleis*) – Corinth, Athens, Sparta, Thebes, to name perhaps the best known – had their heyday several centuries later than this, in the sixth to the fourth centuries BC. What came to be known as Classics is basically the study of the literature, art, history and philosophy of fifth- and fourth-century Athens, where most of the Greek works of literature, philosophy and drama were written. Then, for the sake of schematizing, we have a period known as Hellenistic (roughly coinciding with the period of the *koinē*), lasting down to the expansion of Roman rule, followed by the Roman imperial period.

Was Greece a unity then, as one thinks of modern Greece as one country and one people? Well, the various cities and areas shared a language (Greek), as opposed to, say, Egyptian (demotic) or Persian, but the language was in fact significantly diverse in terms of regional dialects. Not only were vocabulary, pronunciation and grammar of these Greek dialects quite distinct, they also led to 'ethnic' divisions. Ionians felt different to Dorians; Aeolians, Boeotians, Thessalians all celebrated their own ethnicity. And there were pockets of non-Greek-speaking peoples left in Greece: Sikels in Sicily, and Pelasgians on the island of Lemnos, for example. The most significant divide was between Dorians and Ionians, who felt like separate peoples, even if they could more or less understand each other. The Athenian comic poet Aristophanes in one of his plays makes fun of a very Spartan-speaking diplomat who has come to Athens. And in a later comedy by Menander, a doctor uses the dialect commonly spoken by his fellow practitioners, again to comic effect. Much more seriously, one of the famous wars, the Peloponnesian War fought between Athens and Sparta in the fifth century BC, fell along the dividing line between Ionian (the dialect to which Attic, spoken in Athens, belongs) and its ideology, and Doric, embodying Spartan ideology. When we read Herodotus, the 'Father of History', we see that the Greek city-states in the sixth and fifth centuries were anything but united: rather they were constantly warring against each other or engaged in rivalries bordering on war. It was only with a huge effort, and then only partially, that some Greek cities managed to come together in the early fifth century to fight off the threat of Persian dominion in the so-called Persian Wars. A good half of the Greek cities sided with Xerxes, the Persian commander, admittedly under duress, and fought against their fellow Greeks.

LONGITUDE EAST OF GREENWICH
WESTERMANN'S CLASSICAL AND HISTORICAL MAP SERIES
(ANCIENT, MEDIEVAL AND MODERN HISTORY)
ANCIENT GREECE
DISTRIBUTION OF GREEK TRIBES ACCORDING TO DIALECTS
RAND McNALLY & COMPANY, CHICAGO – NEW YORK
ADRIATIC SEA
IONIAN SEA
SICILIAN SEA
MYRTOAN SEA
ILLYRICUM
PAEONIA
MACEDON
EPIRUS
THESSALY
CHALCIDICE
AETOLIA
ACARNANIA
PHOCIS
LOCRIS
BOEOTIA
ACHAEA
ELIS
ARCADIA
ARGOLIS
MESSENIA
LACONIA
Epidamnus
(Dyrrhachium)
Pella
Pydna
Amphipolis
Olynthus
Potidaea
Corcyra
CORCYRA
LEUCAS
ITHACA
CEPHALLENIA
ZACYNTHUS
Delphi
Thebes
Chalcis
Patrae
Aegium
GULF OF CORINTH
Megara
Athens
Aegina
Sicyon
Corinth
Argos
Elis
Olympia
Mantinea
Megalopolis
Sparta
SPHACTERIA
MESSENIAN GULF
LACONIAN GULF
CYTHERA
THERMAIC GULF
SARONIC GULF
ARGOLIC GULF
CRETE
PIRAEUS
GREECE AT OUTBREAK OF PELOPONNESIAN WAR
BLACK SEA
ANCIENT ATHENS
NEW ATHENS
LYCEUM

1 Map of ancient Greece. Insets: Harbours of Piraeus and ship sheds; Greece at the outbreak of the Peloponnesian War (431 BC); ancient Athens; Cyprus.

So, ancient Greece was a relatively small country, and quite divided by geography, dialect and political ideology, but conversely united by a shared language, mythology, religion and sense of 'Greekness', which was a matter of fierce pride. Curiously, Homer does not really distinguish ethnically between Greeks and Trojans in his tale of the Trojan War. The two sides have no difficulty talking to each other, and no one on the Greek side ever talks disparagingly about Trojans as non-Greeks. But by the time of the Persian Wars in the fifth century BC, the Greeks had become extremely sensitized to what they called 'barbarian' peoples and customs and throughout their history felt, frankly, superior. They also felt cleverer, braver, more civilized, better educated and perhaps even more beautiful, as the cult of male beauty was cultivated in male athletics. True, perhaps, every people feels itself superior to all other peoples, and in a way that is true: what people know and are familiar with *is* superior for them. But, looking back, the Greeks were perhaps more justified than most in congratulating themselves on their achievements. This book is, however, anything but a history of Greece. There are many excellent histories of Greece aimed at all levels of specialization. This book is an attempt to show what Greeks were like, what they thought and how they felt. Let us call it a very unscientific attempt to get inside the heads of these classical Greeks from the point of view of a modern person who might wonder about this.

Can we know what the Greeks thought and felt at this distance in time and history? In anthropology, one has become familiar with the curious hybrid expressions emic and etic (from the linguistic terms phon-emic and phon-etic) to describe, respectively, the views of an indigenous people itself, and the views of it from the outside. That is, the observer is always outside, looking in. Even if 'informers' tell the field anthropologist what rites are being performed, and according to what beliefs, there is still the chance that they are tailoring the account for an outsider: what they want the observer to hear, rather than what, for instance, village boys may whisper among themselves in secret. Now we can only gain access to the Greeks' thoughts, feelings and attitudes by listening to what they say: by reading what they wrote and looking at their works of art and architecture. But this is, in a way, an improvement on the field anthropologist's position. For the Greeks were writing to communicate with each other, not as an exercise in public relations, as it were, for future civilizations. Poets were writing for their poetic audiences; historians were recording history as a record for their own peoples. Playwrights wrote plays to be performed before an audience of their own countrymen and citizens. Here there is no emic and etic. If we satisfactorily read the documents and monuments that they produced in the course of their own civilization, then we have direct access to the underlying thoughts and ideals. True, literature is not everyday life but an artistic reshaping of reality according to aesthetic criteria and conditions of reception. But we also have plenty of sources relating to everyday life in ancient Greece. Some genres of literature have everyday life as their focus: comedy, dicastic oratory (lawsuits), inscriptions of all sorts, incidental remarks even in 'high' literature. Other written sources are termed 'documentary' texts, that is, documents of real life written by people during the course of their business. Archaeology has nothing but the bare bones of everyday life, as it were, to work with. Here the values, ideals and abstractions of life are spirited away, leaving only the physical objects that had housed and witnessed these.

In other words, interpretation of sources, hermeneutics: a vast subject with an attendant philosophical discipline of its own. If I find a letter in somebody's attic written two hundred years previously by someone I never knew to someone I never knew, how do I interpret this letter? The first job, clearly, is to see which language it is written in, to decipher the words written by hand (sometimes not a trivial exercise), understand the sentences and then slowly begin to work out the meaning by indications of context within the letter. In other words: to put myself in the place of the letter-writer and try to work out what on earth he or she was communicating, and to whom. If I am lucky (and the letter has some importance), I may investigate concomitant data such as the owner of the attic at that time, perhaps some family history, parish archives, official records, reports from third parties that refer to the matter of the letter: in short, a vast panoply of accompanying data, which I may be able to reassemble and bring to bear on the task of interpreting the letter. With luck, patience and perseverance I may at the end be in a pretty good position to understand that letter.

The case of this one letter has to be multiplied thousands of times when applied to the interpretation of ancient literature and documents, and that at a distance of over 2,000 years, when all equivalents of parish records and witness testimonies have vanished. This is not an easy task but not, to a point, an impossible one either. For ancient authors were trying to communicate their thoughts and feelings (to each other); all we have to do is listen carefully. This is what classicists do: they listen as carefully as possible and discuss among themselves what they think they hear, in an attempt at arriving at a theoretical consensus.

So, what are we listening to in the case of written literature? Well, poetry and prose, in a word, written in Greek in those dialects and over those centuries that I sketched before. This is not the place for a potted history of Greek literature: again, a subject that has been more than adequately addressed for centuries at all levels of specialization. However, the reader needs to have a basic framework to understand what I am referring to in the following chapters.

First: what did Greek literature look like? Books? Papers? Libraries? Clearly we can only read now what was written down. Early on, Greeks learned the art of reading and writing from Phoenicians (in modern Lebanon), who gave them an early alphabet. Its arrival in Greece at a certain place was associated with a mythical king, Kadmos of Thebes, and the early letterforms were still known in classical Greece as 'Kadmeian letters' (Herodotus, *Histories* 5.58). These letters were written (painted) on early clay pots, on writing tablets (*deltoi*) and, later, on papyrus (an Egyptian import and long in use there) and parchment (animal skins). Papyrus was glued together, parchment stitched together, into longer rolls. Papyrus and parchment were first rolled up as books (*biblia*, Lat. *volumina*); later they were cut into pages and bound together like our books (*codices*). Writing on rolls was in vertical columns arranged side by side from left to right along the length of the roll. One read by unrolling the roll progressively. One wrote with a pointed implement on tablets, a chisel on stone, a pen and ink on papyrus. Here we can leave the technical side of writing. Greek papyri survive from as early as the fourth century BC in readable condition; stone inscriptions (epigraphy) from several centuries earlier. Most of our classical literature has survived by way of handwritten medieval manuscripts (for an example see illus. 2): these were simply ancient books written up in the new minuscule script and bound beautifully. The Greeks had a well-developed written culture. Not everyone could read, naturally, but most free citizens presumably could as they went to primary school, where letters ('grammar', *grammatikē*) were a main focus. A market vendor in Aristophanes, for example, says he can read,

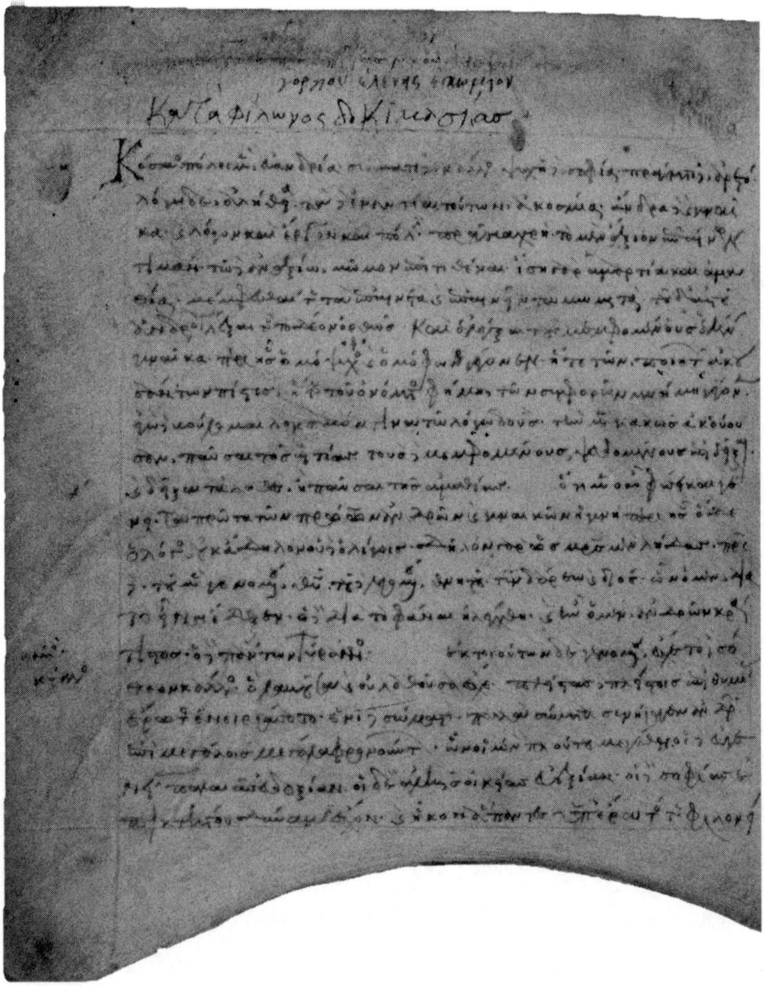

2 Page from a medieval manuscript of Lysias, *Against Philōn*, 1050–1250. Note the lower-case writing and the book format; red ink is used on the title (hence 'rubric').

but poorly (*Knights* 189). Letters were never the prerogative of a class of officials (such as priests, as in Egypt) but rather the basis of city life and laws. The ancient city was called *polis*; just think what words derive from this: policy, politics, polite, to name only the fundamentals.

I said before that Greek literature consists of poetry and prose. Within each area there were numerous subcategories, or genres, for which the Greeks had a word: *genē*, literally 'families'. The complexity of Greek metre requires books to elucidate; types of metre

THE MAIN GENRES AND PERIODS OF GREEK LITERATURE[2]

NAME	DESCRIPTION	FAMOUS NAMES	MAIN PERIOD
Epic	Long mythical narrative in dactylic hexameter verse	Homer, Hesiod	Oral, then written 8th–6th century BC
Solo lyric	Short poems in lyric metres composed mainly for convivial occasions	Sappho, Alkaios, Archilochos, Anakreon, Ibykos	7th–6th century BC
Elegiac	Longer poems in elegiac metre (couplets of hexameter and pentameter)	Archilochus, Mimnermos, Theognis, Solon	7th–5th century BC
Choral lyric	Longer poems in lyric metres composed for performance by a chorus at a public event	Simonides, Pindar, Bakchylides	6th–5th century BC
Tragedy	Dramas with mythical themes in a mix of iambic speech and choral lyric	Aeschylus, Sophocles, Euripides	5th century BC
Old Comedy	Comedies with ribald, political or fantasy themes in a mix of (free) iambic metre and choral lyric	Aristophanes, Kratinos	2nd half 5th–early 4th century BC
History	Narrative of historical events in prose, sometimes annalistic	Herodotus, Thucydides, Xenophon	5th–4th century BC
Philosophy	Treatises on philosophical, ethical or cosmological themes in prose in dialogue form or exposition	Xenophanes, Heraclitus, Sophists, Plato, Xenophon, Aristotle, Theophrastus, Epicurus	5th–3rd century BC

include words that are still familiar, such as iambic, dactylic, hexameter, pentameter. Different metres were associated with distinct poetic genres, which themselves served different cultural contexts: parties, for example, religious congregations, national competitions, funeral laments, victory celebrations and more. And prose, too (*lexis eiromenē*, 'strung-together speech'), had its areas of application. Speeches involved oratory, again of various types; history had its own conventions; letter-writing, biography, political propaganda – all forms of written communications with developed conventions.

NAME	DESCRIPTION	FAMOUS NAMES	MAIN PERIOD
Science and medicine	Treatises on scientific or medical themes in prose	Hippokrates, Aristotle	5th century BC on
Oratory	Forensic (legal), epideictic (public occasions) or symbouleutic (political) speeches in rhetorical prose	Antiphon, Andokides, Lysias, Isokrates, Demosthenes	5th–4th century BC
New Comedy	Domestic comedies on themes from everyday life in mainly iambic metre	Menander, Diphilos	Late 4th–3rd century BC
Hellenistic poetry	Umbrella term to refer to epic, elegiac, iambic and epigrammatic verse written in the age of Alexandrian learning	Apollonius of Rhodes, Callimachus, Herodas, Theocritus	Hellenistic 3rd–1st century BC
Hellenistic prose	Umbrella term covering philosophical, historical, biographical, scientific and scholarly writing	Epicurus, Zeno, Theopompus, Polybius, Dionysius of Halicarnassus	Late 4th–1st century BC
Second Sophistic	Term used to describe a second flourishing of intellectual prose writing in imitation of 5th-century Athens	(Plutarch), Dio of Prusa, Lucian, Philostratos	1st–3rd century AD
Novel	Prose narratives of a young couple's adventures prior to marriage	Xenophon of Ephesos, Longos, Achilles Tatius, Heliodorus	1st–4th century AD

So how did writers in these various types of composition communicate with their contemporaries? First, poetry was always made for singing or recitation. Long narrative works seem to have been spoken rhythmically rather than sung melodically, but there were many types of poetry that were sung either to string (lyre, *phorminx*, *barbitos*) or wind instruments (*aulos*). A lyric song by Sappho (sixth century BC), for example, may have had a very similar status to a modern pop song or perhaps a folk song. Athenians knew these songs off by heart two centuries later, so they were clearly popular. Poetry was never an inner musing, always an expression of stories, ideas, pictures. After Homer, works may have been written down, but that does not mean that people went out to buy their books. Performance was always the thing; writing was a technical aid to performance and transmission. Then there were songs meant for a larger audience at a religious or competitive gathering. Here subjects were less personal and intimate, more suited to a larger audience. And the famous national epics by Homer were recited in Athens by professional rhapsodes (performers) at large public gatherings. Theatre was obviously performed, and reperformed, for centuries after the original performance. Speeches were spoken, even when a written version was circulated later. Even history was read out, we are told in the case of Herodotus (fifth century BC), who assembled a vast compendium of national and international history as if he were writing the first encyclopedia. Another famous fifth-century historian, Thucydides, wrote his book on the Peloponnesian War (431–404 BC) with a view to its endurance; he called it a 'possession' for all time. This may point more to the concept of a book, a thing, a possession. But no Greek ever thought of writing just for themselves, as a meditation or perhaps a kind of self-expression or therapy, and we are therefore entirely justified in reading Greek works as attempts to communicate with contemporary Greeks. And, if we learn the language well enough, we can hear them, too, even if imperfectly and through a crackle of linguistic interference.

So the following accounts of aspects of Greek life are purely anecdotal, devoid of the modern statistical or scientific method. Today, if one appears on the news and wishes to express the opinion that fewer people have been using public transport as a result of the COVID-19 pandemic, one needs figures: a 54 per cent decrease, for example, compared to pre-pandemic. Or, talking about gender equality in pay, one needs a figure such as: women's pay in the public sector is, for comparable positions, on average 86 per cent that of men. Of course, historians of antiquity *do* work as best they can statistically and scientifically, but the evidence is necessarily scant compared to nowadays. This book makes no pretence of science or empirical basis. It is simply a thematic selection, with context and commentary, of the original words and pictures of ancient authors, artists and private people, which, luckily, have a higher-than-average claim to interest as they come from the most creative minds of that age and society. Nor should we forget that opinions then, as now, will have varied from individual to individual. There can be no such thing as 'standard opinion' or 'national average' when talking about the ancient Greeks. All we can do is listen to a variety of opinions, knowing that they are all valid in a way, because they were valid for the mind expressing them. We have one great advantage compared to some modern witness testimonies. Ancient writers were as a rule not setting out to deceive or paint a warped picture, or grind a political axe (though this last might be a possibility among orators!). They are 'straight' in the sense that anything else would have defeated the purpose of writing or expressing it. This is not to say that any statement can be taken as literal truth. We are familiar with the human mind's penchant for shaping experiences of the world according to its own blueprint, desire or selective memory.

As far as we know, the ancient Greeks, and at first especially the Athenians, invented the following things: democracy, freedom of speech, rule of law, secular art and literature, theatre, oratory, and interstate cultural and athletics competitions. And they radically developed poetry and prose writing, philosophy, cosmology, mathematics, astronomy, geography, medicine and anatomy. Their intellectual, artistic, political and theoretical achievements are heroic, and I say that in awe rather than from missionary zeal or academic pride. They are *worth studying*.

But not in everything. One could equally paint a dark side to the picture that seriously detracts from their shining achievements, perhaps so much that we should revise the historical verdict. Their society and economy were based on slave labour. Greeks made slaves of their defeated enemies, whether these were non-Greeks or from other Greek cities. Slaves were property to be bought, sold, traded, whipped and used. And slaves might have children, but they were slaves, too. The chances of being freed were limited, and certainly not a right to which slaves could look forward to after, say, thirty years in service. Slaves had no rights of property, liberty or independence. True, when we meet slaves on the comic stage they are clever, articulate and not in any way depressed (unless by chance through unrequited love). Sometimes their owners are made to look stupid compared to the slaves; but this is perhaps a theatrical trick, a way of making fun of the 'real people'. In art, slaves are also usually depicted as smaller or in some way grotesque by comparison.

The cities endlessly made war on each other. If one reads through the historical record of Herodotus and Thucydides and later historians, one gets the impression that inter-city peace was the exception. And within each city-state, *stasis*, civil war or factional fighting, was also commonplace. War then meant hand-to-hand fighting: brutal, bloody, with no Geneva Conventions defining war crimes or the appropriate treatment of prisoners-of-war. Warriors killed each other with spears, swords, arrows, slings, clubs and short daggers, fighting either on foot (hoplites), as cavalry (*hippeis*) or as light-armed troops (*psiloi*). Great emphasis was placed on bravery and fortitude; Sparta simply did not tolerate cowards. If you fled from the line of battle, you fled to your death at home. Field hospitals were, of course, non-existent and medicine primitive, limited mainly to bandaging up wounds and applying poultices. When we admire a Platonic dialogue set in the shade of plane trees to the seductive chirping of cicadas (the *Phaidros*), we should remember that the speaker, Socrates, had fought in the Battle of Delion (424 BC) and at Poteidaia (432–430 BC), both bloody engagements. Let this brief reminder of ancient warfare linger in the reader's mind like the memory of a nightmare that stays with one during the day. Ancient Greece was anything but an idyll. Forget the atmosphere of a modern university department: hushed corridors, lecture rooms, quiet libraries. Forget the works of Greek art in museums: the frozen, elegant marble; the reverent looks of visitors; the tranquillity. The snippets of life that we encounter in the following chapters played out against a harsh backdrop, civic terrain as rough and precipitous as the Greek landscape and the sea.

Nowadays, statues are being thrown into the sea if the honouree is found to have been deficient in some way: a rich benefactor of a city or university, perhaps, who made his money completely or partly through the slave trade is condemned retrospectively and banished from collective memory. Even Classics itself is coming under attack as being the province of privileged white men (and maybe a few women) who, as if by birthright, go to the best schools and universities and then on to select jobs. Well, there may be something in this, but it is certainly not the Greeks' fault. Anyone who acquires the right language skills can set about interpreting the Greek texts and monuments, whether a clever student climbing the system or a lone researcher desperate to escape a boring day job. There is no intrinsic connection between Classics and the British Empire, or any *Reich* or administration: it is pure coincidence that Latin and Greek were intensively taught at public (that is, private) schools in the heyday of the British Empire and in comparable European education systems. There is nothing intrinsically elitist about Classics; however, it becomes the province of an elite, like any other academic subject, through the time and persistence needed to become acquainted with a foreign sign-system. But unlike a social or financial elite, an academic elite is open to any applicant regardless of class, colour, creed or culture. To 'do' Classics professionally is undoubtedly a niche occupation, but there is general public interest in the cultural explosion that was ancient Greece, and a need for trained guides and interpreters. One thing is certain: it feels very far from white supremacy to me; on the contrary, we classicists feel more like a beleaguered species, coral polyps on a reef shrinking inexorably as the environment deteriorates.

1
LOVE

Epic Love

Greek had two quite distinct words for love, which divide up the range of feeling into two areas. There is *philia,* which is a wide-ranging word meaning the love felt for fellow human beings with whom one is close, bonded. Within the family it is the standard word for the love felt between members of a family, as we use 'loved ones' to refer to those very close. Of course, this love covers a multitude of aspects, too: not only strong affection but responsibility or dependence, solidarity and mutuality, protectiveness or the need for protection, admiration or fear, emotional familiarity – and I am sure one could name other nuances. The other word is *erōs,* also love, but that feeling that initially attracts people for sexual union. Not only desire and lust but that feeling of wanting someone (of either sex) physically but also emotionally, which I probably should not try to describe. The terms are quite well distinguished in Greek but there is overlap. For example, the verb *phileō*, which is obviously related to *philia*, came to mean 'kiss', which one might think is the prelude to *erōs*. And the most famous work on love in classical literature, Plato's *Symposion* (literally 'Drinking Party'; *c.* 380 BC), uses *erōs* for the strong emotional bond between two people, pretty much shorn of the erotic.

The earliest extant poetic work, Homer's *Iliad* (approximately eighth century BC but standing at the end of a long oral tradition), is actually a kind of love poem, although you will not find it described like that in histories of literature. The work narrates just fifty-odd days of events in the final year of the ten-year Trojan War, that famous conflict fought over Helen of Troy between the Greeks and Trojans. Scholars go on debating whether there may be a historical basis to this legendary war; certainly there was a historical city of Troy, which is generally identified with the archaeological site of Hisarlik near the Dardanelles in northwestern Anatolia. A contemporary Hittite inscription even refers to a war that, with an effort, we could interpret as referring to Homer's Trojan War. But it is better to think of Homer's epic as a narrative that has achieved mythical status through an oral tradition lasting centuries. The Greeks themselves considered the poem historical, indeed the basis of their history, and as their bible in questions of religion, and their compass in all manner of ethical questions.

I said that this war narrative is actually a love story. It centres around three instances of *philia*, which are tinged in places with *erōs*. The story starts when the Greeks discover they have captured a pretty girl, Chryseïs, on a raid, who is actually the daughter of Chryses, the priest of Apollo Smintheus (perhaps: 'Mouse-killer') of that town, Lyrnessos (*Iliad* 19.60). Chryses approaches the Greek commander Agamemnon, offering gifts in compensation for the release of his daughter. Agamemnon refuses; desperate, Chryses prays to Apollo to punish Agamemnon. Apollo obliges, sending a plague on the Greek army (expressed as arrows shot from the god's bow; see illus. 12). Agamemnon finally capitulates and agrees to return the captive girl, but only on the condition that he gets another girl in her stead, naming Achilles' own prize, Briseïs, as the object of his desire. Achilles' rage, his *mēnis*, which is the title of the poem, is a combination of fury at the insult, injured pride, hot temper, but also love for Briseïs. When Agamemnon later tries to assuage his anger with the promise of rich gifts, including a selection of women, part of Achilles' response is to say he loved Briseïs just like any other man:

> Why should the Greeks make war on the Trojans? Why has Agamemnon raised an army against them? Is it not because of the fair-haired Helen? Do only the sons of Atreus [Agamemnon and Menelaos] among men love their wives? A good and fair-minded man loves his woman and cares for

> her, as I loved *her* [Briseïs] with all my heart, even though she was a prisoner-of-war. Now that he has robbed me of my prize and tricked me, don't let him come begging: he won't succeed. (*Iliad* 9.337–45)

Now, when the quarrel erupts, Achilles is on the point of killing Agamemnon on the spot, but he is restrained by a divine force and decides instead to sulk in his tent, refusing to fight. His mother, Thetis, a goddess, intervenes with Zeus on his behalf, asking Zeus to honour her son now he has suffered such an insult. He agrees – with some misgivings, as he knows Hera, championing the Greeks, will not like it – and for the next fourteen books of the *Iliad* tips the balance of war in favour of the Trojans. In this way, the tide of war turns against the Greeks, partly through human motivation, as Achilles, the 'best of the Achaeans', withdraws from battle, and partly divine, as Zeus decides (temporarily, at least) to support Achilles' cause.

Then another kind of love tips the balance. The *friend* Achilles loves, his fellow warrior Patroklos, is killed on the battlefield by the Trojan hero Hektor. The intimate bond between Achilles and Patroklos emerges in descriptions of their life together sharing a tent. There is no hint of a homoerotic relationship between the two men, who are said to have their women beside them when they sleep (Book 9), but later reception of the *Iliad*, including art, does develop the theme.[1] In Book 16, Patroklos enters the fray wearing Achilles' armour, as a kind of surrogate, and is killed by Hektor. The pain of his loss stirs Achilles from his inertia and puts an end to his sulk. New armour is made by a god, no less (Hephaistos), and Achilles rampages into battle, fighting Trojans, gods, even the floodwaters of a river. In the course of his rampage he succeeds in killing Hektor, thus effectively ending Troy's chances of winning the war, as Hektor is their champion. Hektor's death causes outpourings of grief on the Trojan side, and it is to these we should turn to learn of the feelings of *philia*, which the women closest to Hektor feel for him. They are representative of the whole population of the city.

Three of Hektor's closest women relatives mourn him when his body is brought into Troy from the battlefield: Andromache,

3 Women (pale faces) and men mourn a dead man on a bier (*prothesis*), black-figure terracotta funerary plaque (*pinax*); below, a chariot race, *c*. 510 BC.

his widow; Hekabē, his mother; and (surprisingly) Helen of Troy. An aspect of their laments is prominent that is typically lacking at modern funerals and wakes: the degree to which the fallen hero was the *protector* of the women, but not only them – also the population of Troy generally. There is endearment in their words – especially in the case of Andromache, as we will see – but the women emphasize particularly their feeling of being bereft and defenceless now Hektor is gone. First Andromache, who laments Hektor while 'cradling the head of man-slaying Hektor in her hands':

> Husband, you have lost your life while still young, you have left me a widow in our home. Our son is likewise still an infant, the child we bore together in our misfortune. I doubt he'll reach maturity. This city will be razed to the ground before that. For you, its guardian, are lost, who saved it. You

> protected its wives and its helpless infants. They will soon be borne away in the holds of ships, and I with them. You, my child, will either be with me where you will endure demeaning slave labour at the hands of a brutal master, or one of the Greeks will grab your hand and pitch you from a turret to a pitiful death, from anger: Hektor may well have killed his brother, or his father, or perhaps son, for many Greeks died at his hands ... But it is to me above all that grief is left. For you [Hektor] could not reach out your hand to me in your dying moments, nor say any last endearment to me, which I might have clung to tearfully during the nights and days. (24.725–45)

Hekabē's words are much as one would expect from a mother who has lost her favourite son, although she too emphasizes the feeling of defencelessness his death has caused. Helen's lament over Hektor's body comes as something of a surprise. After all, it was her complicity in the abduction (if she had any choice in the matter) by Paris that provoked the war in the first place; Hektor might well have hated the woman for endangering his entire people. Instead, apparently, he treated Helen kindly when she was vilified by others. Here we see *philia* as the love Helen felt for a good man who treated her well despite her precarious position as a reviled intruder:

> Hektor, by far the dearest of my husband's brothers to me, yes, my husband is indeed the divinely handsome Alexander, who brought me to Troy, but I would sooner have died! This is already the twentieth year since I came from there and left my home country.[2] But I have never heard a rough or thoughtless word from you in all this time. Rather, if any other member of King Priam's extended family insulted me around the palace – he himself treated me like a father – you restrained them with contrary words out of the kindness of your heart and tongue. So I mourn both you and my own wretched self in my misery. No one else in wide Troy is kind, or a friend, but all revile me. (24.762–75)

What would we say of the girls disputed by the warriors at the beginning of the *Iliad*? That they were trafficked? Abused? Enslaved? Yes, all those things; nevertheless, whatever feelings the men had for the girls, it was not all one to them whether they kept them. Was it, then, simply a matter of pride? Did Agamemnon not want to surrender his girl Chryseïs, who was his prize after a raid? Likewise, Briseïs was Achilles' war prize. Perhaps the quarrel between the men was simply a question of *amour propre*, injured self-esteem. Did Achilles let large numbers of his fellow warriors die at the hands of the Trojans simply because he felt slighted in his honour? Since *kleos*, glory, was the overarching goal and prize for the Homeric warrior, we are probably not far off the mark when we say that what was really at stake in this poem about the 'wrath of Achilles' (*mēnis Achilleōs*) is injured pride: *self*-love, in fact. But will we deny self-love is important today? How many trivial quarrels about parking spaces, rude driving, promotion at work, inheritances, jealousies, even royal successions are in fact about personal insult, the feeling that one has been belittled, demeaned, insulted, overlooked?

But then Homer shows the reverse side of the coin: all Troy loves, admires and finally mourns Hektor, the saviour of the city who fights selflessly to defend his people, to protect his family and dynasty. His love for them is unwavering and altruistic. And the love they feel for him, exemplified by the three women who mourn him when his body is placed on a bier before burial at Troy, is that towards a good, kind, *ideal* man (see illus. 3). There is more to the *philia* in relations within Hektor's family than the average bonding: they stand for family relations, which while intact save the community and when broken undo it. In a way, Homer has shown the best and worst of human love. On the Greek side there is egocentric lust for a compliant concubine combined with an elevated sense of the male ego; on the Trojan side there is family solidarity based on mutual *philia*, which, however, ends in tragedy. This will surprise many readers, I expect, who thought the *Iliad* must be a poem of Greek supremacy. The Hollywood film *Troy* (2004) would prefer it that way. In fact it is the first European tragedy, based on the pain when one loses everything, and everyone, one loves.

Comic Love

Let us move to an area of Greek literature that was all about young love: a young man falls for a young woman and, after some complications, they marry. This is the genre called New Comedy, and it was a type of theatre that flourished at Athens (later, all over the Greek world) from the end of the fourth century BC and never really went out of fashion, to judge from records of reperformances and pictures of the favourite plays in mosaics and wall paintings. The name we must mention here is Menander, although he had many colleagues who probably also wrote amusing plays. However, Menander's fate in terms of survival has been interesting. He was very popular in antiquity, but then his works were lost around AD 500 because – for some reason – the scribes at work at that time did not transfer his plays from the old technology of papyrus and capital letters to the new technology of books and 'normal' writing (Carolingian minuscule, from AD 800). Then, with the expansion of archaeology in the modern era, one began to find papyri preserved in the dry sands of Egypt and – surprise, surprise – quite a number of these papyrus fragments contained parts of plays by the lost author Menander. By now we have enough to fill a good-sized book of pure Greek text.

These plays of New Comedy invariably concern young, romantic love. So invariably, in fact, that some have to stifle a yawn when talking about the plots of Menander's plays. In truth there is much subtlety in his writing, mainly surrounding his attention to details of character and interpersonal relations. One play, *Dyskolos* (316 BC), which means 'Grouch' or 'Bad-Tempered Man', has, remarkably, been preserved more or less intact on a papyrus roll now kept in Geneva. It is the story of an old farmer who is so antisocial that he does not cultivate the edges of his land because it might mean having to exchange words with passers-by. He admires the mythical hero Perseus on two counts: one, that the hero could fly, thus avoiding contact with people on earth, and two, that he possessed the Gorgon's head, with which he could turn anyone to stone who was annoying him: 'If I had that, the world would be dotted with stone statues of people!' (*Dys.* 153–9). One imagines him 'tasering', so to speak, anyone he met with his

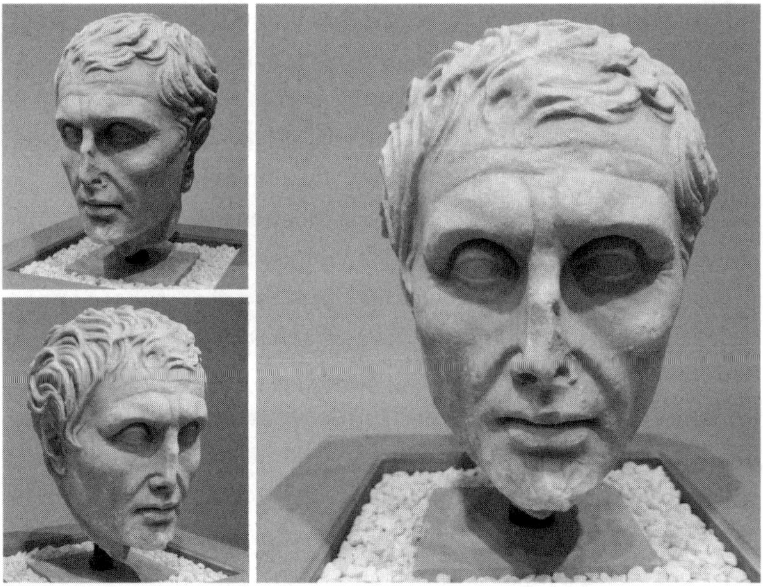

4 Head of the comic poet Menander, first half of the 2nd century AD, copy of a bronze statue dated to the early 3rd century BC.

gorgōneion (Gorgon's face). But the moral of the play is that this attitude is not good enough. He is taught a lesson in the course of the action and forced to repent.

However, our subject is the love story in the play. This old man, Knēmōn, has a daughter who is not described by Menander: we simply assume she is young, pretty and demure. A rich young townsman, Sostratos, encounters her briefly when she is out bringing wreaths to the local cult of Nymphs and is promptly smitten by love. He confides in a 'mate' of his,[3] who asks: 'What, Sostratos? You saw a young citizen girl decorating her neighbours, the Nymphs, and fell in love straight away?' (*Sostratos:*) 'On the spot, yes.' (*Chaireas:*) 'That was quick!' (*Sostratos:*) 'Don't mock! I'm in a bad way, Chaireas.' (*Chaireas:*) 'I don't doubt it.'

At this point we are introduced to a social distinction in young men's love-lives then compared to now: the difference between an affair with a 'bought' woman (a *hetaira*, as she was called) and a girl of 'good family', that is, enjoying citizen rights and eligible to marry (*hetairai* were not). The 'friend', who wants to help Sostratos out, says:

> My position on this, Sostratos, is as follows. If it's a *hetaira* my friend's in love with, I spring into action. I'm fired up, ablaze, I don't take no for an answer. Even before I've found out who she is, I'm onto her. The slow approach is much more conducive to love. Immediate gratification swiftly brings the matter to an end. But if someone mentions *marriage* and a decent girl, then I'm quite a different person. I enquire about her family, income, character, and hand over the results to my friend as a record for the future. (*Dyskolos* 57–67)

Knēmōn the Grudge, the very antithesis of love and friendship, stands throughout between Sostratos and his goal. The impasse is only solved when Knēmōn himself has a very bad accident climbing down his well to retrieve a bucket carelessly dropped by the maid. In so doing, he falls, injures himself and is stuck at the bottom of the well. A local lad rushes to his rescue, and Sostratos helps the rescue attempt, or rather hinders it: he describes how he stood happily, with Knēmōn's daughter beside him (who was distraught), at the rim of the well while Gorgias (the farmer's lad) bravely climbed down the well:

> (*Sostratos:*) Spectators, by Demeter, by Asklepios, by all the gods, never in all my life have I seen someone almost drown at a more opportune moment. What fun! As soon as we got there, Gorgias jumped straight away into the well while, above him, I and the girl didn't do anything. What could we do? Well, she tore her hair in desperation, beat herself on the breast. While lucky old me – I stood beside her as if I were her nurse, by god. I begged her not to do those things, implored her, while I gazed at her – as at the statue of a goddess. I wasn't one bit concerned about the injured man below, except I kept pulling on the rope. That was quite a bore. And I nearly lost him down there, by God. For while I was concentrating on the girl, I let go of the rope at least three times. But Gorgias was an absolute hero. He held on and, with an effort, he's managed to get him out. When he emerged, I left the house.

> I couldn't restrain myself any longer but very nearly gave the girl a kiss – I'm so in love with her! (ll. 666–89)

A number of formalities in ancient relationships emerge from this play. Sostratos employs a kind of go-between to establish contact with the girl's father (he fails). Sostratos falls in love at the mere sight of the girl: there is no first date or walk in the park. Whether Sostratos has a chance with the girl (which means marriage) depends entirely on whether the father agrees, in this case the very *dis*agreeable Knēmōn. When Sostratos stands next to the girl by a stroke of luck, he only has eyes for her and forgets that he's supposed to be helping to pull the father out of the well. He compares his proximity to the girl at the well with that of a nurse: clearly, a free girl was not supposed to leave home without her *trophos*, nurse, who is, incidentally, a stock character in ancient drama. Thus love on the comic stage exaggerates the spontaneous, unexamined fancying stage of a relationship. And, needless to say, this fancying is only in one direction: boy towards girl.

Menander is not all about young first love. There are all facets of love between marriageable individuals and also paid partners (*hetairai* or *pallakai*). There is domestic abuse (*Perikeiromenē* (The Girl with Shorn Hair)); there is a soldier who is rejected by his captive girl (*Misoumenos* (The Hated Man) – remember Chryseïs and Briseïs in the *Iliad*?); there is divorce, reunion, love between partners of all ages. Remarkably, given women's disadvantaged position in society, the women in Menander often outmanoeuvre men, even the most macho among them.

Menander's New Comedy paved the way for a later literary genre, the ancient novel. About five examples of such prose writing have survived, all from around the time of the Roman Empire (but in Greek). Without exception, they all revolve around a type of plot made popular by New Comedy: boy meets girl, falls in love and then spends several hundred pages navigating all manner of perils and difficulties before finally achieving the goal of marriage. There are pirates, mock executions and apparent deaths along the way, all making the happily-ever-after seem impossible until the end. The genre appears to be based on strict conventions; there is little characterization or psychological depth. The plot is everything. Later, we will be considering passages from several of these Greek novels.

Passionate Love

So far we have encountered what might be considered extremes: the solemnity of the women's mourning for Hektor, and Menander's tomfoolery at Knemon's well, hardly calculated to show love in a particularly edifying light. It is time to turn to the popular type of passionate love – akin to that found in a huge number of modern pop, rock and folk songs – expressing strong emotion, disappointment in love, jealousy and all the other facets. I suppose we usually play these songs to ourselves for entertainment or emotional support in some way, certainly not for their informative value or biographical information about the singer. Greek lyric poetry had its acme between the two genres we have pegged out so far (epic and New Comedy): a number of poems (called songs) have survived from the 'archaic' period of Greek history (roughly the eighth to sixth century BC). The music has not survived, only the fact that they were played to the lyre (hence 'lyric') and predominantly by a solo performer such as Sappho, Alkaios, Anakreon or Ibykos. Their compositions also seem to have been performed, and received, for entertainment. What we know points to performance before a relatively small group of listeners: a men's party, perhaps, or a women's gathering at a god's sanctuary. The texts of these poems are composed in a style quite different from that of Homer. This reflects the fact that by then writing was in common use, which moved poetic composition from the oral art perfected by Homer and his predecessors to one of concentrated, precise diction on a small scale. And what did these lyric poets write about for the entertainment of their peers in an evening party atmosphere? Well, love and its variations predominate.

Here we do indeed find all manner of couples: men and women, women and girls, men and men or boys. The goddess of love, Aphrodite, features prominently as she was thought to inspire love; erotic pursuits are called simply *ta aphrodisia*, 'matters of Aphrodite'. With her appear other erotic gods, such as Dionysos, Pan, the

Nymphs, Erōs, all dancing and cavorting as Greeks no doubt did at celebrations. Young Greeks would not have found 'clubbing' particularly alien, once they had got over the technology. One type of male cavorting – the *kōmos*, or drunken revel – must have been quite like a stag night, taking place both inside and on the streets.

Sappho is (still) a very famous name, although not much of her work survives. The first poem in the ancient 'edition' of Sappho, put together by scholars working mainly in Alexandria, is a hymn-prayer addressed to Aphrodite, a *cri de cœur* in which the poet in her own name pleads with Aphrodite to come down from heaven and help her in a difficult affair of the heart: a girl whom Sappho apparently adores is shunning her advances. Aphrodite should intervene with her now and make her change her mind. Aphrodite is pictured descending

5 Sappho and Alkaios, red-figure vase painting by the Brygos Painter, *c.* 470 BC.

from Olympus in her bird-drawn chariot and asking Sappho in a slightly long-suffering tone: 'Who do you want me to work on *this time*?' But let us rather look at a poem that has survived nearly complete (no. 31) and which was copied later by Rome's most famous love poet, Catullus (poem no. 51). In this, Sappho admits to being totally 'smitten' by a girl. She compares her feelings of helpless adoration when she so much as looks at the girl to those of a man seen sitting with her and chatting in a relaxed fashion:

That man seems to me like a god
sitting there beside you, happily
chatting and listening close up
to your heavenly voice

and your sexy laugh, a thing which
sets my heart pounding in my chest.
When I so much as glance in your direction
I lose my power of speech

my tongue is paralysed, and a strange
heat seems to travel through my body.
My vision goes blurry, my hearing
roars in my ears,

I break out in a cold sweat, and shake
all over, I go paler than straw
and have the impression I'm not far
from death itself . . .

Not a very pleasant experience, by the sound of it. Is Sappho exaggerating? Being melodramatic? Each can answer the question according to their own experiences.[4] Certainly Greek poetry celebrated, or lamented, the *power* of Aphrodite. Another archaic lyricist, Ibykos, sang that, while 'plants only grow in spring',

6 The Scourge of Erōs: Erōs stands over a couple having sex with whip raised, relief lid of *pyxis* (small jar) from Italy, 325–250 BC.

. . . my love
does not sleep the whole year round.
[It's like] a northerly gale
with flashes of lightning
stirred by Aphrodite
in dark, irrepressible frenzy,
it seizes hold of my wits and shakes
them to my core . . . (fr. 5)

This power of love, or, put negatively, fatal attraction, was dramatized in Greek tragedy as much as it is in modern drama, whether for film or stage. Euripides' play *Hippolytos* (428 BC) is the story drawn from myth of the Attic hero Theseus' wife, Phaidra, who fatally falls in love with her stepson Hippolytos (who does not reciprocate). Euripides' chorus of women in this play lament this fatal power of inappropriate love and pray for a milder, socially acceptable version of the goddess for themselves:

Erōs, Erōs, who drips longing
over eyes, instils sweet pleasure
into souls of those he attacks:
don't visit harm upon me
or come inappropriately.
No bolt from heaven or burning arrow
matches that which Aphrodite's child
by Zeus releases from his bow.
(. . . In vain we worship all the other gods . . .)
but Erōs, tyrant over human beings,
who holds the keys
to Aphrodite's realm, we omit,
who takes us captive, sends to their undoing
those he singles out. (ll. 525–44)

For his part, Hippolytos' rejection of Aphrodite's realm altogether and his revulsion when Phaidra's shameful love is revealed to him lead to the play's tragic and destructive end.

Wives and Kept Women

One of the things about ancient Greek relationships we find hard to get our heads round, or even translate, is the ancient category of 'kept woman': *hetaira*, *pallakē*. Yet the matter was a simple question of economics, or, even more simply, women's survival in the ancient city. A wife was paid for, protected, housed, fed and everything else, perhaps even loved, by her husband. But only the daughter of an Athenian citizen could marry in Athens according to laws enacted in the fifth century BC. Any other woman was debarred from the social status and economic protection of a legitimate wife. That meant that in order to survive she either had to have the protection of an owner (if she was a slave) or the financial support of a lover (or lovers), if not. Women may have worked in the ancient city, but they did not go out to work and achieve economic independence.[5] And with no welfare state of any kind to support them, they were utterly dependent on men to provide them with the necessities of life. When we talk of prostitutes we tend to think of women in embarrassingly 'tarty' clothes waiting at unsavoury city corners, bullied by pimps and dependent on clients for income. True, there are higher-class escorts, call-girls, masseuses and others, but they all fall into the socially stigmatized class of 'sex-workers'. There were low-class prostitutes in the ancient city, too, called *pornai* (hence our word pornography). They typically worked in a brothel (*porneion*) under the control and ownership of a pimp or brothel-keeper (*pornoboskos*), enjoying no freedoms whatsoever.

There was also, however, a large class of *hetairai*, women living with men 'out of wedlock', as one used to say. But our terms 'civil partner', 'common-law wife' or even 'girlfriend' do not cover this group either. For *hetairai* were economically dependent on their men; they were hired or kept women, professionals if you like, but they were *not* socially stigmatized, except by contrast with the more respectable status of wives. Men fell in love with *hetairai*, treated them very generously, vied among themselves for the prettiest, sometimes kept them for long periods; the type of *pallakē* was a semi-permanent relationship with no particular stigma attached to it, except that citizen children could not be produced from the relationship. Demeas in Menander's *Samia* (The Girl from Samos) certainly loves his *pallakē*, Chrysis, and is pained when he discovers – as he thought – her infidelity. Did the women love their men back? Probably, if they were good to them. And 'good' basically meant giving them generous gifts.[6] The Roman poet Ovid says that he got into trouble with his *amica* (*hetaira*) Corinna when he said poetry was his gift to her: only prostitutes expect payment for their services (*Amores* 1.10). One can imagine Corinna was sceptical about whether she could live off poetry – but her name *is* remembered because of it! There were famous 'courtesans' in ancient Athens who achieved renown through their beauty, wealth, wit and artistic gifts; Perikles' *hetaira* Aspasia is an example, but there were many others. They were held in high regard and probably feared by the wives of powerful and rich men.

Another interesting passage of Menander shows the common perception that a *hetaira* knew more tricks to please and entice a man than did a respectable wife. In his play *Epitrepontes* (The Arbitration), Smikrines, the father of the married woman Pamphile, who has been left by her husband, tells his daughter that it is an uneven competition for a married woman with her husband's *hetaira*:[7]

> [*She*, that is, the *hetaira*, will use]
> . . . poisonous potions and daily threats
> that he'll throw you out. With no money of her own
> to contribute here, but enjoying an equal share,
> she'll live merrily, of course, without a care.
> Then there's this: You'll only encourage her
> with your frowns and endless scolding,
> your position as down-at-heel housewife.
> Finally she'll oust you. It's not easy, Pamphile,
> for a free-born woman to compete with a harlot.
> She knows more tricks, has more experience, knows
> no shame, uses flattery, resorts to one low trick
> after another. (ll. 786–97)

Lucian's *Conversations of Courtesans*

Lucian, a later writer (second century AD) of the so-called Second Sophistic – a period of revival under Roman rule of the intellectual explosion at Athens in the fifth and fourth centuries – wrote some amusing sketches of life among these *hetairai*. They are satirical and meant to be amusing, so they omit all the nitty-gritty of real life (not quite all, actually), but nevertheless they can be relied upon for details of the social background of these women and their lovers. There is nothing sordid about their dealings. True, there is a clear demarcation compared to 'respectable' married life, as we shall see, but there is no hint that their way of life is immoral in any way, or despicable. It was simply a way for these women, who did not enjoy citizen status, whether because they were foreigners to the city or 'undocumented' daughters born to a couple who were not both registered citizens, to exist. In the dramatized story we are going to look at first (no. 2), a *hetaira* called Myrtion – 'Little Myrtle' (the women all have pretty nicknames) – is complaining that her lover Pamphilos ('All-Lover') has left her to marry another woman:

> (*Myrtion:*) What, Pamphilos? You're marrying... the daughter of the shipowner Philon? So all those promises you made and all the tears are gone in an instant, and you've forgotten your Myrtion now? And that when I'm eight months gone already! So that's my only reward from your love: that you've made my belly this size and soon I'll be a mum, which is really tough for a *hetaira*. I won't expose the child, you know, especially if it's a boy. No, I'll call it Pamphilos and keep it with me as solace for your love, and one day he'll blame you that you turned out to be a cheat towards his poor mother. (*Conversations of Hetairai* 2.1.1–13)

We notice a number of things here. Myrtion is already eight months pregnant, so her relationship with Pamphilos was no one-night stand (he's only leaving her now). She calls her big belly the 'reward' of his love, meaning that she has nothing to show from their long-standing relationship but a child, which she is now going to have to raise herself as a 'single mum'. The remark implies that, as a *hetaira*, she would normally expect all sorts of gifts and payments from her lover. There are many instances of lovers boasting of their generosity and lavishness in heaping valuables on their pretty girlfriends. Myrtion's main problem is, of course, that, according to report, Pamphilos has now chosen marriage to a merchant seaman's daughter over her. She goes on to cast aspersions on this girl's looks, implying that she is proud of her own looks compared to this dowdy creature. That was the basic deal between lovers and *hetairai*: material gifts for looks (and sex, of course), much as rich men nowadays surround themselves with pretty girls sporting themselves on their yachts.

When confronted, Pamphilos himself denies the accusation point-blank. He points to the fact that his father had fought a court case against the father of the girl in question (the latter had refused to repay a debt). How could their respective children now be joined in marriage? Moreover, there is another girl of a much better family whom Pamphilos could marry instead of Philon's unattractive daughter. Anyway, he is not marrying anyone. The maid Doris is brought in, who says how she heard the news in the first place. She explains to her mistress how she visited the street in which the marriage was to take place and found it decked out indeed in confetti and flowers in preparation for a wedding ceremony.

Pamphilos is quick to realize the cause of the misunderstanding: it was in fact the neighbours' house in the same street that was preparing for a marriage. He remembered his mother telling him that the son of the next-door neighbours was marrying; she had admonished him at the time for not doing likewise but continuing on in his relationship with the *hetaira*. Myrtion is delighted:

> (*Myrtion:*) You're my saviour, Pamphilos! I would have died if it had been true. (*Pamphilos:*) But it couldn't have happened. I hope I'm not so crazy as to forget my Myrtion, particularly now she's carrying my baby! (2.4.15–20)

A happy ending. Pamphilos prefers his Myrtion, particularly now she's pregnant, to either the seaman's daughter or the general's. This sounds suspiciously like *philia*, fondness for his incipient little family, although *erōs* was the word Myrtion had used for their relationship at the beginning. His mother had blamed him for just that: staying with his *hetaira* instead of marrying a 'good' girl like the boy next door. The word Pamphilos' mother uses for the neighbour's choice, *sōphronei*, 'he's showing sense' or 'being sensible', is one of the loaded words in Greek ethics. One reason why Pamphilos' preference for a *hetaira* is not 'sensible' is financial. A *hetaira* always had her hand outstretched for benefits from her lover and wished to be kept in style, whereas a legitimate wife brought a dowry with her: a good part of her family's fortune. In Menander's comedies we always hear explicitly how large the dowry is to be when a couple marries (and Jane Austen expands on the subject at the beginning of *Sense and Sensibility*). We recall Smikrines' words in the passage from *The Arbitration* above, in which he tells his daughter that it is an unfair competition between a wife and a *hetaira*: the latter brings no money with her but shares the wealth of the man at least equally with the wife, while the wife's dowry is at stake if her husband wastes the money keeping another woman. A minor point also emerges: Pamphilos did not live with Myrtion;

7 A *hetaira* and her lover, with two attendants, Roman mosaic of a love scene, near Rome, 2nd century AD.

after drinking with her in the evening, he went home to his mother, where she told him about the neighbours.

Another of Lucian's *Conversations of Courtesans* (no. 3) shows the realities of a courtesan's dependence on a lover even more starkly. The mother of one Philinna is telling her daughter off for giving her lover Diphilos the cold shoulder at the *symposion* on the previous evening. It turns out that Diphilos had slighted her earlier by going over to another girl, one Thaïs, and 'making out' with her. One must picture the scene: a men's entertainment room, *andrōn*, with couches set out round the walls. Two people fitted on these couches (*klinai*): a symposiast (guest) and his girl. It is not only drinking that is on the agenda: we hear of the girls entertaining the men with music, song and dance. The couples also sleep overnight on these couches. Many vase paintings illustrate the scene, which we should bear in mind for comparison with the men's gathering at Plato's *Symposion*, which follows shortly.

Philinna was offended by Diphilos' behaviour, and when Thaïs' lover Lamprias turned up later the same evening, she went over to him and lavished her affections on him, 'to get her own back on Diphilos', as she says. Both girls show off their dancing skills following these flirtations. When Thaïs dances, Lamprias does not applaud; when Philinna dances, Diphilos lies on his back, staring at the ceiling: the couples are symmetrically estranged that evening. Finally, Philinna's mother accuses her:

> And then you didn't sleep with him! You sang your song while he was lying there in tears! Don't you realize, daughter, that we are destitute? Have you forgotten how much we have received from him [Diphilos]? Or what we would have endured last winter if Aphrodite had not sent him to us? (3.3.10–13)

Immediately we realize that Philinna and her mother (probably a *hetaira* herself in earlier life) are utterly dependent on Diphilos' generosity for their very survival. The mother is saying that her daughter is not wise to play 'hard to get' by making up to other men. She concludes:

> You can be annoyed with him [for making out with Thaïs] but don't humiliate him! Don't you realize that lovers are put off if they're humiliated? They go into their shell. You've always been extremely hard on the man. Take care you don't overstep the mark, as the saying goes. (3.3.16–21)

I hope these examples of (fictive) 'days in the life' of a *hetaira* have acquainted the reader with some of the issues and assumptions here. If we translate the word as 'prostitute' or anything similar, we completely skew our understanding of this social institution. The ancient world of *hetairai* was roughly comparable to modern 'dating', with some relationships lasting a day (or night) and some long-lasting, with the woman advancing to the status of *pallakē*, or long-term partner . There was one essential difference, however: Greek *hetairai* were financially dependent on their lovers; it was their mode of existence, and that, of course, introduces a mercenary component into the relationship largely absent from modern Western dating. *Erōs*, however, was the principal coin of exchange, but, as we have seen in the case of Myrtion and Pamphilos, fondness and attachment, *philia*, extends its roots into the subsoil of *erōs* if given a chance.

Higher Spheres

The great ancient Greek treatise on love is Plato's dialogue *Symposion* (The Drinking Party). What is a dialogue? Plato composed his philosophical works in the form of discussions with Socrates, his own teacher. They take the form of inquiries into ethical questions: what is courage? What is piety? What is justice? The *Symposion* is a little different as it is an account of a drinking party at Athens in the late fifth century, when Socrates (*c.* 470–399 BC) was still alive, and the guests decide to give eulogies of love, *erōs*, as their evening entertainment. Greek symposia were, in essence, drinking parties, but on this occasion the guests decide not to get drunk: it will help their philosophizing. There is some irony in the choice of topic, in fact, because while *erōs* commonly meant erotic love, desire, physical longing, the tone of this conversation aims high rather than low, as one might expect from philosophers. A sophist present (that is, a professional adult educator), Pausanias, makes early on the distinction between physical love, which he calls Aphrodite Pandemos (Aphrodite of the Common People), and a spiritual sister, Aphrodite Ourania (Heavenly Aphrodite). Needless to say, the dialogue is much more directed at the latter. Phaidros, the speaker of the first eulogy of the god, points out how this kind of love makes people altruistic. It makes men brave on the battlefield to save their loved ones. There are even stories of men and women making the ultimate sacrifice of dying for their loved ones. Alkestis, for example, died so that her husband Admetos could live (and was rewarded by restored life for it); Achilles made the ultimate sacrifice for his lover Patroklos (we have already met them) and was rewarded by an afterlife in Paradise; Orpheus, too, descended to the underworld to rescue his beloved Eurydikē, but he was not similarly rewarded as he was not prepared to die for her. A doctor present, Eryximachos, argues that it is love that brings harmony to the world (as opposed to strife) and to the individual body, resulting in health. These speakers all treat *erōs* as an ethical principle actively at work in the world for the good. It has little to do with sexual gratification, and there is no mention of the biological function of sexual attraction: reproduction. When we do come on to individual cases of love (Socrates' account of his 'teacher' Diotima, and Alkibiades' account of his love for his teacher Socrates), the emphasis is all on moral improvement, not pleasure. Elsewhere, Plato makes abundantly clear that the pleasures of the body are vastly inferior to those of the soul. This is inevitable given his ontological dualism: the physical world is an imperfect copy of the ideal.

One speech rather stands out in the *Symposion*, and that is the story told by Aristophanes, who was Athens's most famous comic playwright ever. Plato even indulges in a little joke himself when he comes to Aristophanes' turn to eulogize Erōs. The great poet has hiccups and has to pass initially, letting someone else speak before him. However, he does recover in time to speak later. He chooses a kind of parable form to express what love between two people means. Clearly as a writer for the stage he has to visualize what love means and express it by means of a just-so story:

> Love [*erōs*] is the kindest god to men, being the helper and healer of those who, when healed, enjoy the greatest happiness possible for a human. I'll try to describe its power to you, and you will be the teachers of others. First it's necessary for you to understand about human nature and its condition. For originally human nature was not like it is now, but different. In the beginning there were three genders of mankind, not two like now, male and female, but there was a third which combined both the others, whose name survives, but has disappeared itself: there was an androgynous form back then, whose appearance and name was a combination of both, man and woman; now it doesn't exist as such except as a term of abuse. Back then the shape of each human being was spherical,

> with spine and ribcage in circular form. It had four hands and an equal number of legs, and two faces on a round, symmetrical neck. It had only one head consisting of both these faces looking in opposite directions. There were four ears, two sets of genitals and everything else as one can imagine in this situation. It walked erect as now, wherever it wanted. And when it launched into a run, like gymnasts who tumble with their limbs all turning like a windmill, these creatures, propelled by their eight limbs, moved rapidly by rotating. (*Symposium* 189c8–90a8)

Aristophanes goes on to explain that these early spherical humans constituted a threat even to the gods because they were so mobile and ambitious. Finally, Zeus was moved to limit their powers by splitting them down the middle. He turned the faces of each half round to the cut side and sewed up the wound by pulling the folds of skin together like a leather pouch and drawing the purse strings together at the navel. The narrative continues in comic vein with a description of how the cut halves went round desperately trying to couple up with their missing half. They clung together, but now the problem was that the race of humans was endangered because their genital organs were still facing outwards and they had sex, as it were, with the ground as the only viable receptacle, like cicadas, says Aristophanes. As a solution to this problem, Zeus moved their genital organs round to the front so they could couple with each other. The narrative comes to a preliminary conclusion:

> That's the reason why desire [*erōs*] for one another is imbued in mankind and instils in them a longing for their original condition, attempting to make one of two, and to heal the human state. For each of us is a human half, having been filleted like a flatfish into two halves. So he or she is always seeking their matching half. (191c8–d5)

Following this, we understand why Aristophanes began by saying that humans had originally been of three types: round men, round women, and a combination of the two, the androgynous gender. What follows is an account of diverging sexual preferences, from heterosexual to homosexual to bisexual. One wonders whether this part of the myth is not more tilted towards Platonic preferences than Aristophanic, for heterosexuality dominates in Aristophanes' comedies. Plato's 'Aristophanes' explains that only the split androgynous people are heterosexual in a pronounced way. The male half desperately seeks a female half and vice versa. He even casts the aspersion on them that the men tend to be adulterers and the women nymphomaniacs. The split women, on the contrary, turn out to be more interested in women, and the split men, the best sort, 'Aristophanes' says, prefer the company of men and boys. These split males are the bravest, best citizens; only this sort goes into politics because they don't waste their time on women. Quite unashamedly, he says that these males, as boys, are happy to:

> love men and lie with them in an embrace, and these are the best of the boys because they are the bravest . . . Conversely, as men, they become pederasts and are not naturally interested in marriage and having children, but are forced by convention [*nomos*] and are quite content to live in their community of men without marrying. (191e7–192b2)

This passage, and the entire dialogue, may have had a pernicious influence on the British educational system (of boys) in earlier centuries: the *Symposion* is a famous dialogue, and it promotes a perception that the Greeks happily practised pederasty and advocated the rule of men in their cliques. We have already seen how other authors (for example, Homer and Menander, and Aristophanes himself) convey a quite different picture.

Plato's 'Aristophanes', however, completes his eulogy of *erōs* by describing the happiness true love can bring to a couple, of whatever gender. Again he expresses the story in mythical form, introducing the smith-god Hephaistos, who asks the couple how he can help them join up physically:

> Now when any person bumps into his lost other half, whether a lover of boys or anyone else, then the couple is overcome by remarkable feelings of fondness [*philia*], compatibility [*oikeiotēs*, lit. 'feeling at home'] and passion [*erōs*], and doesn't want to be apart, so to speak, even for a short time. These are the couples who stay together for a lifetime, without being able to say what it is exactly they want from each other. It's certainly not just having sex together [*ta aphrodisia*] which makes them so determined to stick together. No, it is clear that each in their inmost self [*psychē*] wants something else, which it can't exactly express, but is only half-consciously aware of it. And if Hephaistos were to stand over such a couple as they lie together, holding his toolbox, and ask: 'Is that what you want: to be together in the most complete manner so as not to be apart either by night or day? If that's what you want, I'm prepared to weld you together in my forge so that from two you become one, and, as long as you live, you both live together as one. And even when you die you'll still be together in the underworld, joined together as one in death. See if that's what it is that you desire and whether that will suffice, if you achieve it.' We can be sure that no one, hearing that, would turn that down. (192b5–e6)

If one were looking for a text for a wedding ceremony, one might look no further!

Down to Earth

Jilted

If some come away from Plato's *Symposion* with a feeling of inadequacy – 'it's all very well for the philosophers . . .' – voices from very different quarters of love are also audible, showing a much grittier side to the ancient experience. The plaintive voice of a woman badly let down in love is heard in an anonymous fragment of Hellenistic poetry found on a papyrus known as *Fragmentum Grenfellianum* (because it was found and published by B. P. Grenfell; it is also known as the 'Maiden's

Lament').[8] It is the lament of a woman rejected by her 'ex' and can be attributed to the ancient class of poetic text called *paraklausithyron*, or 'facing a closed door', reflecting the situation of a lover metaphorically locked out of a person's affections. Unusual in this composition is that it is a girl lamenting; more commonly, especially in Latin love poetry, it is a man who complains that a woman is not opening her door to him. He stands outside in the street, usually at night, lamenting and imploring her to have a change of heart. The poem here is metrically complex, not fitting easily into any common scheme; the language is direct and down to earth, unlike the high register of tragic laments, for example. For that reason it feels particularly heartfelt. The poetic text was found on one side of a fragment of papyrus, on whose reverse side a loan document dating to 174 BC is found. It was first published in 1896.[9] This girl's plaint had been buried literally under the sands of time for going on 2,000 years. It should be added that the poet is quite likely to have been a man.

Caught, whichever way I turn.
Joined with him as one. Our love
was forged by Kypris. Pain grips me
when I remember
how he kissed me, fully intending
to leave me:
cause of my confusion
and wellspring of my love.
Passion took me,
I don't deny.
Dear Stars and Night, my companions in love,
bring me even now to him, to whom
Kypris drives me helplessly, and
mighty Erōs has me in his grip.
To light me on my way is the pyre
burning in my heart.
This is his crime, this my misery.
Deceiver of my heart,
with his fine words at first . . . (ll. 1–19)

This is not the end of the poem; it continues for another forty-odd lines in similar vein, the last of which are damaged in the papyrus. The text, although spoken from the heart and involving what seem to be real gut feelings, is to be placed in the same milieu as the *hetairai* sketches of Lucian. There is no question that marital infidelity is the issue here. Some telling details firmly identify the man as a 'punter' among *hetairai*. When in line 25 the girl says, 'throw me your crowns at least', she is referring to the crowns of leaves and flowers that men wore when partying at symposia.[10] The girl calls him 'master' (ll. 42 and 48 *kyrie*) and says she will be happy to 'serve' him; she describes how he 'kissed' her but is now ignoring her. The relationship is that of an obsequious *hetaira* imploring a male lover not to shun her now:

> I am going mad
> sleeping alone at night;
> but you shun my touch.
> If we have fallen out, now's the time
> to reconcile.
> Do we not have friends for just this,
> to judge who is in the wrong? (ll. 34–40)

In fact, she is in the same position as the *hetairai* Myrtion and Philinna in Lucian's *Conversations of Courtesans* above, both upset by their lovers' (apparent) infidelity. The poem shows that genuine feelings were involved in such relationships (on both sides), but also that the woman was not protected by the institution of marriage: the man could feel free to move on to pastures new as the mood took him. Nor should we forget that a man's favours towards a *hetaira* brought with them material security: an unspoken factor in such love was no doubt the woman's feeling of peril and destitution if the man withheld his material support.

Love magic

Such constellations were also conducive to potentially more vicious attacks than a poem of recrimination. Magic was widely employed in matters of love, either to attract a lover or to eliminate a rival, or to make oneself irresistible. Theocritus' second *Idyll*, called *Pharmakeutria* (Sorceress; third century BC), is a mimetic poem about a lovesick girl called Simaitha, who performs magical rites with her maid Thestylis in order to recover the love of one Delphis, who had become attracted to another. The situation, then, is similar to that in the 'Maiden's Lament', but here Simaitha resorts to magical arts to try to influence Delphis' heart, instead of howls of misery hurled into the night. Simaitha uses a magical implement, a so-called *iynx*, which seems to have been a kind of spun top, whose spinning motion is supposed to work sympathetic magic on the person to whom it is directed, to spin towards the performer in love. She also uses herbal potions, which her maid is instructed to smear on the threshold of Delphis' home. She uses binding spells and invocations of the typical gods of magic, Hekatē, Sēlēnē (Moon) and Nyx (Night).

Theocritus' poem is a full-length literary dramatization of real-life practices. From Roman Egypt in the imperial period, we possess a number of papyri containing instructions for magical rites, called 'actions' (*praxeis*); they are referred to in common as the Greek Magical Papyri, and they seem to represent a kind of conflation of Greek and Egyptian beliefs and practices, with added elements of Christian and Jewish tradition. Love magic is prominent among the 'actions', whether to induce a beloved person to burn with irresistible love for the practitioner or to eliminate a rival lover from the person's affections. Effigies akin to 'Voodoo' dolls are used to manipulate the emotions of the targeted person at a distance, as well as spells, lamp magic, invocations and magical potions. It is a heady mix. However, before the age of the magical papyri, binding spells were also used throughout Greece in order to cast a spell on a rival or opponent. They tended to be used in the areas of athletics, to weaken or incapacitate a rival; in lawsuits to impede the opponents' power of speech and thought; and, equally prominently, in love, usually where a love triangle was involved: one person tried to 'bind' the charms of a rival in order to eliminate them from the contest. Such spells were typically written (usually very badly) on a thin sheet of lead, which was then folded up and placed in a suitably numinous place such as a person's grave or the bottom of a well, where it would lie hidden and work its nefarious magic in secret and over time. In a later chapter we will also see how binding spells were used in commercial rivalries, where one tradesman or craftsman wished to damage a competitor's business.

The following curse tablet comes from Attica and is written on a lead sheet that was placed, as emerges from the text, in a grave.[11] It aims to thwart a woman called Theodora in her love affair with one Charias. Interestingly, Theodora's *paidion*, child or slave(!), is also mentioned, whom Charias is also said to lust after: was this a particularly devious situation, in which a rival lover wished to remove another woman *and* her slave/child from the competition? We do not know who the author of the curse is; she is likely to be a rival *hetaira*, as in Lucian's dialogues and the 'Maiden's Lament'.[12] This is a voice from the grave with a difference: the person uttering the curse was still alive when her words were placed, like malware in a modern computer, in a dead person's grave, where they were supposed to do their damage surreptitiously.

> I bind Theodora by Hekatē [underworld goddess] and by the unquiet dead. May she fail in her purpose, and whatever she may say to Kallias and to Charias. I bind her works, her words, her actions . . . I bind Theodora so that she may not marry

8 A lead curse tablet, inscribed with a curse and a person's name on the inside surface, folded and then pinned with a nail, Hellenistic period.

> Charias, and Charias may forget Theodora and her slave/child [*paidiou*] and his sexual union [lit. 'bed'] with Theodora.
>
> And as this corpse [in the grave] lies powerless, so should everything fail for Theodora, her words, her actions towards Charias and to other people. I bind Theodora by Hermes of the Underworld and by the spirits of the dead, and by Tethys [another underworld god]: all the words she utters and the deeds she does towards other people and with regard to her sexual intercourse with Charias. And that he forget that intercourse. And that Charias should forget the slave/child of Theodora for whom he feels desire (*erāi*).

Before we begin to suspect that the text has not been properly deciphered and interpreted where it mentions Theodora's child (whose sex in the Greek of the tablet is indeterminate), whom Charias is also said to lust after, one could point to other cases of men having relations with women *and* their daughters. A case in point is described by the orator Andokides in his speech *On the Mysteries* (turn of the fourth century BC), in which he describes how one Kallias took one woman to wife, then took a fancy to her daughter (from a previous relationship) and ejected the older woman, but later took her in again, plus the child she had conceived by him, when the daughter tried to commit suicide. Who are we to judge when Hollywood celebrities are alleged to have had affairs with the daughters of their partners? But Theodora's child may also have been male, and the relation one of pederasty (as Auguste Audollent suggests).[13]

2
STATUS

It is, perhaps, an unpleasant aspect of human society that interactions between people are very much based on status. That is, their perceived standing or position in the hierarchy in society. Perhaps we can forgive ourselves by comparison with animals such as wolves or primates, which also live in groups (societies) and are extremely status aware. There, fights to establish status are often physical and may even result in death. If we consider human warfare as motivated either directly or indirectly by status ('whose power is greater?'), then that is also, and fatally, true of us as humans. However, there are much more subtle expressions and reflections of status in human intercourse. We all know stories of certain people who seem to exercise a magnetic influence in a group; people for whom a room of chatter goes quiet when they enter.

Gods

Let us start again from the beginning of literature. In the last chapter we saw how Agamemnon and Achilles fell out over prerogatives and prizes of battle. Self-love, or self-esteem, was an important factor. By taking a prize from a warrior, one reduced his self-esteem and standing in the eyes of others. It would be safe to say that the epic poem *Iliad* has, as its core dynamic, this system of honour (*timē*) among warriors, their fame (*kleos*) and their standing (*kūdos*). But this system operating on earth, and particularly on the battlefield, had its corollary in heaven, or on Olympus, the residence of the gods grouped as a family around

Zeus. Human honour was modelled very much on divine honours, or, no doubt, one could reverse the relation: the Greeks chose to depict the gods in their polytheistic system as just as interested in rights and prerogatives as humans were (and are). For the gods in Homer are a bit like the manager, coach and trainers of a football team: a whole range of powerful operators in the background, watching events on the field, selecting accordingly and developing game plans and tactics. On Olympus, Zeus is the head man, and on one occasion, after other gods intervened on the battlefield, he calls a council of the gods – appropriately, on the 'highest pinnacle of Olympus' – and explains that his power is supreme and the others must obey his will:

> If one of you tries to help either the Trojan or the Greek side . . . then he will come to understand that I am far and away the most powerful of all the gods. Just try me, and you'll all understand. Hang a golden chain from heaven and all of you – gods and goddesses – grab hold of it. But you won't succeed in pulling Zeus to the ground from heaven, Zeus, the commander-in-chief, even if you try with all your might. But if *I* choose to pull on it in earnest, I could pull you all up, sea and earth and all. Then I'd tie the golden chain from a peak of Olympus and all would dangle from it in mid-air. I am *that much* superior to gods as well as humans! (*Iliad* 8.10–27)

Zeus' supremacy stemmed from a myth, or sacred tale, that was universally known in Greece and has been shown to have affinities with neighbouring Near Eastern cultures: the succession myth. It was narrated in great detail by a Boeotian poet called Hesiod, who was a rough contemporary of Homer. Put simply, the myth of his *Theogony* explained why and how it came to pass that gods and men now live under the reign of Zeus. It traces the world, if one wants to call it that, back to a primeval state called, appropriately, Chaos, then narrates a genealogy of gods starting with the divine couple Ouranos (Heaven) and Gaia (Earth), who are succeeded by Kronos (not Chronos: Time) and his partner Rhea, in turn violently deposed by Zeus, who takes Hera to wife. The myth then records a division of realms between

Zeus and his siblings: he gets heaven, Poseidon the ocean, Hades the underworld, and the earth is (theoretically) held in common between Zeus and Poseidon (cf. *Iliad* 15.185ff.). Following this basic apportioning of realms, Hesiod goes on to describe all the other branches of the divine family and their particular provinces. Further definition of divine prerogatives is narrated in a collection of so-called *Homeric Hymns*, attributed to Homer in antiquity but not necessarily so in fact. Four long ones to Demeter, Hermes, Apollo and Aphrodite, but also the shorter ones, contain myths that explain how these gods acquired their typical areas of power and worship. In the high classical period, the historian Herodotus says, quite simply, that 'Hesiod and Homer' gave the Greeks their 'theogony' (family tree of gods), named the gods and divided up their powers (*Histories* 2.53).

The fourth, *Homeric Hymn to Aphrodite*, for example, shows how the major goddesses each acquired a particular province or area of power. The story told is that of Aphrodite, who irritates Zeus by subjugating all the other gods and goddesses – and humans and birds and beasts – by love (sexual attraction) but does not herself fall victim to its power. He teaches her a lesson by uniting her with Anchises of Troy on Mount Ida, thus humiliating her by making her fall, temporarily, for a mortal and experience the strange sting of love. Incidentally, the union produces Aineias, who, in a different life, becomes Virgil's hero in the *Aeneid*, Rome's national epic. It is said at the beginning of the hymn that only three goddesses have no truck with Aphrodite: Athena, who loves warfare rather than typically feminine pursuits but does involve herself in creative activities through handicrafts – she inspires men to build war chariots and women to weave fine textiles. In other words, in contradistinction to all the goddesses and women, Athena does not participate in the works of Aphrodite but instead has chosen a different prerogative. Similarly, Artemis is said not to obey Aphrodite but to prefer hunting and celebrations in the 'great outdoors'. Finally, let us see how Hestia (*Histiē* in Ionic dialect; Latin Vesta, or Hearth) acquired her compensatory status, having declined love:

> Nor did the works of Aphrodite appeal to the decorous maiden Histiē, whom Kronos of the crooked mind fathered

> first, then again as his youngest,[1] by the will of Zeus the holder of power. Poseidon and Apollo both courted her, but she strongly resisted and flatly refused. She swore a great oath, which she has stuck to, touching the head of Zeus the Father, the wielder of power, to remain a virgin for all time, a prominent goddess. Zeus the Father gave her a different prerogative instead of marriage: she took her place at the centre of the house, taking pride of place. She receives honour at all the temples of the gods [on their altars] and among all mankind she counts as venerable. (*Homeric Hymn to Aphrodite* 21–32)

A great deal of epic poetry, then, is concerned with structuring the divine family into relations of graded honour: Zeus at the top with his partner Hera, then the others of the first generation descended from Kronos – Poseidon, Hades, Hestia – then the next generation descended from this, and so on. The *Homeric Hymn to Apollo*, for example, shows how Apollo's younger brother Hermes has to negotiate with his father Zeus for an appropriate distribution of honours as both are interested in herding, and both in music. But it is not simply a question of seniority; it is also a question of the specific power wielded jealously by each god. Mount Olympus itself, with its highest pinnacle and lesser crags and promontories, appears to have been a visualization in space of the hierarchical relations of the gods. They all (with exceptions such as Hades and Poseidon) have their homes on Olympus, but these are arranged – where a poet cares to mention this point – in ascending order to Zeus at the summit. This is not the place to delve deeper into the anthropology, or psychology, of polytheism, but clearly the Greek gods of Olympus are, at some level, a conceptualization on the part of human society of the powers to which their lives are subject, or to which they subject themselves within society.

In fact, of course, things seldom went smoothly within Zeus' extended family. The *Iliad*, as we have seen, centres on the fight for status between Agamemnon and Achilles, after Agamemnon has insulted Achilles. And the gods take sides in this conflict, which also affects the course of the Trojan War. Thetis, a daughter of Nereus who is also Achilles' mother, petitions Zeus following the insult to her son, to so steer the war that her son regains his honour. Zeus sighs, conscious that this will annoy his scold of a wife Hera, but agrees to let the Trojans win for a while so the Greeks will clamour for Achilles to return to the fray, now that he has withdrawn from active service and gone off to sulk in his tent. But this championing of the Trojan side – albeit temporarily – brings Zeus into direct conflict with other gods, principally Poseidon and Hera. We have just heard Zeus' reaction to challenges from the other gods to his authority: his boast that he is stronger than all of them even pulling together. In Book 13, Homer pauses a moment in the battle narrative to summarize the relative status of the gods acting behind the scene:

> And these two mighty sons of Kronos [Zeus and Poseidon] took opposite sides in the bitter conflict of the heroic warriors. Zeus on the one hand favoured victory for the Trojans, wishing to raise fleet-footed Achilles' esteem. Not that he wanted the entire Greek host to be defeated before Troy – no, he merely wanted to honour Thetis and her warlike son. Poseidon on the other hand was backing the Greek cause, having secretly emerged from the grey-blue sea. He was displeased to see them being beaten by the Trojans, and he was mightily angry with Zeus. Mind you, these two were children of the same parents and the same family tree, but Zeus was the first-born and knew more. Hence Poseidon avoided direct confrontation and chose rather to employ stealth tactics in the shape of a human being. (*Iliad* 13.345–57)

In other words, Poseidon defers to Zeus' higher status, but that does not deter him from trying to influence the course of battle. Later in the poem (Books 13 and 14), we find him impersonating first a hawk, to give a favourable omen to the Greeks, then an old man acting as personal adviser to Agamemnon.

Likewise Hera, who is also maddened by Zeus' decision to honour Thetis' request to tilt the battle in her son's favour. She too employs devious means to achieve her purpose. One of the books of the *Iliad* (14) was dubbed in antiquity the 'Deception of Zeus'. It describes how Hera decided to use a woman's wiles to distract Zeus' attention from the human arena. She visits Aphrodite, goddess of sex appeal, and asks her to give her a love charm – but on a false pretext. She tells Aphrodite she needs it to reconcile Tethys (an infernal river) and Okeanos (Ocean), who are at loggerheads in the underworld. Aphrodite hands her her *kēstos*, a kind of magic girdle, it seems, in which are bundled all her seductive powers. She also touches down on her divine journey on the Greek island of Lemnos, where she meets Sleep (*Hypnos*), Death's brother, to request a donation from him. He hesitates, citing an earlier occasion when he had got into trouble with Zeus by giving Hera a dose of sleep with which to trick Herakles on his adventures. Hera bribes Hypnos by promising one of the younger Graces (Charites) as a wife. Hypnos agrees, having extracted an oath by all the underworld powers from Hera to keep her word.

Thus equipped, Hera meets up with Zeus where he is observing the Trojan War from a vantage point on Mount Ida (a local mountain in the Troad). He falls for her ploy, they sleep together and afterwards Zeus falls into a deep sleep, unable to continue his vigil over the human battle below, like a watchman asleep on duty. Hypnos rushes to Poseidon and tells him: 'Now's your chance' (14.357–60).

It is worrying, and no doubt deliberate on Homer's part, that the fate of humans in the theatre of war is dependent on these antics of the gods. While Zeus and Hera are enjoying a second honeymoon in a mountain resort, fates of whole cities are being decided. It is not that Homer is deriding the divine apparatus he has built up. He is merely showing their unencumbered existence compared to humans. In epic poetry, gods are 'easy-living' (*rheia zōontes*) compared to long-suffering humans.

The simple message we can take from these scenes of gods' behaviour is that status, whether expressed as strength among males or beauty and allurement among females, was everything on Olympus. It is a relatively small circle of potentates, but they decide everything on earth like a court at which there is one king but many lords and ladies. Such a scheme invites rivalries, intrigues, alliances and feuds. It is both a mirror of human society on earth and a model for that society by providing a paradigm. The two realms are mutually exclusive in existential terms but also interdependent in terms of behaviour. Hierarchy, status, strength, special skills: these are the governing principles, not peace, harmony, cooperation.

Homer

Beneath this canopy of divine powers, Homeric heroes in the *Iliad* fought and competed for honour, wealth, power and success. The basic conflict of course was for victory in battle: would the Greeks succeed in sacking Troy and thus reclaiming Helen and amassing vast treasure from the city? Even the *casus belli*, the abduction of Helen, was more of a slight to Menelaos' honour than any real dent in Greece's power or wealth. It was fought according to a code of honour: when a husband was sought for Zeus' daughter Helen, suitors arrived from all over Greece to compete for the honour. They swore an oath, as condition of the competition, that they would come to the defence of the victor in the competition should anyone take Helen from him subsequently.[2] Well, Paris did just that, so the leading Greek warlords were obliged to help Menelaos and his brother Agamemnon retake her. Achilles complains in the course of his argument with Agamemnon in *Iliad* Book 1 that he himself has no quarrel with the Trojans; his participation in the war serves merely to increase the *timē* of Agamemnon and Menelaos. And now Agamemnon wants to steal his prize girl, Briseïs, from him if he is forced to return his own prize, Chryseïs, to her father, priest of Apollo:

> We followed you [to Troy], shameless man, to make you happy, securing honour [*timē*] for Menelaos, and you, dog, from the Trojans. And now you completely disregard that. Indeed you threaten to take away my prize from me, for which I fought hard, and which the sons of the Achaeans [Greeks] awarded me. I *never* receive an equal share compared to you whenever the Achaeans score a victory over the well-populated citadel of Troy. And yet *my* hands do the lion's share of the fierce fighting. But when it comes to dividing up the spoils, *you* get the lion's share whereas I return to camp

> with a small, albeit cherished, share, after I have exhausted myself in battle. Now I will sail to Phthia, since it's obviously to my advantage to return home with my warships. I will not be dishonoured there, nor will you be able to siphon off my wealth. (*Iliad* 1.158–72)

Agamemnon's angry reply to this challenge shows that it is personal honour and standing that are primarily at stake in the quarrel:

> Run away if that's what you want! I won't beg you to stay on my account. There are others on my side who will honour me [*timēsousi*], above all Zeus the Governor. You are the most hated of the royal kings to me. You love nothing more than a quarrel, wars and battles. You may be very strong, a god may have granted you that: well, go home with your ships and your men and lord it over the Myrmidons. I don't care about you and your temper. But I tell you this. Since Apollo is robbing me of Chryseïs, I'll return her with a ship manned by my men, but I'll come in person to your encampment and take *your* prize, pretty Briseïs, from you so that you realize how much stronger I am than you, and anyone else in the future will hesitate to speak back to me like an equal and to challenge my authority. (1.173–87)

In the following books, Zeus' plan to honour Achilles by giving the Trojans the upper hand leads to despair in the Greek camp. Confronted by their losses, Agamemnon repents and declares that he is prepared to make it up to Achilles in an attempt to repair the damage caused by their quarrel and induce the great warrior to return to the fight. As he says, 'A man who is favoured by Zeus is worth a large army' (9.117). Agamemnon concedes that in their initial quarrel in Book 1 he was guilty of a serious mistake: the word he uses is *atē* (and in 9.119 the verb *aasamēn*, 'I screwed up'), which indicates a kind of mental seizure, sometimes inflicted on men by gods. Now he is prepared to atone for this by heaping riches and honours on Achilles in the hope of making him change his mind. It is worth looking at the list of goods that Agamemnon promises, to see clearly what constituted wealth and honour for a nobleman at that time (9.121–56).

First comes a string of valuable objects: seven brand-new tripods; seven talents of gold; twenty shining cauldrons. These should be seen not just as pricey objects desirable in themselves but also as valuable for their cult value: tripods and cauldrons made common donations to the gods for favour: if a man had such treasures, he was not merely rich but possessed the means to curry favour with gods.

Next, twelve fine racehorses that have won many prizes: 'A man would not be destitute who won so many prizes, nor poor in valuable gold.' Here the point is not merely the monetary value of prizes won in horse races but participation in the aristocratic field of horse breeding and racing (seen also in Aristophanes' *Birds* 1443). One need only compare the enthusiasm of Sheikh Mohammed bin Rashid Al Maktoum, prime minister of the United Arab Emirates, for horse racing as an entry into the British aristocracy, even the royal family. In ancient Greece such races were also part of the Panhellenic institution of state games: most famous were the Olympic Games, but there were others: the Pythian Games at Delphi and the Isthmian Games at Corinth, for example. Leading statesmen and dignitaries were very keen to win at these games for the status and fame that it brought.

Agamemnon next promises seven very pretty women from Lesbos and, in addition, the girl whom he had taken from Achilles initially (Briseïs). Agamemnon now swears he has not slept with the girl in bed yet, 'as is the custom for men and women'. So clearly the possession of a harem of pretty women counted as a status symbol, but not only for sex. Agamemnon promises that the girls from Lesbos will also be 'skilled in crafts'; in other words, they contributed to the wealth of a man's estate.

Next, a promise of the gifts Achilles will receive if and when they capture Troy: a ship full of gold and bronze and twenty of the most beautiful women 'after Argive Helen'. This promise reflects what was, in fact, the main motivation for ancient warfare: booty.

Then Agamemnon promises one of his three daughters to Achilles as his wife, so that he will become his son-in-law.[3] This offer reflects one of the major routes to enhanced status: marriage into a leading family or clan. As we will see below, there was much competition for a rich or powerful man's daughters, as indeed there was in European royal families until fairly recently.

As dowry for this daughter, Agamemnon offers an extraordinary thing: no fewer than seven important cities to rule over. He lists these by name, saying they are all close to the sea (that is, they enjoy trade) and have citizens rich in sheep and cattle. These, Agamemnon says, will honour Achilles 'like a god' and pay high taxes. In other words, they will be a power base in terms of manpower and money.

Agamemnon finishes his speech with a veiled threat about 'dire Death'. The meaning seems to be that Achilles should take advantage of Agamemnon's offer while life lasts. Perhaps it is also a pointer by the poet to the *datum* of myth that Achilles would die before Troy was taken. Agamemnon finishes with a final flourish: 'And he should acknowledge to me how much more of a king I am and how far superior my lineage.' That may be a diplomatic mistake on Agamemnon's part. Having promised Achilles all these riches and adornments, he ends by saying as a kind of condition that Achilles should nevertheless defer to Agamemnon as the greater king. Perhaps these two components in his speech – the veiled threat of death and the demand that Achilles defer to the greater king – are meant by Homer as pointers towards the reaction we might expect from Achilles. And when an embassy conveys Agamemnon's offer to Achilles, that is what happens: it fails. The episode encapsulates what is at stake in the Homeric status games: wealth and power are all well and good, but hierarchy is perhaps the deciding factor. Even accepting Agamemnon's offer would be a sign of deference on Achilles' part, something he is not prepared to do. As we have already mentioned, it takes the death on the battlefield of his beloved friend Patroklos to wake him from passivity to a burning desire for revenge.

Most of the status factors we have identified so far are familiar enough to the modern world: money, power, trophy wives, property empires and so on. We may miss some things that are valued today: justice perhaps, fairness, kindness, generosity – although whether these are status markers nowadays may be open to question. Anyway, the more cooperative virtues that enhance an individual's status are evident enough in the ancient state, too, as we will see later. However, one status marker in the Homeric world that was very important then but which has since receded to an infinitesimal level, at least in the Western world, is the question of divine patronage. That is, characters in Homer receive aid and assistance from gods, which clearly elevates their standing. We have already seen in passing how Agamemnon observed that Achilles seemed to be being 'favoured by Zeus'.

In fact, the Homeric text is peppered by divine interventions and individual favouritism on the part of the gods. This comes out most clearly in the *Odyssey*, Homer's 'other' epic. Here Odysseus may be buffeted by fate on his return journey from Troy – it takes ten years! – but he could never have survived the roller coaster at all if Athena had not intervened on his behalf. True, he also draws the anger of another god, Poseidon, upon himself because he blinded his ogre son Polyphemos in the cave. But Odysseus is clearly very special to Athena (she says so), and his life's journey is unthinkable without this perceived relationship.

Similarly, in the *Iliad* the gods frequently lend a hand to a warrior in a tight spot, almost like a boxer's second. A few instances: Athena stops Achilles in the first book from killing Agamemnon outright when Agamemnon insults him, as his temper has run away with him (*Il.* 1.194); Zeus is said to 'favour' Agamemnon and to give him *timē* (2.197); Aphrodite rescues Paris from imminent death at the hands of Menelaos (we recall the 'Judgement of Paris', when Paris awarded her the prize) (3.374ff.); in the duel between the Trojan Aineias and Diomedes, Aphrodite backs Aineias, Athena Diomedes (5.248–56); later in the same duel, Apollo spirits Aineias from death in battle to the safety of his temple in Troy (5.445); Poseidon intervenes in the duel between Achilles and Aineias in order to save the latter (Virgil's *Aeneid* could not have been written if he had not!) (20.259). A particularly detailed account occurs in 22.545ff. when Apollo gives personal assistance to Agenor on the Trojan side in a duel with Achilles. First he instils courage in Agenor to stand up to Achilles so as to enable the remaining Trojans to flee to safety within Troy's walls, then he takes his place after Agenor has thrown his spear ineffectively and lures Achilles away from Troy by running away, always keeping just ahead of him. Apollo's purpose is to prevent Troy falling to the Achaeans before the appointed day; he uses Agenor as his agent.

Once, in battle, a hero's fate hangs in the balance. The Trojan Sarpedon and the Greek Patroklos are engaged in combat, first in their war chariots; then they jump to the ground to fight it out, watched by Zeus, to whom Sarpedon is dear. Zeus turns to Hera and complains:

> 'Woe is me, that Fate decrees that Sarpedon, who is most dear to me of men, must now die at the hands of Patroklos, son of Menoitios. I am in two minds whether I should pluck him still living from the tearful battle and set him down safe in Lycia, or whether I should let him die at the hands of Patroklos.' And Lady Hera, cow-eyed, answered: 'Wretched son of Kronos! What are you saying? You want to save a mortal man who has long been fated to die and release him from obnoxious death? Well, do it. But we other gods will not approve!' (*Iliad* 16.433–43)

The greatest example of divine favour as status marker also marks a turning point in the narrative – the *peripeteia*, in ancient terminology – when Achilles rejoins the fray. This also corresponds to the divine plan of the *Iliad*, which is constructed around Zeus' decision to enhance Achilles' *timē* as the 'best of the Achaeans' after he has been needlessly insulted by Agamemnon. When Achilles is goaded into battle once again by the death of Patroklos, his goddess mother Thetis intervenes on his behalf. His suit of armour was lost on the battlefield when Patroklos fell. Now Thetis decides to obtain a new suit of armour for her son from no less a source than the divine armourer himself, Hephaistos. This occurs in Book 18 and, as I said, marks the turning point in the narrative. From now on, the impetus will be with Achilles. He will kill Hektor and the war will be as good as won for the Greeks.

If these are the attributes of the high-status protagonists of the *Iliad* – prowess and power – what might be the defining attributes of the less richly endowed? Homer does not often mention the 'little people' of life, although many of the similes are drawn from everyday farming and fishing life. In one scene shortly after the quarrel, however, we are given a vignette of the 'lower classes' in the Greek camp. Tricked by Zeus, Agamemnon has given the order to abandon the mission and sail off home. The army is delighted, and they rush to the ships. Odysseus, however, instructed by Athena, realizes the mistake and hurries through the camp, telling them: 'Hold your horses!' He cajoles the high-ranking officers (called 'kings') and lambasts the common soldiers:

> But whoever among the commoners [*dēmos*] he encountered shouting out loud, at these he brandished his stick and railed at them: 'Fool, stand still and listen to what your superiors say. You're no warrior! You're weak! You don't count either in war or in council. Not everyone who is Achaean can be a commanding officer. Nor is a plurality of commanders good. There should be *one* commander, one king, he to whom Zeus the son of wily Kronos gave the sceptre and the command, so that he might lead them.' (2.198–206)

Odysseus manages to call another general assembly of the camp in order to rally the spirits of the men for renewed battle. One of the lower classes, however, comes forward and baits Agamemnon. Tellingly, his low status is depicted through his physical appearance. He is ugly and almost deformed:

> Only Thersites went on shouting abuse. He was always shooting his mouth off in an unseemly, insubordinate way against his superiors, saying anything which he thought would make the men laugh. And he was the ugliest man at Troy, bow-legged, lame in one leg, his shoulders hunched forward. Above them his head was pointed, his hair thinning on top. He was particularly spiteful to Achilles and Odysseus, being in the habit of goading them. But on this occasion he aimed his jibes against mighty Agamemnon, shouting them loudly. The Greeks disliked him very much and felt anger in their hearts.

> But he shouted out now, baiting Agamemnon with his words: 'Son of Atreus, what's wrong now? What are you lacking? Your stores are full of bronze, a string of choice women fill your tent, given to you as our commander by us Greeks whenever we capture some settlement. Is it gold you want . . . or a pretty girl, perhaps, for you to have sex with? Whom you'll then refuse to part with? It's not right that you as commander get the Greeks into trouble.' (2.212–34)

We note how Thersites fixes on Agamemnon's recent embarrassment over Chryseïs, asking him whether he is about to repeat the performance and bring another pestilence down on the army. His taunts are answered by an angry riposte from Odysseus, who tells him to shut up. Otherwise, he threatens to humiliate him in a way that is revealing for perception of status:

> 'If I catch you uttering nonsense like this again, may the head not rest on Odysseus' shoulders, may I no longer be called the father of Telemachos, if I don't grab you and strip the clothes from you, coat and undergarment, which cover your private parts and send you squealing back to the ships, chased from our midst by vicious blows!' With these words, he struck him with his staff on the back and shoulders. And he doubled up and howled with pain. Bloody weals stood out on his back from the blows of the golden staff. He fell on the ground, cringing, wiping the helpless tears from his eyes. And the others, who had been annoyed, laughed out loud. (2.258–70)

In other words, Odysseus has stripped him down to his naked 'shame' – the Greek word for 'private parts' is exactly 'the shameful things' – and beaten him like a slave (although he was not one), and everyone had laughed at him. Such humiliation in physical bearing clearly was the opposite of the manly ideal that the 'heroes' were striving after.

The Great and the Good

Homer has often been called the 'Bible of the Greeks', and there is some truth in that, although it was never read at church services (I mean festivals of the gods), nor was it cited as a moral instance, although frequently as an authority on all sorts of matters. The Greeks of the Second Sophistic were still citing Homer as their authority in all manner of things. In short, the values we have traced in Homer's gods on Olympus, and Greeks at ground level, remained relevant for centuries. There was, however, considerable development in the structure of society, in civic institutions and in politics.

This is not the place for a history of Greece, in however potted a form. We need to have a scaffold, however, on which to hang other observations. The Homeric age takes us up to about the seventh century BC. Following this 'heroic' age with its kings and vassals, the Greek city-state, *polis*, gradually emerged: Sparta, Corinth, Athens and Thebes in Greece, Miletos and Ephesos in Ionia (on the west coast of Asia Minor, modern-day Turkey) and Syracuse in Sicily are only the most famous. There were myriad others. A Greek *polis* consisted of an area of land, *gē*, feeding and supplying a town in which civic institutions, including temples with their cults, could develop. After the kings, who modelled themselves on Homeric kings, came the tyrants (*tyrannoi*). Politically, the seventh and sixth centuries BC were the 'age of tyrants'; these men invariably came from the powerful aristocratic dynasties. Eventually, and not everywhere, the tyrants were ousted and more democratic forms of government introduced in stages. Particularly in Athens, fully fledged democracy was in place by the second half of the fifth century BC. Other cities, notably Sparta, developed an oligarchic form of government, where a governing elite, with two nominal 'kings' at its head, ruled over an upper class of Spartiates (men of Sparta), with a vassal population beneath them (*helots*).

While some of these cities turned out to be hotbeds of political development and of the arts, sciences and architecture, it also led to a fragmentation of Greece. There was little sense of national unity, only vigorous competition and, unfortunately, wars between the vying states. The Greek *poleis* (plural) defended themselves with massed ranks of hoplites (armoured foot soldiers), who fought in line, some, like the Spartans, achieving legendary standards of discipline and bravery, as we will see. Hoplites were citizens in arms. It was expected of citizens of these *poleis* that they would fight in their town's army. Socrates fought in the army and had a reputation for bravery. Likewise Sophocles, the tragic poet, and the historian Thucydides, who were generals no less. This hoplite army meant the end of individual chivalry as we find it in Homer. It also led to an identity of interests between individual citizen and his *polis*. Its survival and success guaranteed the living conditions of citizens, and the reverse was also true. Fifth-century Athens was the *polis* par excellence.

However, we should not think that the aristocratic values of the Homeric age vanished overnight. On the contrary, the great families continued to play a vital part in these cities for centuries. They traced their ancestry back to heroes and gods mentioned by Homer. Their ethical code was grounded in the epic poems, even when the city, like a tide, was rising around them. In terms of status, this meant that you were either a member of one of the aristocratic families, the *eupatrides*, or 'of good fathers', or you belonged to the craftsmen and artisans or were a farmer or sailor. We find the expression 'pillars of society' (literally 'tiles', *kaluptēres*, meaning the top echelon) referring to the social elite, 'giving themselves airs because of their birth', in a much later composition (Herodas' *Mimes* 2.31–2; third century BC). Intellectual pursuits later led to other groups of specialists. These were the free citizens. There were at least an equivalent number of slaves, and, as people moved around from one *polis* to another, there developed a class of 'resident aliens', Attic *metoikoi*, or 'house-movers', who were free but did not enjoy full citizen rights.

Epic poetry, for example, knew the story of Helen's suitors who gathered from all corners of the Greek world at its 'capital', Argos, and competed for her hand. The model was repeated in the sixth century BC when the tyrant of Sikyon, Kleisthenes, put out a call to likely young aristocrats to compete for the hand of his daughter. Clearly, he was looking for an exceptionally high-status groom for his daughter. Herodotus' narrative of the event in his fifth-century *Histories* is part of his account of the rising star of the Alkmeonid family in Athens.

Herodotus explains how Alkmeon, founding father of the family, came into his wealth by helping the Lydian king Kroisos, a man of legendary wealth, when Kroisos consulted the Delphic oracle. This wealth enabled the Alkmeonids in the early sixth century to bribe Delphi into giving an oracle that persuaded the Spartans to help the Alkmeonids oust the rival clan of Peisistratids (family of the tyrant Peisistratos) from Athens (*Histories* 5.62–3). As with the leading European aristocratic families, wealth was the original basis of power and influence; a certain aura of 'nobility' is only the result of the family's standing in society over multiple generations, combined with the trappings of wealth such as a grand house and excellent stables. In Kleisthenes' search for a son-in-law we have an account of what life was like in such aristocratic circles, and what were the marks of excellence.

> Kleisthenes had a daughter called Agaristē ['By-far-the-best']. He wanted to marry her off to the man he found to be the best of all Greeks. When Kleisthenes won the prize at the Olympic Games in the chariot race for quadrigas, he made a proclamation that whoever among the Greeks thought himself worthy to be his son-in-law should come within sixty days (or earlier) to Sikyon, where Kleisthenes would settle the question of his daughter's marriage within a year starting from this sixtieth day. At this, all the Greeks who were proud of themselves and their country came as suitors. (*Histories* 6.126)

Herodotus then lists all the worthies who came to Sikyon for the competition, including two from Athens: 'Megakles, son of that Alkmeon who was acquainted with Kroisos, and another, Hippokleides, distinguished at Athens for his wealth and his handsome appearance' (6.127). Kleisthenes had a special racetrack and *palaistra* (wrestling place) constructed for the men's competition. Now it is worth looking at the status markers singled out by Kleisthenes in weighing up the young men's qualifications:

> First he asked each man where he came from and from what family. Then he kept them all there a whole year testing their

> manliness [*andragathia*], their spirit [*orgē*], their education [*paideusis*] and character [*tropos*], interviewing them both individually and in a group. He tried them in athletic competitions, the younger among them at least, and most importantly in their social skills [*synestō*, lit. 'being together'] . . . And the two candidates from Athens pleased him most among the suitors, and, of these, Hippokleides more because of his valour and because he was related to the Kypselids [a famous Corinthian family] by descent. (6.128)

Having come to this provisional choice at the end of the year, Kleisthenes celebrated his daughter's betrothal by sacrificing a whole hecatomb (one hundred) of cattle – another bow to Homeric society, as that is what they did then to mark important occasions – and inviting the suitors and all the Sikyonians to a feast. At this we find Hippokleides committing a faux pas that makes Kleisthenes change his mind about him.

> After the feast, the suitors engaged in a contest of song and after-dinner speaking. As the drinking party progressed, Hippokleides was far outdoing the others. He told the musician to play a certain dance music, and when the music started, he began to dance. And he was clearly pleased by his own dance performance, but Kleisthenes, watching, took a dim view of the whole thing. Then, after a while, Hippokleides asked for a table to be brought in. When it arrived, he first danced a number of Spartan dance steps, then some Athenian ones. Finally he balanced on his head on the table and danced with his legs in the air. During the first two dances Kleisthenes began to hate the idea of Hippokleides ever becoming his son-in-law because of this exhibitionism in dance but restrained himself, not wanting to make a scene. But when he saw him dancing with his legs in the air, he could no longer keep silent, but said: 'Son of Teisandros, you have danced away your marriage!' Hippokleides merely answered: 'See if I care!' And these words became his nickname. (6.129)

Hippokleides' drunken display, however adroit, was evidently *not* a status marker in the eyes of the bride's father when it came to choosing her husband. All the other virtues – nobility, wealth, looks, bravery, lineage – are suddenly annulled by a 'shameless' piece of exhibitionism. Restraint, *sōphrosynē*, was the chief Spartan virtue, and Kleisthenes, although he was not a Spartan (but from the same part of the world), clearly thought that Hippokleides was lacking the necessary dignity for the role. Interestingly, this mentality may also be a reflection of Homeric values as, on one occasion (*Iliad* 16.617), Aineias on the Trojan side taunts a Greek, Meriones, for being an *orchēstēs*, 'dancer', in battle, as he had elegantly dodged a spear thrown by Aineias. A 'dancer' was obviously meant as the opposite of a stalwart fighter, however sensible it was to dodge the spear! That dancing was considered undignified for an Athenian gentleman is also mentioned in Xenophon's *Symposion* 2.19 (*c.* 360 BC).

Kleisthenes chooses Megakles as Agaristē's groom; he is an Alkmeonid, and his rocketing to the very top of Greek society

9 Red-figure column krater (wine mixing bowl) depicting an older man dancing between two youths, by the Florence Painter, *c.* 460–450 BC.

through marriage helps elevate the status of the Alkmeonids. We note how the clan's wealth derived originally from Alkmeon's contacts with the Lydian king Kroisos. This episode is steeped in aristocratic values. Olympic Games, chariot racing, men vying for status, a symposion, displays of cultural 'polish' – this was upper-class Greek life at the time. These Alkmeonids at Athens supplied some of the most famous historical figures: Peisistratos, tyrant of sixth-century Athens; Kleisthenes (not the tyrant of Sikyon), who was responsible for a huge political reform, paving the way for fifth-century democracy; and Perikles himself, the political leader of Athens in its democratic heyday. The Alkmeonids were not the only leading aristocratic clan in Athens; there were others, but here let the Alkmeonids stand as exemplary.

New Men

The expression *novus homo*, 'new man', is a Latin expression for men who 'made it' at Rome without belonging to the *nobilitas* of Roman society. A similar phenomenon can partially be observed in fifth-century Athens, as individuals climbed from the ranks of the artisans, tradesmen and farmers to achieve prominence in politics. The key to political success at Athens was speech, *rhētorikē*, or the art of oratory, because that was how one made one's mark in politics: by speaking at the democratic institutions of the general assembly (*ekklēsia*) or the council (*boulē*). Rhetoric was taught by teachers, so-called sophists (*sophistēs*), which originally meant simply 'skilled person' or 'expert' (in some field) without any connotation of 'tricky'. They came from various cities in Greece – Gorgias from Leontinoi in Sicily, Hippias from Elis, Prodikos from Kēos, Protagoras from Abdera, many from Athens – and plied their trade as itinerant experts all over, but predominantly at Athens. And anyone could pay for a sophist's training if they had the funds. Hence success in any occupation, whether manufacturing or trade or mining, opened the door to political power – as long as one had the nerve to address large public gatherings. One young man, Charmides, confessed to Socrates in a conversation recorded by Xenophon that his nerves were not up to the challenge.

Socrates tried to persuade him that he had the makings of a statesman in him, but Charmides clearly lacked, or felt he lacked, this essential attribute (*Memorabilia* 3.7.1–9).

So we find in the fifth-century BC challenges to the 'blue blood' of aristocracy. A new set of brash politicians arose who made their mark in the political arena by influencing the people, *dēmos*, in their decision-making. These were not the horse-racing, lavishly entertaining, internationally networking upper classes but were populists in a very modern sense: men from the people who appealed to the people. And, of course, they were hated by the aristocracy. In a way, they were like Thersites in the *Iliad*: brash and vulgar but with the gift of the gab. But by the fifth century they had the people on their side, so they were not hounded from the dispatch box by an Odysseus wielding his staff.

The Ranter and the Sausage-Seller

The most famous was one Kleon. He was the butt of a comedy, *Knights*, by Aristophanes, performed in Athens in early spring of 424 BC. That is, on the stage of the Theatre of Dionysos in Athens, watched by an audience of thousands, the comic poet dared to lampoon a leading demagogue in mask-play with a thinly disguised plot involving a character called Paphlagōn, who, we learn, stood for Kleon, being linked to the verb *paphlazō*, meaning splutter, seethe, of Kleon's style of public speech.[4] The play opens with two slaves discussing their woes.[5] One explains that since Paphlagōn, the 'newly bought' (that is, a newly acquired slave), has entered their master's household, they suffer endlessly from beatings, because the newcomer denounces them to their master. They explain that their master is someone called Dēmos (signifying the Athenian people), describing him as follows:

> We serve under a master with a foul temper, a popcorn eater, irascible, called Dēmos the Plebeian, a bad-tempered old man, hard of hearing. Well, last month he bought a slave, a tanner by trade, called Paphlagōn, an absolute rascal, snitching on everyone. This hide-beater understood well his master's character and grovelled at his knees, flattered him, buttered him up, deceived him with little snippets of truth. (*Knights* 40–49)

Kleon was not a slave, of course. In fact, he came from the class of artisans (leather-tanning) and was rough in manner and coarse in speech. Thucydides the historian calls him 'the most radical of the demagogues' (3.36.6). In Aristophanes' play, a distinction is made between the 'great and the good' (the *kaloi kāgathoi*) and the 'low-down' (*ponēroi*), with a strong connotation 'of bad character' (l. 185). In other words, the distinction in real life between the aristocrats and the commoners is translated on the stage into the distinction between free and enslaved. The 'master' is the Athenian people themselves; the speakers before the assembly are the slaves of this master. One Paphlagōn denounces his fellow slaves to this master and enjoys watching them being chastised.

Now our two slaves in the play wonder how they can escape the tyranny of Paphlagōn. One suggests they pray to god. His friend asks incredulously: 'Do you really believe in god?' To which the other replies: 'Well, judging by how god seems to treat me . . .', meaning his misery must be a sign of divine punishment. Having stolen some wine to pour a libation and pray for deliverance, they next decide to steal an oracle from Paphlagōn, which they have heard he keeps secretly. 'Kleon' is asleep inside, having drunk and eaten, and one slave easily steals the oracle, written by the mystic Bakis. It gives an account of how the working classes have taken control of affairs of the state at Athens: 'Public office is no longer the province of the educated and the fair-minded; it's for the uneducated scum,' as slave A observes (ll. 191–3). The oracular form in the following discussion reflects both the traditionally cryptic language of oracles and certain politicians known to the audience:

> (*Slave A:*) It says here he [Paphlagōn] is going to die! (*Slave B:*) How? (*Slave A:*) How? Well, the oracle says that in the beginning, a hemp rope-maker is born who will be the first to decide the affairs of state. (*Slave B:*) That's one tradesman. What next? Go on. (*Slave A:*) After him, a sheep-dealer is the next. (*Slave B:*) That makes two tradesmen. What will happen to this one? (*Slave A:*) He governs, until another, more despicable man than him is born. Then he must go, succeeded by

> the leather-monger Paphlagōn, extortioner, soap-box orator, with a voice like a cataract. (*Slave B:*) So the sheep-dealer was fated to die at the hands of the leather-monger? (*Slave A:*) That's right. (*Slave B:*) I'll be damned! Where might yet another tradesman be found? (*Slave A:*) There is one with a remarkable craft. (*Slave B:*) Who? Please! Tell me. (*Slave A:*) I should tell you? (*Slave B:*) Too right! (*Slave A:*) It's a sausage-seller who'll oust this one. (*Slave B:*) A sausage-seller? Poseidon! What an occupation! Tell me, where might we find this man! (ll. 126–45)

Thus, the play turns into the drama of the Sausage-Seller versus Paphlagōn. The oracle stolen and read by the pair of slaves shows clearly how the 'affairs of state' have been taken over by the working classes: a string of market traders is cited by the prophet Bakis, culminating provisionally in Kleon, but he too will be deposed in time by the Sausage-Seller. Aristophanes has staged in this lively opening scene a discussion among the slave class of Athens how one among them is tyrannizing the rest. It is a comic allegory of the state of democratic politics at Athens in the time of Kleon.

The Populist

What is fun and games in Aristophanes is in bitter earnest in the pages of the historian Thucydides, who wrote a *History of the Peloponnesian War* fought between Athens (and her allies) and Sparta (and hers) from 431 to 404 BC. Thucydides calls this war the 'greatest upheaval' in history (to date). At one point (425 BC), a subject state of Athens, the city of Mytilene on Lesbos, defects from the Athenian alliance. The rebellion is quashed, and Kleon is the speaker at the assembly, who advocates killing all adult male citizens of Mytilene and enslaving all the women and children. His proposal is passed by the assembly and a ship bearing the order to execute the Mytileneans sets sail. On the very next day, however, the Athenians begin to regret their over-hasty decision. There are Mytileneans present in Athens, and they persuade (bribe, probably) the relevant officials to reconvene the assembly for a second hearing. At this, Kleon again advocates the harshest possible punishment of the Mytileneans in a famous speech that is given in full by Thucydides (but not word-for-word, of course). In it, we see Kleon's political style in action, and it is a far cry from Aristophanes' fun and games. Here are his opening remarks, in which Kleon sets the tone, telling the Athenian assembly not to soften their hearts. They illustrate Thucydides' introductory comment that Kleon was 'the harshest of the citizens in other matters, too, and enjoyed the confidence of the people most at that time'.

> On many occasions in the past I have observed that democracy is incapable of ruling over others. This is especially clear now in view of your vacillations concerning the Mytileneans. Because of the lack of danger and discord in our own daily lives, you assume the same applies to our allies. Whenever you mistakenly allow yourselves to be persuaded by them, or indulge in clemency, you fail to grasp that this softening of the heart is dangerous for you and beneficial for the allies. Don't forget that your rule over them is in fact tyranny over people who wish you ill and resent your rule. They obey you not when you pander to them – to your own detriment – but when you show your superior strength, not your benevolence. (*Histories* 3.37.1–3)

Kleon continues in the same vein, advocating a show of strength rather than clemency. He criticizes the Athenian assembly further, accusing them of becoming like spectators at a debate, enjoying the verbal cut-and-thrust instead of giving serious consideration to the issues at stake:

> You've become like spectators of political debate, an audience to events. You regard future developments as possibilities if they're well expressed by speakers, and you judge past actions not so much by the visible facts as by listening to the well-chosen words of analysts. You're masters at being taken in by newfangled formulations, reluctant to believe the tried and trusted; you're slaves to absurdities, suspicious of convention

> . . . You approve a clever speaker, are quick to anticipate a train of thought, but slow to grasp what will come of it, seeking, as it were, some parallel world to that in which we are living, without properly judging the present one. Put simply, you're victims of your love of words, like seated spectators of debates between sophists rather than men advising on matters of state. (3.38.3–7)

The point of showing a 'self-made man' on the Athenian political stage both through the eyes of comedy and political history was to show the opposition between the Athenian aristocracy and the working class, which became an important factor in the fifth century. On the one hand these tradesmen were scorned by the gentry and looked down upon for their coarse manners, but on the other they clawed back a considerable degree of status through the institutions of the democracy, which allowed their rise. As already mentioned, the route was through effective oratory in the decision-making bodies of assembly and *boulē*. Rhetoric was a *technē*, a skill that could be taught, and teaching it was big business for the professionals purveying this skill. The above paragraphs of Kleon's speech illustrate sophistic (that is, rhetorical) training at every turn. There are countless oppositions, parallels, juxtapositions, abstractions and counterpoints, all illustrating the relatively new art of polit-speak. Kleon lambasts speakers for their political 'spin', while being the biggest 'spin-doctor' himself. Democracy opened the door to a rising class of ambitious workers, and secondary education offered them the tools to achieve their ambitions. What had been low social status could now be turned on its head and even turned to an advantage. Men like Kleon clearly did not suffer from any weakness of resolve or temper their words according to some aristocratic code of restraint and decency, *sōphrosynē* (think of Kleisthenes choosing his son-in-law).[6]

Salt of the Earth

I have set up an opposition between the old aristocracy and a new class of self-made men who became empowered first by manufacturing and trade, then by the education their money bought. Socrates, we might point out, was the son of a stonemason. Kleon, Thucydides' least favourite politician, had made his money by curing leather. The picture Kleon paints, however, of an assembly full of Athenian citizens all loving displays of verbal skill without much thought for the old-fashioned virtues of hard work and honest living, is, of course, an exaggeration. Like today, although we may despair of the political classes, the huge majority of the population is concentrating on trying to lead an upright life with a decent standard of living, get on with their neighbours, raise children and 'do their bit' for society. Many people are not desperate for high status; they are either content with their lot or recognize their limitations, or simply want a quiet life. There was an Athenian word for such people: the *hēsychazontes*, literally those 'keeping the peace', 'the tranquil'.

The last of the great trio of authors of tragedy in fifth-century Athens, Euripides, manages to combine the subject-matter of tragedy – myth – with the 'modern' city-state of contemporary Athens. His characters, women included, speak like orators trained by the sophists. His plots are family dramas, even if they do involve Herakles and his wife Deïaneira rather than citizen X and his wife. One could express this differently: he updates mythical stories to make them relevant to his contemporary audience. One of his plays, *Elektra* (*c.* 415 BC), contains one of the simple, good people I just mentioned, surrounded by some famous names of Greek myth: Elektra, Orestes, Klytaimestra. The myth of Orestes' revenge on his mother Klytaimestra for murdering her husband Agamemnon when he returned from the Trojan War was one of the central myths of the heroic age, one dramatized by all three tragedians: Aeschylus, Sophocles and Euripides. Now we find Elektra at the beginning of Euripides' play married to a simple farmer, a salt-of-the-earth type, a good man who has not touched his princess bride but rather looked after her like a friendly uncle. In short, Euripides has 'demystified' these icons of myth and brought them down to earth. The *autourgos*, farmer, in the play can stand for the silent multitude of Athenians who were not trying to climb the status ladder either by noble birth or ambition.

This farmer speaks the prologue of the play. Having sketched Agamemnon's fate and explained the power structure in the land now – Aigisthos has usurped the throne – he explains how he became Elektra's 'keeper'. Aigisthos had wanted to kill her, but Klytaimestra had stood in his way. So Aigisthos decided to send her to Siberia, as it were, by giving her to the farmer as his wife:

> So he gave her to me as wife. I'm a Mycenaean by birth: I don't deny that. My roots may be noble, but I'm destitute of money, and that's the end of nobility. He thought if he gave her to a nobody, he'd have nothing to fear. If a man of good standing took her, he might wake the sleeping dogs of Agamemnon's murder and justice might finally catch up with Aigisthos. But I've never laid a hand on her: may Aphrodite be my witness! She's still a virgin. I'm ashamed to bring dishonour on a rich man's daughter, as I am not worthy . . . But whoever calls me a fool for not touching a girl I take into my home, let him know that he is judging upright character [*to sōphron*] by crooked standards and that he's no better himself. (*Elektra* 34–53)

At the end of the prologue, he catches sight of Elektra approaching, bearing on her head a pitcher of water that she has fetched from the well.

> (*Farmer:*) My poor dear! Why are you doing menial work on my behalf, who is used to a life of privilege? And that after I told you not to? (*Elektra:*) I consider you a friend, like a god. In my misfortune you have not abused me. For the sick it's a boon to find a doctor, as I've found you. So, while there's strength in my body, I must lighten the burden by sharing in the work with you, even if you don't ask me to. You have quite enough work in the fields. The housework is my job. For

> a labourer it's pleasant to come home and find everything in order. (ll. 64–76)

Whether Euripides is advocating the simple life as opposed to that of the corrupt nobility (Aigisthos and Klytaimestra) is impossible to say. An artist is not a political pamphleteer. It is only of importance here that he includes such a scene in a drama set in the mythical age of royalty by way of connecting with contemporary life in Attica, where the majority of people were still farmers. When Elektra's brother Orestes does in fact appear (without revealing his identity initially), there is a great to-do as to whether this simple farmer can invite these guests into his humble home. Orestes muses to himself:

> There's no true marker of virtue. Men's natures are mixed up somehow. I've seen men born of noble fathers who are nobodies, conversely good children of bad fathers, poverty in the mind of a rich man, great wisdom in a penniless person. This man is neither a grandee in Argos nor does he boast of a palace for a home. He's one of the common people, but a saint. Won't you cease this stupidity, you who walk about with heads full of empty prejudices, and judge the noble by the way they treat their fellow men and their character? . . . Let us accept this man's hospitality. Proceed inside, attendants. I prefer a poor man who offers his warm hospitality, over a rich man. (ll. 367–95, with omissions)

So here we have another gradation of status: a good man with none of the trappings of birth, power or wealth. By Euripides' time, philosophy, figure-headed no doubt by Socrates, was identifying true markers of nobility of character divorced from outer appearances. This was progress in thought and marked a departure from the heroic ethos of the *Iliad*. In the coming centuries, schools of philosophy, such as the Stoics and the Epicureans, addressed themselves to the question: what, truly, is the good life?

Status Symbols

It seems universally human to build a cocoon of status symbols around oneself to impress others, and not least oneself. An address, a make of car, designer clothes, a holiday destination, one's choice of partner and friends, cultural status markers too – such as one's choice of university, what books one has read, knowledge itself – are bought, chosen, acquired: partly, no doubt, as a matter of personal taste, but equally perhaps to impress others. Things, attributes, qualifications are the cover one places between oneself and the outside world, a suit of armour that should gleam maximally. Theophrastus has a charming portrait of a wannabe in fourth-century Athens. He calls this character the Boastful Man (*Alazoneia*, literally, perhaps, 'ostentation') and defines such a person as one who boasts of his riches or influence, with no substance to his claims:

> The Boastful Man is one who . . . tells strangers that he has a fortune coming to him from overseas. He talks about the size of his money-lending business, how much he's made and lost. And, exaggerating that, he sends his servant to the bank, where he has one drachma to his name.
>
> He likes nothing better than to tell a travelling companion how he served under Alexander [the Great], how he stood with him, how many jewel-studded cups he came away with. He maintains that foreign craftsmen are so much better than home-grown ones. He goes on about that without having ever travelled abroad.
>
> He says he's already received his third written invitation from Antipater [King of Pella] to come to Macedon. That he's turned down the offer of a duty-free concession to export timber [from there], so as not to be troubled by a single informer. The Macedonians should have been a bit cleverer than that [that is, to tempt him].
>
> In the time of food shortages [330–326 BC] how he'd given more than five talents to the poor: he just couldn't say no . . .

> How he doesn't even keep count of the public services he's performed, all the warships he's sponsored.
>
> When he mixes with exclusive horse-breeders, he acts as if he's interested in buying. When he goes out shopping, he chooses clothes worth two talents [a lot!], then tells his slave off for not bringing the money with him. He lives in a rental but tells strangers it's his ancestral home. He says he's thinking of selling it as it's not big enough for his entertaining needs. (*Characters* 23)

If we analyse the salient points in this sketch, we find the man boasting of: 1) wealth and business acumen; 2) military service with distinction; 3) international business contacts; 4) excellence in public service; and 5) extravagant lifestyle. His strategy in each case is interesting: he says he's received some generous offer or promise but has either declined it or given some excuse. Most of these points sound familiar enough today, too, except perhaps the military service. This is different from snobbery, as in fact it is all lies. A snob looks down on others from a position of superiority (real or imagined); this man is a poser. Conspicuous by their absence are any kind of intellectual or artistic pretensions. But these could easily have been supplied either by Theophrastus or another author. In fact, most of Socrates' career as a philosopher, as reported by Plato and Xenophon, seems to have been spent debunking various types of intellectual and cultural snobbishness: the sophist who doesn't know what justice is (Gorgias); another who teaches 'virtue' without knowing whether it can be taught (Protagoras); the religious expert who cannot define piety (Euthyphron); the young man proud of his book learning who knows less than he thinks (Euthydemos in Xenophon's *Memorabilia*). The regard for and seeking of status may be universally human, but it is not always something to smile at. In ancient Greece, the class rivalries between the haves and have-nots – very approximately between the aristocrats and the people – translated into the political factions of the *oligoi*, the few, and the many, *dēmos*. The factional fighting, *stasis*, that stemmed from that caused as much bloodshed in the ancient *polis* as interstate wars.

3
Sail and Oar

> And Telemachos urged his men on with a command to man the ropes. And they obeyed his order. They raised the pine mast in its mast step to an upright position and tied the supporting stays. Then they raised the white sails by their twisted halyards. And the wind filled the belly of the sail, and the blue bow wave creamed beneath the ship's motion. And she ran over the ocean wave, making good way. And they fastened the running rigging all round the swift ship, then set up bowls full to the brim with wine. They poured a libation to the immortal, deathless gods, first and foremost to the blue-eyed daughter of Zeus [Athena]. All night long until morning she was under way. (*Odyssey* 2.422–34)

Thus Homer describes Telemachos, son of Odysseus, setting off on his first voyage as an adult to search for news of his father, who has not returned from Troy for ten years. There is something fresh and invigorating about this description, although it is composed in formulaic epic language. This was the way to discover the world: to set sail and travel the world, albeit with precautionary prayers to the gods.

If one wanted to get around in Greece there were few options compared to our networks of rail, road, sea and air. One could walk, ride or sail. Walking was slow and arduous; riding was only for the rich, and roads suitable for carriages were poor or non-existent over the mountainous terrain. That left, for longer journeys and all intercity travel, arduous and time-consuming walking – or sail. Only myth knew of flight for humans: Daidalos, a mythical craftsman, flew from Crete with his son Ikaros, having fashioned wings of feathers and wax. For Ikaros it was fatal, as he flew too close to the sun and the wax of his pinions melted. Phaethon's joyride in his father's (Helios, Sun) chariot was equally disastrous. Myth, and satiric fantasy: the second-period sophist Lucian wrote a very entertaining spoof called *Ikaromenippos*, which is a playful combination of the mythical winged man Ikaros and Menippos, Lucian's philosopher-hero. Ikaromenippos explains to a friend how he has just returned from a trip into outer space. None of the philosophers knew the truth about the celestial bodies, he says, so he decided to cut himself wings, one from an eagle, one from a vulture, and fly up to the sky. After some practice sessions he learns the art of flight and flies first to the moon, then on to the sun, where he interviews Zeus himself and accompanies him on his daily round of evaluating men's prayers and oaths.[1]

But this is a spoof. The reality was: sail or stay! The Greeks appear to have learned the art of seafaring and navigation (although they preferred to sail along coastlines rather than across open sea)

10 Model reconstruction of a Roman cargo ship found near Marciana Alta (Elba), 1st century BC.

from the Phoenicians (in modern-day Lebanon), who were already accomplished navigators, just as they learned writing from them, too. Sailing ships were known already to the Mycenaean Greeks as we find representations of them. Homer is ample witness to the seafaring skills of Greeks from the 'Dark Ages' on (eleventh century BC), and indeed the period of colonization of East and West that began then would have been unthinkable without ships for transport. Although Odysseus has a different purpose in his journeying round the Mediterranean – to return home to the island of Ithaka – many readers of the *Odyssey* have felt that descriptions in his epic poem (like the one above) reflect the feeling of adventure and enterprise of this period of colonial expansion.

Ships were basically of two types: cargo ships and warships. Cargo ships were rounder, of greater draft, and suitable for transporting commodities such as olive oil, wine, wheat grain and pottery. The recent find of a Roman ship off a Mallorca beach ('Ses Fontanelles') was a cargo boat carrying jars of wine, olives, oil and garum (a sauce or condiment). The boat was 12 metres (40 ft) long and 5–6 metres (16–20 ft) at its widest point, so about yacht-size, but very beamy to give greater buoyancy (see illus. 10). On average, Greek cargo ships were larger than this, around 30 metres (100 ft) in length with a carrying capacity of around 100 tonnes. Warships were longer and sleeker and equipped with rows of oars to make them faster and more manoeuvrable, particularly when the wind dropped or blew in the wrong direction. But they also had masts and sails for use when moving from one place to another. There were also many gradations of smaller craft meant for inshore work and shorter distances. The catch-all word for 'boat' is *ploion*, from the verb 'to sail'. A cargo boat is *holkas*, from the verb 'to draw', and a classical-age warship was a *trireme* (Greek *triērēs*), derived from 'three-banks-of-oars'.

Sailing and seafaring became so integral a part of life that it entered the language and consciousness of the Greeks in a deep and pervasive sense. Of course, the main factor here was the danger of crossing potentially stormy seas in a relatively small boat. As we shall see, storms and shipwreck were a universal and constant danger for the enterprising Greeks. Although the navigational season was theoretically restricted to the warmer, calmer summer months, storms could strike then, too, and anyway cargo transports were needed the year round. In particular, a fair wind blowing from the right quarter was used as an image of good fortune: *ourios*, literally 'fair wind', could be applied metaphorically to any favourable thing or event; the god Zeus even acquired the name Ourios, meaning 'Zeus who gives good fortune'. In Euripides' play *Andromache*, the heroine is about to be led away to her death when an old man, Peleus, appears at the last minute to save her: 'First I will blow for her like a fair wind filling sails,' he says (ll. 554–5). And rescue, when it comes, is like a harbour to a storm-tossed ship: 'You, poor woman, who found yourself in a violent storm, have reached the tranquillity of the harbour' (ll. 748–9).

Anchors were a symbol of security; a poem by Pindar uses the metaphor of a 'double anchor' to indicate increased security (*Olympian* 6.100–101). A procuress in Herodas' fourth mime tells a woman: 'a ship moored by a single anchor is not secure' (ll. 41–2), meaning the woman should get another lover. A troubled train of thought leading to no good conclusion is compared to a ship that has 'run aground' (Aeschylus, *Suppliants* 438). A giant who has been deliberately fed wine to dull his wits says drunkenly to himself: 'I'm loaded to the gunwales like a fully laden cargo boat. The cargo's leading me a merry dance' (Euripides, *Cyclops* 505–8). An old woman is compared in an erotic epigram to a ship whose timbers and rigging have become bent and leaky (Meleager, *Greek Anthology* 5.204). A father bringing his children to safety indoors compares himself to a ship towing smaller barges behind it (Euripides, *Herakles* 631–2). Shipwreck became the classic image of disaster in any form and its concomitant, being saved from drowning at sea, an image for salvation or rescue generally. An extended simile in the *Odyssey* illustrates this. The comparison is with Penelope's joy and relief when Odysseus returns to her in Ithaka and she recognizes her husband:

> And just as when welcome land appears to people swimming at sea whose well-built ship Poseidon has broken up at sea, when it was being driven by the wind and the breakers. Only a few have escaped the leaden ocean by swimming towards

11 Votive plaque of an *archigrammateus* (sports official) from Ephesos as a thank-offering to Zeus Kassios for saving him from shipwreck, 2nd century AD.

> land. Happily they reach dry land, their bodies encrusted with salt, escaping death. So welcome a sight was her husband to her when she saw him. She wrapped her pale arms round his neck and would not let go. (*Odyssey* 23.233–40)

In short, all aspects of seafaring – sailing, anchoring, setting sail, reaching harbour, being shipwrecked, foundering, being laden with cargo – came to be applied metaphorically or by simile to everyday experiences and occurrences. Clearly seafaring pervaded the Greek mentality because of its familiarity and because of its intrinsic drama with associated emotions. We use metaphors of motion or travel in English, too: something gets off to a 'bumpy start', a campaign 'takes off', a market 'crashes', we go 'full steam ahead', are 'in the same boat', 'sailing close to the wind', 'flying high', and many others, all taken from modes of transport familiar to us. Perhaps it is precisely the aspect of movement, transition, of transport or travel that makes it suited to comparison with changes, reverses and generally events in our lives. Passage through space provides an analogy for passage through time, or temporality, as philosophers call it.

The comparison of community life with seafaring resulted in a common motif ('trope') in poetry, oratory and political philosophy: the ship of state. Community life on land with all its trials and tribulations came to be compared with life on board ship, where captain, crew and passengers were all 'in the same boat', whether this arrived safely in port or was perhaps wrecked mid-voyage. The archaic poet Alkaios, who lived in Mytilene on Lesbos, was a member of a political grouping that found itself in opposition to the ruling tyrant, Myrsilos. His poetry belongs to those texts that survive as poorly preserved pieces of papyrus that have been dug up in Egypt. The following poem (fragment 6) is not complete, but it shows how the political turmoil experienced by Alkaios' group is compared to rough seas (I translate in prose, as the verses are quite damaged):

> Again a heavy sea from the same quarter as before is coming, and will give us much work bailing, when the ship runs into it . . . Let us prepare as quickly as we can, and head for a safe harbour. Let there be no cowardly hanging back.

Although much is missing, clearly this is a rallying cry to take up arms and fight a perceived challenge. The poet expresses the imminent threat as 'heavy seas from the same wind direction', which presumably means from the same source as before. He advocates 'running for harbour', though whether that implies flight or fighting their way to safety is not clear. What is clear is that this island community and factions within it easily identified civic strife with what they knew of storm winds and high seas. The Mytileneans could do nothing, whether it be engaging in trade, travel or alliances, without crossing the sea: it was their gateway to a wider world, and a dangerous one. Another of Alkaios' poems uses the same image of a storm-tossed ship of state (fragment 208):

> I don't understand the commotion of the winds: one sea rolls in from this quarter, and another from that. And we're caught in the middle in our dark-timbered ship, storm-tossed to an extreme degree. Water we've taken on is swilling round the mast-step; the sail is showing holes already and is ripped to shreds; the anchors do not hold.

Here again, a dramatic picture of distress at sea is used as an image for political turmoil. When Athens and the whole of Greece was thrown into panic by Philip II of Macedon's invasion in 339 BC, the orator Demosthenes says that he could hardly be blamed: 'It is as if one were to accuse a ship's captain of causing a shipwreck, after he had done everything he could for the ship's safety, but who ran into a storm which led to the ship's rigging and tackle failing' (*De coronā* 194). A recently discovered papyrus now kept in Florence uses images of calm and stormy seas to draw the distinction between war and peace: war is equated with storm at sea; peace, like a gentle west wind, allows people to flourish (*Hymn to Eirēnē*, PSI XV 1482).

For Those in Peril

A taste of what real-life voyages at sea meant for people is given in the course of a law-court speech by the Athenian orator Antiphon sometime after 428 BC. The case concerned Euxitheos, a man from Mytilene who was charged in Athens with the murder of an Athenian, Herodes, while the two of them were engaged in a sea voyage. The case was tried in Athens because Mytilene, as we have noted incidentally in the discussion of Kleon, was subject to Athenian jurisdiction at the time. Antiphon defended Euxitheos against the charge. Interestingly, we learn in the course of the speech that Euxitheos' father had been involved in the uprising of Mytilene against Athenian rule but had not been among those executed as leaders of the uprising. Politically, it is not irrelevant that Antiphon, who was on the 'oligarchic' side in Athenian politics, chose to defend this Mytilenean whose father had been one of those involved in rising up against the Athenian *dēmos*. Herodes had disappeared one night when the boat on which he and

Euxitheos had been sailing was forced to put into the harbour town of Mēthymna, on Lesbos, to shelter from a storm. Here is Euxitheos' account of that incident as formulated by Antiphon. One should know that lawyers in those days did not speak their speeches for clients but rather wrote them for the clients to learn and deliver.

> My journey took me from Mytilene, gentlemen of the jury, on the same vessel as this man Herodes, whom they accuse me of murdering. We were bound for Ainos [in Thrace]; I was going to my father, for he happened to be there at the time, whilst Herodes was ransoming some slaves to some Thracian people. These slaves whom he was selling were on board with us, as well as the Thracians who were going to pay the ransom money. I now call witnesses to these facts. (*On the Murder of Herodes* 20)

The details given incidentally are what interest us here. It is not said how Herodes acquired these slaves whom he was ransoming. They appear to have been Thracians (so not 'proper' Greeks), and their Thracian relatives who were going to pay the ransom money sailed with Herodes, probably to make sure he really brought them home. Euxitheos, by contrast, said he was sailing to Ainos to meet up with his father. In the course of Euxitheos' account, we hear how they ran into bad weather on sailing from Mytilene and were forced to put into a smaller port, Mēthymna. There the men (all of them?) moved from their boat to another, which afforded shelter from the rain. Some sort of drinking party ensued. Herodes apparently got off the boat, though for what reason is not said. We can imagine the scene that stormy night with the men hunkering down in the cabin of one boat, getting drunk. In the course of the speech, it is never revealed what really happened to Herodes; the case is an ancient whodunnit without a solution. An obvious thought would be that he drowned in the night, being drunk. Alternatively, there were people on board that ship who would clearly have wanted Herodes dead: the Thracian relatives of those captives being ransomed. These guesses are not aired in Antiphon's speech. We do not hear precisely what sort of ship was involved: probably a small cargo boat; certainly not a warship. When Euxitheos says 'conditions improved' after the night in question, that points toward a moderate wind blowing from the right quarter to reach Ainos in Thrace. We should imagine not a galley but rather a sailing ship with its square rig. Note the traffic involved: a number of ships were sheltering from the storm at Mēthymna that night: they were all criss-crossing the Aegean for one reason or other.

Sea voyages, pirates, shipwreck, kidnapping, enslavement and ransoming – realities of life – became stock elements in what one might call 'adventure fiction'. This is first developed in the genre known as New Comedy (late fourth century BC), in which everyday life plays out against a theatrical tradition established by Athenian tragedy. Where Orestes and Pylades, mythical characters, are washed up on the north coast of the Black Sea in Euripides' play *Iphigeneia at Tauris*, the heroine of Menander's play *Sikyonians* (People from Sikyon), for example, is captured as a girl by pirates and taken from the Peloponnese to the west coast of Asia Minor and sold on the slave market at a place called Mylasa. Another example from New Comedy: the father Pataikos in Menander's play *The Shorn Head* loses his wealth when his merchant ship founders at sea, cargo and all; his resulting poverty leads him to give away his two infant children to foster parents; the story of the play concerns how they grew up and discovered who they really were. Thus adventures at sea, horrific in real life, became almost standard motifs in ancient fiction, whether this took the form of plays for the stage or, later, prose narratives for reading.

The novel that follows the fortunes of a young couple, Leukippē and Kleitophon, by an author called Achilles Tatius contains a narrative of storm at sea and shipwreck that is so sustained, detailed and realistic that one suspects the author had experienced something similar himself.[2] An ancient author, needless to say, lacked the entire infrastructure of media allowing instantaneous 'access' to far-flung places, times and people. Modern 'publication', whether in print or increasingly online through the Internet, permits circulation of a work without direct contact between creator and recipient. Ancient authors, by contrast, reached their public by travelling round

Greece giving readings, showing off their education and knowledge on display in their works, and becoming known through personal appearances and contacts. The era of the Second Sophistic (early centuries of the Roman Empire) was a period of great mobility around the Mediterranean world. Novelists were among these travelling intellectuals; their novels are full of passages showing off their special knowledge of geography, science and local colour. Achilles, for example, in his novel includes a long excursus on the Egyptian phoenix, on the geography of the Nile Delta and the amazing street plan of Alexandria in Egypt. They came from all corners of the Greek-speaking world, showing the wide spread of Greek *paideia* (education) and the mobility of individuals. Lucian, whom we have already mentioned, came from Samosarta (Samsat nowadays) (in Turkey); Heliodorus, author of the novel *Aithiopika* (Ethiopian Tale), from Emesa (in Syria); Dio, with his nickname 'Golden-tongued', from Prusa (in Turkey). Dio's 36th oration, *Borysthenitikos* (Man from Borysthenes, ch. 1–3), for example, contains a vivid description of approaching Olbia and Borysthenes, on the north coast of the Black Sea, by ship; the detail and understanding of navigational hazards shown point towards personal experience. Achilles Tatius himself is said to have been from Alexandria.

His novel concerns the adventures of one Kleitophon, who tells a chance acquaintance his tale, and Leukippē. The story starts in Sidon (in Lebanon) but moves to Egypt by means of a sea journey, from there to the offshore island of Pharos (of light-beacon fame), and ends in Ephesos on the (now) Turkish coast. All travel is by sea on merchant sailing vessels carrying passengers, as was the case in the speech of Antiphon just mentioned. The navigation begins for the young couple – who are escaping family tensions – at Berytos (modern Beirut) in ancient Phoenicia. When they set sail, the mood is of hope and optimism. Kleitophon narrates:

> I was pleased when I saw the sea. The ship was not yet at sea but was riding in the harbour. When the wind appeared to be favourable [*ourios*] for departure [that is, from the north or the west for sailing south to Alexandria], there was

> much commotion on board with the crew bustling hither and thither under orders from the helmsman, pulling on the ropes. The yardarm was brought into position, the sail was unfurled, the ship began to stir, the anchors were raised, and we left the harbour behind us. Gradually we saw land growing smaller in the distance as the ship made way. A cry to Paian [Apollo] went up, with it prayers, as the men called on the saviour gods, praying that the voyage might be fortunate. The wind got up, the sail filled and powered the ship on its way. (*Leukippē and Kleitophon* 2.32)

Events on board are narrated at length, in particular a conversation with one young man, Menelaos, on the pros and cons of heteroerotic versus homoerotic love. Then, on the third day, the ship runs into a terrible storm. The following description is a tour de force of dramatic narrative. It is meant literally, but it also symbolizes the extreme difficulties that the young couple encounter on their journey towards ultimate salvation. The description is peppered with technical nautical terms; these contribute to the atmosphere but also serve to show off the writer's technical knowledge, a quality valued among the sophists.

> On the third day of our voyage, clouds gathered out of a clear sky and darkness fell in broad daylight. A headwind blew up, striking our ship on the bow, and the helmsman gave the order to jibe the yardarm. The crew obeyed with alacrity. They reefed the sail on one side of the arm by force (the strength of the wind prevented them pulling against it), on the other side they kept as much sail as would let the wind help them bring the yard across. The ship keeled over on one side as a result, while the opposite side rose into the air and the deck angled steeply. Most of us thought she would capsize completely any second in a gust of wind. So we all moved over to the weather side of the ship, so as to lighten the lee side and, by increasing the load on the weather side, gradually bring it down to the level.
>
> But that didn't help at all. The weather rail of the ship's hull lifted us higher into the air rather than our weighing

it down. For a while the ship seesawed in the waves in this manner while we fought to stabilize it. A sudden wind change, however, from the opposite quarter nearly capsized the ship and the side which had been lowermost was heaved upwards with sudden momentum, whilst the upper side plunged into the water.

A great wail went up from the ship, and a panicked rush amid shouts to move back again to our original places. This happened three or four times more; each time we shifted over with the wild movement of the boat. And before we had got settled on one side, a reverse move in the opposite direction was necessary. So we spent a whole day shifting ourselves plus baggage around on the ship. It was like running an endless marathon. Fear of death was constantly upon us. And, to be sure, it was never far off.

Around mid-afternoon the sun finally disappeared completely. We saw each other only by a sort of moonlight. Flashes of lightning struck, thunder boomed in the sky and rumbled round; the tumult of waves thundered from below. Between sea and sky the gusting winds howled. The air sounded out like a trumpet. The rigging cracked as it lashed against the sail. The ship's timbers groaned frighteningly under the strain, making one think the hull might be going to break up as the rivets gave. The deck houses were everywhere awash as a downpour of rain was also coming pelting down. We hunkered down under the shelters as if in a cave, resigning ourselves to our fate and abandoning hope.

Giant waves came frequently from all directions, some on our bows, some from astern, crashing into each other. The ship rose up on the crests of waves and plunged down in the troughs. These were like mountains and chasms respectively. Even more worrying were the waves which struck us amidship. These seas broke over the ship and ran in a torrent through the deck houses, inundating the ship. Each wave towering on the horizon seemed to touch the low cloud. From afar as it approached the ship it looked like a mountain; seeing it get

> nearer one thought it was going to swallow the ship entirely. There was a tumult of both wind and waves. We could not stay still because of the ship's tossing. A hubbub of cries was everywhere. The waves roared, the wind howled, the women screamed while the men shouted, and the crew shouted orders. The air was filled with laments and wailing.
>
> Then the helmsman gave the order to jettison the cargo. No distinction was made between the silver and gold and the cheaper things. We threw everything alike overboard. Many of the merchants took hold of their wares on which their hopes rested and pushed them overboard. Already the ship was stripped of any encumbrances but still the storm did not abate.
>
> Finally the helmsman gave up the struggle and let go of the steering oars, abandoning the ship to the seas, and began to make the lifeboat ready. Giving the crew the order to get on board, he was first down the ladder. And they immediately jumped to it. Then began a terrible hand-to-hand struggle. For those who were already in the lifeboat tried to cut the line that made it fast to the ship. Everyone left on board made haste to jump when they saw the helmsman pulling on the tow rope. But those on board the lifeboat didn't let them get on board. They had axes and knives and threatened to use them if anyone tried to board. Many still on board the ship armed themselves as best they could, one grabbing hold of a piece of old oar, another a piece of the ship's benches. For the sea turned might to right; this was a new kind of naval battle. Those on the lifeboat struck those jumping ship with their hatchets and knives for fear the boat would be swamped by the numbers of people trying to board, whilst the others swung at them with their clubs and oars even as they jumped. (3.1–3.3.4)

Perhaps the reader needs a short break from the drama. In the next couple of paragraphs, Achilles combines further narrative with some typically sophistic analysis of the situation from a psycho-theoretical point of view: for example, what an unpleasant death drowning is. However, despite the gloom and doom, the modern reader should know – and the ancient reader knew anyway, as it was programmed into the genre of the ancient novel – the couple would be saved and live to fight another day (in fact, many other days in the rest of the book). Here we find a combination of narrative that I feel can only be based on the personal experience of the author, as well as the shared experience of his Greek readership, with features associated with the genre: display of technical language, analytic acumen, powers of observation. Incidentally, at this time a new subspecies of literature arose, the so-called *ekphrasis*, or 'description'. We find long passages in prose writings where the author describes down to the last detail a painting, sculpture or natural phenomenon in front of him. It is as if these authors wanted to wrap up a visible work of art or object in a word-net that would fix it as vividly in the mind's eye as vision itself. Similarly here with the ship, part of the point is undoubtedly the drama, but equally important is the display of linguistic elaboration, sometimes to the point of obscurity.

> Some clinging to the gunwales of the ship slipped off. Others trying to get on the lifeboat were already fighting with those on it. There was no more room for friendship or consideration; each looked to his own salvation and had no regard for kindness towards others. In this way, great dangers break down the rules of comradeship. At one point a spirited youth on the ship grabbed hold of the line and tried to pull the lifeboat towards him. And when it was already close to the ship, everyone got ready to jump into it, should it come within reach. Two or three managed it, not without injury, but many fell into the sea as they slipped off the ship in their attempts to jump. For the sailors quickly freed the lifeboat by chopping through the line with an axe, and then let the storm carry them downwind. Those still on the ship tried to sink the lifeboat.
>
> The ship continued to pitch and roll in the waves like an acrobat. No one noticed an underwater rock approaching. The impact shattered the ship. As it dragged free, the mast fell on its side, partly smashing the ship, partly sinking it. Those

> who sank with it and drowned immediately had an easier death in the dire circumstances, as they were not faced with the lingering fear of death. Drowning at sea is a slow death by anticipation before the actual moment. For the horrific sight of the sea prolongs the feeling of panic indefinitely, so that one dies a far worse death in this manner. As vast as the sea is, so great is the fear of death.
>
> Some tried to swim but were killed when the breakers smashed them against the rocks. Some fell on splintered timbers and were skewered like fish. Some tried to swim, already half dead.
>
> But when the ship broke up, some guardian angel saved for us a section of the bow, to which Leukippē and I clung, letting ourselves be carried by the sea swell. Menelaos and Satyros managed with other passengers to grab hold of the mast and use that to stay afloat. We saw Kleinias [Kleitophon's cousin] swimming round the yard and we heard his cry: 'Hold on to the wood, Kleitophon!' Even as he shouted a wave from behind hid him from our sight, and we let out a wail . . . I cried out in desperation: 'Lord Poseidon, have mercy and relent towards the survivors of the shipwreck you've caused. We have already died many deaths in our fear. If you wish to kill us, don't separate us in death! Let one wave drag us under! And if we must be swallowed down as food for sea monsters, let one whale finish us, one fish gut contain us, so that even among the fishes we share a tomb!' (3.3.5–3.5.4)

At the end one has to smile at the ludicrous pathos of Kleitophon's prayer to Poseidon. Here again, genre obtrudes into dramatic narrative. On the other hand, some of our modern romantic verse or fiction involves figures similarly removed from real life. It is, in fact, a feature of genre that tropes can grow and become exaggerated by repetition and expansion so that an originally good idea – 'may we stay united even in death' – finds itself transferred to the unlikely intimacy of a whale's belly.[3]

Gateway to Elysium

While seafaring could lead to disaster, death or commercial ruin, it was also the gateway to adventure, profit and gain of all kinds. It was a gamble but one that could pay off. The chorus of Euripides' play *Iphigeneia in Tauris* asks the question how people came to this 'uncivilized' land on the Black Sea (Tauris) where human sacrifice is offered to Artemis at her temple:

> Who were they who once left the reed-banked waters of the River Eurōtas or the sacred waters of Dirkē [a spring] and travelled to this godless land where human blood stains the altars and columns of the temple of Artemis? Did they sail over the ocean wave in their sea chariot with its twin banks of pine oars, letting the wind fill its linen sails, aiming to grow their family wealth? Insatiable optimism lies at the heart of human endeavours. Men criss-cross the ocean in their quest to bring great wealth back from uncivilized countries. (*Iphigeneia in Tauris* 399–419)

Seafaring was an area of life calling for particularly intensive prayers. As we have seen, Telemachos prayed when he set off from Ithaka; the ship on which Euxitheos sailed from Mytilene in Antiphon's speech is said at one point to have revealed bloodstains on its bow on examination: was this perhaps the clue to Herodes' murder? No, it was merely the traces of a sheep sacrifice performed at the commencement of the voyage (Antiphon 5.29). And, as we have just seen, Kleitophon prays to Poseidon for the salvation of the pair of them when their number really seems to be up. There was a Sanctuary of the Great Gods on the island of Samothrace at which seafarers dedicated votive plaques to the gods if they were saved at sea. There hung a great number of these before the gods' altar, we are told, but the Cynic philosopher Diogenes (fourth century BC) still saw fit to point out sardonically that 'There would have been a good deal more of them if those *not* saved had also dedicated plaques' (Diogenes Laertius, *Lives of the Philosophers* 6.59.1).

A work that shows the spirit of adventure and discovery involved in seafaring well is the *True History* of Lucian, another of the second-wave sophists. I pointed out above that Homer's *Odyssey* already in the seventh century BC reflects the spirit of adventure in Odysseus' wanderings round the western Mediterranean that characterized this age of expansion and discovery in Greece. Lucian makes the comparison explicit in his fantasy adventure entitled *True History*, with heavy irony. He introduces the work with the comment that serious readers need a little relaxation from time to time. He might have used the term *jeu d'esprit* for his fantasy narrative: a form of escapism through reading, one following a fantastic sea voyage to wondrous lands. The *Odyssey*, he says, provides sufficient precedent in the amazing tales that Odysseus told of his adventures to King Alkinoos when he landed on his island, Scheria:

> The great inventor and teacher of such nonsense is Homer's Odysseus, when he tells Alkinoos' court about the tying up of winds, one-eyed giants who eat men [Cyclopes], monsters with many heads [Skylla], drugs causing men to change into animals [Circe], and other such tall tales which he told the Phaeacians. (*True History* 1.3)

Although Lucian emphasizes that nothing he will relate of his fantasy journey is true, he says that makes him more honest than many other 'historians' in that respect: 'In one respect I *am* telling the truth – when I admit I'm lying' (4). Lucian's narrator tells how he made preparations for a journey starting at the Pillars of Herakles. This landmark, the Straits of Gibraltar, was, for the Greeks, already the end of the known world. Their ships plied the Mediterranean, even if they knew that Phoenicians had gone further, even, by then, circumnavigating the continent of Africa, as they claimed.[4] So when Lucian's narrator says that he set off from Gibraltar to discover the 'end of the world', this project was equivalent to that of Columbus in 1492: it was a voyage into the unknown. Although invented, the spirit in which he undertook the adventure is typical of the real-life spirit of Greek exploration by sea:

> Once upon a time, I set sail from the Pillars of Herakles and steered towards the Western Ocean, carried by a fair wind. The reason and basis for my voyage was a curiosity of mind and desire for new discoveries, coupled with a desire to learn what the end of the ocean is and who the people living over yonder are. (*True History* 5)

No sooner had they set sail than they ran into the obligatory storm, which carried them for eighty days to an island where they encountered wonders such as vines with female torsos and grapes at their fingertips. These tree-women tried to captivate the men by seducing them, and two who did embrace them were promptly rooted by the genitals to the trunks. The men sprouted shoots and became male vines, as it were. The incident shows that the story is set at a mid-point between fantasy and absurdity. On journeying further, their ship encounters a whirlwind, which, as in *The Wonderful Wizard of Oz*, carries them up into the sky. A jet stream there fills their sail, and they journey through the sky until coming to an island-like place glowing brightly: it is the moon. There they meet Endymion himself (a mythical character) and are caught up in a battle between the moon-men (*Selēnitai*) and the sun-men (*Hēliōtai*, with their leader Phaethon, also a mythical character like Endymion). As Lucian had announced at the beginning, his story is partly a spoof of well-known books. The battle that ensues, with its catalogue of the forces ranged against each other, is a parody of historians such as Herodotus, who elaborately listed the forces deployed on the Greek and Persian sides in the Persian Wars. Further wonders of moon life are described, along with weird anthropological data (such as that the *Selēnitai* have no women at all, but men give birth from their thighs): all an elaborate spoof of Herodotus and perhaps other geographers such as Hekataios, whose works are largely lost to us. The spirit of discovery here has taken us to a never-never-land of strange wonders and freakish phenomena. Sailing itself has become space travel.

The 'I' takes his leave of Endymion (who gives him guest-presents, as in Odysseus' journeys) and they descend (with many wondrous sights along the way) from the moon back down to sea level. There all goes well until they encounter a shoal of sea monsters, the largest of which swallows them down, and they 'wake up' in its belly. When the whale opens its mouth and lets in light they see all manner of debris – bones, dead fish, wrecks of ships – but also a green island where trees seem to be growing in the mud swallowed by the whale. They explore the forest and come upon an old man and his son, living in comfortable accommodation and cultivating the land. The old man explains how they too were swallowed and so suppose they are dead, but they pray they are alive. His story is worth listening to, as it is no doubt meant to be based at least on some familiar elements of the 'merchant's story', who sets sail hoping to trade overseas for profit.

> Friends, I am a Cypriot by birth. I set off as a merchant seaman with my son here, whom you have met, and many household slaves, bound for Italy with a rich cargo of merchandise on a sizeable ship. You no doubt saw the remnants of this in the monster's gullet. Well, as far as Sicily we had fine weather. But then we were engulfed by a storm, which after two days carried us out into the [Atlantic] Ocean. There we encountered the sea monster which swallowed us down, men and all. Only two of us survived while all the others perished. We buried our comrades and built a sanctuary to Poseidon, then lived the life you see here, tending a vegetable patch, eating fish and fruit . . . It is now twenty-seven years since we were swallowed down. (1.34)

The old man's tale cannot have been so rare (apart from the setting in the whale's belly): a merchant who sets out with his son hoping to make his fortune by trade, only to have his dream shattered, with his ship and its cargo, by a storm. The survivors who make it to dry land first thank Poseidon for having escaped with their lives; then, from merchants, they become settlers, living as simple farmers. His tale is also a tale within a tale, hence a step towards the literary device of *mise en abyme*, or infinite regress. One feels the old man's account might easily have included someone else's story, and so on ad infinitum: Lucian employing another trick of the storyteller's art.

Finally, after further adventures and wonders, the ship comes to an island surrounded by a heavenly scent. It turns out to be paradise, no less, to the Greeks: the Isle(s) of the Blessed (*makarōn nēsos*). This island is a feature of Greek eschatology from Homer on: particularly famous heroes made it here instead of descending to the usual Hades, which was a dingy, inhospitable place. The Isle of the Blessed, by contrast, was everything one could hope for in paradise: a sort of permanent holiday in the Seychelles, with wine brought to one's beach lounger while a crystal clear sea laps at one's feet. Both in myth and in Lucian's story, entry was gained by, among other things, justice in one's lifetime: Rhadamanthys, the divine judge, judged an individual's merits on his death. In Homeric epic, Menelaos, rather surprisingly, is named as a hero who gained entry (*Od.* 3.561ff.). In Lucian's story, Odysseus is also there, rather wishing he had stayed with Kalypso instead of returning to his faithful wife Penelope. Indeed, when the narrator departs, Odysseus hands him a note to take to Kalypso on her island Ogygia, as a billet-doux, which he duly gives her when putting in to Ogygia on his return to reality, bringing tears to her eyes: this is Lucian's irreverent little joke. My point here is the fact that the sea voyage of Lucian's hero takes him to the pinnacle of good fortune, a blessed existence. This paradise is, as it were, the gleaming Eldorado that tempted the ancient sailor to risk everything on a small ship in the hope of making his fortune.

4
Signs

> The Lord whose oracle is in Delphi neither speaks nor hides but gives a sign.
>
> Heraclitus, fragment 93 DK

The above is a fragment preserved from the writings of a famous philosopher of the late sixth century BC called Heraclitus, who lived in the Ionian city of Ephesos. Talking about the Delphic oracle, and specifically about Apollo, the god whose mouthpiece the oracle was supposed to be, he says that the god gives signs rather than speaking plainly or giving no indication of his will. The verb for 'gives a sign', *sēmainō*, gives our word 'semantics', which, put simply, means that a sound (word) 'stands for' or 'points to' a meaning. This chapter looks at a huge difference between our modern 'post-Christian' Western society and ancient Greece: while we are much more inclined to attribute unplanned occurrences and phenomena to chance or some scientific principle ('there must be a rational explanation'), the Greeks throughout antiquity believed that the gods were communicating with us as recipients by giving signs of their mood and intent.

Of course, this raises the question: did all Greeks always believe in their gods? How could anyone seriously believe in a bearded god sitting on a mountain and hurling thunderbolts (see illus. 13), or a female god being born in a suit of armour from the head of this god (Athena)? Weren't the Greek gods just pretty literary figures, or fairy-tale figures from a bygone era in whom supreme rationalists such as

Socrates and Plato could hardly believe? Well, libraries of books have been written about Greek religion, and I have contributed one or two myself. The answer is that we will never see inside the heads of anyone, let alone the ancient Greeks, to know their private beliefs. But on the strength of external evidence, which includes written testimony and pictorial art and iconography, it would seem perverse to think that they were lying to themselves and others so constantly and consistently when they offered these gods reverence and worship. The world *is* a very remarkable place, and nature (*physis*), animate and inanimate, must inspire awe and wonder in anyone. We express our wonder of nature partly still in art, but mainly in the elaborate pursuit of science: we are much further along this path than the Greeks. But they began it. And it is doubtful whether, however far along the path we progress, we will ever come upon a sign saying 'Ultimate Truth', like Pooh discovering the North Pole. As we shall see, the Greeks' rationalism did not lead them to deny the existence of gods or the signs they appeared to give, but rather to apply their intelligence to the interpretation of what they took to be the divine. Rather than trying to pin down the elusive question of 'faith', attention here is focused on the phenomenology of signs.

Birds and Beasts

As always, it is sensible to start from where the Greeks themselves took their lead: Homer. We have already seen at the beginning how the Greek seer Kalchas 'read' the plague that afflicted the Greek army at Troy as a sign of Apollo's displeasure. How did he 'read' the situation? Well, it was no great leap of the imagination to guess that the Greeks had incurred some god's displeasure, which was being expressed by plague. Apollo was well established as the plague god, and Kalchas knew that Chryses, whom Agamemnon had humiliated, was Apollo's priest: one might say that his reading of the situation was almost self-explanatory. Already in the Homeric poems the mantic art of the seer was a developed art. Signs were read in sacrifice, bird flight, meteorological phenomena (such as claps of thunder and lightning: *diosēmia*, lit. 'sign from Zeus'), dreams. Armies took a resident seer

12 The plague- and healing-god Apollo with bow and libation bowl emerging from his temple, red-figure krater from Tarentum, early 4th century BC.

with them on their campaigns from Homer on throughout antiquity, whereby his role was only consultative, offering general advice rather than deciding strategy himself (Plato, *Laches* 198e). Homer knows a variety of words to describe different branches of the holy man's art: *hiereus*, priest, was a general term, linked to the word for 'holy' (*hieros*). A seer, *mantis*, was an interpreter of signs; the word is etymologically related to *sēmainō*, give a sign. An *oneiropolos* is literally a 'dealer-in-dreams', that is, a dream interpreter, but it was used also more generally of a seer, as was *oiōnopolos*, literally a 'dealer-in-birds', an interpreter of bird flight (Latin *augur*).

Kalchas was also responsible, according to myth, for a sign-reading at the beginning of the Trojan expedition. In Book 2 of the *Iliad*, Odysseus makes a speech (with Athena backing him up in person) to try to persuade the Greeks not to abandon their mission:

> Friends, endure! Stay for a while so we may see whether Kalchas prophesies truly or not . . . Beside a spring [at Aulis], standing round the altar, we sacrificed a full hecatomb to the gods under a handsome plane tree where the spring water

> flowed. There we saw a great sign: a terrifying snake, with yellowish-brown skin, sent by Zeus himself, slid out from under the altar and snaked its way up the plane tree. There, at the tip of a branch among the leaves, was a bird's nest with young chicks in it, eight of them, and their mother made up the nine. The snake swallowed down the chicks, cheeping pitifully, while their mother flapped around in consternation. The snake coiled up and struck the mother on its wing, drawing a squawk. Then, when it had devoured chicks and mother-bird, the god who had sent the snake turned it into a clear sign: the son of cunning-hearted Kronos [Zeus] turned it to stone! And we stood there, dumbfounded by what had happened.
>
> Thereupon Kalchas immediately spoke his interpretation: ... 'As this creature ate up the eight chicks, and the mother who bore them as the ninth, so we will fight the war here for that number of years but in the tenth we will take the city with its wide streets.' (*Iliad* 2.299–329)

This performance by Kalchas involves a bit more creativity. For one thing, he has to add a year on to the number nine that the portent suggested: the Greeks were already in the tenth year of their siege of Troy when the events of the *Iliad* took place, so, to fit portent to the mythical *datum*, a year has to be added. Then, it was by no means self-explanatory that the snake was sent by Zeus; snakes tended to be associated with other gods: with Athena in Athens; and Asklepios, of course, as the healer-god. Then there is the curious detail of the snake turning to stone. The point of that seems to be that the snake will be frozen in action, as it were, as an enduring sign. The fact that the portent will have lasting significance is emphasized with two words in the Greek original. Finally, one might observe that the creativity is not all on Kalchas' side. On the contrary, it is Odysseus now who harks back to the portent at Aulis as a rhetorical device to persuade his fellow soldiers not to abandon their plan. Perhaps he is the clever one who added a year onto the magic number nine embedded in the omen. However, all sophistry aside, the basic point here is how the Greeks immediately took this startling piece of animal behaviour for a sign. They thought the natural world was speaking to them – not, as we would, that we were incidental witnesses of an event in the natural world that would have occurred anyway, indeed with greater likelihood if we had not been there: if there was anything surprising, it was that the snake had not allowed itself to be deterred by our irritating presence.

The episode reflects two 'takes' on an occurrence in the animal world. First Kalchas' then Odysseus' recall of the initial one in order to apply it to the present situation. Later in the *Iliad* another case of augury reveals two opposing views of a bird omen. What happens in the natural world just happens; how men interpret that behaviour with reference to themselves becomes the point at issue. The potential validity of an interpretation depends on the assumption that gods are communicating with humans through nature. The Stoics developed in the Hellenistic period the doctrine of *sympatheia*, sympathy, to explain the action of divinities on the physical world: these exert a kind of force field that draws nature in its train. Much later, in the fourth century AD, the theologian Proclus' illustration of the process is the sunflower (Greek *heliotrope*, literally 'sun-turner'), which turns its head towards the sun as it moves overhead. Since the sun is a heavenly body, this is an example of nature's slow dance to the music of the spheres without physical touch. I suspect that Homer's gods were probably thought to be a bit more hands-on in their actions: that they caused natural phenomena rather than inducing them remotely by a kind of invisible force field. Poseidon was known as the 'earth-shaker' and Zeus as the 'cloud-gatherer', 'high-thunderer'; Apollo shoots with his 'gentle arrows'. In other words, they were active agents, not mere influencers.

Because of Zeus' plan in the *Iliad*, the Trojans under Hektor's command have been making inroads into the Greek lines. They have driven the Greeks back to the defensive wall around their camp and now wonder whether to breach this wall and attack the beached ships. At that moment a bird omen is spotted:

> A bird appeared to them as they were determining on breaching the defences [of the camp]: a high-flying eagle approaching

> the host on the left, carrying in its claws a large blood-red snake, which was still alive and squirming and had not yet given up the fight. It twisted its head back and struck the eagle clutching it on its breast, close to the neck. The eagle dropped the snake to the ground, shocked by the pain, and it landed right in the middle of the attackers. The eagle flew off with a cry, riding the currents of air. The Trojans were struck dumb when they recognized the wriggling snake lying in their midst as a sign from Zeus the Ruler. (12.200–209)

Again, the humans immediately took the incident in the animal kingdom for a sign from Zeus meant for them. That the bird appeared on the left was inauspicious, as, no doubt, was the sight of the squirming snake bleeding from the lacerations from the eagle's talons. Poulydamas and Hektor, on the Trojan side, read the omen in opposite ways, or rather, Hektor chooses to ignore the sign as being subordinate to the greater will of Zeus, which he claims to know and which is favouring him. How he knows this is not clear, but it does in fact correspond to the plan of the *Iliad* as given at the beginning: to favour Achilles and humiliate Agamemnon, Zeus will *temporarily* favour the Trojan side. First Poulydamas gives a reasonable interpretation of the omen, claiming that experts would agree with him. He draws attention to the fact that Hektor never listens to him as he is of common stock, hence lower status:

> Hektor, you're always criticizing me in public even when I'm talking sense. It is clearly not done to speak against you as a commoner either in council or ever in war, but rather always to support your position. But now I'll tell you what I think makes most sense. Let us not do battle with the Greeks around the ships. If this omen was really meant for us Trojans as we prepare to enter the defences, then this, in my opinion, is what it portends. The eagle . . . dropped its prey before it got back home to the nest and did *not* succeed in bringing it to its chicks. Thus with us: if we breach the gates and wall of the Greeks by brute force, and the Greeks retreat, it will be no

orderly withdrawal when we return from the ships. We will leave many dead Trojans behind, killed by the Greek weapons as they defend their ships. That's how a diviner would interpret the omen, one with expert knowledge of portents, and the ranks would believe him. (12.211–29)

Poulydamas' words rile Hektor, as he is keen to press home their present advantage. He claims to know Zeus' plan for the war and ridicules Poulydamas' anxiety about the portent:

'And you tell me to pay heed to birds with their long wings? I have no regard for them, nor do I pay them attention, whether they fly to the right, towards the light and the sun, or to the left and the shady darkness. *We* will obey the will of great Zeus, who rules over all men and gods. There's only one true omen: to defend our fatherland!' [He further threatens and cows Poulydamas] . . . Thus he spoke and led the charge. The men all followed with a huge cheer. And Zeus who loves thunder stirred a storm wind from the heights of Mount Ida, which blew a dust cloud towards the ships. He dulled the wits of the Greeks and gave glory to the Trojans with Hektor. (12.237–55)

13 Zeus with thunderbolt and eagle, two of his most potent signs, *skyphos* (cup), 500–475 BC.

According to this, Hektor was right to ignore the eagle portent, at least as Poulydamas interpreted it, because Zeus confirmed his will by blowing dust in the Greek defenders' eyes. However, there is tragic irony in this, as Zeus is only temporarily supporting the Trojans, and that only because of Achilles' injured pride. Soon the tide of battle will turn, and Hektor will be dragged as a corpse behind Achilles' chariot round the walls of Troy for all to see. In this way Homer uses a bird omen as a literary device to heighten the emotional charge of his battle narrative. Poulydamas urged caution. Hektor threw his advice to the winds, preferring to pursue what he saw as his advantage, but he was in fact only hurrying on his death. Here Hektor simply disregards the bird's behaviour. Below we will see that different interpretations of the same omen or oracle sometimes vied for acceptance.

A professional interpreter of bird flight was an *oiōnoskopos*, an 'observer of birds'. *Oiōnos* itself meant 'bird' but came to mean 'omen' by transference. A kind of archetypal bird-diviner in myth was Teiresias of Thebes. A passage of tragedy (Euripides' *Bacchae* 347ff.) describes the prophetic seat of Teiresias from which he observed bird flight. Direction, type and number of birds and behaviour were all important. The quarters of the heavens were mapped out relative to the seat, turning the seer's vantage point into a kind of observatory. We will have more to say on the pseudosciences of divination below. Clearly the practitioners enjoyed prestige among laymen and soldiers, but their reading of an omen was often open to challenge. Hektor pooh-poohed Poulydamas' reading of the eagle omen. In the *Bacchae* passage just mentioned, the young hothead Pentheus is annoyed by something Teiresias has said and gives the order to vandalize his mantic seat from which he makes his pronouncements. In the final bird omen we will look at here, there is also talk of 'rejecting the seer' as a possible reaction to his advice.

In Aeschylus' great tragedy *Agamemnon*, the story of Agamemnon's fateful return after conquering Troy, we encounter a different version of the omen at Aulis that helped the Greeks on their way. Kalchas makes another appearance, as in the *Iliad* omen we have just looked at, but, interestingly, Aeschylus chooses to vary the omen. The chorus (fifteen men) sing when they enter the theatre (the entry song is called

14 'A high-flying eagle, and it held a trembling dove' (*Odyssey* 20.243). Eagle portent: an eagle seizes and devours a bird (a dove?), Roman floor mosaic, Lugdunum (Lyon), 2nd century AD.

parodos), telling how a bird omen appeared to the Greek commanders (Agamemnon and Menelaos) and all the Greek forces when the fleet was assembled at Aulis. First comes the omen itself, then Kalchas' reading of it:

> A black eagle, king of birds, and another white-backed eagle appeared to the kings of ships close to their encampment on the right-hand, spear-brandishing side in a very propitious quarter. They were devouring a mother hare, heavy with her young, stopping their future runnings. Cry Shame, Shame, but let the good prevail!
>
> The good seer of the army [Kalchas] saw the connection between the two sons of Atreus [Agamemnon and Menelaos] with their divergent temperaments and the meal of hares auguring in the expedition. This was his reading of the omen:

> 'This expedition will take the city of Priam in time; Fate will brutally subdue the city's flocks, its former thriving populace. Only let not some curse from heaven darken this great military bridle-bit of Troy from the outset.' (*Agamemnon* 114–35)

Kalchas reads the omen as being ambivalent: it signifies on the one hand ultimate success for Menelaos' expedition to retrieve Helen, because the eagles are Zeus' birds and they strike it lucky on the hunt. On the other hand, Kalchas suspects that the divine protrectress of animals, and the young in general, Artemis, will object to the eagles' gory meal and will demand another sacrifice to appease her anger. This may reveal itself, Kalchas says, through headwinds delaying the fleet's departure. When these duly materialize, Agamemnon reluctantly agrees to sacrifice his daughter Iphigeneia to Artemis, instead of trying to wriggle free from the noose of causation and necessity tied by his seer (l. 186). This, in turn, stirs the household 'curse of infanticide' into life again (l. 155: the reference is to a previous child-killing incident in the mythical prehistory of Atreus' family), resulting in Agamemnon's own death when he returns from Troy to his wife's murderous arms.

Of interest in this complex is, firstly, the visual analogy between the pregnant hare falling prey to the eagles and Troy's towers 'full of people'. It seems that Kalchas sees in the killing of the pregnant hare by Zeus' brace of eagles a picture of Agamemnon and Menelaos conquering and plundering the city of Troy, emptying it of its people and treasures. He also, however, sees in the eagles and hare portent an image of tension on Olympus. Zeus may be egging on the kings with his pets, the eagles, but Artemis is offended by the death of the hare family and does her best to obstruct Zeus' purpose by preventing the fleet's departure. The opposing purposes of Zeus and Artemis, then, symbolize the eventual victory over Troy combined with a spirit of revenge, which is awoken within his own palace. Stirred to murderous rage over her daughter's sacrifice in the name of war, Klytaimestra plans infidelity (with Aigisthos) and ultimately murder when Agamemnon returns. Aeschylus' treatment of the portent at Aulis also reveals a willingness to rework myth creatively if it serves his purpose. Where before in the *Iliad* the portent of the snake and chicks served a purely numerical purpose according to Kalchas' interpretation in counting the years down to Troy's fall, now the change to eagles (very clearly Zeus' birds) and a young innocent family of hares as the victim (dear to Artemis' heart) reflects the structure of Aeschylus' tragedy: victory in Troy, yes, but with fatal consequences for Agamemnon. Aeschylus has not changed the constellation of animals completely (a predator kills the young of an animal) but sufficiently to give the omen a new slant.

Oracles

At this point the reader may think: this is literature. Bird and animal omens may have their place as colourful adornments in poetry and myth, but surely they cannot have had a place in serious real life? On the whole, it is surprising to what extent signs and portents obviously did play an enormous part in the Greek mentality, whether in peacetime or indeed in warfare. It is remarkable how often the historian Herodotus, writing in the later fifth century BC, records a dream or an oracle, or another divine manifestation, which played a part in influencing commanders' decisions throughout the Persian Wars (490–479 BC). However, one should add immediately that this does not mean that these commanders were irrational or stupid; they were superstitious, in our terms, undoubtedly, but what is conspicuous is the rational intelligence they applied to the interpretation of what they perceived as divine signs. This section will concentrate particularly on oracles. These were pronouncements by oracular mouthpieces given on the occasion of an enquiry: should we make war against the Persians? for example. The answers were usually given in the form of short poems, either in dactylic hexameters (like Homer) or in elegiac couplets (an alternate-line variation of hexameters). The language of these responses was highly allusive, sometimes riddling. Simply understanding what the poem meant was a challenge – and open to challenge. As we shall see throughout this chapter, the mantic art was indeed an art, hardly a gut reaction, even if it may start from some visceral reaction to an unusual event (like the snakes and eagles we have just been looking at).

Oracle is the Latin word (*oraculum*, prayer-place); the Greek is *manteion*, which means 'where a *mantis* (seer, diviner, prophet) is'. It applies both to the place, or shrine, where the oracle sits, and the answer given by the god or his representative. Thus one consulted an oracle and received an oracle. There were famous oracular seats in Greece from the archaic age (seventh century BC). The most famous was at Delphi, where Apollo was thought to dispense oracles. Delphi is quite central in Greece, being accessible both from the mainland and the Peloponnese. A myth indeed described how two crows flying from the perimeter of the world met at Delphi, thus marking its centre point (*omphalos*, 'navel', the Greeks said). But there were others: there was the oracle of Trophonios in Lebadeia; of the Abai in Phokis; the oracle of Zeus Ammon in Libya; of Zeus at Dodona (northern Greece); of Apollo Ismenios at Thebes; and of the Branchidai at Didyma (Ionia). Again, details and history of these oracles, together with editions of their oracular responses, are to be found in many handbooks and should not hold us up here.

There were also portable oracles, as it were. That is, short texts or collections of such texts that travelling seers carried around with them and purveyed to anyone requiring an 'expert' opinion on a problem or threat. Again, these tended to be in the form of short, hexametrical poems. They were attributed to legendary, inspired figures such as Orpheus, Mousaios or Bakis, whose historical existence is distinctly open to question. We saw above how Aristophanes' Kleon figure carried an oracle of Bakis around with him. Their oracles were collected into books (scrolls), and these were then marketed by figures called *chrēsmologoi*, chresmologues or purveyors of oracles. On the whole they were not very highly regarded, since they clearly had their eye on profit and were in competition with each other. They are often the butt of Aristophanes' humour in his plays. Apart from the *Knights* passage discussed above, the *Birds* (ll. 959ff.) contains a chresmologue who is clearly on the make in the newly founded City of Birds with his collection (*biblion*) of oracles of Bakis. The hero of the play sends him packing, comparing him unfavourably with Apollo (l. 982). Here we should make a distinction between the official oracles of Greece, which had international standing, and the motley ranks of itinerant chresmologues, who sold their oracles to individuals requiring guidance from above in all life questions.

All oracles claimed to stem from a divine authority, whether it was Apollo in Delphi or the magician Orpheus, who was not himself a god. The claim was that divinity was speaking to men through an oracle given by sacred transmission. The only problem was: oracles were verbal formulations in Greek (as a rule), by Greeks and for Greeks. That is, the human component in the transmission of oracles was open to challenge, and frequently was challenged if the message was not palatable to the recipients, as well as open to manipulation by selection, tendentious interpretation, perhaps even forgery. What proof was there that Apollo had really uttered these words or that this hexameter couplet really stemmed from Orpheus? Absolutely none, and the Greeks were keenly aware of this. What is in a way more interesting is the authority that such sacred texts continued to exert throughout antiquity. On the one hand people questioned them, but not the *idea* itself. That idea was that there were routes to divinity, channels of communication, if only one could find and trust them. Nowadays we rely on experts, scientists and pundits in all areas who make prognoses about illnesses, economics, wars, football matches, elections and so on. Their opinions are based on reason and experience, but then so were those of the ancient experts. Authority for us stems from science; for the Greeks it stemmed from their gods. That is an essential distinction, but neither is particularly reliable when making predictions about the future.

The historian Herodotus is very thorough in his reporting of oracles before and during the Persian Wars. He also occasionally comments on 'god's will' himself. Frequently this is to express scepticism as to whether the actors had understood god's will correctly, but sometimes to give his own view on what god intended: for example, that the Battle of Plataia (summer, 479 BC) took place on the same day as the battle for Mykalē in Ionia (one in the morning, one in the afternoon) was 'a sure sign of divine providence (theodicy) at work' (*Histories* Book 9.100). Of another momentous occasion, the sea Battle of Salamis (480 BC), also won by the Greeks against the Persian fleet, he comments that the oracle predicting such a victory, given by

Mousaios and Bakis, 'turned out true' (8.96); likewise another oracle, given long before that, about the wreckage of the Persian ships that would be washed up on the coast of Kōlias in Attica. He quotes the oracle (one hexameter): 'The women of Kōlias will roast with oars' (8.96). Note the typically riddling language of the oracle: roast? with oars? What could be meant? Well, reasons Herodotus, not without satisfaction: the wrecked ships were washed up at Kōlias, where their wood was used for roasting by the local women.

He was equally capable of reporting underhand practices when it came to oracles and their use in international warfare and politics. In the build-up to Xerxes' invasion of Greece in 480 BC, he describes how the Persian general Mardonios, in cahoots with representatives of the Athenian tyrant Peisistratos, worked on Xerxes to persuade him to attack Greece and, in particular, Athens. One method used was to employ a famous seer, Onomakritos, an Athenian who, Herodotus says, was a purveyor of oracles (*chrēsmologos*) and an 'editor' of the oracles of Mousaios (*diathetēs*) (7.6). This Onomakritos had a previous record of tampering with oracles when he was caught adding an oracle to those of Mousaios – that is, inventing an oracle and passing it off as genuine Mousaios. Now he was employed by the Peisistratids (sons of the Athenian tyrant Peisistratos) to use his skills to help persuade Xerxes to attack Athens. Herodotus describes his procedure:

> He [Onomakritos] then joined them [the Peisistratids] in Susa [royal seat of the Persian king], in order to meet the King. They introduced him with glowing words, and he recited from the oracles. If there was one that pointed to a setback for the King, he omitted it. He chose the most propitious and recited them, to the effect that the Hellespont was fated to be bridged by a Persian man, explaining about the invasion. So he worked on the King by reciting oracles, and the Peisistratids and the Aleuads [another influential Athenian clan] by giving their advice. (7.6)

So much for the 'word of god'. Onomakritos was exploiting the institution of sacred oracles in order to influence momentous decisions.

One way or another, Xerxes was persuaded and decided to invade Greece. Another case shows Herodotus applying an oracle, which may have been well-known at the time or he dug it out of the archives, so to speak, to an event in his narrative of the Persian Wars. When Xerxes invaded with an immense force via Thrace and Macedonia in 480 BC, a first naval battle was fought at Cape Artemision (the northernmost tip of Euboea). Herodotus describes how the Athenian commander Themistokles told the Greek forces to gorge themselves on the flocks of goats on Euboea before the battle as it was 'better that *they* ate them rather than the enemy'. In so doing, Herodotus says, they disregarded an oracle of Bakis, which ran as follows: 'Watch out, when the foreign-tongued throws a yoke of jute across the sea, to keep the bleating goats from Euboea' (8.20.6–7). Little wonder that the Greeks 'disregarded' such a couplet, as it was enigmatic in the extreme. Who was the 'foreign-tongued'? What is a 'yoke of jute'? How could one keep the goats off Euboea? But after the event, when Xerxes had built a rope bridge (a yoke of jute) across the Hellespont and led his army across it as far as Euboea, and the Greeks ate the goats, things became clear. Herodotus comments that the Greek side ignored the oracle to their sorrow, as 'great evils were about to befall them.'

We begin to get the idea: a great number of these 'political' oracles circulated at the time. None were expressed in clear news-headline form; they were all expressed in the riddling language Heraclitus meant when he said 'the god neither speaks nor hides but gives a sign.' As with the women of Kōlias 'roasting with oars', it was a question of groping in the dark to predict what the oracle meant; *post eventum* it became easier to recognize a likely sense. Herodotus is full of such incidents. Oracles theoretically predict the future. But their meaning is open to dispute. Only afterwards can one fit prediction to perceived event. I cannot help seeing an analogy with modern military intelligence. From the air, spy satellites can recognize troop movements and suspicious construction works; but what these mean is still a riddle.

Perhaps the most famous Herodotean oracle is Delphi's reference to 'walls of wood' on being asked whether Athens should fight the approaching Persian horde. Herodotus prefaces his account with a remark he says will be unpopular 'with the majority', namely that if

Athens hadn't resisted Xerxes at the sea battle of Salamis, but had fled, all of Greece, including Sparta, would have fallen to the Persians as no defensive walls across the Isthmos (the neck of land dividing north from south Greece) would have helped if the Persians controlled the sea (7.38–9). The reference to Athens' subsequent unpopularity is due to the empire it built up after the Persian invasion known as the Delian League, in which Athens began progressively to leach its subjects' wealth and to act like a tyrant (see Kleon's remark earlier). But that was later, when Herodotus was publishing his *Histories*.

When Xerxes approached in 480 BC with his army of some three million all told, according to Herodotus, Athens sent envoys to Delphi to get advice. They performed the correct ritual ablutions, then took their seats in the inner sanctum, where the officiating Pythia (priestess), one Aristonikē, spoke in uniquely blunt words, not veiling her message in the usual riddles:

> Wretches, why are you seated? Flee from your homes and the rugged hills of your ringed city to the ends of the earth. Neither the head nor the body will remain unharmed; from the soles of your feet to your hands, and what's in between, nothing remains, all is woe. Fire and violent Ares [war god] driving his Oriental chariot will destroy it. And he will destroy many another citadel, not only yours. He will burn down many temples of the gods with destructive fire which are now breaking out in a sweat of fear and trembling; dark blood pours from the rooftops. I foresee the iron grip of death. But go from the sanctuary: cloak your woes in courage! (*Histories* 7.140)

An unambiguous message from Delphi to the Athenians to flee the Persian onslaught. Instead of departing the sanctuary, however, the Athenians took suppliant branches in their hands and put their question to the oracle for a second time. 'O Lord', they said (note how they addressed Apollo directly, not the priestess), 'Give us a better prophecy for our city. Have mercy on us, who come to you as suppliants! Otherwise we will stay here and not leave until we die' (7.141). Extraordinary defiance! The priestess (answering for Apollo) did indeed issue a second oracle, and it was this one that was subject to 'creative interpretation' once it became known:

> I will give you this second prophecy, set in stone. All else will be lost in Kekrops' land [Attica] and on the slopes of sacred Mount Kithairōn. A wooden wall alone – Zeus grants this to Athena – will survive unscathed, which will be a boon for her children . . . O sacred Salamis [island off Attica], you will be the death of women's children both when Demeter is scattered [seedtime] or when she collects herself [harvest time]. (7.141)

The envoys, says Herodotus, wrote down the oracle and brought it back to Athens. There it seems to have been interpreted both by private citizens as well as 'professionals' (*chrēsmologoi*, oracle interpreters), and rival interpretations sparked debate. Some older citizens took Apollo to mean by 'wooden wall' the Acropolis itself, as in early days this had been surrounded by a protective wooden palisade. Others believed that Apollo had meant ships, the Athenian navy, as these were made of wood. However, the last couplet of the Pythia's words were an obstacle to this reading, as they seemed to hint that a sea battle off the island of Salamis would lead to defeat (the 'deaths of women's children'). A contradiction presented itself: a 'wall of wood' pointed perhaps to a naval defence, but 'O Salamis, you'll be the death' pointed towards defeat. At this point a young Athenian, a rising star on the political stage at the time, pointed out that the oracle said 'O sacred Salamis'. It would never have addressed the island in such respectful terms (*ēpiōs*, literally 'kind') if defeat for the locals – the Athenians – was meant. Rather, it would say something like 'O baneful Salamis'. So the enemy had been meant by 'deaths of women's children', not the Athenians. And the rest is history, as they say. Themistokles persuaded the Athenians to prepare to do battle at sea off Salamis, but to evacuate Attica itself. The Greek navy (mainly Athenians and Aiginetans) defeated the Persians by their superior training and fighting tactics, and Xerxes decided to retreat.

Let us examine the chain of transmission of such an oracle. Theoretically, it stemmed from Apollo himself. But it was uttered by his mouthpiece, the *promantis*, or 'mantic proxy', one might translate. Her words were written down, then pored over by the recipients. Here *chrēsmologoi* played a role in interpreting the god's words. Nor should the words themselves be disregarded in this hermeneutic chain. For frequently they were ambiguous, allusive or obscure, by no means an unequivocal message. Here, as we have seen, one word, 'sacred' (*hiera*), permitted Themistokles to twist what one might call the surface meaning to a more far-fetched, but more favourable, message. Finally, the democracy had to decide between the different interpretations. All in all, a long and precarious chain of transmission. But what remains is the Athenians' determination to obtain a favourable word from Apollo supporting their purpose. Clearly this was a huge moral boost, a 'god-with-us' rallying cry. Once they had determined the favourable message behind the oracle, by fairly tortuous reasoning, it accompanied the Athenians like a standard or mascot: Apollo was with them! Sometimes one reads sceptical opinions about ancient oracles: all a cheat! Well, not really, in terms of belief, despite possible weak links in the chain of transmission from god's mouth to client state or individual.

Were oracles corrupt in the sense of venal? There was one famous case involving Delphi and the Alkmeonidai, the rich clan of Athenians whom we have already met. Herodotus records the case, as does the documentary *Constitution of the Athenians* attributed to Aristotle. The members of this extended family were banned from Athens by the Peisistratids (sons of Peisistratos, tyrant of Athens) on the pretext that they had incurred religious pollution (*agos*) by killing conspirators on the holy ground of the Acropolis. Now, Herodotus narrates, the Alkmeonidai strove to get help from Sparta in ousting the Peisistratids from Athens. To achieve this aim, they agree with the authorities responsible for the Delphic oracle to renovate the temple, adorning its facade with Parian marble instead of inferior *pōros* stone. And, it was said, they bribed the priestess (*promantis*) with money to tell any Spartan delegation, whether private or public, to 'free Athens' from the tyranny of the Peisistratids. And they succeeded. The influence of the Delphic oracle was sufficient to persuade Kleomenes, a Spartan leader, to 'liberate' Athens, thus facilitating the Alkmeonids' return.

Lest we think, however, that the Delphic institution was purely venal, it is worth noting that the route to its favour was through investment 'to the greater glory of Apollo': his temple was made more magnificent by the Alkmeonids. They traded in sacred capital, as it were, not merely money (Herodotus, *Histories* 6.62–3). Later, the machinations of the Alkmeonidai came to light, to the displeasure of the Spartans (6.74).

Oracles were not only consulted in matters of state. Private petitions were also very common, concerning all manner of personal concerns: health, wealth, children, wives, business, farming – the god might help in every department of life. Aristophanes' comedy *Wealth* opens with a scene involving a private consultation of Delphic Apollo about how to prosper in life. The play begins with two men, master and slave (Chremylos and Kariōn), walking along behind a third person, who is apparently blind. Kariōn explains what has just happened:

> I have the following justified complaint to make to Loxias [Apollo], who 'prophesies from his golden tripod': he's supposed to be a clever doctor and prophet, but he's sent my master away acting crazily. He's following along behind a *blind man*, which is the opposite of what he should be doing. (ll. 8–14)

Kariōn challenges his master as to what he thinks he's doing, and Chremylos explains:

> I'm a god-fearing and fair man but I was doing badly and was poor. Others were the ones prospering, the temple-robbers, orators, sycophants and rogues. (*Kariōn:*) I agree. (*Chremylos:*) So I set off to consult the god, thinking my own miserable life might be over, but my one and only son, well, I wanted to enquire whether he should change his character and turn to the bad, to crime, become a ne'er-do-well, as that seemed to help in life. (*Kariōn:*) And what did Phoibos Apollo 'cry from his holy crown' [a quote from tragedy]? (*Chremylos:*)

> I'll tell you. He told me clearly: whomsoever you encounter when you leave my oracle, don't let them out of your sight but persuade them to accompany you back home. (*Kariōn:*) And this is him? (*Chremylos:*) Yes, it's him. (*Kariōn:*) So, stupid, don't you understand what the god is trying to tell you? He's saying as clearly as he can that your son should do what everyone round us does. (*Chremylos:*) How do you work that out? (*Kariōn:*) Well, that it's obvious even to a blind person that for the present generation it's most advantageous not to be morally upright. (*Chremylos:*) Oh no, the oracle can't mean that! (*Wealth* 28–50)

At this point the two men decide to question the blind man to find out who he is. They discover that he is none other than Wealth (Ploutos), and the play then pursues the theme of blind Wealth who regains his sight, with all the implications of that. For present purposes, the salient points are: Chremylos consults the Delphic oracle in order to try and establish the correct course in life for his son, his closest family member. Apollo does not answer directly but says enigmatically that Chremylos should persuade the first person he encounters on leaving the oracle to accompany him home. Then the master and slave question this first person they meet to see how Apollo's response may have been meant. The area of consultation – personal prosperity – is exemplary, as is the necessity of interpreting the god's riddling response. We will return to Aristophanes' play *Wealth* when considering the acquisition of wealth in a later chapter.

Dreams

Throughout ancient history, dreams were thought to open a window on a truth normally kept hidden, as if the gods spoke to humans while they were asleep, or perhaps that by entering the strange, subliminal state of sleep, the human mind has access to a kind of 'backstage' of the world, where the directors are at work. In the *Iliad*, Zeus, having decided to honour Achilles by humiliating Agamemnon for a limited duration of time, sends a 'dire dream' (an *oulon oneiron*; Book 2) to

Agamemnon. His plan is to encourage Agamemnon to launch an attack the following day, which will be doomed to failure (without Achilles fighting on his side). Dream is personified in the account:

> So spoke [Zeus], and Dream hurried to the swift ships of the Achaeans, making for Agamemnon, son of Atreus. He found him sleeping in his camp, and holy sleep held him in its grip. Dream stood over his head, taking on the appearance of Nestor, son of Nēleus, whom Agamemnon favoured among his elders. So, in this guise, divine Dream spoke: 'You sleep, son of Atreus, the wily horseman. A leader responsible for armies and momentous affairs should not sleep away the night. Now listen to me. I am a messenger from Zeus who from afar cares much for you and is sympathetic to your cause. He orders you to arm the Achaeans with their flowing hair, the whole host. Now is your chance to take Troy with its wide streets.' [Dream gives further instructions] . . . With these words, Dream left him with these thoughts, which were not destined to be fulfilled. Agamemnon imagined he would take the city of Priam that very day, poor fool, nor did he understand what Zeus was planning. (*Iliad* 2.16–38)

Again we see the elusive nature of divine signs. On the one hand there is trust that they *are* divine – Dream told Agamemnon he was Zeus' messenger – on the other, an inability on the part of humans to grasp their true significance. One can be tricked by divine signs, just as oracles were the subject of intense scrutiny in the effort to construe the true sense behind their riddling language. That was presumably the reason professionals, *oneiropoloi* or *oneirokritai*, were often consulted: perhaps they could read the dream better than the layman who had the dream. An example in Pindar, *Olympian Ode* 13 (early fifth century BC), relates how the mythical king Bellerophon saw Athena in a dream, who gave him a golden harness with which to harness the magic horse Pēgasos. On waking, he 'gladly' consulted the local seer Koiranidas, who gave him precise ritual instructions about how to cope in this situation. A technical treatise on the interpretation of dreams, *Oneirokritika* by Artemidoros (second century AD), has survived.

The orthodoxy was that dreams were god-given, if only one could grasp their significance. Staying with Herodotus' narrative of events during the Persian Wars (the 'early classical' period), we find an extraordinary nexus of dreams allegedly had by the Persian king Xerxes before he decided to invade Greece. As in the political debate that accompanied this decision, it seems that Herodotus used the 'foreign' context of the Persian court to reflect a contemporary debate about the 'veracity' of dreams. Xerxes has just listened to a lively debate among his top advisers as to whether he should lead an army against Greece. Mardonios, his top general, says the Greeks are hopeless fighters; Xerxes will win hands down (*Histories* 7.9). Artabanos, a wise elder with much experience at the Persian court, corrects him and advises caution (7.10). Xerxes is irritated by Artabanos' lack of fighting spirit and declares that he will invade. But at night he begins to have second thoughts, as Artabanos' arguments sink in (7.12). At this point he has a dream ('so the Persians say,' says Herodotus, but one wonders). A handsome young man appears to him and tells him he is making a mistake to change his mind about the invasion. The only dreamlike element of this direct communication is that the young man appears to 'fly away' once he has spoken. Xerxes wakes, disregards the dream, and announces to his inner circle that he has had second thoughts about invading Greece and is calling off the invasion. But then he has a second dream. The same young man appears to him and tells him that as he has risen to prominence quickly, so he will fall quickly into obscurity if he does not conquer Greece. Xerxes 'jumps out of bed in alarm' and summons Artabanos to discuss the dreams with him (7.15). When he arrives, Xerxes explains how he had decided against the expedition, then the dream figure had twice appeared to reprimand him. 'If it is god sending this,' he says to Artabanos, 'and it is entirely according to his will that the invasion of Greece happens, he'll fly to you too, with exactly the same message' (7.15). In an attempt to test god, Xerxes tells Artabanos to dress in his clothes, sit on his throne, then sleep in his bed; then surely they will see whether the god sends the same message to Artabanos as to Xerxes.

Artabanos remonstrates that the god will hardly be tricked by his disguising himself as Xerxes ('he'll see through that') and lectures Xerxes on the dubious status of dreams as missives from god:

> Now that you have changed your mind for the better, and decided not to invade Greece, you say you've had a dream by divine ordinance which prevents you from cancelling the invasion. But such things, my boy, are not divine. From my position of seniority, I will explain to you what is the true nature of dreams which appear to men. Dream visions are usually of matters that concern us by day. In recent days we have been intensively involved with discussions about the expedition. If what I say is not the case here, but really has a divine component, you yourself have said what's to do. Let the thing appear to me, as to you, with its message. But it is no more likely to appear to me if I wear your clothes instead of mine, nor if I sleep in your bed instead of mine. For this thing, whatever it is that is appearing to you in your sleep, is hardly so naive as to be deceived by my wearing your clothes. (*Histories* 7.16)

Finally, however, Artabanos does exactly what Xerxes wants, and, sure enough, dreams of the same young man, who first asks him if he is that person who has sought to dissuade Xerxes from invading: 'Neither in the future nor in the present will you escape punishment for attempting to avert what is fated to happen. What Xerxes needs must suffer if he fails to obey has already been made clear to him' (7.17). And, to underline his point, the dream figure threatens to blind Artabanos with a hot iron. Not surprisingly, Artabanos wakes from the nightmare and runs to Xerxes to tell him that he takes back his previous advice not to invade Greece: 'If divine will is really at work here, and it is written in heaven that the Greeks must perish, then so be it' (7.18). Again, the rest is history: Xerxes invades and is defeated; this dream, which has persuaded both him and Artabanos that the invasion is in accordance with god's will, is like Agamemnon's dream in the *Iliad*. It seems to say one thing, but the ultimate result is the opposite. It is quite possible that Herodotus even had the *Iliad* precedent in mind when he wrote this episode: god punishes those guilty of *hybris*. Agamemnon was guilty of *hybris* in humiliating his best fighter Achilles. Artabanos tells Xerxes quite clearly that it is *hybris* to attempt to conquer the whole world. We can perhaps take from this discussion the belief, held by Herodotus and perhaps his readers, that human affairs are indeed subject to divine will ('theodicy'), but that attempts on the part of humans to ascertain what that is through signs are inadequate and, for that reason, fallible. What is never questioned is the belief structure established by Homer – and no doubt generations of poets before him – that there *are* gods, but their purposes are opaque to us. Sign-reading is the only way for humans to read their minds, but the art itself is subject to human limitations.

Another saying of Heraclitus, whose words began this chapter, ran: 'The Age of Man is a child playing draughts: all power [lit. 'kingship', *basileia*] to the child!' (fragment 52 D–K). This may mean that Life itself (Aiōn, the age of man, is a divinity in later theology) plays with us as if we were pieces in a board game. This puts us into a passive role, subject to the whims of the child playing a strategy game. The picture suits the *Iliad* quite well, where life is in tragic earnest for the human actors, while the gods seem to be altogether more frivolous. Herodotus, however, in his *Histories* introduces the serious theme of *hybris*, aiming higher than is permitted to a mere human (*thnētos*, mortal), and inevitably falling foul of it.

A Little Theory

Xenophon (*c.* 430–355/354 BC) was not a philosopher himself, but he moved in philosophical circles, being a so-called Socratic, that is, a pupil and close associate of Socrates. Xenophon's main Socratic writing is a collection of 'memoirs' of Socrates, called in Greek *Hypomnēmoneumata* (Latin *Memorabilia*). Its chief purpose is to exonerate Socrates posthumously from the charges raised against him at his trial of 399 BC: 'corrupting' the youth of Athens and not worshipping the traditional gods of Athens. Otherwise, he wrote a slightly weird *Upbringing of Kyros* (the founder of the Persian empire), weird because it makes Kyros seem like a young Athenian aristocrat. His most famous work is the *Anabasis of Kyros* (Kyros the Younger), a gripping narrative of the so-called Return of the Ten Thousand Greek mercenaries who had joined Kyros' expedition to depose the Persian king. In the same historical vein, Xenophon wrote a *Greek History*, picking up where his predecessor Thucydides left off (411 BC). There are also a number of minor works, for example the *Symposion* and *Home Management* (*Oikonomikos*). So, Xenophon was a writer who spread himself widely in terms of both genre and the geographical scope of his works. At every turn he reveals a fairly traditional Greek piety, which is useful here for examining his justification for believing in divine signs. It is less useful for assessing the historical Socrates, as Xenophon was an ardent supporter of Socrates and defender of his reputation after his death.

A character called Hermogenes in Xenophon's *Symposion*, or 'Party Talk', recording the after-dinner conversation of a group of Athenian notables and representing Xenophon's companion piece to Plato's work of the same name, is called upon to give an account of the benefits of listening to divine signs. He says:

> That both Greeks and foreigners believe that the gods know everything that is and will come to be, is obvious. All cities and all peoples enquire through the mantic art of the gods what they should and should not do. That we believe that they can do good and harm is also clear, I believe. All people call upon the gods to avert harm and to bestow blessings. These gods, then, who are all-knowing and all-powerful, are such good friends to me that their care for me means that neither by night nor by day do I escape their notice, on whatever I embark and whatever I intend to do. Through their fore-knowledge of what will be the result of each of my actions they send me messages in the form of reports, dreams, bird-omens, saying what's to be done and what not. When I pay attention to these, I never regret it. Occasionally I have not taken any notice, and suffered for it. (Xenophon, *Symposion* 4.47–8)

Hermogenes' reasoning seems to be: the gods govern the universe and have a concern for humans. Because of this, they try to prompt human action in the right direction by sending signs. Hence one should study and follow these signs. This makes explicit what is implicit in the passages looked at so far: divine signs are a functional element of Greek theology or belief. Omens, portents, bird flight, animal entrails are the gods' way of communicating with us through natural phenomena. The same interdependence – if the gods exist, there is divination; if there is divination, there must be gods – plays a large part in later Stoic philosophy (Chrysippos is the main name here), as reported in the Roman statesman Cicero's treatment of the subject in *On Divination* (*De divinatione*, 44 BC).

In the *Memorabilia*, Xenophon's 'Socrates' at two important points explains why we may assume gods exist and why divination is the way to discover their will. Both passages show Socrates to be a fervent believer in the Greek gods. As noted above, this may be a distortion of the historical truth.

The first conversation in the *Memorabilia* shows 'Socrates' persuading a religious sceptic, Aristodēmos, of the existence of the gods and their concern about human welfare. Aristodēmos, he had noticed, 'did not sacrifice or pray to the gods'. Socrates launches into a full-scale 'proof' of the existence of gods, and of their care for us. The main argument is the teleological one that both the world and, in particular, we humans seem to be designed on purpose rather than by chance. Take our eyes, for example. Socrates points out that they not only allow us to see all the marvels around us, but they are protected by eyelids against damage, by eyelashes against particles that might be blown in by the wind, and by eyebrows which keep out the sweat if it drips down our foreheads from exertion. Surely such a design reflects intelligence on the part of our creator rather than mere chance (Darwinians, take note!). Furthermore, Socrates asks Aristodēmos, why do you imagine your soul (*psychē*) is not part of some cosmic soul, intelligence or rational power, when the material parts of your body are mere portions of the earth, air and water around us? Haven't the gods given us sense organs to enjoy all the sights, sounds, tastes, smells and sensations (including a year-round appetite for sex!) all around us? Divine signs are evidence that the gods are concerned for the welfare of humans, Aristodēmos included:

> (*Socrates:*) What action of theirs *does* make you think that they care for you? (*Aristodēmos:*) [*reluctantly*] When they send – as you say they do – advice what to do and what not to do. (*Socrates:*) And when they send signs to the Athenians when they consult them through divination, don't you think they are also communicating with you? Or when they predict the future for the Greeks generally, or the whole of mankind, by sending portents, do you imagine they make an exception of you and neglect to think of you? Do you imagine the gods would have implanted in men a belief that they are capable of working good and harm, if they were not? Have humans been deluding themselves the whole time and not noticed? (*Memorabilia* 1.4.15–16)

Later in the work (4.3), Xenophon returns to the theme of divine providence in providing for all life's needs, and has Socrates argue that, although one cannot see the gods, their works are very much in evidence, as are the visible effects of other unseen forces. He points out that one cannot see winds, but their effects are obvious. Nor can one look the sun in the eye; it is, so to speak, unseeable. Similarly, the human *psychē*: invisible itself, but undeniable in its importance. 'You should realize', Socrates says to Euthydemos this time, 'that the gods show themselves in a subliminal way. Like other things that give us benefits without showing themselves, so too the governing principle of the entire universe, in which all manner of fine and good things occur, provides these for our needs tirelessly and unceasingly . . . He makes himself apparent in his majestic works but remains invisible to us as he provides them.' Finally, in 4.7.10, in a peroration on Socrates' piety and morality, Xenophon's Socrates gives the advice to anyone wishing for higher-than-human knowledge to employ divination.

Why don't we believe in divination any more? Well, that is only true to a degree. Many believe they had better pay attention to their dreams as these offer some kind of privileged insight into what is going on. Media channels were prepared to put on air an octopus called Paul to predict the outcome of World Cup matches in 2010. Some believe in horoscopes and astrology. Many believe that strange occurrences have a supernatural explanation. Some still ask themselves when diagnosed with a serious illness, 'What did I do to deserve this?' It is very difficult really to believe that nature and the universe are utterly indifferent to us and our doings. If there is no higher power, no superior instance, what is the point of morality, obedience, devotion, self-sacrifice, all the other virtues? Who is going to reward us? Who cares if we behave dreadfully? But what I think can be said, is that the recognized institutions of divination, augury and extispicy, no longer play a part in the modern Western state as they did in Greece or Rome. Not everyone in antiquity was like Theophrastus' Superstitious Man (*Characters* no. 16, *Deisidaimonia*, *c.* 300 BC), whom one might call neurotically sensitive to anything that could be construed as a sign. Yet Euxitheos, the defendant of Antiphon's speech *On the Murder of Herodes*, was presumably speaking to a public consensus when he said:

> You have heard the evidence and the witness testimonies, gentlemen of the jury. But you should also have regard for the signs from the gods relating to these matters when you come to pass judgment. For you conduct public business most securely when you place your faith in these, both those pertaining to our security and those not. (5.81)

Pseudosciences

Extispicy

One area of divination that was widespread and respected in antiquity appears seriously alien to us now. That is the inspection of animal entrails in the course of sacrifice to see what they tell about the future. Nowadays, if one searches 'sheep entrails' on the Internet, one is presented with an array of recipes for cooking sheep's liver or Scottish haggis, for example (and, admittedly, a few cranky sites on divination). The thought that the appearance of these bloody organs extracted from a sheep that had just been slaughtered might predict

15 Kalchas the seer inspecting a sheep's liver, Etruscan mirror, 5th century BC, bronze. The lungs and trachea lie on the table.

the future seems, as I said, bizarre, if not plain barbaric. To be fair, it was barbaric: the Greeks acquired the art from their Mesopotamian neighbours, whom they called *barbaroi*, at an early stage of their history; in Rome later, *haruspices*, priests who performed the rite, were also prominent. The main use of extispicy, as it was called (from *exta*, 'entrails' in Latin), was for the quick, on-the-spot examination of the divine lie-of-the-land, as it were. Was an army preparing an attack? A ship about to sail? A colony to be founded? A business trip planned? Before all such enterprises, an individual could apply to a priest and 'take the omens'. A sheep was slaughtered in a religious rite called sacrifice, *thysia*; its entrails, the liver and lungs mainly, were extracted, and the priest would take these in his hands, furrow his brow and utter a string of pronouncements on whether the 'Head' was present, whether the 'Sweetness' was intact, whether the 'Way' was bifurcated, and other such mumbo jumbo (see illus. 15). But not mumbo jumbo to the priests and their clients, then.

The stars

A remarkable find from Etruscan Italy, the so-called Piacenza Bronze Liver, after the place where it was found, shows us a bronze model of a sheep's liver marked according to the quarters of the sky. In other words, the parts of the liver examined in extispicy had their corollary in the heavens. This points strongly towards the belief – originating in Babylonian extispicy – that the animal's liver in sacrifice reflected the heavenly constellations, which, in turn, were influential on human affairs. To read the liver was to read the heavenly bodies, which was to understand the constellation of forces operating on human beings at that time. Astrology, like extispicy, was an import into Greece from Mesopotamia (Babylon), where it was a highly developed pseudoscience (as we say).

An author in late antiquity (fifth century AD), Hephaistion of Thebes, wrote an astrological treatise called *Apotelesmatika* (Astrological Phenomena). By his time, astrology and extispicy had become complementary branches of divination. The constellations of the heavenly bodies influence the appearance of the inner organs of animals, which in turn have a bearing on human fate. Both the stars, then, and the entrails of animals can be 'read' in an effort to determine whether the time is 'right' or 'wrong' for a certain action or decision. Here is a short extract:

> The Moon [Sēlēnē] being the closest [heavenly body] to earth rapidly affects conditions here more than the other heavenly bodies. If she is in phase with Hermes at the moment of the animal's immolation, she affects the inner constitution of the entrails variously at various times and in accordance with the nature of the stars with which she is commingled. She gives [the entrails] a healthy colour and appearance when she combines with the coordinates and lights of, and is in accord with, the Kindly [stars]; a livid, pallid and watery appearance,

> conversely . . . when she is waning and is in accordance with Kronos. (*Apotelesmatika* 3.6.8–9)

In the divinatory arts of ancient Greece we see a concerted attempt, with the help of 'professionals', to read an individual human's present standing in the cosmos. From Homer's birds and snakes, the examination of nature for signs relating to man extended to the interior organs of animals and the positioning of stars at night. We may scoff at such 'superstition' based on the belief that differing forms of terrestrial and celestial existence are interconnected and interdependent. The gradual displacement of this belief by modern science, however, brings with it a new kind of *hybris*: that humans are somehow above nature, and not an integral part of the whole.

5
The Daily Round

Days are where we live.
Philip Larkin, 'Days', 1953

The ancient Greeks had to live in their days, too. While history tends to filter out remarkable events and people from the humdrum daily round like mountains rising out of a plain, we can be sure that there was a lot of routine in ancient Greece too, boredom even, and a lot of repetitive days without much drama. On the other hand, most of us appreciate such uneventful routine. Such days are indeed 'to be happy in', as where else if not in these? The Greek day was less determined by precise timekeeping than ours is, with our quartz watches and GPS time-tracking. We do hear about two forms of clock: one, the *klepsydra*, or water-clock, was a way of timing durations, for example the length of a speech permitted in a lawcourt, but not the time of the day. Two, there are occasional references to sundials and the lengths of the shadow that their *gnōmōn*, or rule, casts. A character in Aristophanes' comedy *Assemblywomen* (l. 652), for example, mentions that it is dinnertime when the sundial reads 'ten feet' (that is, a long evening shadow). But most times are given very approximately by the basic divisions of dawn or morning (*orthros*, *eōs*), midday (*mesēmbria*), afternoon (*deilē*), evening (*hespera*) and night (*nyx*), modified by adjectives like 'early' (*prō*) and late (*opse*). Sunset and sunrise are also used as reference points, with qualifications such as 'after', 'before' and 'sometime after or before'. 'Before dawn' is expressed as 'deep twilight' (*batheos orthrou*). 'Full marketplace' (*agorās plēthōra*) was likewise used for 'later in the morning'. There were basically two meals in the day, one usually translated as 'breakfast' (*ariston*) but taken late, and an evening meal (*deipnon*).

One can piece together Athenian daily life quite well from the orators and the authors of comedies among literary sources. Forensic oratory (lawsuits) usually have a section of narrative (*diēgēsis*) in which the defendant gives his account of events surrounding the charge, and this frequently involves descriptions of daily events and places. Already we have seen in Antiphon's speech *On the Murder of Herodes* how the speech gives a good account of the seafaring involved. Comedy, likewise, is based on everyday life as opposed to myth (tragedy), history or fantasy. True, the plots of Aristophanes' plays have plenty of fantasy in them, but the dialogue and texture were what Athenians could identify with. Much evidence of real life can also be gleaned from art and archaeology, of course. However, I am not an art historian or archaeologist, so the emphasis here, as throughout, is on Greeks talking about their lives.

At Home

A case of adultery

Lysias, a speechwriter who lived and worked in Athens at the turn of the fourth century BC, although his family came from Sicily, composed speeches for lawsuits. The first in our collection is called *On the Homicide of Eratosthenes*. It concerns the killing of one Eratosthenes for adultery, by the cuckolded husband. Athenian law permitted this as long as the killing was not premeditated and was committed, as it were, in good faith (and not because of a personal vendetta, a debt or otherwise). The speaker, who is not named, describes his family life leading up to the homicide, giving us a good picture of what typical middle-class Athenian life looked like. The man has land in the country and farms it, no doubt with the help of slave labour. But he lives in a house in Athens that has two storeys, as he describes. He describes his marriage to a good woman, as he thought. The couple are clearly not rich but have one maid (a female slave). The husband describes how at first his wife seemed excellent in all respects. She bore him a child and, he says, he treated her fairly. He describes how, so as to make her life easier, he let her sleep downstairs in a bedroom while he slept upstairs, thus turning normal sleeping arrangements on their head. The move, he says, was to avoid the necessity of her climbing down the 'ladder' to wash and feed the baby, perhaps risking falling and hurting herself. He considered their domesticity to be perfect.

Things went wrong, he says, when his mother died (the wife's mother-in-law), reflecting a feature of Greek life we hear about elsewhere that the mother-in-law could be a formidable figure of authority in a woman's marriage. The speaker tells us that he subsequently found out that his wife had first been approached by the maid of the adulterer Eratosthenes at the funeral. This reflects another feature of family life in Greece: women normally stayed at home and only had contact with the outside world at funerals and women's festivals. These, then, were times when women could interact and perhaps misbehave. Greek women did not (have to) cover their faces and hair in public. This maid, acting as go-between for Eratosthenes, worked on the wife and eventually persuaded her to admit Eratosthenes. Things were made easier by the fact that she slept downstairs and the husband upstairs.

The speaker describes how on one occasion he returned from the farm (*agros*) unexpectedly and the wife acted as if she was pleasantly surprised. They ate the evening meal together upstairs, as we learn, then the baby started crying downstairs, where it was being looked after by the maid. Later it emerged that the maid poked the child deliberately to make it cry: that was the signal for the wife to come downstairs and join Eratosthenes, who had made his entry. The wife made a play of locking him up in the upstairs room where they had eaten, so that he would not 'make a pass at the maid'. The wife jokes: 'I know you grabbed her on a previous occasion when I left the room.' Another common feature of domestic life: we hear quite often how fathers and husbands treated the female staff (slaves) as sex objects when the mood took them.[1] On this occasion the husband, locked in playfully, sleeps upstairs. Next day, he asks his wife why he heard the front door opening in the night. She says that the lamp beside the child had gone out and she had to fetch a light from the neighbours.

In fact, we may assume, the front door squeaked when Eratosthenes either arrived or left. He also notices that she seems to be wearing make-up that morning, which surprises him, as it is not a month since her brother had died. Again, the case reveals details of everyday household affairs.

The actual crime does not concern us here. Sufficient here is to explain how the husband heard of his wife's infidelity from an old maid who confronted him once on the open street, telling him that his wife was cheating on him with one Eratosthenes. She was sent on this errand by another woman friend of Eratosthenes, who was annoyed that he wasn't paying *her* enough attention any more! The old maid told the speaker that Eratosthenes was a serial adulterer: 'That's his habit,' she says. She tells the speaker to torture his maid-servant if he wants proof. He takes the maid aside and threatens to beat her and send her to the workhouse if she does not tell him the whole truth. Eventually she caves in and confirms the old slave's account. The husband catches Eratosthenes one evening in flagrante and, assisted by friends, dispatches him with blows. We don't know the outcome of the trial, but Lysias gives a very convincing account of the defendant's actions as being in accordance with Athenian laws on adultery.[2] The speech reads like the plot of what could now be filmed or televised as a domestic drama: telling detail and snippets of dialogue interspersed with the narrative all contribute to a lively picture. This was no grand house. There is no glamour, no conspiracy, just a sordid little affair with a lover who, allegedly, was a frequent offender. One does notice the wile of the wife in various respects. Apart from the material circumstances – the sleeping arrangements, the slaves, the lamp – and, of course, the drastic punishment that could legally be meted out to the adulterer by the injured party, the story strikes one as all too familiar. That seems to be roughly what happened in the O. J. Simpson case.

Wedding preparations

Another interesting domestic interior is given in Menander's *Samia* (The Girl from Samos) (*c.* 300 BC). As mentioned, Menander authored over a hundred comedies of the type known as New Comedy to distinguish it from the more political and fantastic Old Comedy of Aristophanes. In *The Girl from Samos*, a well-off Athenian, Demeas, returns from a business trip to the Black Sea (Byzantium) to discover – as he thinks – that his adoptive son, Moschiōn, whom he loves dearly, has been cheating on him with his common-law wife Chrysis, the girl from Samos of the title. Chrysis was a so-called *pallakē*, that is, long-standing partner (mistress or 'kept woman') without the sanction of marriage. She was not eligible to marry as she was not an Athenian citizen. That did not mean that Demeas did not love and respect her. On the contrary, he was horrified when he thought his adoptive son had had a baby with her secretly during his absence.

He discovered this 'fact' in the course of preparing his son's wedding to the girl next door, the daughter of his neighbour Nikēratos. It was, however, all a misunderstanding – read the play to discover the truth! This is how he describes the scene when the whole house was busy preparing the wedding feast:

> As soon as I got home, enthusiastic to make the wedding preparations, I told everyone at home of our decision [that is, the betrothal] and told them to get everything necessary ready, to do the cleaning, to bake the cake and get the basket ready. Everything was proceeding nicely, at such a speed that there was some confusion, as is natural. The baby [which Demeas thought up to that point was his, by Chrysis] had been put somewhere on a couch out of the way, and it was crying. The women of the house were all shouting simultaneously: 'Flour! Water! Pass the olive oil! Charcoal!' And I tried to do my bit by passing this and that. At one point I went into the walk-in larder, from which, in the course of choosing a number of things and looking round, I didn't emerge for a while. While I was inside, a woman came downstairs from the upper floor into the room that adjoins the larder. That's a utility room for sewing through which one passes to go upstairs and to enter the larder. The woman had been Moschiōn's nurse. She was older now and had become my servant but is now a free woman. Well, she saw the baby crying because

16 Menander's *Samia*, Act Three. Left: cook (for Moschiōn's wedding feast); centre: Demeas; right: Chrysis, his *pallakē*. Floor mosaic from Mytilene, 3rd century AD.

> no one was paying it attention and, not knowing I was in the larder, thought she could speak freely. She goes over to the baby and starts saying those typical bits of baby-talk, 'You little dear! What a sweetie! Where's your mummy?' She picks it up, coddles it. When it had stopped crying, she says to herself: 'My, my! Just yesterday I was feeding dear little Moschiōn when he was your size, but now that *he's* had a baby . . .' [text missing] She says to a maid who happens to come in: 'Here, you clean up the child. What can it mean? You're not looking after the little one at the wedding of its own father?' And the maid goes: 'Shh! What are you saying? *He's* inside there in the larder!' 'No! Where?' 'In the larder!' Then, changing her tone: 'She's calling you, nurse. [Then, aside again:] Go on, hurry up! He hasn't heard anything, thank God!' And the old nurse says: 'Dear me, why can't I keep my mouth shut!' and goes outside. (*Samia* 219–61)

Again, a vivid interior scene evoked by Menander with a similar mix of telling detail and quoted speech as we found in the Lysias speech. The type of dramatic scene here reminds one of a modern farce: someone hiding in a bedroom closet overhears a conversation and gets the wrong end of the stick. And, as in modern theatre, the scene puts a domestic interior with members of the household going about their business before our eyes: the women all working busily; the man of the house trying to do his bit but probably getting in the way more than he is helping; a baby crying; people coming and going with quick entries and exits; plenty of scope for a mix-up. We also hear about the wedding cake (a type of bread) and the charcoal needed to bake it. All very familiar, if we replace the last detail with a split-level electric oven. And we encounter a whole range of varying degrees of servitude and civic status that we cannot translate into modern equivalents: the citizen father and his adoptive son; his common-law wife; an old wet-nurse who has been given her freedom, no doubt for her faithful service over many years; and true servants, that is, slaves owned by Demeas. However, they all talk to each other, it seems, on quite equal terms. And Menander seems to know how bread is baked: flour, water, olive oil and a charcoal oven. Later in the play, when the plot of mistaken identity gets even more convoluted, there is equally lively action played out between Demeas and his neighbour Nikēratos. Perhaps I should add that Menander's stage shows the street in front of the two houses involved as background (literally 'the scene', *skēnē*). Demeas' narrative here is an example of how Menander shows interior scenes: by narration after the event.

Pots and pans

An interesting inscription from the Athenian Agora (marketplace) records the property of certain individuals who had been found guilty in a conspiracy.[3] Their property was confiscated and sold, and the proceeds paid into the public purse. These so-called Hermokopids were a group who, one night in 415 BC, defaced all the public statues of Hermes that stood like humanoid fire hydrants around its streets and squares. On the whole they belonged to the well-off propertied class of Athens, and some were prominent. For example, the famous Alkibiades is among them. We hear in his case of three bronze pots (*chytra*) that were sold, another bronze vessel of indeterminate type (the inscription is damaged), the harvest from a farm in Thria and one in Athmonon. A metic ('resident alien' in Athens) called Kephisodōros, who lived in the harbour town of Piraeus, had a small army of slaves, which fetched a price: three female Thracians, two male; two Syrians; an adult Carian and two boys; two from Illyria; a Scythian; one from Kolchis (Georgia); a male or female from Cappadocia; and a Lydian. The price that each fetched is noted in the left column. The average for all slaves (45) listed in the inscription is 170–80 drachmai. One notices that these slaves were of foreign origin, all from countries neighbouring Greece and, no doubt, bought on the slave markets there.[4] Respectable Athenians do not seem typically to have owned Greek slaves. The nationalities of these slaves correspond closely to the slaves of comedy, who tend also to be Thracians, Syrians, Carians and so on – but, in comedy at least, fluent in Greek. The situation might be compared to all the people from Eastern Europe, the Philippines and South America, employed (or exploited) in menial work by wealthy Western households nowadays.

Many of the goods are agricultural. This does not mean that the owner was a farmer, rather that he owned a farm in Attica, which was worked by an estate manager and slaves. We recall that the speaker of Lysias' first speech lived in Athens but also worked a farm, or supervised the work, in the country. This is mentioned as a typical pattern in Theophrastus' portrayal of the 'Flatterer', who tells the person he is flattering 'how well-built his house is [in town] and how well-appointed his farm' (*Characters* 2.12). The novel mentioned earlier by Achilles Tatius has an episode that shows clearly the relationship between a rich woman, her country estate run by an estate manager, and the slaves who do the hard work (*Kleitophon and Leukippē* 5.15–20). In other words, farming was a common source of income for well-off Greek town-dwellers. The inventory of Panaitios' property here in the inscription lists: jars of pure (not diluted) Attic wine, seven *choes* (jugs), beehives in the field, two working oxen, two more oxen, four oxen and calves, sheep and their offspring, goats and their offspring, and more: all agricultural produce. Or another, Adeimantos, owned a farm and farmhouse on the island of Thasos, a slave called Aristomachos (so a Greek), nine *pithoi* (wine jars) in good condition and [? others] in poor condition, with lids, amphoras of wine, three *choes*.

An episode in Aristophanes' play *The Assemblywomen* shows a similar inventory of personal possessions, more detailed and poetic this time. The situation is that the women of Athens take over the government and institute communism: all wealth and material goods will be held in common. A character in the play ('First Man') announces that he will empty his house of its utensils and line them up neatly outside his house. He addresses the individual items as if they were members of a company about to take part in a procession. It is a play on a well-known religious procession, the Panathenaia, at Athens, performed annually for the figurehead goddess Athena Polias ('Of the City'). We should imagine the man on stage outside his house and directing extras (slaves) as they carry the things out:

> Come on, let's be having you, my pretty sieve,
> come outside, first in line of my home utensils.
> Nicely powdered, you'll be a basket-carrier[5]
> (who've upended many 'bags' of mine![6])
> Who'll be chair-bearer? Stewpot, come out now!
> God, you're black! You wouldn't be that black
> if you'd boiled the hair-dye used by Lysikrates![7]
> Stand beside her. Come out, make-up artist!
> Bring out the pitcher, pitcher-bearer, and set it
> here. And you, minstrel of the house, come out.[8]
> You've often woken me up for Assembly
> at an ungodly hour of night with your reveille.
> And you, tub-bearer, quick march! Fetch
> the honeycombs, put the olive branches next,
> bring out the tripods and the flask of oil.
> Never mind the crockery and the riff-raff.
> (*Assemblywomen* 730–45)

This list is a combination of (mainly) kitchen utensils with the typical participants in a procession for Athena, to comic effect.[9] Rather than just listing things, Aristophanes equates pots with people, with various cases of innuendo and allusion. In this way, the pots and pans of everyday life are made to come to life, as it were. Incidentally, it is a well-known psychological phenomenon how one becomes attached to household objects and forms a kind of bond with them, far beyond their materiality. There is a sentimentality associated with dumb objects, however cheap or charmless, which allows Aristophanes this parade of pots.

The Agora

Agora, or marketplace, is actually an abstract noun meaning meeting place. It comes from a verb, *ageirō*, meaning to collect, gather. However, *agorā* came to be seen as the physical, social, political and religious hub of the ancient city. It was where people gathered to shop, attend the law court, make political decisions, do official business, meet people, gossip, receive various services, meet for conspiratorial purposes and so on. Most of what is said here applies to the Athenian Agora, as we are best informed about that, but no doubt much would have been applicable to the agora of other cities. One could approach the subject from an archaeological direction, as the Athenian Agora has been the subject of intensive archaeological excavations and analysis, but I leave that to others. This introduction is through the mouths of Greek sources, living witnesses to their social experiences, not an attempt at historical synthesis. Most of the remarks collected here are incidental, much as modern reporting, or indeed fiction, might mention Trafalgar Square in connection with the National Gallery or Nelson's Column, as a concert venue or exhibition centre, or as a meeting place for a demonstration, without describing its physical features in detail.

The agora was the hub of the ancient city, physically and conceptually. In Aristophanes' play *Birds*, which develops the fantasy of a 'bird city', Metōn, a well-known astronomer in Athens, appears at one point to sketch out a ground plan for the new city in the sky for birds. His plan is circular, with an agora at its hub, and streets radiating out from this like spokes of a wheel. It is possible that the plan has a connection with a Panhellenic settlement in southern Italy that was undertaken around this time (443 BC), a place called Thourioi, but Metōn's plan is likely to have general applicability to a simplified, ideal plan of the ancient city, not allowing for specific topography (hills, valleys, harbours, rivers). We have to imagine him talking to Pisthetairos in mid-air, as it were: 'I'll measure the space using my straight rule, in order to square the circle, so to speak [an old joke, it seems!], and in the middle I'll put the agora, and, leading to that, straight roads radiating out, just as straight rays of light radiate out in all directions from a round shining star.' (*Birds* 1004–9)

Shopping

One shopped in the agora. We have to imagine a jumble of market stalls and shops arranged around the agora and adjoining streets. The marketplace was the open-air supermarket of the ancient city. Products were laid out on tables (*eleos*) and long counters (*klinē*, literally 'bed'). The stalls themselves were afforded shade by wickerwork coverings (Demosthenes, *De coronā* 169). There were also money-lending tables (*trapezai*) for people to draw cash (Theophrastus, *Characters* 5.7). One walked there from one's house, but no doubt there were some horses and donkeys, and occasionally we hear of a fancy carriage, usually for a rich *hetaira*.[10] Usually the servants (slaves) of a household did the shopping, as in Lysias' *On the Murder of Eratosthenes* (16.5), where the maidservant arranged trysts for the wife, her mistress, when she went shopping for them in the agora. The Peripatetic philosopher Theophrastus wrote, perhaps for relaxation, an amusing collection of sketches of oddball types in fourth-century Athens called *Characters*. In one of these, *The Flatterer*, a man who tries to be (over-)obliging – to people he wants something from – is said to be prepared even to shop for them at the 'Women's Market' without batting an eyelid (2.9): this was clearly thought to be beneath a man's dignity normally. We are not told what women normally bought at the Women's Market: presumably clothes, cosmetics and other items.

Theophrastus' Friend-to-All type (no. 5, *Areskeia*, 'obligingness') 'does not shop for himself but buys olives to send to friends in Byzantium, Laconian dogs to send to Kyzikos [on the Black Sea] and honey from Hymettos to send to Rhodes, and tells everyone around him as he does so' (5.8). In other words, he buys regional specialities of Attica to send to friends abroad, but only so as to make a good impression among fellow citizens. One may wonder at these dogs which he intends to send all the way to Kyzikos! The Shameless Man (no. 9, *Anaischyntia*, 'shamelessness') also has interesting shopping habits: 'When he goes shopping he reminds the butcher if he's ever done him a favour in the past. He stands by the scales [at checkout] and tosses in a bit of meat or bone into the sauce [while it's being weighed]. And if he gets away with it, well and good. If not, he picks up a bit of tripe and, with a laugh, walks off' (9.4). In other words, he tries to pull a fast one on the stallholder, and laughs it off if he's caught. No. 11, the Inept Man, also reveals his character while shopping in the Agora:

> And around midday he goes over to the stands selling nuts, or myrtle berries, or plums, picks something up and samples it, all the while chatting to the vendor. Or he calls over to someone by name, who he's not friends with. When people are hurrying on their way, he calls over to them to stay a while, or, seeing someone leaving the law court who's just lost an important case, he goes over and revels in the details of the case. He shops for himself, and hires a stripper [literally a 'flute-girl'] and shows what he's bought to anyone he bumps into, and invites them round. And standing beside the barber's or the perfume counter he announces he's having a party [lit. 'drinking', or getting drunk]. (11.4–6, *Bdelyria*)

It is a vivid picture of this man's maladroit behaviour at market. One notices what foods are mentioned, but of course they are just a sample of all the different stands. He casually samples the products on offer, talks to complete strangers and even invites them round to share what he has bought. As someone leaves a law court, having lost an important case, he asks them to share the details. The point of the last sentence – announcing in a busy place that he's going to party – seems to be in line with the previous ones: a sort of inept invitation no one is meant to take seriously. It is commented upon that he does his own shopping and not a slave: Theophrastus' Suspicious Man (no. 18) sends one slave to do the shopping and then a second to check up on prices, to make sure the first slave did not short-change him. Home-helps were hired at the market, too: cooks and waiters for dinner parties, and flute-girls, as here, for the entertainment of guests: there is one in Xenophon's *Symposion*, and at the dinner in Theophrastus' *Characters* 19.10.

Characters in Aristophanes' comedies have a great deal to do in the Agora. In the play *Lysistrata*, centring on a women's sex-strike, designed to force their men to abandon their warlike mindset and become more domestic, the crazed men are described as going shopping in the Agora wearing their armour. The ringleader of the women conspirators is shown, with another woman (Kleonikē), in conversation with an official (*proboulos*):

> (*Official:*) What should we do? (*Lysistrata:*) If we first stop them shopping in the Agora (*agorazō*) fully armed in this crazy manner. (*Kleonikē:*) Good idea, by Cypriot Aphrodite! (*Lysistrata:*) As it is they're going round the pottery stands and vegetable market in the Agora in their armour like berserkers. (*Official:*) Of course! As befits brave men. (*Lysistrata:*) But it's ludicrous when someone carrying a shield with a Gorgon on it buys fish! (*Kleonikē:*) Yes, and I've seen a ranking officer with a warrior haircut *on his horse* buying cereals from an old woman and putting them into his bronze hat! And another, from Thrace, brandishing his shield and spear like Tereus in person [a violent Thracian king in myth]; he scared the girl selling figs as he stuffed his mouth with them. (*Lysistrata* 555–64)

The joke hinges on the ludicrous sight of macho men in arms shopping at market stalls, a job usually done by female servants. The women conspirators want to demilitarize their men. This description serves to characterize their extreme attachment to all things martial at present. We might compare the scene with demonstrations in the USA in support of the Second Amendment, attended by men and women all carrying the most lethal of firearms.

A final taste of Athenian shopping. In Aristophanes' *Assembly-women*, which we have already met, two men, Chremylos and an unnamed man, are discussing recent changes in coinage. Chremylos is reminded of the recent vote to introduce copper coinage.[11] He sighs and describes his bad experience with those coins: 'That bronze currency was a disaster for me. I'd just sold my grapes [that is, at market] and gone home with a cheekful [against pickpockets?] of bronze change. Then I went to the marketplace to buy some flour and was just about to fill my sack when the town crier [literally 'herald'] announced that bronze coin wasn't being accepted any more. "We deal in silver coin"' (ll. 816-22) (see illus. 20).

Gossip

We have already seen how Theophrastus' Inept Man displayed his (lack of) social skills in the Agora. Not surprisingly for a place where goods were exchanged, this was also the place where news and gossip were exchanged – between men (and slaves), of course; women citizens did not roam the streets of Athens, although female slaves did. Dikaiopolis in Aristophanes' comedy *Acharnians* complains that he is standing there alone on the Pnyx (where the assembly met) while the Athenians 'are all busy gossiping in the Agora about all manner of things and trying to avoid getting roped into going to the assembly' (21–2). A character in Menander's *Samia* (see illus. 16) boasts to his neighbour that if *he'd* been in his neighbour's embarrassing position (cuckolded, as he thought), he would have acted like a man, and been the talk of the town:

> You're her servant, Demeas [the neighbour]. If she'd cheated on me . . . I would have sold the whore forthwith. No barbershop, no stoa, would have been empty! From dawn they'd have been full of people sitting talking about me, saying, 'Now, there's a man who knows how to fight injustice!' (*Samia* 506–12)

This proverbial 'barbershop' (in fact, a cluster of hairdressers), we know from other sources, was a well-known spot in the Athenian Agora where men met not only, clearly, to have their hair and beards trimmed but to exchange gossip. It was close to a landmark in the city known as the Herms (a group of statues of Hermes; Lysias 23.3). Fathers gossiped about the aberrant ways of their sons there (Aristophanes, *Birds* 1441–3), for example how someone had led his son astray and made him mad about horse racing (a drain on family finances!). Theophrastus' Inept Man (*Characters* 11.7) announces his forthcoming party to all and sundry 'standing beside the barber's' (*koureion*). Demesmen, that is, members of one deme (roughly: borough), chose the 'barbers' quarter' as their rendezvous (Lysias 23.3).

The Stoas, elegant colonnaded halls situated around the Agora (see illus. 17), were also men's meeting places, where they could exchange views, gossip and also, in the course of time, even develop such discussions into philosophical schools. The Stoic school, for example, was named after the Stoa Poikilē, 'Painted Stoa' (famous for its large wall paintings), on the Agora. A glimpse of informal conversations conducted there is given in Theophrastus' *Flatterer*: this man typically tells someone he is walking with and wishes to flatter:

> Don't you notice how people are looking at you? This happens to no one else in the city except you. You excelled yesterday in the stoa. There must have been upwards of thirty men sitting there and when the conversation turned on who was best among them, everyone present, starting with me, came round to your name. (*Characters* 2.2)

Interestingly, Socrates used to meet up with one of his protégés, Euthydemos, in a saddler's shop (selling riding equipment) *off* the Agora, as Euthydemos was 'too young' to frequent the Agora itself. The young man used to stop by this saddler's shop, apparently, 'whenever he had some business in town', so Socrates went to meet him there. Xenophon reports their extended conversations there (*Memorabilia* 4.2.1). We learn from this that one had to be a certain age to participate in 'adult business' in the Agora. In the *Constitution of the Athenians*, an interesting constitutional history of Athens found on a papyrus in the late nineteenth century, the author describes how youths are 'inducted' into the city's civic institutions at the age of eighteen (42). The 'coming-of-age' was called *ephēbeia*, roughly equivalent to 'majority'. We also learn from this scene in Xenophon that such conversations took place in public rather than privately (that is, that Socrates was not a private tutor) and that Socrates was not averse to the company of very young men.

There were, of course, pubs scattered round the ancient city, too, not only in the Agora. Menander's plays frequently involve pubs or inns (*pandokeion*, public house) where the men meet and talk. In Lucian's *Life of Dēmōnax*, the philosopher once found a ring and placed a note about it (*grammation*) in the Agora to find the owner (17) . One can imagine many such notes with various announcements and snippets of mini news in the Agora.

Public life

By far the most important function of the Agora, however, was as civic centre, a kind of City, Bank, St Pauls, Gray's Inn, Westminster, Covent Garden, all rolled into one, in London terms. There were important religious buildings: temples of Apollo, the Great Mother, Hephaistos (nearby) and Ares, and altars for public sacrifice to the Twelve Gods, of Apollo Pythios and Zeus Agoraios, among others. The street along which the great civic pageant of the Panathenaia passed ran through the Agora on its way to the Acropolis. The courthouses, apart from the Areopagos (for cases of homicide), all sat in the Agora; we just saw how Theophrastus' Inept Man, while shopping in the market, buttonholed someone who had just lost his lawsuit. When the sophist Protagoras expressed in writing his doubts about the existence of the gods, his works were burnt in the Agora following a public proclamation by herald (*Testimonium* 1.15–17 D–K). There were banks here where money was exchanged and lent (Theophrastus, *Characters* 5.7). Above all, there were the gracious colonnaded buildings known as Stoa: roofed gathering places housing works of art, commerce and meetings. We have already mentioned the Stoa Poikilē, Painted Stoa, famous for its artwork with a national theme, such as the *Battle of Marathon*. The Council Chamber (*bouleutērion*), the upper chamber, if you will (a very inexact comparison), of the Athenian democracy was adjacent to the Agora, next to another sacred building, the Tholos, or Roundhouse. A statue of Harmodios and Aristogeiton,

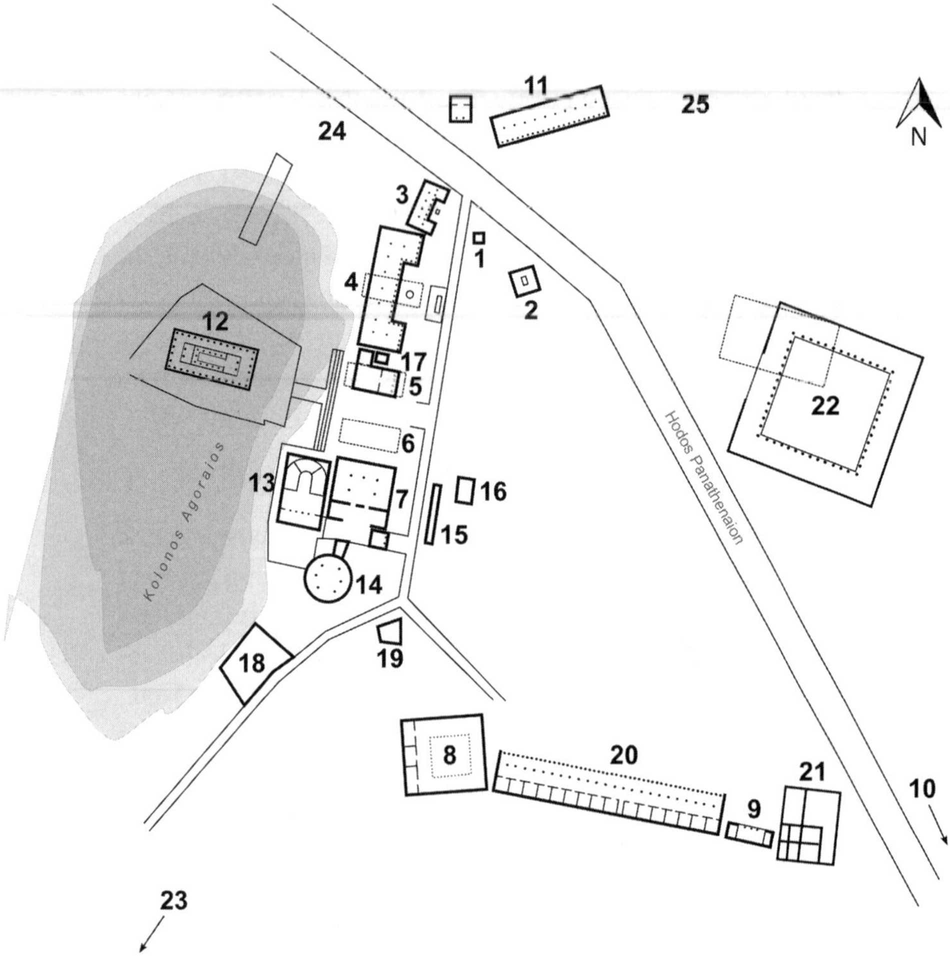

17 Plan of the main buildings in the Athenian Agora, *c*. 300 BC:

1 Leokoreion 2 Altar of Twelve Gods
3 Royal Stoa (Stoa Basileios) 4 Temple of Zeus, later Stoa of Zeus
5 Old and new Temple of Apollo Patrōös 6 Old Metrōön
7 Bouleutērion 8 Aiakeion (not Heliaia as previously thought)
9 Southeastern fountain house (often Enneakrounos)
10 Eleusinion (outside the map) 11 Stoa Poikilē
12 Temple of Hephaestus 13 New Bouleutērion
14 Prytanikon, later Tholos 15 Monument of Eponymous Herōs
16 Altar of Zeus Agoraios 17 Temple of Zeus Phratrios and Athene Phratria
18 Strategeion 19 House of Simōn and agora boundary stone
20 South Stoa I 21 Mint 22 Columned court
23 State prison (outside the map)
24 Temple of Aphrodite Ourania (location uncertain)

the tyrant-assassins, stood in the Agora, commemorating the fall of tyranny in the city in the sixth century. If a man was even accused of bloodshed he was debarred from the *nomima*, civic institutions, of the city, which essentially meant the temples and Agora (Antiphon 6.4). In Roman times there was an Ōdeion, concert hall, in the Agora. In short: it all happened in the Agora. It had central physical, political, commercial, historic, artistic and social importance.

At this point we could return to the story begun in Aristophanes' comedy *Knights*. There we met Kleon, a man from the 'working classes' who became big in Athenian politics. Two slaves, who work in the household of Dēmos, the People, were saying they hate Kleon because he is always denouncing them to their master, and they get a beating. They discover an oracle, which Kleon keeps secret, predicting both his rise to power in Athens and his demise at the hands of a 'Sausage-Seller'. The episode that follows in this play gives a good idea of the turbulent atmosphere that characterized the Agora. The scene is a kind of slanging match between two tradesmen – Paphlagōn (representing Kleon), who comes from a family of leatherworkers, and a Sausage-Seller – but with a political slant. The Sausage-Seller comes on stage with his table, knives and meats, about to set up stall in the market. Slave A tells him about the oracle predicting his rise to power and encourages him to challenge Paphlagōn: 'You've got all the qualifications of a demagogue: a nasty voice, dubious background, you're a man of the market' (ll. 217–18). When Paphlagōn appears, the two lay into each other with all manner of insults, slights and accusations, as well as a physical scuffle.

Although the stage is the conventional one of Greek comedy – two houses (one is that of Dēmos) on a street in which all the action takes place – there are clear markers that the audience was meant to imagine the slanging match taking place, as it were, between two stall-holders in the market. There are references to well-known landmarks in the Agora: the Altar of the Twelve Gods (l. 235), the Prytaneion (l. 281), an oath by Hermes Agoraios, 'Of the Marketplace' (l. 297), an oath by the altar of Zeus Agoraios (l. 410) and a short prayer to Zeus Agoraios (ll. 499–500). To close the scene – which the Sausage-Seller has nominally 'won' – the two combatants march off to the Council

Chamber, which abuts the Agora, to make their respective accusations of the political depravity of the other. The Agora is shown as the beating heart, as it were, of Athenian public, commercial and political life. In this scene it is the place where a challenge is made for political leadership, witnessed by the Athenian people, who are sitting watching the play. The Agora here can be compared to the Roman Forum later, which was the scene of much political drama.

Messaging

The Greeks were not so hopeless at getting messages to each other as we might suppose now, with our smartphones, World Wide Web and virtual nearly everything. Theoretically at least, they knew instant worldwide messaging, too: both Hermes, equipped with wings, and Iris (also meaning rainbow) had the power of instant message-bearing flight from the gods on Olympus down to earth. As early as Homer we find the use of writing tablets to convey a message, although it is disputed whether the 'dread signs' (*sēmata lygra*) written on Bellerophon's writing tablet in the *Iliad* were normal writing (of sorts) or magical signs of some kind (6.168–9). The tablet there is said to be 'folded' (*ptyktos*), so it had two layers that folded together. Messengers were the usual bearers of messages, of course, whether slaves in a town or runners in wartime, or complex chains of communication with staging posts, as Herodotus describes within the Persian Empire (*Histories* 8.98). Fire or smoke signals famously bore the news of the fall of Troy from the Troad back to Argos in Aeschylus' play *Agamemnon*. It seems fire signals (that is, night lights) were used rather than smoke signals. Ships could carry messages, as in the revolt of Mytilene during the Peloponnesian War. Coded messages could be sent via a system associated with Sparta: a stick, *skytalē*, wrapped with a strip of leather on which letters were written (as for example in Aristophanes' *Birds* 1283). The recipient had a stick of the same thickness, so he could wrap the leather strip round his and read the otherwise incomprehensible message. Arrows with messages wrapped round them could be shot within range of the intended recipient in a siege situation (*Histories* 8.128). In Herodotus we hear once of a messenger who had a message tattooed onto his shaved skull, then his hair was allowed to grow and cover the message before he was sent on to the intended recipient (5.35). Themistokles in the Persian invasion of 480 BC thought up a creative way of getting a message to the Ionians, who were coerced into serving with the great king Xerxes. He had his men write messages on rocks at Cape Artemision, which only the Ionians, being Greek, could read: 'Do not kill your ancestral relatives!' (the Ionians were originally colonists from Attica), they read (8.19). Let us look at some of these means of daily telecommunications more closely.

Tablets and notes could only be used after the introduction of writing, obviously, in the eighth century BC. Bellerophon's tablet in the *Iliad* has already been mentioned. In the *Odyssey*, too, there is mention of 'tightly fitting, folding double writing tablets' in Odysseus' storeroom (2.344–5), which is watched over day and night by a female housekeeper. This sounds like a reminiscence of the archives of Linear-B tablets found in excavations of the Mycenaean palaces, at Mycenae and Pylos, for example. In that case the writing would be Greek in syllabic script, but they were writing tablets no less. Security seems to have been an issue: the tablets are 'sealed' and watched day and night. Presumably, as in modern-day bank vaults, such records contained sensitive information about riches and reserves.

Letters themselves were written on these wooden tablets, and later on papyrus, when that material became more widespread. Papyrus finds in Egypt have turned up a large quantity of ancient letters with

18 Scarab with Herakles holding a club and a bow set in a swivel ring, Greco-Phoenician, green jasper in gold mount, late 6th century BC. Gems were used as seals but also as jewellery.

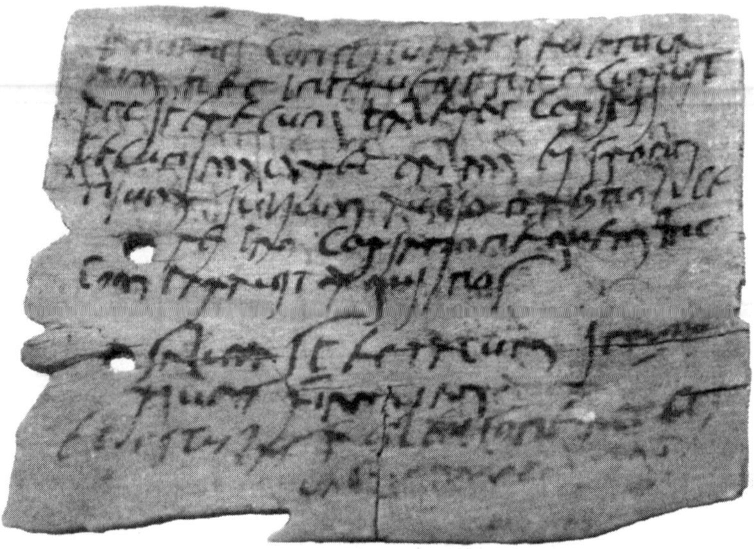

19 Example of a wooden writing tablet with ink writing from Vindolanda, 1st–2nd century AD.

both official and personal content: friends and relatives keeping in touch, some as official (and officious) as any letter today from a country's tax authority. One wrote on a tablet by coating the wood surface with wax or gypsum (white), then scratching the letters with a stylus. The leaves of the tablet could then be folded together and sealed. The tablet could then be reused indefinitely by renewing its coating.

The Spartan Dēmarātos, who was staying with King Xerxes in Susa just before the Persian Wars, sent a secret message back to Sparta by scraping the wax off a wooden tablet, writing on the bare wood, then resurfacing it with wax. The message he wished to convey was the imminent invasion of Greece by Xerxes. In Sparta, Leōnidas' wife Gorgo alone understood the trick, and deciphered the news (*Histories* 7.238). It was in fact common for the sharp stylus to mark the wood under its wax covering even in normal circumstances, leaving some tablets still legible now. Later, ink was used on tablets as on papyrus and parchment. The famous collection of tablets from a Roman military station on Hadrian's Wall known as the Vindolanda tablets (illus. 19) (first–second century AD, in the British Museum) are ink on wood.

Writing tablets had multiple purposes, of course, not just letter writing. They could be used for note-taking; for announcements, for example that a philosophical school was closed for the day (Lucian, *Hermotimos* 750); as curse tablets (these were usually of lead; see an example in illus. 8); for putting questions to oracles; for school exercises (Herodas, *Mimes* 3.14); and, as we saw in the *Odyssey*, for keeping records. It was the start of the 'extended mind', which psychologists are addressing now in respect of the transfer of our lives, thoughts, secrets and messages onto digital devices and services. Letters, too, had multiple functions and types, as they still do. Of official uses, we hear of military news and instructions travelling by writing tablets, and of oracles written down on writing tablets at the oracular site to be read and interpreted in the community for whom the response was intended (such as in *Histories* 8.135). A secret message from the Persian king Artaxerxes to the Spartans during the Peloponnesian War was intercepted en route; its Assyrian message had to be deciphered before it could be read (Thucydides 4.50). This was a case of military intelligence gathered by the interception of enemy communications. Methods and materials change, but the human nexus remains constant.

Letters also began to play a role in literature as part of the *mīmēsis* of real life. Both in tragedy and comedy, information conveyed by letters (*grammata*) was used as a device at crucial moments in the plot. When poor Orestes and Pylades are about to be sacrificed to the 'barbarian' Artemis at Tauris on the north Black Sea coast in Euripides' play *Iphigeneia at Tauris*, a letter written on a tablet reveals the true identity of Iphigeneia – who is the officiating priestess at the sacrifice to Artemis – to her brother Orestes, and saves the day (584ff.). Incidentally, the letter was written for Iphigeneia by a helping hand, perhaps indicating that she could not write herself. In the later play by Euripides on Iphigeneia (*Iphigeneia at Aulis*), her father Agamemnon lures her to Aulis on a false pretext by sending her a letter by messenger. A third example from Euripides: in his *Hippolytos*, the suicide note written by Phaidra seals the fate, tragically, of Theseus' son Hippolytos. Likewise in comedy. Menander makes much use of *grammata* (or *grammateidion*) to convey vital information to characters at key moments in the drama when verbal communication is not possible. Similarly, in a late novel by Heliodorus (*Aithiopika*, Ethiopian Tale), the girl Thisbe is carrying a letter, which is read only after her death (2.10). I do not know of an example of false information conveyed in a literary letter as a distraction or deception. Rather, such missives are thought to convey discretely truths that people are reluctant to say out loud.

We have already seen in Lysias' *On the Murder of Eratosthenes* how amorous trysts could be arranged by a go-between, usually a male or female servant. Here the secret information was entrusted not to any writing material but to a trusted servant. In drama, Phaidra's nurse tries to mediate between her mistress and the stepson Hippolytos. In Menander's *Bad-Tempered Man* we saw how Sostratos' buddy Chaireas acted as his go-between in arranging meetings with girls.

Commonly, however, such liaisons were arranged by the secret exchange of notes (carried by a go-between). Odysseus' love note to Kalypso in Lucian's tale of magical realism *True History* has already been mentioned. An epigram of Asklepiades (*Greek Anthology* 12.162; 23 Gow-Page) clearly alludes to the freight of love commonly associated with messages on writing tablets:

Not yet an archer, nor a youth, but babyish,
  my Erōs runs back to Aphrodite
with a golden tablet. He lisps the love spells
  of Diyllos to Antigenes in her ear.

Diyllos, the older lover (*erastēs*), delivers a message (*philtra*, love charm) to Aphrodite concerning his love (*erōs*) for a boy, Antigenes (the *erōmenos*). However, perhaps here we should see behind the epigram not so much communication between lovers as a reference to prayer plaques hung, or placed, at the sanctuaries or statues of gods by way of expressing a wish. Here the poem mentions 'my Erōs' placing a petition, as it were, before Aphrodite, concerning the love of one Diyllos. Perhaps by 'my Erōs' the poet means his poetic gift, which has formulated the epigram as a kind of love note on Diyllos' behalf. Such prayer plaques are well known; love spells are also very common in the so-called Greek Magical Papyri. A spell might say, 'Let so-and-so [*ho* or *hē deina* in Greek, a placeholder] burn with love for me,' or something similar. Such a spell is called a *philtron*, as here in the epigram.

Then as now, written messages of love find a way to the heart as if by a secret entrance. Internet traffic nowadays might, at a guess, be halved if romantic and erotic content were removed. We can follow an interesting use of the ancient tablet used as love note in the Roman poet Ovid. His work *Amores* (Loves) is devoted to the subject of love and lovers' strategies, in particular his own towards a woman whose status is that of a Greek *hetaira*. Poem eleven in Book 1, in elegiacs, is addressed to his trusty maid, Napē, the go-between:

> You, of proven worth in ministrations of the furtive night, inventive in conveying my messages and encouraging Corinna when she hesitates to come to me, trusty aid in my troubles – take this written message I wrote to my mistress early this morning and bring it to her. Hurry! . . . If she asks what I'm doing, tell her I live in anticipation of the night. The wax will tell the rest of what I wrote. 'While I speak, time flies.' Make sure to give her the letter when she's alone, and that she reads it there and then. Watch her face and her expression as she reads: one can read the future even on an unspeaking face. Tell her to write back at length immediately: I hate it when the shiny wax yawns emptily . . . But why should she tire her hand by holding the pen? Let the whole tablet bear but the one word: 'Come!' Then I'll deck my victorious tablet with laurel and dedicate it in Venus' temple with the words: 'I, Ovid, dedicate this trusty tablet to Venus. Before it was but humble maplewood.'

The whole system is on view: the trusty maid who takes the billet-doux to the girlfriend. The tablet written with such hope. The process of writing and reading: how Napē should watch Corinna's expression when she reads it. Then the reply. First Ovid hopes it should be extensive, then says one word ('Come!') will suffice. How, if his hopes are answered, he will dedicate the tablet to Aphrodite as a thank-offering (this ties in with Asklepiades' epigram above). And how did Corinna answer, we wonder? Poem twelve tells us: she declined! Ovid curses the wood from which the writing tablet was made.

Business

The money economy

One needed money in the ancient city as nowadays. Bartering no doubt took place, particularly in the country, but business at the agora was conducted using the legal currency, *nomisma*, as we saw in the *Assemblywomen* passage, where Chremylos describes how the currency was suddenly changed from copper to silver. As a shoemaker in Herodas' seventh mime says: 'What the market needs is money, not words' (*Skyteus* 49–50). The philosopher Dēmōnax once teased a magician who was proud of the coercive powers of his magical

20 Hoard of silver Greek coinage (from Sicily, Tarentum, Corinth, Leukas), late 4th century–280 BC.

spells by saying that he only had to say one magic word and hand over one magic token (he meant a coin) to the baker in the market for him to hand him over a loaf of bread (Lucian, *Life of Dēmōnax* 23). This was, no doubt, how most business was done in the ancient city: direct production and market trade. Chremylos had sold his grapes at market, received copper coins in exchange, then had wanted to buy flour with his earnings. Already at the beginning of the fifth century BC the Ephesian sage Heraclitus was saying that the physical world involved change (for example, water evaporates or freezes), just as goods change hands using a currency of exchange (he calls it 'gold'; Fr. 90 DK). The word for money-making was *chrēmatistikē*, from the verb *chrēmatizomai*, I make money, all based on the word for money, *chrēmata*, which, interestingly, has the basic meaning 'things', 'material goods'; the whole family of words is derived from the root *chrē* or *chrā*, which means 'use' or 'need', and is connected with a word meaning 'necessity' (*chrē*). This whole string, then, runs something like: need – things – money, or 'one needs money for things (that one needs).'

'Wealth is blind'

Aristophanes' comedy *Wealth* turns on the importance of money in the ancient city. Chremylos has consulted the Delphic oracle to learn how his son should behave in order to prosper in the present generation at Athens. He and his slave Kariōn agree that nowadays the worst types seem to prosper and the best to suffer from poverty. Apollo answers them that they should take home with them the first person they encounter on leaving his oracle. They bump into a blind man and follow along behind him. Using threats, they extract from this dour, blind man who he is: Wealth (Ploutos). The point is: because Wealth is blind, he can no longer distinguish the righteous from the rogues, and so distributes wealth without any guiding ethical principle. In an early scene, Chremylos and Kariōn show Wealth how he rivals Zeus in power, as everything, simply everything, depends on money:

> And, by Jove, if people have acquired anything splendid and fine, it's through you [Money]. Everything is dependent on wealth. (*Kariōn:*) [*bitterly*] For a few coins I became

> a slave having been free before. (*Chremylos:*) And they say Corinthian call-girls turn up their noses if someone poor tries to approach them, but if it's a rich man, they immediately offer them their bottoms. (*Kariōn:*) And boys, they say, do exactly the same, for the money, not because of their admirers ... (*Chremylos:*) All men's trades and tricks-of-the-trade have been discovered because of you. (*Wealth* 143–61)

Chremylos and Kariōn promise Wealth that they will help him recover his sight, by incubation in the healing cult of Asklepios. However, the possibility of Wealth recovering his sight and bestowing his largesse fairly throughout the city's population opens up new potential problems, as Poverty (Penia, also personified in the play) explains to Chremylos and Kariōn. The premise is that, at present, people have to work to avoid poverty with all its privations. If Wealth distributed the nation's GDP fairly between individuals, the necessity to work would be removed – with disastrous consequences, according to Poverty:

> If what you want [that is, equal distribution of money between citizens] happened, it wouldn't help you, I tell you. If Wealth got his vision back and shared himself round equally, no one would bother learning a trade or a skill. If both of those disappeared, who would want to forge bronze or build ships or sew or make chariots or shoes, or bricks, or to launder or tan hides? Who would break the soil with ploughs or harvest Demeter's grain if you could all live a life of leisure without bothering about those things? (ll. 509–16)

Poverty's interlocutor objects: 'No problem, slaves would do the work,' to which Poverty answers that there would be no slaves available as slave traders, too, would have enough money without risking their lives by enslaving others.[12] Then she (Penia) continues her litany of shortages:

> And you won't have a bed to lie in – there won't be any – or blankets: who's going to want to weave when they have

> enough money? And no distilled scents for perfume whenever you want to marry a girl, no expensive, beautifully dyed clothes to dress the bride in either. What use is it to be rich if you don't have any of these things? Whereas with me all these things you need are readily available. For I sit beside a workman like his *dominatrix*, forcing him by the necessity of want to seek a way to make a living. (ll. 527–34)

I wonder whether Karl Marx had read his Aristophanes as he sat preparing *Das Kapital* in the reading dome of the old British Library? Penia's logic seems incontrovertible to me, and the Soviet 'economy of shortages' goes a considerable way to proving her words prescient here. In this section let us look at some of the trades mentioned by Poverty, and others that are not specifically.

War

War, too, which Poverty does not mention, was undoubtedly a major source of income, not to say vast wealth, throughout antiquity. Quite simply, one helped oneself to the resources of communities one conquered: money, jewellery, jewel-studded silver drinking vessels (Theophrastus, *Characters* 23.3), fine clothes, valuables, women, slaves – it was all booty, to be divided up according to rank once an enemy had been defeated and a town captured. The soldiers in Menander's plays who heaped valuables and finery on their girlfriends acquired these on campaign: Polemōn in *The Shorn Head* and Thrasōnidēs in *The Man She Hated* both boast of how they had spoiled their women with jewellery and finery – so why, they lament, are the women rejecting them now? Agamemnon and Achilles in the *Iliad* fall out ostensibly over the division of spoils after a raid, as we have seen. When Agamemnon tries to persuade (bribe) Achilles to change his mind, one of his promises is: 'If the gods grant that we take Troy, you'll sail home with a ship full of gold and bronze' (9.278–80). A tenth share (*dekatē*) of the spoils of victory was traditionally given to the gods as a thank-offering, or perhaps we should say, to appease the conscience. Usually the money was turned into a fine statue or a valuable cauldron. War offered endless opportunities for huge gain – and loss.

21 Model of a transport ship filled with *pithoi*.

However, war was perhaps not the daily round but rather a bloody adventure, the opposite of peacetime activities. Let us here look at more everyday forms of business in peacetime, what kept the wheels of the ancient city turning more or less smoothly.

Trade

An unexpected glimpse of ancient overseas trade has been gained through maritime archaeology. The sunken ships that have been discovered and excavated in the course of recent decades show the cargoes they had been transporting round the Mediterranean for sale at the market of their destination. Usually their holds were filled with *pithoi*, large jars with pointed ends to sit securely in holes in boards of the ship's bilges.

These *pithoi* could transport olive oil, wine and sauce (garum). Dry goods were shipped in sacks: grain, spices and so forth. Theophrastus' sketch of a Boastful Man, based in Athens, mentions a concession offered to him by the king of Macedon to export timber duty-free. We saw how the sailors in Achilles Tatius' *Leukippē and Kleitophon* had to jettison their cargo when the ship was about to founder. There we hear about 'silver and gold and less costly goods'; the merchants pushed the crates and sacks of cargo 'on which their hopes rested' overboard. Pataikos, a character in Menander's *The Shorn Head*, tells how, as a young father, he had lost his fortune when his ship had gone down, forcing him to put the children up for adoption now that he can no longer support them. Wonderful bronze statues, for example the Riace Bronzes (discovered in 1972 off the Calabrian coast), have also been recovered from the seabed, where the ships that were transporting them went down. The Antikythera wreck, named after the island of Antikythera between Crete and the Peloponnese, near which it was discovered in 1900, contained among much else the famous Antikythera mechanism – a complex mechanical calculator whose sophistication is still amazing researchers. We also hear of horses and other animals being transported in special transport ships to accompany armies. Cattle are stolen in a pirate raid at the end of Book 1 of Longos' (2nd century AD) novel *Daphnis and Chloē*. Chloē is rescued when the cowherd's piping causes all the cattle in the ship's hold, drawn to the music, to move over at once and capsize it. It must have been pretty sizeable to hold a herd of cattle. Cargo ships designated 'worth a hundred talents' – probably referring to the weight it could carry in its hold – are mentioned by the historian Thucydides (7.25.6).

The trading of goods is not always purely mercantile. Sometimes political factors also play a role, for example in trade embargoes or sanctions. Conversely, trade could be a way of furthering the interests of a city or nation, delivering goods to support the cause of a community or party within that community. The Athenian orator Andokides was exiled in 415 BC for his part in a notorious conspiracy, the Mutilation of the Herms (statues of Hermes).[13] He describes in his speech *On His Own Return* how he left Athens and took up the life of a merchant seaman, having been an Athenian aristocrat with all the social trappings, such as horse racing. He describes in this speech of 411 BC how, after time, he yearned to return to Athens and to participate once more in the Athenian democracy. To that end he determined to do Athens a favour by providing much-needed supplies for the war effort (against Sparta and its allies):

> In view of this, I decided it was better for me either to be done with this life or to help this city so much that you would be willing to let me live among you again as a citizen. From then on, at great personal risk and financial outlay, I began supplying your army, which was stationed in Samos, with timber for oars . . . Archelaos [of Macedon] was an old family connection of ours and he let me fell and export as much timber as I required. I transported this timber for oars and sold it to you at cost price. I also delivered corn and copper [for making bronze]. Thus equipped, those men [the army in Samos] subsequently defeated the Peloponnesians in a sea battle, and they alone saved this city at that time. So if they were the cause of great good fortune, I might rightly claim to have played no small part in that success. (*On His Own Return* 10–11)

However, having performed this service for the Athenian democracy, as he thought, Andokides was unlucky enough to find, when he sailed into harbour at the Piraeus hoping to collect his reward, as it were, that the Four Hundred were in power, who considered the army in Samos their enemies for siding with the *dēmos*. Andokides was had up by one Peisandros before the council, accused of supplying timber and corn to the enemy, and was thrown into prison and suffered much (but survived). Later, however (in 400 BC), he did succeed in securing his reinstatement at Athens by employing the same tactics: using his merchant ships to supply a much-needed commodity, corn (wheat), this time:

> You know how you were told that no corn was to arrive here from Cyprus? Well, I, personally, with the means at my disposal, succeeded in thwarting those who had planned and done this against you of their purpose. You do not need to know how this was achieved. Suffice it for you now to know that fourteen corn transporters are already about to put into harbour at Piraeus, and all the remaining ships from Cyprus will be here shortly. I would give anything to be able to reveal openly what I secretly told the council, for the sake

> of transparency. As it is, you will know when it happens, and you will immediately reap the benefit. (ll. 20–22)

Attica could not grow sufficient corn for its own needs in the fifth century, necessitating imports of corn from Egypt, the Black Sea and Cyprus. We see here how Andokides twice used his resources as a merchant seaman to secure his political, or perhaps we should say civic, ends. Note the size of his fleet: fourteen ships are mentioned first, then an unspecified flotilla to follow them. Clearly he had not been idle in his exile but had amassed a fortune. He tells us that family connections had helped, for example, in securing a licence to export timber from Macedon. One wonders what he told the council when he explained how he had managed to counter those who had opposed supplying corn to Athens from Cyprus: some questionable deal with the enemy, no doubt – whoever these may have been – or perhaps plain bribes.

Shady practices

Staying with the question of the corn supply to Athens, we find in Lysias' 22nd speech, *Against the Corn Dealers* (386 BC), a fascinating insight into insider trading and price-fixing among the so-called 'corn dealers' who bought grain (wheat) from merchants (*emporoi*) putting into Piraeus harbour, and sold it on through outlets in Athens at the grain market (*sitikon emporion*). They tended to be foreigners (metics); that is established at the outset, the implication being that they did not have a particular loyalty to Athenian interests. We do not know who the speaker of the speech is, but he accuses the corn dealers basically of price-fixing and extortion at a time when corn was scarce at Athens. He accuses them of buying as a cartel, in one lot, more than was allowed (fifty *phormoi*, or baskets, a measure), fixing the price, then selling on, although the law (cited in the case) prohibits such mass wholesale buying. They say they were doing it in the interest of Athenians, to keep prices down. The speaker then cites instances of price fluctuation upwards on the same day, showing that the dealers had not bought wholesale and kept the price down to help the city. He then describes the malfeasance of the corn dealers to show they were out for their own profit, not to benefit Athens:

> They profit most whenever there's news of some disaster threatening the city and corn prices soar. They view your impending crises with such glee that they get wind of some before anyone else, or spread rumours about others: 'the ships from Pontus have sunk.' 'The Spartans have seized the ships as they left port.' 'They've closed the ports,' 'The peace-treaties will be revoked.' They go so far in their hostility, in fact, that in times of crisis they attack you, just like the enemy. When your demand for corn is greatest, they hoard it and are reluctant to sell, so that we won't haggle about the price but will consider ourselves lucky if we can buy it from them at whatever price. Even in peacetime it's sometimes as if we are being besieged by them. For so long now has the state been aware of their malpractice and malevolence that for all other merchandise you've appointed the so-called 'market supervisors' as overseers, but for this sector alone you appoint by lot special officers to oversee the corn trade. (Lysias 22.14–16)

It is a fascinating vignette of trade practices. One imagines the ships coming into port; the corn dealers vying to buy the cargo, possibly in bulk although that was prohibited (more than fifty *phormoi*); the *sitophylakes*, overseers, elected by lot, trying and failing to prevent this; and, at the end of the chain, consumers desperately chasing after short supplies, possibly in times of war or famine. Two types of business are involved: the merchants and the vendors; there does not seem to have been an intermediate class of wholesalers. At one point, Lysias refers to corn dealers as 'shopkeepers' (*kapēloi*), indicating they not only bought the grain as it was imported but also sold it at the grain market, but that may not have been the case: quite possibly the actual vendors at market were like the Sausage-Seller and Paphlagōn in Aristophanes' *Knights*, plain stallholders. It also gives an insight into demographic questions: the foreign traders against the Athenian people. And, for economics students, a classic case of prices obeying the laws of supply and demand.

Businesses today still vie in rivalry with one another, and advertising is a prominent above-board way of promoting one's own product or system over its rivals. Advertising seems to have been more or less unknown in ancient Greece, probably mainly because of the lack of technological means (printing, television, even reading). When potters signed their pots, as they commonly did, with the formula 'So-and-so [name of potter] made it/me,' they were perhaps bringing their name into circulation: anyone seeing or using the article would know in whose workshop it was made. However, there was one widespread practice in ancient Greece that (with bizarre exceptions, no doubt) is not at the forefront of modern business practices: the curse placed on rivals. Curse tablets, usually written on sheets of lead, then folded up and dropped into a well or someone's grave, have been recovered in large numbers from sites all over Greece. The usual formula is, at its simplest, 'I curse so-and-so' or 'I bind so-and-so'. For this reason, such texts are commonly called 'binding spells' (Lat. *defixiones*, pinnings down), as the verb used to incapacitate a rival or enemy is 'I bind' (*deō* or *katadeō*, with variants): the sense is that a binding spell should be placed on the victim so as to render him or her helpless or incapable. Commonly an underworld deity or several are invoked to enforce the curse. Sometimes the victim's body parts and members are mentioned explicitly: their hands, feet, brains, tongues, sexual organs and so on. Such curses are commonly used in love magic (to stymie a rival; we saw an example earlier), lawsuits (to incapacitate one's opponent and his supporters) and in business.

So-called commercial binding-spells have been thought to have been written or commissioned by an artisan or a tradesman wishing to harm a rival. For this reason they have been termed 'commercial'. The writer of *SGD* 52 (Attic, third century BC), for example, binds two fishing-net makers (*stigmatias*) as well as their workshops (*ergastēria*) and slaves.[14] Presumably the curse was written by a rival net-maker hoping to drive his rival out of business. *SGD* 88, from Camarina in Sicily from the mid-fifth century BC, is written *boustrophēdon*, that is, backwards and forwards. It runs: 'The following people are marked down [*gegrabetai*] for a loss of profits,' followed by a list of names, ending, 'they are all doomed.' Here we do not know whence the 'profits' derive.

A fourth century BC Attic curse tablet (*DTA* 69) runs: 'I bind Dionysios the helmet-maker and Artemis his wife, who is a gilder,

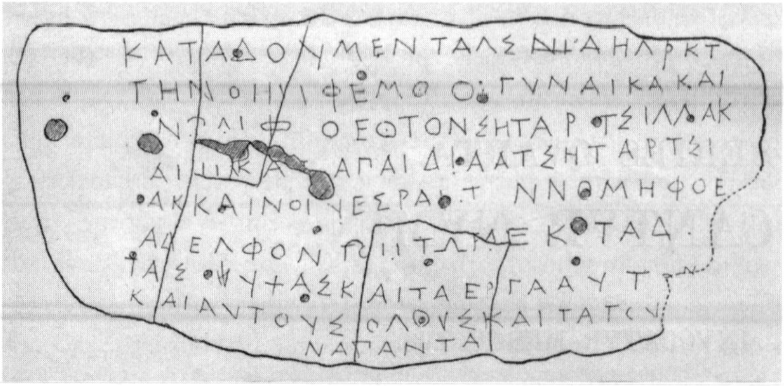

22 Transcript of an Attic curse tablet directed at the wife of one Theophēmos and her body parts.

their house and their business [*ergasia*], and their livelihood [*bios*].'[15] Not a nice message by whoever wrote the *defixio*! We note the different crafts of the husband, who makes helmets, and the wife, who is a gilder: perhaps she gilds some of her husband's helmets or parts of them to make these ones particularly precious. Their workshop, business and livelihood are placed under a curse. We do not need to ask whether the curse worked: the victims were not even aware that they had been cursed. But the placer of the curse felt that he or she had at least done something to promote their own business and to stymie that of their rivals; and if the business of Dionysios and Artemis did indeed start to suffer, which businesses often do, well, that was proof of the efficacy of the curse, and the worth of the outlay in commissioning the tablet.

Mining

Mining was big business for those owning mining rights. The hard work was of course done by slaves in atrocious conditions. A Corinthian plaque (illus. 23) depicts the slaves at work in a mine. Likewise one could farm out slaves as a line of business. We hear about someone in Andokides' speech *On the Mysteries* who wanted to go to Laureion in Attica to collect his 'rent' (*apophora*) for slaves labouring in the mines there (38 Diokleides). Most lucrative, no doubt, were the gold and silver mines we hear about occasionally. Silver and gold were used for coinage as well as costly drinking- and dinner-sets, sacred art (chryselephantine – of gold and ivory – cult images) and many other things. Both were very much the 'gold standard' of value and status. If one wanted to impress someone, one brought out one's silver dinner service, as the Segestans (in Sicily) do to trick an Athenian embassy by putting on a (deceptive) display of wealth (Thucydides 6.46).[16]

A major source of wealth for Athens were the silver mines at Cape Laureion (just mentioned). During the Peloponnesian War we hear that the fortification and occupation of a place called Dekeleia in Attica by the Spartans cut Athens off from Laureion, thus depriving it of an important source of money (Thucydides 7.27); 20,000 (!) slaves deserted to Sparta on the same occasion, no doubt most of them miners. Later in the fourth century, the orator Hypereides mentions the horrendous number of 150,000 slaves in the silver mines at Laureion; he proposes that they be manumitted.[17] At one point Perikles, the famous statesman, in Thucydides (2.13), gives a rundown of Athens' wealth in temple gold and silver on the Acropolis, which might, if necessary, be melted down to finance the war against the Spartans and their allies. The family of the historian Thucydides

23 Corinthian black-figure terracotta votive tablet of slaves working in a mine, late 7th century BC.

himself seems to have acquired its fortune through possession of gold-mining rights in Thrace (4.104–5). Gentility has its origin in wealth. Both Herodotus (6.46–7) and Thucydides (1.100) mention the wealth of the island Thasos through its silver mines. A place on the mainland opposite Thasos called Datos was famous for its gold mines (Herodotus, *Histories* 9.75). There were, of course, mines for other things: copper, salt (4.185), clay (illus. 23) and bitumen (6.119) are all mentioned. Let us leave this topic with a quote from Aristophanes' *Birds*. As we mentioned, the play imagines a 'city of birds' with bird-gods as well. The chorus leader of the birds asks Pisthetairos, who represents the human race on earth: 'And how should we give them [humans] wealth? They love that, you know.' Answer: 'When they consult the birds through divination, they'll give them those profitable silver mines!' (ll. 592–3). In other words, augury, which we have looked at, will prophesy where to dig for valuable minerals. Pisthetairos also mentions trade. Augury by means of bird flight will help with that 'by informing the diviner where the profitable trading posts are, so that no merchant seaman will fail' (ll. 594–50).

Craftsmanship

Poverty's list of trades comes into its own here. All things in ancient Greece had to be manufactured, as today, by some manual process. Without industrialization, men and women rely on hands and tools. In general, women made textiles by spinning and weaving, wreaths for all festivities, and possibly pottery, and men, with the muscle power of slaves, all the rest, from weapons to ploughshares, to jewellery, bridges, houses and everything else. Most manufacture will have been of the sort we call 'cottage industry', that is, one family, one workshop. Below, we will look at a shoemaker's shop. The general word for all forms of manufacturing is *ergasia*, derived from the verb *ergazomai*, to work, which comes from *ergon*, work. Some insight into a somewhat larger operation is provided by a speech by Lysias again, this time in his own personal cause. As we said, his family came from Sicily (on the invitation of Perikles) and lived in Attica as metics, resident aliens, free but without full citizen rights. Lysias' father Kephalos had made the family rich by manufacturing shields for the hoplite army of

Athens. When the so-called Thirty Tyrants grabbed power in 404 BC at the end of the Peloponnesian War, supported by the victors, the Spartans, they began a rule of terror over their own countrymen, as tyrants and dictators are wont to do. In particular they grabbed rich people's property and money on a pretext, in order to enrich themselves. Unfortunately, Lysias' family was singled out for this treatment because of its wealth. Before we begin to imagine Kephalos as some kind of Elon Musk of Athens, it is worth mentioning that various members of the family, Kephalos and Lysias included, feature in Plato's dialogues as friends of Socrates: clearly these were cultured industrialists. Slave labour enabled them to philosophize and lead the good life while others toiled in their workshop.

Lysias' twelfth speech, *Against Eratosthenes* (one of the Thirty), was delivered in person to prosecute Eratosthenes, mainly for the murder of Lysias' brother Polemarchos, who had been killed when the family's property was seized. Lysias could only give the speech as he was granted citizenship after the ousting of the Thirty (revoked later). Lysias describes how Eratosthenes' lackeys came round one night in order to seize the family's money, earned, as noted, from making shields. The narrative allows us some insight into the house and adjacent workshop:

> They [the Thirty] divided the families [of their chosen victims] among themselves and set off. They found me entertaining friends. They threw the friends out and handed me over to Peisōn [working for the Thirty]. The others went into the workshop and made a list of the slaves. I asked Peisōn if he'd spare me for money. He said, yes, if it was a lot. I answered that I could give him a talent of silver. He agreed to the terms . . . After he had given me his word . . . I went into the office and opened the safe. Peisōn saw what I was doing and came in too. When he saw the contents of the safe, he called two slaves and told them to seize the entire contents . . . On our way out, Mēlobios and Mnēsitheidēs met us as they were coming out of the sweatshop . . . That night they seized seven hundred of our shields, an equivalent amount in gold and silver, more

24 Workers in a textile factory, black-figure wine jug (*oinochoē*), *c.* 550 BC.

> bronze and jewellery and furniture and women's clothes than they ever hoped to lay their hands on, and one hundred and twenty slaves, of which they took the best themselves and sold the rest. They even went so far as to rip the earrings from the ears of Polemarchos' wife. (Lysias 12.8–19, with omissions)

As mentioned, Polemarchos is killed during the episode. Leaving the cruelty and injustice of the actions of Peisōn's men to one side, we learn of at least three spaces in Lysias' property: a dining room (*andrōn*), a workshop (*ergastērion*) and an office (*dōmation*). We learn that the brother Polemarchos lived separately. We hear how many shields were seized; seven hundred sounds like a large number. Likewise the one hundred and twenty slaves: a small army. Lysias says the Thirty 'kept the best of these themselves': perhaps a pointer to some being young and strong, others less so. These will have been mainly Thracians, Carians, Phrygians and others, as we saw in the property lists of the Hermokopidai. Hoplite shields were made of layers of, respectively, bronze, wood and leather, with a leather grip, so one can get some idea of what work in the workshop would have involved. Those hundred and twenty slaves will have needed a small warehouse (factory) to do the work, and presumably also sleep and everything else. The estate was located in the Piraeus, we hear in other sources. No doubt that expedited importing materials and exporting the finished product. The personal riches of the family surely reflect great prosperity as a result of this arms trade. For the reader's interest: Lysias did not fall victim to his arrest; he managed to escape to Megara and return to prosecute Eratosthenes.

The Greeks had quite a few works of technical, or didactic, poetry supposedly informing the reader how to do or make something. It starts with Hesiod in the seventh century BC, who wrote a poem called *Works and Days*, which, apart from much else of general interest, is basically poetic instruction on how to cultivate the fields (*Erga*, Works) in accordance with the seasons. Later, in the age of Alexandrian scholarship (Hellenistic age, roughly last three centuries BC), there were poems on fishes and fishing (Oppian, *Halieutika*, Fishing), astronomy (Aratus, *Phainomena*, (Celestial) Phenomena), snakes (Nicander, *Thēriaka*, Bestiary) and much else. An interesting fragment of this tradition of didactic poetry survives on a piece of papyrus found at Oxyrhynchus (P.Oxy. 3536) describing, poetically, the work of a glass-blower. One can imagine his shop (as in modern-day Murano) open to public viewing, and probably in or near the agora of whatever city the poet has in mind. The papyrus itself dates from the third century AD, and glass-blowing in this manner commences in the Augustan period (Roman), so we should imagine this glass-blower's shop around that time. The style of didactic poetry, however, is Hellenistic. It describes how the glass-blower melts a chunk of glass in his furnace, then blows it on the end of a tube, turning it all the time so that a spherical shape emerges. One doubts, somehow, that an apprentice glass-blower would reach for a didactic poem for instruction; this tradition of didactic poetry seems aimed more at the educated reader who can appreciate well-crafted verses on technical subjects, as well as the more typically poetic subjects. The text is, unfortunately, far from complete as papyri rarely survive intact.

> First he heated the pointed tip of the iron . . . Then he took an unworked lump of glass [which was lying] at hand. Then he placed this expertly inside the hollow of his kiln. The crystal glass, feeling the heat of the roaring fire, softened, like wax, under the blasts from the fire god Hephaistos. And after blowing out a moist breath from his mouth, the man inhaled, like a flute player practising his art. And the glass took in [the exhaled breath] and swelled into a round sphere before his eyes. And it was subjected to another force of divine [motion at the same time]: for, as he blew repeatedly through the tube, he twirled it as one twirls a shepherd's crook.

In other words, the glass-blower turned the tube as he blew repeatedly into it, to ensure a symmetrical round shape as the glass inflated. The bare technical process is embellished with various poetic devices, notably the two similes: the glass-blowing process is likened first to a flute player who blows into his instrument while using fingerwork to modulate the notes, then to the twirling of a shepherd's crook. The mention of the fire god Hephaistos as well as a 'divine' (force, probably, or skill) removes the description from the purely mundane and reminds the educated reader of Homer's description of Hephaistos working the new weapons of Achilles in the *Iliad*, a very famous passage of literature. In other words, the everyday is given attributes of the bucolic (flute playing and shepherd's staff) and the heroic (the epic verse itself, and Hephaistos). We can well imagine a real-life glass-blower at work as we read the description (*ekphrasis*), but we are also firmly in the realm of poetry rather than the grime and sweat of a workshop. This style of Hellenistic poetry makes a tourist of the reader, one who visits in his mind's eye a glass-blower's shop or a fisherman with his net, or a herdsman with his flock.

The Hellenistic poet Herodas (sometimes known as Herondas) wrote a series of *Mimes*, that is, poetic sketches of scenes of people interacting in real life, in a slightly outré metre called the *skazōn*, or 'limping iamb'. The work was lost in late antiquity, like so much, but has been recovered in good part by the discovery of a papyrus (now in the British Library) and the assiduous work of papyrologists in deciphering it. The sixth mime, called *Women Friends* (*Philiazousai*) or *Women Alone* (*Idiazousai*), shows two women talking together about leather dildos; Mētrō visits one Korittō to ask her where she got her excellent dildo. The answer is from a shoemaker called Kerdōn, who makes them as a sideline in a backstreet workshop to avoid the attentions of the *telōnai*, tax collectors, who frequented the marketplace. Then in the next mime, called *Shoemaker* (*Skyteus*), the same woman, Mētrō, visits Kerdōn's premises with a group of women interested ostensibly in buying shoes. In the scholarship on this mime there has been debate whether the two mimes are in fact a pair, despite the coincidence of names, as there is no explicit mention of dildos in mime seven. It is fair to say, however, that those arguing for a connection between the two mimes have won the day: the women in seven are definitely interested in Kerdōn's dildos, even if the topic is only

25 Attic red-figure amphora with a woman (entertainer) with a dildo, Myson Painter, 480–475 BC.

referred to by innuendo and allusion. What in fact seems to be happening is that Kerdōn shows his wares to the women with a heavy nod and a wink and tells them at the end of their visit to return to him 'if they need anything else in future' (that is, other than shoes). He also says more or less explicitly to Mētrō at the end that he will reward her (with the gift of a dildo?) for bringing in new custom when, in a few days' time, she picks up the shoes she has ordered.

We can imagine, then, this middle-aged shoemaker – he refers to himself at one point as white-haired and balding on top (ll. 71–2) – in his workshop in a backstreet where he uses his skills in shoemaking for a sideline in sex toys, which could not be sold openly but only discreetly, in neutral packaging, as it were. He is married, with thirteen children (l. 103; 44), or so he claims. He has at least two slaves to assist him, and the women come accompanied by their slave, too. When the women arrive, a bench is brought out for them to sit on, so it seems there is no shop as such. Perhaps this detail, however, is owed to the mime genre, itself an imitation of theatre, which only played outside in the street. His slaves open the 'large chest' for the women and bring out all the shoeboxes for them to inspect his wares. The conversation that then ensues between Mētrō and him in mime seven is peppered with coy phrases regarding prices and wares. Most of the mime is taken up by haggling over prices. First Kerdōn softens up his clientele by saying how expensive his raw material, leather, has become; how hard he has to work from morning to night; how he has thirteen hungry (and lazy) children to feed. Challenged to choose a pair, Mētrō asks him how much the last pair he had shown them costs ('and don't frighten us away by too outlandish a price!'). Kerdōn says:

> Set your own price, if you want. Decide yourself what's a fair price. A man allowing this is not likely to cheat you. If you want a real pair of shoes – by this grey and balding pate of mine – fair lady, you'll say something that will feed an honest working man. [*aside*] O Hermes, God of Profits and Lady Salesmanship, unless something lands in our net, it'll be the worse for our cooking pot. (*Mētrō:*) Why are you mumbling like that to yourself and not stating in plain language what

> the price is? (*Kerdōn:*) Lady, this pair is worth a *mina* [a hefty price], whichever way you look at it. Not a farthing less even if Athena herself was doing the shopping. (*Mētrō:*) Now I see why your little place is full of luxury goods and fineries! (*Skyteus* 67–85)

Kerdōn's name itself is related to *kerdos*, 'profit', and here he swears by two gods with 'profit' in their names. Kerdōn's speech is all glib sales talk, the kind associated with sales pitches at market stalls combined with the haggling over prices when the stallholder has got a customer interested. Flattery is an important part, as we see when Kerdōn lets one woman try on a pair of shoes for fit:

> Now, no protesting! Ah – you could lend me, a cobbler, lump of clay, wings to fly up to the gods! It's not a voice you have but a pleasure-strainer. Ah – that man is not far from the gods for whom you part your lips both night and day. Put your little foot here, against the sole. Perfect! Neither too small nor too big. Nice things fit nice people! It's as if Athena herself [divine seamstress] had cut the sole. (ll. 107–17)

Kerdōn continues on in this style as he lets the women try on shoes. It's when Mētrō comes to pay for hers at the end that he adds his remark: 'if you ever need anything else, ladies . . .' and promises Mētrō her bonus when she collects the shoes. The reader of the previous mime, six, knows exactly what the hint means: the women should contact him privately for their other needs. Herodas has brought the scene of an ancient shoemaker making his sales pitch to a group of women to life. *Mime* (*mīmos*) means both an actor ('mimic') and the mime itself; the cognate verb *mimeomai*, imitate, and *mīmēsis*, imitation, point to the ancient aesthetic of drama as an imitation, or perhaps model, of real life.

Dinnertime

With religious ceremonial, eating in the company of others is perhaps the central social institution. It is not just taking in calories and vitamins and minerals – one could do that on one's own – but rather a kind of shared celebration of the good things in life (food and human company). Because of modern production and retailing methods, we are becoming less sensitive to the miracle of food and survival, but the Greeks were keenly aware that some very beneficent powers must be at work for food to grow so conveniently for us, whether meat or vegetable. Different foods were assigned to individual gods: cereals of all kinds to Demeter; wine to Dionysos; Pan was the herdsman god. The eating of meat generally involved the intricate ritual of animal sacrifice, by which an animal was consecrated to one or more gods at their altar, killed in a ritual manner, and divided between the gods and men according to an archetypal myth: that of Prometheus in the works of Hesiod (approximately contemporary with Homer). Eating at dinnertime always involved a certain amount of interaction with gods, even just within the family. However, dinner parties of varying sizes and degrees of lavishness were very common. When combined with a drinking party, *symposion* (literally from 'drinking together', *sympinein*), the divide between dinner and drinking was fluid, one leading to, some might say degenerating into, the other.

For that reason, Theophrastos, in depicting quirks of social behaviour among Athenians in the late fourth century BC, quite often mentions aberrant behaviour at dinnertime. The 'Scrooge', for example (*Characters* 30, *Aischrokerdia*), is conspicuous in serving too little bread with dinner. One can just imagine the bread basket set on the table with one small piece of bread for each guest! The Disgusting Man (19, *Dyscheria*) commits all manner of sins over dinner. At the opening ceremony of prayer and libation he drops his wine glass (cup, actually) and laughs, saying it must be a sign. He behaves irritatingly when an animal is sacrificed. Over the meal itself he talks with his mouth full, spits food while talking, burps while drinking and, when he means to spit at table, he spits into the wine jug by mistake. When the flute girl performs for the entertainment of the friends after the meal, he alone claps out loud, whistles along with the tune and protests that she has stopped too soon. The litany of his sins gives one a sense of the order of events at such a dinner, from initial prayer and libation through the meal itself, to the drinking afterwards and after-dinner entertainment. His antisocial behaviour denotes, by contrast, what was considered good manners at dinner: the absence of all these obnoxious traits!

Less overtly gross than the previous case is Theophrastus' Offensive Man (20, *Ahēdia*), who nevertheless succeeds in rubbing people up the wrong way with his dinner-table manners. First he boasts of the fine fresh spring water he has at home and lovely fresh vegetables; he boasts about his cook (*mageiros*; one is pictured in illus. 16), and how his home is like a restaurant: it's always full and his guests are like the proverbial leaky jars that can't be filled. How he cannot get enough of entertaining them. Then, over dinner, he parades his 'parasite' – a friend who scrounges off him but performs services as well – to the other guests. After dinner he says he has something very entertaining in store for them and says, if they so wish, he can send to the brothel owner straight away, and get a girl to play for, and *with* (nod-and-wink), them. Again, good behaviour was clearly *not* that: one should not boast of one's lavish dinner parties or act as if one were an impresario or pimp. Seemly behaviour must have been to show modesty and restraint.

Bad behaviour at dinner seems to have been considered so contrary to propriety that it even had its own mythology. 'Herakles at Dinner' seems to have been a stock theme of comedy. Being a larger-than-life figure, Herakles was also entitled, one assumes, to indulge in excesses of eating and drinking.[18] Aristophanes (*Wasps* 60) refers to such a scene in Euripides, where Herakles is guilty of an inadvertent faux pas at dinner. Euripides' *Alkestis* (431 BC) is the story of Alkestis, wife of Admetos, who alone of his family members is prepared to die in his stead, for that is the condition which has been granted to Admetos by the god Apollo: he must die unless he can find someone who is prepared to die in his stead. Very unusually for Athenian stage conventions, Alkestis does actually die on stage, accompanied by suitable outpourings of grief from her children and others around her. However, at that absolutely grief-stricken moment for the family, Herakles turns up at their house, not knowing what has happened. As a guest of honour, he is not told about the family misfortune but rather is sat down to dinner and told to tuck in. While the rest of the family is plunged into sorrow in a different room, Herakles indulges himself. An indignant servant describes the scene:

> I've known many guests come from all over Greece to Admetos' house, whom I have served with dinner. But I have never known a worse guest come to our hearth yet. First he dared to darken our door although he could see that Master was grieving, then he showed no restraint when accepting the hospitality shown him, although he knew of the misfortune. If we did not serve something, he called for it. Taking a drinking cup of ivywood in his hands, he drank the juice of the black grape unmixed until the alcohol ran through him and heated his blood. He set a crown of myrtle [a distinctly aphrodisiac choice of plant] on his head and bayed off-tune. Two songs could be heard. He sang one of them, totally disregarding Admetos' grief, while we household staff wailed for Mistress, although we did not show our tears to him. (ll. 747–64)

In fact, the whole point in the play is that Herakles does not know Alkestis has died. When he hears about it, he changes his manner immediately and shows his heroic mythical persona. He wrestles with Death himself and rescues from his clutches Alkestis, who, we are led to understand in a distinctly ambivalent ending of the play, is reunited with her husband. Altogether it is an unusual tragedy: for those interested in literary genre it may be added that it is not in fact a tragedy. Euripides seems to have written it instead of the obligatory satyr play (a kind of mythical romp) that was staged as the fourth item in a playwright's entry in the annual dramatic competition (Dionysia). That to one side, we see in this episode again the possibilities for offending social norms by not behaving properly at the dinner table. As a social institution, dinner should proceed according to accepted protocol, which one contravened at one's peril.

As an antidote to rogue hosts and guests at dinner we can turn to the country idyll of Longos' *Daphnis and Chloē* (second century AD), with a plot based on bucolic poetry (such as Theocritus), that is, love among country folk. One Daphnis, fifteen, is a goatherd who falls in love with Chloē, thirteen, a shepherd(ess). Their love develops in charming and rather gauche innocence as they herd their flocks in nature and feel, but do not succumb to, Erōs' proddings. In the winter of the third book, heavy snow falls, preventing the young people meeting outdoors. Getting desperate to see Chloē, Daphnis walks to her house and starts hunting birds with snares and birdlime in the clumps of ivy and myrtle outside her parents' cottage, hoping that someone will come out and see him. As evening approaches, no one has, and Daphnis is about to go home when the father comes running out of the house chasing one of the sheepdogs, which has carried off his portion of meat from their evening dinner table. He sees Daphnis, greets him heartily (they know each other) and invites him in. What follows is a kind of Hardyesque scene of country life as they break bread together:

> They [Chloē's parents] invited him [Daphnis] to share what the dog had left of their meal, and they told Chloē to pour Daphnis some wine. She happily served the others with wine, leaving Daphnis to last; she pretended to be cross with him because he had been about to leave without showing his face. However, before she served him, she took a sip from the cup, then gave it to him. And he, despite his thirst, drank slowly, so as to prolong the pleasure. Soon the table was emptied of its bread and meats. (*Daphnis and Chloē* 3.8.2–9.1)

We note here that the usual order followed at dinner parties – first the food, then the wine – is not followed here. Rather, the family with their guest Daphnis eat and drank simultaneously. Only bread and meat are mentioned as food, but this may be because Longos is not interested in the precise menu. The conversation takes a pleasant course as Chloē's parents congratulate Daphnis' parents (who are not there) for having such a good boy to look after them in their dotage, and they invite him to share their sacrifice to Dionysos the next day.[19]

Overjoyed, Daphnis empties his rucksack of the honey cakes he was carrying with him as a gift, and the birds he had caught in the bushes outside. At that point they decide to serve up more food and draw out the enjoyable meal:

> They immediately began preparing the birds for a nocturnal feast. A second bowl of wine was mixed and the fire stoked for a second time. As the night grew quite late, they feasted on the second serving, after which they told stories and sang together before turning in for the night, Chloē with her mother, Daphnis with Dryas [her father]. (3.9.3–4)

The young people sleep the night with thoughts only of each other. We are told that Daphnis dreamed he was lying beside Chloē and kissed her father repeatedly, imagining it was her. One wonders whether the father woke! On the next day, the meal that follows the sacrifice to Dionysos is more formal than the impromptu meal of the previous evening. If we make allowances for the idyllic nature of the description, we can perhaps imagine what a rustic festive meal might have been like in reality:

> On the next day there was a heavy frost and a biting north wind. The family rose and sacrificed [killed] a yearling ram to Dionysos [a rural god]. They stoked up a roaring fire and prepared their meal. Napē prepared the dough for bread and Dryas cooked the lamb. With some time on their hands, Daphnis and Chloē went outside to where the ivy grew [and caught some more birds]. They kissed each other repeatedly and indulged in lovers' talk. [*Their dialogue.*] As Chloē echoed Daphnis' declaration of love, Napē called them to come, and they ran in, taking in their catch of birds, which was bigger even than on the previous day. First they poured a libation to Dionysos and then ate, wearing crowns of ivy [Dionysos' plant] on their heads. When it was time, they sent Daphnis on his way accompanied by the ritual Iakchos chant, having filled his rucksack with helpings of meat and bread. (3.10.1–11.2)

This meal, then, is accompanied by ritual formalities. The animal is consecrated to Dionysos before being cooked. They pray and pour libations to Dionysos before eating and wear wreaths of his sacred plant, ivy, in his honour. When Daphnis leaves, the family utter the ritual cry of 'Iakch' Ō Iakche', which we know from other sources. Iakchos was a divinity associated with the Mysteries of Demeter and sounds like Bakchos. Again, we are not given the gourmet details of the meal; only freshly baked dough and meat are mentioned, but we can be sure other *trōgōmata*, side dishes, were served too. Again, there is no mention of after-dinner drinking. We assume they sat at table close to the fire, since reclining on *klinai*, couches, was for townsfolk. As we saw at the meal on the previous evening, table talk was very important: stories (*mythoi*) were told and songs (drinking songs were called *skolia*) were sung. Pleasure was shared with the wine god Dionysos, who, after all, set the precedent for human celebration with the parties he celebrated with his band of satyrs (*kōmos*) in myth and vase painting. Human indulgence on such an occasion is very much in accordance with the divine precedent, rather than representing one side of the divide between the sacred and the profane.

Bedtime

There are in-depth studies on all aspects of ancient Greek sexuality, from heterosexuality to homosexuality, pederasty, wives, prostitutes and pornography – and this is not one of them. The Greeks were certainly no prudes; if anything, the gods encouraged sex in all forms rather than restricting it to 'holy matrimony'. Zeus was a notorious lecher; an unreliable witness, admittedly, in Aristophanes says that adulterers should be excused because of the precedent set by Zeus (*Clouds* 1080). Aphrodite boasts in a hymn in her honour that she subdues all the other gods to her will; virginal goddesses such as Athena, Artemis and Hestia (Hearth) have compensating gifts and weapons to make up for the lack of sex in their careers, so to speak. Women are thought to enjoy sex just as much as men, if not more. Teiresias, a mythical figure who experienced life both as a man and woman, declared that women enjoy sex 'nine times more than men'.

Fragments of the woman poet Sappho declaring passionate love for a girl are presumably the origin of the modern term 'lesbian', as Sappho was from the island of Lesbos. Certainly there was no taboo about sex, no feeling that it was intrinsically degrading or animal. There was no legal age of consent, which no doubt led to ghastly abuse of girls and boys. Although, as we have seen in Lysias' first speech on the murder of Eratosthenes, adultery with a married woman was a crime for which a man could be killed if caught in flagrante, and adulterers were looked down upon, there were certainly not the same standards of fidelity and monogamy as underpin much Western fiction, film and TV. A man could, and did, have various sexual partners, from the girl slaves in his household to the *hetairai* we met earlier, as well as common prostitutes (*pornai*) in brothels (Aristophanes, *Knights* 1280–87). And women shopped around, too, if we can take Aristophanes' comedies seriously (of which more below).

As often, the tone, and precedent, is set by Homer. One scene in the *Iliad* known as the 'deception of Zeus' (*Dios Apatē*) shows Hera using a woman's wiles to subvert Zeus' agenda regarding the Trojan War. As we saw, Zeus decided to honour Thetis' request that her son Achilles should not be allowed to be humiliated by Agamemnon in that way. He will support the Trojans for a while so that Agamemnon will be taught a painful lesson. Zeus' 'wife' Hera, however, is displeased when the Trojans drive the Greek forces right back to the beaches. She decides to distract him from his battle plan by sleeping with him and sending him to sleep. To achieve this aim, she visits Aphrodite and borrows her irresistible 'girdle' (*kēstos*) (14.201) so that Zeus will desire her greatly. She also calls in on Hypnos (Sleep) on the island of Lemnos, to get a dose of his power, too, before flying on to Mount Ida in the Troad, where Zeus is refereeing the Trojan War in a very biased way. The scene then described by Homer is part domestic comedy, part 'Sacred Marriage' (*hieros gamos*), which was a religious rite in some cults. First Hera spins Zeus a yarn about where she is headed. He replies in a way that might surprise modern wives:

> Hera, you can go there later. Now let's go to bed together and enjoy sex. Never has lust [*erōs*] for a goddess or woman taken

> such hold of my feelings. Not when I had that affair with Ixion's wife, who bore Peirithoos, a quite unrivalled strategist. Nor when I went with Danaē with her beautiful legs, who bore Perseus, most famous of men; nor with that far-famed daughter of Phoinix, who bore Minōs and Rhadamanthys, nor that time with Semelē or Alkmēnē of Thebes, whose child was mighty Herakles. And Semelē bore Dionysos, no less, delight of mankind. Nor with Queen Demeter of the beautiful hair, or renowned Lēto. Nor with you yourself, as I fancy you now and sweet desire possesses me. (*Iliad* 14.313–28)

Hera demurs, saying 'someone may see us,' and lures him away from Mount Ida to a secret bedchamber made by the divine craftsman Hephaistos. There 'the heavenly ground sprouted fresh green grass under them, a carpet of lotus flowers, crocuses and bluebells sprang up from the ground. There they lay, enveloped in a golden cloud' (ll. 347–51). One wonders whether Homer is being tongue-in-cheek when Zeus lists his previous amours to Hera, as a way of highlighting his feelings now (the stylistic device is called priamel). But the idyll is genuine enough: true marital bliss – and Hera has achieved her purpose of distracting Zeus from his war plan, until he wakes up, that is. A thoroughly ambivalent affair, involving trickery and deceit even within 'holy matrimony', and the woman wins out.

We already met the wife of the defendant in Lysias' *On the Murder of Eratosthenes*, who had an affair with the titular character, even meeting up with him secretly downstairs while her husband innocently slept upstairs. A woman in Aristophanes' play *Thesmophoriazousai* (Women at the Thesmophoria) comments that men generally have become so suspicious of their wives – particularly under the influence of Euripides, who, according to this comedy, denigrated women – that they 'use all manner of seals and locks on our bedrooms to safeguard us, and keep terrifying mastiffs as a deterrent to adulterers' (ll. 414–16). The plot of this play involves Euripides' relative Mnesilochos dressing up as a woman in order to infiltrate the festival of women called Thesmophoria, to see what they are plotting against him. The women accuse Euripides of defaming them in various ways: he has spread malicious rumours that they are all adulteresses; he has undermined their business as wreath-binders for religious festivals by persuading men that gods don't exist any more. Euripides' relative Mnesilochos, pretending to be a woman, tries to put their complaints into perspective by saying, well, some of us have done some pretty awful things. (S)he narrates the following (obviously fictitious) account about herself. It contains some shocking details but was obviously supposed to make Aristophanes' male audience laugh:

> I count myself among them [the wicked women]. I know I've done some bad stuff. The worst thing was as a young bride: I'd only been married three days. My husband was asleep at my side. I had a friend who'd been with me when I was only seven. Still fancying me, he came to the door and scratched at it, and I recognized the sound at once. I tiptoe downstairs and my husband asks: 'Where are you going?' I'm like, 'Where I'm going? I've got a bellyache, my husband. It hurts. I'm going down to the toilet.' 'Okay. Go ahead,' he says. Then he starts crushing juniper berries, dill and sage-apple [for a herbal remedy], while I pour water over the door handle [to stop it squeaking] and go out to my boyfriend. Then I bend over and lean against Apollo's statue, holding onto his laurels. Now, Euripides never said *that*. (*Thesmophoriazousai* 476–90)

A domestic scene with a difference! She tells a tall tale to her husband about belly cramps, and while he solicitously makes her herbal tea, she goes out and has a quick one with her ex-boyfriend. There is no need to ask whether an Athenian girl might actually do that. The point is, the audience got the joke. Aristophanes' plays are full of what used to be called 'filth': sexual positions, anal intercourse, masturbation, cunnilingus, fellatio, you name it, it's all there (for example, *Knights* 1280–87). It meant Aristophanes was an unpopular author in public schools, and still leads to embarrassment in all teaching situations. Even in today's 'enlightened' age, students blush or shy away when called upon to translate such passages aloud. The great Greek–English

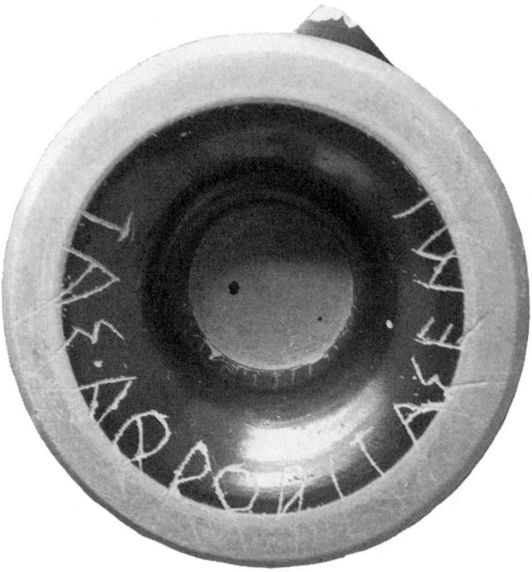

26 Inscribed lamp: ΤΑΣΑΦΡΟΔΙΤΑΣΕΜΙ, 'I belong to Aphrodite.'

dictionary known as *Liddell and Scott*, a pillar of the establishment, if ever there was one, used to content itself with defining Aristophanes' sex vocabulary with '*sens. obsc*'. This has now been rectified in the new *Cambridge Dictionary of Ancient Greek*.

In a play by Aristophanes that we have already touched upon, *Assemblywomen*, Praxagora sets the women's uprising in motion at the break of day by addressing a lamp that is illuminating their secret gathering. She eulogizes the lamp as being privy to the women's sex life, as now it is witness to their conspiracy:

> O shining eye of my wheel-thrown lamp, finest invention of high tech. Let us dwell on your pedigree and your lot. Thrown on the spinning potter's wheel, you hold the sun's shining light in your nozzles – send the agreed signals of your light. We're sharing with you alone, as is proper, since you're at our side in our bedrooms when we practise Aphrodite's moves. When our bodies are bent, heads back, no one bars your watchful eye from our home. Alone you illuminate our secret crannies when the hair that sprouts there is being singed. (*Assemblywomen* 1–13)

Although the lamp is a theatrical prop being used to signal the women's gathering, it is eulogized as the bedside light that knows the women's bedroom secrets. As the lamp is the women's domestic friend, so now it should light their nocturnal gathering. The lamp in illus. 26 bears the inscription, part of a line of lyric poetry in Doric dialect, τᾶς Ἀφροδίτας εἰμί: 'I belong to Aphrodite.' It seems to be the thought underlying Aristophanes' episode here.

Bedtime is not all about sex, of course. There are all those unremarkable bedtimes, then as now, as routine and unerotic as putting the cat out or locking the front door. Theophrastus describes how his Suspicious Man (*Characters* 18), on getting into bed beside his wife, asks her:

> whether she has locked the chest [some kind of safe, it seems], whether the [unknown word] is properly sealed, and whether the front door is bolted, and even if she says yes, he still gets up from the bed undressed and without shoes, lights a lamp, and goes round checking everything before he finally manages to get to sleep. (*Characters* 18.4)

Street Crime

While the good folk were asleep, or not, in their beds, criminals were roaming the streets and alleys in the very under-policed ancient city. There were policemen on the beat: they carried bows as weapon and were called 'bowmen' (*toxotai*). In an unlit ancient city without any form of telecommunications, their effectiveness must have been very hit-and-miss. Words denoting thieves, muggers, burglars, rapists and others give an indication of their main areas of operation:

> *kleptēs*, thief, or *fōr*, were the common words for thief. From the first we derive words such as kleptocracy and kleptomaniac; from the second words like furtive, lit. 'like a thief', derived via Latin *fur*.
>
> A *toichōrychos*, literally a 'wall-tunneller', was a housebreaker or burglar generally, one who forces an entry into property in order to burgle.

> A *lōpodytēs*, literally 'clothes stripper', and properly applied to someone who stole clothes from bathers, for example, came to mean generally thief, robber, mugger – someone who stripped a victim of their possessions.
> A *ballantiotomos*, literally 'cutpurse', means a thief or pickpocket generally.
> A *bōmolochos*, properly an 'altar lurker', someone who hung around altars hoping to pick up some of the offerings, might be equivalent to loafer, scrounger.
> An *andrapodistēs*, literally 'slave dealer', came to have the wider sense of kidnapper.
> An *hierosylos* meant literally 'temple robber', that is, a specific type of robber who stole sacred property.

The most common form of street crime was undoubtedly mugging at night. As nowadays, people going home late at night, perhaps after a party, were vulnerable (women less so – they were not allowed out!). Euelpides in Aristophanes' *Birds* 494ff. tells how he attended a friend's party on the occasion of his son's recent birth. He was beaten up on leaving the party by a *lōpodytēs*, thief, as soon as he left the city perimeter. The thief struck him on his back with a club and, when he had fallen to the ground, robbed him of his coat (*chitōn*) of Phrygian wool. We note that the danger was greater when he left the city proper – so the police do appear to have afforded some protection within the city perimeter. In another play of Aristophanes, *Assemblywomen*, which posits a communist state with a parliament of women, the leader of the women, Praxagora, says there will be no more mugging in the streets by night:

> (*Blepyros:*) Won't there be any more nocturnal muggings?
> (*Praxagora:*) Not if you're asleep in bed. Nor if you walk out by night just as before. Everyone will have enough to live on. If someone does rob you of your coat, he'll just hand it back. Why put up a fight? He can always go along to the common store and get another one better than the first. (ll. 668–71)

Both passages show the phenomenon of street robbery was a known factor.

The orator Antiphon wrote not only forensic speeches for delivery in lawsuits but also model speeches, presumably for didactic purposes. The first so-called *Tetralogy* (sequence of four speeches: two for the prosecution, two for the defence) involved the case of someone murdered on the street by night, with his slave. The defendant is a man who was known to have an enmity towards the victim, as he was facing prosecution by him: so he had a motive to kill the man. The first speech for the prosecution argues, then, that the killing was no normal piece of street mugging by a *lōpodytēs* but was in fact a deliberate murder. He cites as evidence the fact that the victim was not stripped of his clothing, showing the perpetrator had no interest in robbing him of his clothes. To this, the first speech for the defence counters:

> It is not, in fact, unlikely – as the prosecution claim – but quite understandable that he was killed for his clothes while out walking at some ungodly hour of the night. That he was not *stripped* of his clothes is hardly a counter-argument. For if they [the muggers] were not quick enough in stripping him but were frightened by the approach of people and made off, they were simply acting sensibly and were not so foolish as to put profit before their own safety. Or if he was not killed for his clothes, who knows, he might have seen others committing some crime and been killed by them so that he could not be a witness to their crime. (*Tetralogy* 1.b.5–6)

Nowadays, people are not usually mugged for their clothes but for money or valuables or their smartphone. Clearly, good clothes had a higher relative value then and were, perhaps, more easily stripped off a person than modern clothes with their sleeves and legs, buttons and zips. One notes the defendant's line of defence: the man might have been mugged, but the attacker was disturbed before he could strip the man; alternatively, the man might have become a chance witness to another crime and been killed as a potential witness. In any event, he makes such street crime sound like a relatively common event. The third *Tetralogy* of Antiphon also involves a case of street crime. The defendant is a younger man who claims he killed an older man in a brawl at night in self-defence. The prosecution argues that it is not likely that the older man would have attacked the younger man, but the defendant claimed it was the aggression of the older man that had started the brawl. Incidentally, the older man died, in fact, owing to faulty treatment by the doctor he attended for his injuries. Nevertheless, another incident of street violence at night. That makes two out of three of Antiphon's model speeches revolving round this theme: presumably he chose the subject as being a relatively common offence.

Another thing people had to watch out for when they were out at night was the possibility of running into rowdies, drunk and disorderly. The *symposion* or men's drinking party was often followed

27 Attic black-figure *oinochoē* with a *kōmos* scene of four bearded nude dancers, *c.* 510 BC.

by a semi-formal exodus of the participants onto the street, where they roamed as a vocal, and highly volatile, band called a *kōmos*. In origin this was a celebration of the god Dionysos. Pindar of Thebes (early fifth century BC), for example, could refer to his highly stately lyrics celebrating an athletic victory as a *kōmos*. However, drunkenness combined with personal enmities or rivalries led not infrequently to street brawls. Aristōn in Demosthenes' speech *Against Konōn* (no. 54; 346/5 BC) tells how the members of a drinking club around Konōn set upon him when he was walking in the Agora one night. The encounter was not accidental, as Konōn's son had called the revellers out from their drinking party after meeting their enemy Aristōn in the Agora:

> They attacked me, first stripped me of my coat, then kicked and beat me where I lay in the dirt. Then they jumped on me and thrashed me so severely that I sustained a split lip and my eyes swelled up and closed. They left me in such a sorry state that I could neither stand nor even speak. Lying there, I heard them utter all manner of insults, which I hesitate to repeat here . . . I will tell you, however, how he crowed over me like a prize cockerel, while his friends egged him on to flap his elbows against his sides in lieu of wings. Finally I was carried away, naked, by passers-by, while they ran off with my clothes. (*Against Konōn* 8–9)

Aristōn says that Konōn 'sang' like a cock (9.4 *ēide*), a play on the usual role of the *kōmos* to sing songs as they roamed the streets. The combination of song, drunkenness and possible violence explains an aspect of New Comedy, which, in general, imitated contemporary city life. Between each of the five acts of a New Comedy, a chorus, described as drunken revellers, sang (and danced, presumably) an interlude or entr'acte. The words are not recorded, and they did not play an integral part of the plot. At the end of act one in such a comedy, just before the chorus was about to make its first entry and sing its first song, the actors on stage invariably give some kind of warning, of the form: 'I'd best be off as I see a group of drunken rowdies approaching.' End of act one, choral interlude. This theatre convention must reflect real life to a degree: such groups of riotous young men, 'under the influence', must have been a real hazard to contend with, but also one sanctioned by society and not banned, for example.

6
A Better World

From our position in time, it is easy to admire the 'Greek miracle' for the rapid advances made within a few centuries, in a small geographical area, in almost all the important areas of civilization: literature, politics, art, philosophy, technology, science and medicine, among others. There were, of course, downsides as well, as was pointed out in the Introduction; equality, freedom of expression and the rule of law were only for one group, even in Athenian society: the citizen men. In this chapter I wish to indicate tendencies even within this dynamic and experimental culture to branch out and to form groups separate from the mainstream with their own rarefied ideals and beliefs. Two such groupings involve philosophy: Plato and the Epicureans. Philosophy as a whole can be seen as a ship of discovery, casting off its moorings in myth and traditional society and sailing off into uncharted intellectual waters.

In fact, we find instances throughout Greek history of elitism and a wish to rise above what one might call marketplace morality, a desire for a higher, purer, more moral existence, frequently with an eye on the rewards on offer in the afterlife. Already in Homer we met Elysium, or the Elysian Fields: a kind of paradise in the afterlife for select individuals, and below we will see how the concept developed. In the *Odyssey* there is also an example of a kind of ideal society separate from the rest of humanity, on the island of Scheria. This was the kingdom of Alkinoos, king of the Phaeacians, and his wife Arētē, whose name, perhaps not coincidentally, is almost identical with the word for virtue itself (*aretē*). This island community is not normally accessible to the rest of mankind but leads a kind of charmed existence by itself. Odysseus reaches it only by being washed up on its shore while drifting in the ocean, clinging on to a spar of wood. In other words, a kind of fairy-tale place reached by an arduous and unrepeatable journey, like the legendary Shangri-La in the Kunlun Mountains.[1] Naked and salt-encrusted, Odysseus encounters the beautiful princess Nausikaa on the beach where he has landed: another fairy-tale motif of the prince – albeit in an unrecognizable state – meeting the princess in a kind of never-never land.[2] Nausikaa is of distinctly marriageable age and inclination, and throughout Odysseus' stay among the Phaeacians there is an undercurrent of courtship between the two, despite Odysseus' goal of returning to his wife Penelope.

On Odysseus' way from the seashore to Alkinoos' palace, led by Nausikaa, he learns how the Phaeacians arrived at Scheria. They had lived elsewhere (Hypereia) but had been molested by their neighbours, the Cyclopes, a particularly brutal tribe, and their king Nausithoos (Swift Ship) had led them to the edge of the world, 'far away from the rest of mankind', where they lived in splendid isolation. 'There is no man alive,' Nausikaa explains, 'nor will there be, who will come to the land of the Phaeacians bringing war. For we live under the protection of the gods, far away across the billowing sea, at the world's edge, and no stranger molests us' (*Odyssey* 6.201–5). Instead of bows and arrows, they trusted in their swift ships, which travelled the ocean as fast 'as a bird or a thought'. Their boats, drawn up beside their settlement, were effectively their home and hearth (6.265). They were suspicious of strangers, and Athena casts a cloak of invisibility over Odysseus when he makes his way through their city on his way to the king's palace, for fear of being molested by the locals. In short, the Phaeacians are a people living apart, deliberately keeping away from the rest of mankind and cultivating a peaceful existence without weapons, dependent on seafaring. We are not told how this seafaring provides them with a living, whether through trade or fishing. In the course of his sojourn at Alkinoos' court, Odysseus is invited to recount his adventures thus far: an opportunity for narrative analepsis (recall of past adventures in the language of narratologists) on Homer's part, but also a way of placing Scheria firmly in the land of make-believe and wonder, as

Odysseus tells of one-eyed monsters (the Cyclopes), an enchantress on her island (Circe), a visit to the underworld and communion with the dead, and many more such adventures. By the time the Phaeacians provide Odysseus with a crewed ship and provisions to return to his island home on Ithaka, he has effectively 'caught up' for the benefit of the listener and is ready for the next stage of his journey with a clean narrative slate. Like the hero of a fairy tale, he has travelled to never-never land and can return, restored and strengthened, to reality: a

28 Athena (centre) facilitates the meeting between Odysseus and King Alkinoos' daughter Nausikaa after Odysseus is washed ashore naked on the island of Scheria. Odysseus holds a couple of branches to cover his nakedness. Attic red-figure amphora, *c.* 440 BC.

reality in which he must kill a horde of suitors to achieve reunion with his wife Penelope and homecoming.

Elysian Fields

While the Phaeacians are clearly conceived as living in this world, their peaceful existence on a distant island bears some resemblance to Greek concepts of a charmed existence in the afterlife. Later we will be meeting the so-called Orphic-Bacchic religion, documented by inscribed gold leaves placed with the dead and giving them instructions how to find their way as souls to the 'blessed place' in the underworld. These documents go back at least as early as the fifth century BC (some two or three centuries later than the *Odyssey*), and it is early in this century (476 BC) that we find the Theban poet Pindar writing about the existence of charmed souls in paradise in a so-called victory ode. Pindar wrote many religious works (hymns), which have survived only as fragments; what have survived are his poems celebrating the athletic victory of an aristocratic patron at one of the Panhellenic athletic competitions: so-called *epinikia*, victory odes.[3] When the title of such a poem reads 'For Thērōn of Akragas in the Chariot Race' (*Olympian Ode* 2), this does not mean that Thērōn himself piloted the winning chariot but rather that he financed the team. Pindar wrote these victory odes to butter up the tyrants and dynasts who commissioned them, but he wrote in an extraordinarily elevated style, including many myths with which to illustrate heroic deeds (like those of the patron) and much moralizing sentiment (*gnōmai*, sayings, containing conventional wisdom).

In the second *Olympian Ode* we find praise of Thērōn in plenty but also an undercurrent of trouble in the background. What Thērōn or his family had done wrong is not spelled out, but a comparison is made with Oidipus' family at Thebes, which was stained by Oidipus' inadvertent killing of his father Laios; here Pindar adds, 'in accordance with the Delphic oracle' (ll. 39–40), meaning that Delphi had predicted this course of events. Oidipus' children Eteokles and Polyneikes killed each other in battle as the family curse went on. A later descendant, however, Thersandros, is said to have clawed his way out of trouble by virtue and civic service. Thērōn, tyrant of Akragas in Sicily (modern Agrigento), is said to be descended from this very Thersandros of Thebes.

Crime in life is also the theme of an excursus by Pindar in this poem on the punishment of sinners in the underworld. The poet says that 'wealth adorned with virtues [*aretais*; l. 52] is good for many things' – and Thērōn had wealth in abundance – but one should always bear in mind the consequences of wrongdoing for the afterlife. One feels that Pindar's flattery of Thērōn in this ode is somewhat two-edged: you may be a wealthy tyrant, but remember Judgement Day! Then Pindar launches into a description of the underworld and the punishment of sinners. The important point here is that 'goodness' has become the criterion for avoiding punishment in the afterlife; not fame, wealth or prowess on the battlefield, but virtue and goodness. In other words, Pindar is holding out a reward in the afterlife for moral rectitude in this life. This represents a considerable advance on the Homeric situation, where even the 'best of the Achaeans' (Achilles) laments in Hades that he would rather be a 'day-labourer on earth' than King of the Shades in Hades (*Od.* 11.489–91); in other words, Achilles' fame and prowess bring no reward with them when he falls finally.[4]

Pindar's eschatology here holds out the prospect of a better lot both in the underworld and in future lives (he assumes the doctrine of transmigration of souls) through virtue in the sense of moral and behavioural righteousness. One can earn oneself both a better life in one's next incarnation, as well as ultimate paradise in the Isles of the Blessed, through avoiding wrongdoing over three full cycles of life, time spent in the gloom of Hades, followed by rebirth. In other words, there is an escape for the fortunate few from 'original sin', to use a Christian expression, through virtue and righteousness. If we equate 'original sin' with what one might call 'human nature' or 'the weakness of the flesh', one sees that the Greeks, too, knew the wish to escape from, or transcend, the bounds of corporeal existence. Following on from his comment about the uses of wealth, Pindar says:

> The good [*esloi*] receive a less arduous lot, not having to plough the soil with the strength of their arm, nor the ocean

> wave, a vapid existence. No, those who followed the commandments of the gods lead a happy existence among the esteemed, whilst the rest bear unimaginable toil. And whoever manages to complete this cycle [of life and death] thrice, keeping their souls free from all wrongdoing, they travel Zeus' path [of justice] to Kronos' Tower. There the ocean breezes waft over the Isle of the Blessed. Golden flowers blossom, some on land on lovely trees, while water nurtures others. They make chains of these [flowers] for their hands and garlands for their heads, living according to the ethical code of Rhadamanthys. (*Olympian Ode* 2.62–75)

There is much that is obscure in this eschatology, but we should not let that detain us here.[5] What is clear is that Pindar envisages a kind of Purgatory, a cleansing of polluted souls by punishment in the afterlife. Good souls have an easier lot in the next life; truly exemplary souls who manage to complete three rounds of life, death and rebirth without blemish are rewarded with Paradise. What has happened here is that Pindar has absorbed what we might call 'Western' ideas – I mean 'Western' in the context of ancient Greece, where Sicily and southern Italy were in the West – in a poem meant to please a tyrant of Akragas (in Sicily). Both the Orphics (more on them below) and Pythagoras (southern Italy) are associated with the doctrines of transmigration of souls (*metempsychōsis*, reincarnation of soul) and paradise in the hereafter. Pure, unsullied souls will be rewarded in the afterlife. This life is seen more as an obstacle race, or array of temptations, sent to try us. Virtue (*aretē*) is the avoidance of injustice (*adikia*) and the keeping of oaths (sanctioned by the gods). For this, Homer's Olympians were hardly models, as we have seen, so we have here a movement away from traditional religion towards a sect of the true believers, away from 'gather-ye-rosebuds-while-ye-may' towards asceticism and self-denial. It is for psychologists to explain the interplay of appetites and constraints, indulgences and feelings of guilt, which seem to be universally human.

Celibacy

One young man's desire to escape the clutches of Aphrodite forms the basis of a tragedy by Euripides towards the end of the fifth century (*Hippolytos*, 428 BC). The son of the Athenian king Theseus, Hippolytos rejects Aphrodite and prefers the company of Artemis and her hunters in the wilds. Unfortunately, his stepmother, Phaidra, has fallen in love with his youthful beauty (on Aphrodite's instigation) and is deeply ashamed of her secret passion.[6] The erotic impasse leads in the course of the play to the suicide of Phaidra, and the death of Hippolytos when his father Theseus curses him, thinking he is the cause of Phaidra's death. It is Aphrodite's way of punishing Hippolytos for rejecting her, a mighty goddess. In the prologue, Aphrodite explains her resentment of Hippolytos:

> The son of Theseus, Hippolytos . . . alone of all citizens of this Trozenian land [Trōzen: a town in the northeast Peloponnese] says I'm the worst of the gods. He refuses sex and shuns marriage. Phoibos' [Apollo] sister, however, Artemis, daughter of Zeus, he honours and thinks her the greatest among the gods. In the company of this virgin goddess he spends all his time in the greenwood, hunting wild animals with a pack of hounds. He prefers her company to that of his fellow humans. I don't resent *that*. Why would I? But I'll avenge what Hippolytos has done to offend me this very day. (*Hippolytos* 10–22)

Euripides has set up an opposition between Aphrodite, champion and cause of procreative love, and Artemis, who is celibate and prefers nature over culture, to use Lévi-Straussian terms. However one wishes to interpret the Greek pantheon, there is clearly an element of human psychology in the division of powers among the gods. Aphrodite 'stands for' sexual passion, Artemis the opposite: virginity and celibacy. This opposition is a way of expressing a no-go relationship in one (famous) man's family: his wife conceives a passion for his son (by another woman). It is a way of dramatizing 'sinful Aphrodite', as it were. However, it is not just that Hippolytos rejects Phaidra but rather that he rejects all women, and all sexual love. In other words, when he claims to be a devotee of nature, he is in fact at odds with human nature. When he first walks on stage at the head of a band of huntsmen singing a short hymn to Artemis to set the tone, he utters an 'entrance monologue', clearly stating his agenda:

> My Lady [Artemis], I come bringing you a woven crown which I have made for you from an untouched meadow. No herdsman dares to graze his flock there, no scythe has ever touched it, only the honey bee in spring traverses this untouched meadow. Modesty tends the garden there with waters of a stream for all those unspoiled by learning, to whom purity of mind comes naturally always: they may pluck there, the wicked not. But, dear Queen, accept this golden headband from my reverent hand. I alone of mortals have this right, for I dwell with you and speak with you in words. I hear your voice, though I don't see your face. May I reach the finishing line in life just as I began it. (ll. 73–87)

The servant who greets him at the palace entrance (Theseus' home) questions him about his reluctance to salute the 'gracious goddess' Kypris (Aphrodite), who stands at his own doorway.[7] Hippolytos replies that he salutes her from afar but wants nothing further to do with her. The servant insists that she is much honoured among men, to which Hippolytos answers: 'I don't like any god who shows herself at night.' (*Servant:*) 'Yet it is our duty to honour the gods.' (*Hippolytos:*) 'Each to his own, among gods and men.' (*Servant:*) 'Good luck with that. I hope you're thinking straight.'

The opposition between sexuality (Aphrodite) and chastity (Artemis) plays out in the course of the play. Hippolytos spurns Phaidra, whose unrequited love afflicts her like an illness. She, too, rejects the illicit *erōs* and wastes away. Her Nurse, when she discovers the root cause of Phaidra's ailment, says she is fighting a natural force. Aphrodite is responsible for love and reproduction in the world; to reject her is to reject nature. The chorus sing an escapist ode, wishing for the wings of a bird to fly away to another land, one not bedevilled by the misfortune caused by Aphrodite (ll. 732–51). The land they describe is like the paradise envisaged by Orphics in the afterlife, a sunny and untrammelled place. It is also reminiscent of Hippolytos' flowery meadow at the beginning of the play. There is a connection between the escapist longings of young men like Hippolytos seeking to steer clear of what he perceives as the corruption of the body, and the hope of finding purity and bliss in the afterlife, as we have seen in Pindar's eschatology.

When Phaidra, in desperation after the Nurse has revealed her secret to Hippolytos, hangs herself, leaving a suicide note accusing Hippolytos of rape (the motif is that of 'Potiphar's wife' in Genesis), Theseus finally returns home and discovers the tragedy. He takes the suicide note with its denunciation of Hippolytos at face value and lambasts his holier-than-thou son (as he now thinks):

> Look me in the eye, now you have stained your honour, face up to your father. You claim to be exceptional, do you, a companion of the gods? You – well-behaved? A stranger to wickedness? I can't believe your boasts: I'd have to think the gods are stupid, not thinking straight. Go ahead, boast about your vegan diet, spread the word about your food! Claim Orpheus as your guiding light, join the Bacchic club [Dionysos], hide behind the smokescreen of your treasured books! You've been found out! I advise everyone to shun your sort. They sound off with lofty words but stoop to sordid deeds. (ll. 946–57)

Theseus inveighs against Hippolytos as one of *those* people, followers of Orpheus and Bakchos, devotees of esoteric knowledge, vegetarians, claiming to be better than others but acting worse. Whether the accusations are just or not, we cannot really tell; what is particularly relevant here is Theseus' identification of his son here as a member of a particular sect, the so-called Orphics, who kept themselves aloof from common humanity. These 'Orphics' have long ghosted around in studies of ancient Greece without finding accurate definition, to such an extent that some have doubted they really existed as a coherent

29 A rich woman's grave in Roman Londinium, 3rd–4th century AD: embossed coffin, grave offerings and a reconstructed bust of the Spitalfields Woman.

body of believers in any particular doctrine. The situation has, however, become more tangible in recent years with the discovery and publication of the so-called Orphic-Bacchic gold leaves and other documents (papyri, mainly). By Roman times, initiation into the Orphic-Bacchic Mysteries was widespread and significant. The Villa of the Mysteries near Pompeii is eloquent and elegant testimony to the cult in Rome. In London, the excavation of the grave of the so-called Spitalfields Woman (named after the market site) revealed grave offerings pointing to her initiation into the Dionysiac Mysteries. Visitors to the Museum of London can see these and gaze on a model of her face as she has been reconstituted using 3-D modelling techniques from her bones (illus. 29). Christian doctrine shows remarkable affinities with the Orphic-Bacchic Mysteries: death and rebirth of a saviour figure, the promise of heaven in the afterlife, aversion to 'pleasures of the flesh' in one's lifetime.

Out of the Dark

It feels like *hybris* to dip into Plato and his philosophy, but nevertheless, here goes, even if in absolutely summary fashion. For reasons that psychologists might be best placed to fathom, Plato had a profound aversion to the body and its senses. For him, the body (*sōma*) was a kind of tomb (*sēma*) for the soul (*psychē*), from which it could be freed only by death (and reincarnation) or, to an extent, philosophy (*Gorgias* 493a3). Sex, for him, particularly between men and women, was just a kind of rubbing of bodies. The senses were second-best to thought, and profoundly deceptive. They offer a kind of unreliable picture of pictures of reality. That is, objects themselves are just copies (imperfect ones at that) of forms that exist only in the mind, a sort of mental paradigm giving a thing or concept its shape and justification. Plato called these forms Ideas (*ideai*), or pictures (*eikones*), or shapes (*eidē*). Beings of all kinds are what they are by 'participation' in a Form, like reproductions coming off a mould. Abstractions, too, like justice, beauty, courage, even the Good itself, 'exist' only by participation in metaphysical Forms, like a kind of hierarchy of ontology. For those interested in such connections, the Neoplatonists (for example Proklos in the fourth century AD) coined the term 'chains' (*seirai*) to denote these upwardly mobile chains of being leading up to ultimate truth. The concept might even derive ultimately, even if unconsciously, from Zeus' 'golden chain' in the *Iliad*, which we have already encountered, from which he wished to hang all the other gods, dangling like yo-yos in space.

For Plato, then, the goal of philosophy was to escape from the material world into the sphere of intellectual cognition (*to noētikon*, from the verb *noeō*, think). The material, or sensible, world is but a poor copy of the absolute Forms, which are accessible only by thought. In Raphael's famous fresco of the School of Athens, Plato and Aristotle stand centre stage like two gods, with lesser philosophers sprawled on the steps below them (illus. 30). Plato is pointing upwards towards the realm of the metaphysical, Aristotle is pointing down to earth, meaning that is what we must observe and analyse. It is the opposition between metaphysical and natural philosophy.

30 Raphael, *School of Athens*, 1509–11, Apostolic Palace, Vatican City. Plato (left) and Aristotle (right) are centre stage.

Plato, then, was the great escapist: we should spend our lives attempting to transcend our physical incarnation, meaning the body and its senses, and attain a higher order of being through thought. Although Socrates was Plato's teacher, hero and spokesman in many of the dialogues he wrote, this metaphysical turn was quite alien to Socrates, who asked principally how we should live well in this life, in this city, under these laws. There was perhaps some escapism traceable in Plato's own life, too. He made repeated attempts to found a better order in Sicily, associating with successive rulers of Syracuse and attempting to convert them to his philosophy, but was ultimately frustrated in his attempts and returned to Athens with his tail distinctly between his legs. In Athens, however, he founded the educational establishment called the Academy, named after the Attic hero to whom the land belonged (Akadēmos), which became the most influential university in world history to date. Plato did not fail in his mission, but he has had his critics, particularly in the field of political philosophy.

Life in the cave

In perhaps the central work of Plato, the *Republic* (Greek *Politeia*, or *The State*), Socrates, acting as Plato's mouthpiece, illustrates his vision of intellectual cognition as the goal towards which we must strive in order to free ourselves from mere opinion (*doxa*) with a sequence of vivid allegories: the Sun, the Line and the Cave. In it we see an extreme example of how Greek thought did not always embrace the here and now but showed a strong leaning towards otherworldliness, a yearning for a better or truer world. So far we have seen this yearning showing itself in the legendary community of Phaeacians in the *Odyssey*, in Pindar's depiction of heaven for the virtuous in the afterlife, and in Hippolytos' embracing of a natural lifestyle at odds with the seaminess of real human relations (not that I am advocating affairs between stepsons with their stepmothers!).

Plato's Socrates depicts our life on this earth as imprisonment in a dark cave in which we only see shadows flickering on its walls and think them real. In fact, he says, we must be released from our chains and forced to climb the arduous passage out of the cave into the brilliant (metaphorical) sunlight, in which we can begin to apprehend true reality and see how abject our guessings and shadow-existence in the cave have been. By 'sunlight', Plato does not mean the real sun: he means intellectual perception. We must ascend from the cave of sense perception, which is a poor and deceptive illusion of reality, to the bright light of thought. This is extreme otherworldliness: our lives on earth here are as nothing compared to the illumination an education in Platonic philosophy can provide. Here is how he puts it at the beginning of Book Seven of the *Republic* (Socrates talking to Glaukōn):

> Now compare our nature as regards education and lack thereof with the following situation. Imagine people living in an underground cave with a long entranceway connecting the whole cave with the daylight. From childhood they live there with chains around their legs and necks so they have to sit tight and only look in front of them. They can't

> turn their heads round on their necks because of the chains. There's a fire burning behind their backs at an elevation and at some distance from them. Between the fire and these prisoners is a high walkway with a parapet, like at a puppet show where there's a screen in front of the people, above which the operators show their sketches . . . Now imagine people carrying all manner of things and statues and model animals along this walkway, protruding over the parapet . . . and the prisoners see only their shadows on the wall in front of them. (*Republic* 514a1–515a7, abridged)

Some people have jokingly compared Plato's vision of people trapped in a cave and seeing only moving images on the screen in front of them with the audience in a cinema. However, his picture is meant existentially. In the world of sense impressions we are reliant on images, sounds, scents and feelings to assemble a picture in our minds of reality. Plato's prisoners in the cave see not only shadows of objects moving in front of them but shadows of *models* being held in front of the artificial light source behind them. What they are seeing are shadows of images of people and things. Then Plato pictures someone escaping from the cave by crawling up the narrow passage towards the light. He describes how that person would initially be dazzled by the blinding light of day and at first would see worse than in the cave. With time, however, they would adapt to the changed conditions and see the world as illuminated by the sun. Then they would see that the cave existence (our existence in terms of intellectual perception, don't forget) was a poor substitute for the enlightened world they have now reached.

We must not forget that Plato's cave is not meant literally. It is an allegory of the enlightenment that philosophy provides. The rest of mankind are prisoners in the cave; philosophers – or rather, those who have seen Plato's Forms through a process of intellectual effort (climbing the steep and narrow passage from the cave) – have liberated themselves from darkness and emerged into the sunlight of true perception. In other words, Plato's brand of otherworldliness involves philosophical discipline. It is the route from the 'normal' human condition to an existence contemplating eternal truths in the pure light of intellectual reason. Most of us, on the terms of this image, are content, in one way or another, to stay in the cave: doing our business, painting our pictures, writing our writings, building our houses and tending our back gardens. We will not be pleased to be told that all these things are guesswork based on shadows of models of reality, lit by artificial light. However, we may agree with Plato that study of any subject whatsoever gives us greater insight into how it works, how it is constituted, and according to what natural or physical laws it functions. Incidentally, this appears to be what Socrates preached in his discussions with fellow Athenians, if we are to believe the picture in Xenophon's *Memorabilia*: that we trust and believe experts in any branch of knowledge. Practice, experience and study make us into such experts, who earn recognition among our fellow citizens for expertise in a particular field. For Plato that is not enough: for him, philosophy is a higher field altogether, one not based on the here and now but the opposite of empirical. It is a flight from the transitory to the eternal, a passage and flight adopted by many later religions and ideologies, not always happily or for the benefit of mankind.

The Garden

Where Plato yearned for a life spent contemplating eternal and unchanging Ideas free from the distractions of sense perception, thus essentially denying the validity of 'normal' life, a philosopher appeared hard on his heels in Athens who advocated the precise opposite. This was Epicurus (341–270 BC), founder of the Epicurean school of philosophy, which in the Hellenistic age became the chief rival and opponent of the Stoics. Epicurus bought a plot of ground to the northwest of Athens (not far from Plato's Academy) in 307–6 BC and there founded his 'Garden' (*kēpos*), where his followers met to philosophize and live together. Women were also welcomed, and slaves, marking a radical exception to the rule of female exclusion in male institutions at Athens.

Epicurus' recommended course to avoid life's trials and tribulations was pleasure (*hēdonē*). One should be happy, content, at peace with oneself, free from disturbing thoughts and worries. The great goal in life was *ataraxia*, 'unperturbedness', a kind of serene peace of mind comparable in some ways to Buddhist nirvana. How was one to achieve this bliss? By avoiding anything that troubled one: getting involved in quarrels and rivalries with one's fellow humans, politics, wars, unhealthy competitions, ambition, greed and so on. In short, what occupies most people most of the time was to be avoided by the Epicurean. The Epicurean was to lead a life in relative obscurity, among friends, discussing philosophy in the Garden and avoiding – the modern word – stress.

This was escapism of a thoroughgoing but also virtuous type. When Epicurus said pleasure was the goal of life, he did not mean wine, women and song in abundance. No, these types of pleasure only brought discomfort in their train: hangovers and all other concomitants of overindulgence. The type of pleasure Epicurus advocated was abstemious, ascetic, modest. He said that a good piece of cheese was a feast, water was the best drink, and so on:

> When we say that pleasure is the goal of life, we do not mean the pleasures of the degenerates or those involving overindulgence, as some believe who either do not know us or disagree with us, or deliberately distort our message. No, we mean by pleasure the lack of physical pain and the absence of mental distress. It is not drinking and endless carousing, sex with boys and women, nor caviar [lit. 'fishes'] and all the other delicacies of a gourmet table, which produce an enjoyable life, but rather sober thought that reflects on the rationale of moral choices and which drives out the erroneous beliefs from which stem the greatest perturbation of the mind. (Diogenes Laertius, *Lives of the Philosophers* 10.131.8–132.6)

And what did Epicurus chiefly have in mind when he referred to 'false beliefs which lead to worry'? It was the fear of death itself, which he saw as the greatest bane of human life, its chief scourge and torment. We must remember that the Greeks had a lively picture of the punishments awaiting wrongdoers in the underworld, which added to the fears about death and what might await one. Epicurus combated the very human and widespread fear of death with elaborate physical theory defining the human condition. Drawing on earlier philosophers, he adopted the materialist view of the physical world labelled atomism. The only components of the world (universe) were, according to the Greek atomists, atoms and the void. The atoms were the smallest indivisible particles of matter, and they floated, or bounced, around in the void, forming combinations and compounds, which, in their variety, produced the range of animate and inanimate things and beings in the world. Since these were all there was to the physical universe – soul, for example, was just super-fine atoms in their own particular constellation – it followed that death was the dispersal of these atoms back into the void from the particular agglomerations which we had called ourselves. 'Death is nothing to us,' Epicurus proclaimed, 'as, when we are, death is not, and when death is present, we are not' (*Lives* 10.124–5, condensed). Or, put differently: 'Death is nothing to us. What is dispersed has no feeling. What has no feeling has no relevance for us' (10.139).

When Epicurus died – excruciatingly painfully, of kidney stones, it is said – he left a will specifying that his very considerable estate was to pass to his successors in the school, who were to maintain the Garden and Epicurus' house as they had been in his lifetime, to support certain individuals who had been close to the school and to maintain the philosophical habits founded by Epicurus, including his birthday celebrations. It seems that Epicurus' wealth (*prosodoi*), which was, no doubt, inherited, perhaps partly from land ownership in Samos, had supported the oasis of calm and tranquillity outside the hurly-burly of Athenian life that was the Garden. He is said to have been extremely generous to friends, some slaves and a number of women *hetairai*. The image of an oasis seems to have been very applicable to this refuge from trouble offered to followers of Epicurus.

For this reason it had its vehement critics. Philosophically, the Stoics with their advocacy of fortitude and selfless engagement in public service praised a quite different goal in life. Others turned the Epicurean advocacy of 'pleasure' unfairly against them, saying they were self-indulgent hedonists devoted precisely to those feasts and frivolities that Epicurus specifically rejected. The Roman philosopher and statesman Cicero (106–43 BC) later wrote extensively against the escapism of the Epicureans, their otherworldliness, which was basically a shunning of responsibility. While today most of us spend a lifetime behind a desk or a machine earning a living to support ourselves and our families, with *hēdonē* usually reserved strictly for the weekend and the few weeks of holiday a year, it is worth calling to mind the ideals behind recent pacifist and hippy movements. John Lennon's songs 'All You Need Is Love' and 'Imagine' are not far from the ideals of friendship and non-aggression advocated by Epicurus.

Orphic Initiation

Orpheus himself is a figure of myth, or legend. There he had the reputation of a poet and musician with magical powers, whose playing could charm all nature into obeying its call. He sailed with Jason and the Argonauts to far-flung Colchis (in modern Georgia) and performed magical feats along the way. The Hellenistic poet Apollonius of Rhodes (third century BC) introduces him in his epic known as *Argonautika* as follows:

> Let us mention Orpheus first, whom, they say, Kalliopē [Muse of epic poetry] bore to the Thracian Oiagros near to the Rock of Pimplēïs [one of the homes of the Muses]. They say he could charm rocky mountain crags and flowing rivers by the sound of his singing. Dense ranks of wild oaks still bear witness to his song on the Thracian shore of verdant Zōnē, where he lured them down from Mount Pieria [another seat of the Muses] by the magic of his music. (*Argonautika* 1.23–31)

The myth told of his marriage to Eurydikē, her death by snakebite, and Orpheus' descent into the underworld in an attempt to rescue her. According to Virgil's famous version (in the fourth *Georgic*), he failed because he could not keep to the condition imposed by Hades, king of the underworld, not to turn round to check that Eurydikē was really following him (she was). Nevertheless, we note his *katabasis*, descent, to the underworld, as it is relevant to Orphic promises of a better lot there for initiates. He is said to have 'died' by being torn apart by the Maenads (women followers of Dionysos) but continued singing as his disembodied head floated over the sea and landed on the island of Lesbos, where an oracle of Orpheus was founded. His remains were said to have been gathered up and buried by the Muses. In the Orphic Mysteries he was closely associated with Dionysos, Bakchos, who likewise suffered dismemberment at the hands of the Titans but whose heart was rescued by Athena and resuscitated with the help of Apollo. Thus both central figures of Orphism underwent a form of death and resurrection.

Plato refers disparagingly to ritual practitioners, or wandering priests, known as 'Orphic initiators' (*orpheotelestai*), who spread the oracular utterances of Orpheus and Mousaios (another legendary singer) in conjunction with cathartic initiation rites for both individuals and towns. The rites consisted of sacrifices and 'childish play' (*paidia*; perhaps this linked up with the toys offered to the child Dionysos by the Titans) performed by initiates in their lifetime as a way of securing a privileged existence in the afterlife. Plato writes:

> And they [the *orpheotelestai*] parade a whole hubbub of books by Mousaios and Orpheus, children of Sēlēnē [Moon] and the Muses, as they claim, according to which they conduct their magical rites, persuading not only private individuals but also cities that there are remissions and cleansings from the stain of guilt by means of sacrifices and the pleasures of revelry for people while still alive and after they are dead, which they call 'initiations' [*teletai*], which release us from sufferings in the hereafter, but that terrible things await those who fail to sacrifice. (*Republic* 364e3–365a3)

The Orphic initiators apparently cited the authority of 'sacred' books by the poet-seers Orpheus and Mousaios as the myth underlying the rituals of initiation that they offered to communities and individuals. The myth, as we learn from assembling a 'hubbub' of sources from the fifth century through to late antiquity, told of the reign of Dionysos, which succeeded that of Zeus: a clear break with 'conventional'

31 Orpheus mosaic from a Roman floor in Cagliari, second half of the 3rd century AD. Orpheus was surrounded by wild animals in the original, which he charmed with his singing to the lyre.

theology, which said that we (humanity) are living under Zeus' reign. Dionysos himself was said in the Orphic cosmogony to be the son of Zeus by Persephone; that, too, went against the traditional account that Semelē was his mother. As a child he was tempted away from the protection of a mythical group called Kourētēs by vicious Titans with toys and mirrors. Once they had him in their power, they dismembered him, according to the myth, and ate parts of him. For this, Zeus blasted them with his thunderbolt; we humans are said to have been born from the soot of this blast. Either Athena or Rhea (goddesses) were said to have collected up the rent parts of Dionysos and the young god was revived, according to one version by Apollo (Paiōn) at Delphi. Humans, originating from this violent crime, must atone for the 'original sin' of the Titans by celebrating the Orphic rites in honour of Persephone. If they do this, the promise is that they will receive a far superior fate in the afterlife. The story of Dionysos and the Titans, by the way, and the precise wording of the ritual, was a secret: hence the ancient term 'Mysteries' (*mystēria*), which comes from *muō*, 'shut the eyes': the Mysteries are what initiates see when they open their eyes in a ritual epiphany.

This story departed from mainstream theology as represented by Homer and Hesiod at almost all points, and shows a desire to be 'different'. We saw above how Hippolytos' father Theseus accused him of trying to be different in his lifestyle choices as a follower of Orpheus. That the present generation lives under Dionysos, as children of Dionysos (born of the ash of Titans who had eaten Dionysos), that a god can die and be reborn, that there is paradise after death for the chosen – all this stands in deliberate opposition to the traditional cornerstones of belief: Zeus the father of gods and men, the descent of man from Deukalion and Pyrrha as sole survivors of the flood, immortal gods, gloomy Hades after death. The name Hades is etymologically opposite to the eye-opening experience of the Mysteries: it derives from *a-id-*, 'not see'.

The discovery of the gold lamellae (leaves) in graves in Sicily, Crete and the Greek mainland from the fifth century BC on has done much to underpin these rather nebulous 'Orphic initiations' and the accompanying myth. Like Dionysos himself, the evidence for his rites had been dismembered over the centuries and the extent of Greece so that reassembling them and acquiring a coherent (and plausible) account still relied on considerable leaps of the imagination and credulity. Now, the lamellae prove that Dionysos was deeply involved in the eschatology of this faith, and that people died who had been initiated in the Orphic-Bacchic Mysteries and were confident of a better lot in the next world. With them were buried fine gold leaves, often hung round their neck, inscribed with specific instructions to their souls how to proceed in order to find the Garden in the underworld. One of the oldest and most explicit was found in the cist-grave of a woman buried around 400 BC:

> This is a work of Memory [aide-memoire], when you are about to pass into the roomy halls of Hades. There is a spring on the right and beside it stands a white cypress. There the souls of the dead refresh themselves on their descent. Do not go near this spring! Before [you get to] it, you will find fresh water flowing from the Pool of Memory. Guards stand over it. In their superior wisdom, they will ask you why you are seeking the dark of gloomy Hades. Tell them: 'I am a child of Earth and starry Heaven. I am parched with thirst and dying. Let me drink of the cool water from the Pool of Memory.' They will tell it to the Lord of the Underworld. They will allow you to drink from the Pool of Memory. When you have drunk, you proceed along the Sacred Way which the other elect Initiates and Bacchoi tread.[8]

The key point here is the instruction *not* to drink from the fountain from which all the other souls of the dead are drinking, but rather to take the path less trod to a Pool of Memory, answer the challenge of the guards standing watch over that with an appropriate password ('I am the child of Heaven and Earth'), and then proceed along the way reserved for the chosen initiates. These latter are called *mystai*, initiates, and *bakchoi*, showing they are devotees of Bakchos (Dionysos). The Pool of Memory relates to the necessity of obtaining enlightened consciousness in the afterlife as opposed to the forgetting (*Lēthē*) that afflicts the souls who do not drink of this water. Once the souls of the blessed have drunk of this water and answered the guards' challenge correctly, they may walk the 'pilgrims' way', presumably leading to a happy existence in the afterlife. Orphics and Pythagoreans believed in reincarnation, so it is likely that initiates (as Pindar had professed) are privileged in their future existences.

In short – and there are a multitude of hermeneutic issues involved with the corpus of these Orphic-Bacchic gold lamellae, which cannot be dealt with here – initiates in this cult are choosing the way 'less travelled by', to use Robert Frost's expression, in the hope of escaping the gloom of Hades and instead joining the Blessed, who are also equipped with good hope for a future round of existence. What is there not to like about this prospect? As already mentioned, the Orphic-Bacchic Mysteries became very popular over the centuries prior to, and including, the Roman Empire and may be thought to have handed the torch, when the time came, to Christianity.

7
WARFARE

> War is the father of all, and the king of all. Some it reveals as gods and some as humans, some it has made slaves, and some free.
>
> Heraclitus, fragment 53 DK

Thus a rather dispiriting saying of Heraclitus of Ephesus, to which we may reluctantly assent, but deplore. Those looking to find a better, different, more peaceful and natural life in the last chapter will seem to have had a point in the course of this chapter. As stated in the Introduction, Greece was never a nation-state in the ancient course of its history, even though it was temporarily united by the Macedonian conquest in the latter decades of the fourth century. It consisted of city-states, *poleis*, which competed, quarrelled and fought with each other incessantly, though primarily round the axis of the major players: Athens, Sparta, Thebes, Corinth. Pella in Macedonia crept up on these city-states rather stealthily in the fourth century and, under the leadership of first Philip II in 338 BC and then Alexander the Great, conquered all. The vast swathe of territory conquered by Alexander was divided after his death in 323 BC into separate kingdoms and ruled by the so-called Successors (Diadochoi, from the verb *diadechomai*, succeed to), until they, too, were relieved of the command by the Romans. This fragmented world, living on the edge of the Persian Empire and often engaged, directly or indirectly, in conflicts with that, was seldom at peace, and the internecine fighting was exacerbated by inner-state fighting, *stasis*, or factional fighting, as it was called. The courses of these wars, campaigns and conquests are for the history books. Here what concerns us is, as throughout, what it may have felt like to have fought in them: the personal perspective.

Epic

Towards the end of the *Iliad*, Achilles needs a new suit of armour to re-enter the fray. His bosom friend Patroklos has died in his stead, wearing his armour, which has been stripped for spoils. Incensed, Achilles decides to set his *mēnis*, rage (at being insulted by Agamemnon), aside and return to fighting, if nothing else to take revenge on Hektor. His mother Thetis, a goddess, handily, goes up to Olympos and visits the divine craftsman Hephaistos and asks him to fashion a new suit of armour for her son. Rather grimly, Hephaistos accepts the commission. The shield, in particular, is singled out for special attention. Made from bronze and pewter, with a relief embossed in gold and silver, it becomes an emblem of the entire epic world, as Hephaistos depicts a kind of microcosm in repoussé technique on it. First comes the sky with heavenly constellations, and below it, earth. There, Hephaistos hammers out two cities, one at peace and the other at war, as if to show both sides of the human condition. The scene of war has points in common with the story of the *Iliad* itself, as it concerns a city under siege. One army intends to sack the city; the defenders have not yet conceded defeat. While battle rages in the plain below the city, the elders, children and wives man the city walls – as the Trojans themselves do in the *Iliad*. The scene Hephaistos depicts concerns an ambush at a ford. The defenders of the city ambush the enemy as they drive their herds to the watering place. First they fall on the animals and herdsmen, but soon the opposing army hears the alarum and hastily joins battle:

> When they [the other army] heard the commotion surrounding the cattle [where the ambush was], they jumped up from where they had been sitting around in camp, mounted their spirited horses and rushed towards the spot. There they did battle beside the banks of the river, throwing their

> bronze-headed javelins at each other. Fight was among them, and Battle-Cry, and dire Death held one freshly wounded man in his grip, another as yet unwounded, and another already dead, dragging him by the feet through the moil. Death's cloak was stained with the blood of humans over both shoulders. Like living people, these spirits ranged among them and joined in the fight. (*Iliad* 18.530–39)

Hephaistos' work is an allegory of war, with the war gods shown fighting among the two armies. We must imagine his workmanship as so consummate that the illusion of movement and action was perfect. Although the figures were all metallic – and, of necessity, static – nevertheless it was as if they were 'living people fighting'.

Hand-to-hand fighting

Homer in the *Iliad* made a point of not depersonalizing the fighting between Greeks (he called them Achaeans, Danaans or Argives) and the Trojans. He never described their engagements impersonally along the lines of: 'On that day the Trojans got the better of the fighting. Some four hundred Greeks fell while the Trojans only lost one hundred and fifty.' Or: 'An incursion of Greeks secured an outpost of the Trojan defences in a day of intensive fighting.' That would be to reduce the brutality of war to facts and figures, mental tokens that strip events of their meaning in terms of human experience. He insisted on what historians are terming 'experiential' or 'immersive' narrative: an account that draws the listener in to experience vicariously what the actors themselves experience. Some readers of the *Iliad* tire of this approach. There seem to be endless detailed descriptions of slaughter and death. Do we need them all? Is the aesthetic effect not somewhat numbing, almost a distraction from the larger tragic movement of the epic?

Some deaths on the battlefield are embellished with literary devices such as similes and personal details of the victim, like that of Imbrios. The context is the battle 'for the ships', where the Trojans, helped by Achilles' inactivity, have advanced to a position where they can attack the Greek camp itself, where the ships are drawn up on the shore:

32 Homeric battle around the body of a dead warrior, probably Patroklos, Attic black-figure calyx krater (flared-rim mixing bowl), *c*. 530 BC.

> The others engaged in battle and a huge cry arose. Teukros, son of Telamōn, was the first to kill his man, one Imbrios, a spear-fighter, the son of Mentōr who owned many horses . . . Teukros struck him with his long spear just below the ear and yanked the spear out again. He fell like an ash tree which, growing afar, high on a prominent mountaintop, falls to the axe-blade, bringing its fresh foliage crashing down to the ground. Thus he fell, and the bronze armour he was wearing clashed. Teukros rushed to strip it off him. (*Iliad* 13.169–82)

Here the gory details of the killing are kept to a minimum while the act is illustrated by the felled tree simile. Even the detail of where the tree grows – far away on a mountaintop – reflects the fact that Imbrios had lived far away in Pēdaion before the war. Thus Homer dwells, if briefly, on the sad circumstances of one man's death on the battlefield.

Imbrios' story is not quite over, however. When Hektor, the greatest warrior of Troy, sees Teukros making to strip Imbrios' armour (armour was valuable – and a trophy), he hurls a spear at him. Teukros is alert enough to dodge it, but the spear hits one Amphimachos behind him and kills him. Hektor then, in turn, rushes forward to rip the helmet off Amphimachos (as a trophy, presumably), but Aias (on the Greek side) stops him with a spear-thrust, which failed to penetrate his armour but succeeded in repelling him. At that point, the Greeks grab the two bodies – those of Greek Amphimachos and Trojan Imbrios – and drag them from the field: Amphimachos for seemly burial, but here is what they do with Imbrios:

> But Imbrios the two men called Aias, fired up by the heat of battle, like two lions that wrest a goat from the jaws of ravening hounds and carry it off through the dense undergrowth, holding it aloft in their maws – thus did the two helmeted Aiases shoulder Imbrios and strip him of his armour. And the son of Oileus, enraged by the death of Amphimachos, cut off the head from his soft neck and threw it like a ball through the melee of battle. It landed in the dirt before Hektor's feet. (13.197–205)

Again, a simile to heighten the immediacy of the battle scene: like two hungry lions, two Greek fighters carry off Imbrios' body and strip it of its armour, while a third, grieving for the loss of Amphimachos, mutilates the corpse by beheading it and lobbing the head into the ranks of the enemy. The head rolls up to Hektor's feet, returning to taunt him, as it were, for his attempt to strip Amphimachos of his armour. In cinematic terms, Homer zooms in on details of the action rather than panning out over the battlefield: individual death and disfigurement rather than a blur of action in which details are lost in the general confusion. And we note that pathos is the keynote rather than glory: it is Imbrios' fate that Homer evokes sympathetically, rather than the valour of his killer or mutilator. With Wilfred Owen ('Strange Meeting', 1918): 'The pity of war, the pity war distilled.'

Other battlefield deaths in the *Iliad* are not embellished with literary devices but are told in plain, gory detail. In Book Five, the Greek fighter Diomedes has what was termed by ancient critics his *aristeia*, his winning streak, when all attention focuses on his achievements to the exclusion of others. It is rather as if, on a football field, the camera zooms in on a particular player and shows an inspired passage of play, perhaps culminating in a goal. We say 'inspired', but in the case of Diomedes, this is literally true, as the goddess Athena accompanies Diomedes on his rampage, guiding his aim and breathing fire (*menos*, lit. 'courage') into his heart. As he slashes and thrusts his way through the Trojan ranks, two Trojans, Aineias and Pandaros, determine to mount a joint attack on him from a chariot of war to put a stop to his killing spree. They debate at length who should be charioteer and who the warrior, weighing up tactical advantages. They decide that the horses will respond best to their accustomed driver, Aineias in this case. That leaves Pandaros with hands free to fight. As they approach Diomedes, Pandaros declares that he had wounded Diomedes earlier in the battle with an arrow; now he intends to finish the job with his spear.

> He spoke, and, gathering himself for the throw, hurled the long-shafted spear and struck Diomedes in the shield. Its bronze tip pierced right through the shield and came close to his chest plate. Pandaros, brave son of Lykaōn, let out a shout which carried across the battlefield. 'You're hit in the flank. I don't think you'll last long. You've given me great glory!' But mighty Diomedes was not cowed, and spoke: 'You're wrong: you missed. I don't think we'll stop before one of us is dead, quenching Ares' thirst for blood, that warrior with the bull's hide shield.' With these words he threw his spear, and Athena guided it to the nose between the eyes, where it smashed through the white upper teeth. The hard bronze cut through the base of his tongue and its point emerged just below the jawbone. Pandaros fell from the chariot, his glittering armour clashing, the horses reared in terror. His life and strength drained from him. (5.280–96)

One count of individual deaths in the *Iliad* arrives at a total of 240 (188 Trojans, 52 Greeks).[1] These endless scenes of violent death in battle do wear on the reader, who feels one gets the idea after about ten of them. However, Homer does everything to vary the individual scenes according to the wound inflicted, the precise sequence of each fight, the words exchanged by the combatants, details of their pedigree and so forth. Such variety (*poikilia*, Lat. *varietas*, is the ancient critical term) goes some way towards mitigating the monotony, but clearly Homer believed that the many deaths were conducive to the epic effect of his narrative, which could hardly be over after a handful of duels. As we already said, he has anyway radically reduced the length of the whole war (from the mythical ten years) to a mere 52 days at a critical juncture in the fighting (the rage of Achilles). Moreover, the detailed descriptions of wounding and death have a cumulative effect of repulsion: it was not Homer's intention to glorify war, as has already been noted, despite the fact that the warriors declared they were seeking above all else 'glory' (*kleos*) on the battlefield. The wounds reveal, rather, the vulnerability of the human body despite armour, the ease with which a brave soul is 'released' from its body. They also contribute to the *enargeia*, immediacy or vividness, of the fighting, making at least this reader flinch at each spear-thrust or sword-cut. Individual duels are also the way vase painting in the archaic period depicted war: like Homer, not as a seething mass of bodies but rather as vignettes of two warriors locked in combat. As Vladimir Putin's Russian army relentlessly reduced Ukrainian cities to rubble, causing thousands on thousands of deaths, both civilian and military, imagine if each individual death was described in a news bulletin instead of statistics and generalities: 'The bomb landed on the shelter, penetrating half a metre of reinforced concrete. First the explosion took off Maria's head, her limbs and all her skin, then the shock wave threw the child she had been holding with such force against the shelter wall that its body was flattened into a dark red human-shaped mark on the wall.' This imagined description, by no means exaggerated or fanciful, shows how the details of wounding and suffering are the reality of war, which Homer wanted to show.

The fall of Troy

Homer's *Iliad* does not include the fall of Troy; its subject is the limited one of the 'ire of Achilles' (*mēnis*). Nor does it even include the death of Achilles, although there are many pointers towards this. The fall of Troy was featured in other (largely) lost epic poems, in particular *Iliou Persis* (Sack of Troy). However, a passage of Attic tragedy by Euripides contains a song by the chorus of Trojan women lamenting the night Troy was finally sacked and the Trojans either killed or enslaved. The theme of Euripides' play, titled after Troy's queen Hekabē (*Hecuba*, *c.* 424 BC), is the fate of the women and children of Troy now their menfolk have been defeated. In a way this does follow on directly from where the *Iliad* left off, as the last book of that contains the mourning for Hektor. With him, Troy's best defender, gone, the feeling is that all is lost. His death is, as it were, the harbinger of the fall of Troy. The women collectively lament:

> Troy, my home, you no longer
> number among the standing cities.
> The Greeks have cast a cloud over you,
> spear on spear has taken you.
> Your turrets have been destroyed,
> alas, all blackened now by fire.
> I will no longer walk your streets.
> Destruction came at night . . .
> I was arranging my hair in stays,
> looking into the mirror's endless depths
> before falling into bed.
> A shout went up around the town
> a battle cry rang out: 'Sons of Greeks,
> when, oh, when, will you take
> the citadel of Troy, at last go home?'
> Dressed in just an undergown,
> like a Spartan girl, I left my bed
> and supplicated Artemis – in vain.

I saw my own husband's death
and was led down to the shore.
I looked back over the ship's stern
as it took me from Troy my country . . .
(*Hekabē* 905–41)

A follow-up play by Euripides (*Andromache*) shows the fate of Hektor's wife Andromache when she is taken as Neoptolemos' prize back to Phthia in Greece, where she lives in slavery. Neoptolemos is Achilles' son.

Lyric: Love and War

The lyric poets of the seventh and sixth centuries BC who placed erotic love at the heart of their work often contrasted this theme with the horrors of war. We have already made acquaintance with poems by Sappho and Ibykos on the subject of passionate love and seen how Alkaios used the theme of 'storm at sea' to describe the political battles that were fought between factions on the island of Lesbos. Even the forms used by the lyric poets were at war with Homeric epic. While he used the 'heroic' metre of the dactylic hexameter (what the Greeks themselves called *epos*, meaning literally 'speech') – a long, flowing line endlessly repeating itself (though with infinite subtle variation) – they chose short, chiselled forms and metres suitable for song sung to the lyre. Altogether, 'lyric' poetry, meaning originally the verse that was sung to the lyre, was inappropriate for heroic epic as lyre music was the accompaniment of merriment and celebration, not suited to battle or macho exploits at all. One of Sappho's unfortunately badly preserved poems explicitly contrasts the warfare typical of epic with her preferred theme, love. As far as is possible, it translates:

Some say cavalry, some say infantry,
some say a navy is the finest sight
on the face of earth, but I reply
it's what one loves.

This is easy to make comprehensible
to anyone, as Helen, who far outshone
all the rest in beauty, left her husband
[who was a great man]

behind, and sailed away to Troy
without a thought for her child
or her own dear parents – no, [love]
had her in its grip . . .

[*lines missing in the text*]

. . . reminds me now of Anaktoria
who is not beside me.

I would rather see her sexy walk
and the lovely sparkle in her eye
than all the chariots of the Lydians
or their infantry in action
[*more text missing*]
(fr. 16 Voigt)

Sappho seems here clearly to be taking a swipe at Homer, or rather what one might term the masculine battle ethos, as she turns his tale against him, saying any fool can understand that love is stronger than war because Helen absconded with Paris, precipitating a war. In other words, she means Helen's attraction to Paris was stronger for her than the consequences, which, immediately, were the loss of child and parents, and, just down the road, what was then a world war. In fact, this is unfair to Homer, as we have seen how the tragedy of war rather than its glory is his main theme. True, there are descriptions of gleaming ranks of warriors, and the individual protagonists thirst for glory, *kūdos*, on the battlefield, but the overall impression is the pain and loss caused by war. Sappho is pointing up the basic opposition between war (with its god Ares) and love (represented by Aphrodite), but it is interesting to note that Homer himself sends both these divinities into battle at Troy, and both emerge far from unscathed. Aphrodite suffers a slight wound to her immortal curves at the hands of Diomedes, who also manages to wound Ares himself (both episodes in Book 5). When Ares withdraws from the battlefield distinctly crestfallen, Zeus tells him not to come running to him for aid, as he is 'the most hated of the Olympian gods' (*Iliad* 5.890). It is as if, on the one hand, Homer is saying that these two forces – Ares and Aphrodite – are stirring up the war on earth, and, on the other, that both sides do not emerge with their honour intact from the narrative but suffer humiliations through their involvement in it. The theme of Ares and Aphrodite (Mars and Venus) lying together in repose – with Ares looking distinctly post-coital – is known in art both in antiquity and the Renaissance, for example in the painting by Botticelli that hangs in the National Gallery, London.

The Heroic and the Not-So-Heroic

Homer, like the background sound of surf crashing on a seashore, is ever-present in Greek (and Latin) poetry, from beginning to end, and internationally. In a poem, rediscovered in 2006, by the archaic poet Archilochus of Paros, the Homeric cycle of epic poetry is used for comparison with a contemporary military event. We do not know the precise context. It seems the side in a battle that Archilochus supported had performed less than gloriously, choosing flight rather than fight. Archilochus compares this flight with a story of a setback on the Greek fleet's voyage to Troy. By mistake, the fleet landed at a place in Mysia called Teuthras, which is south of Troy on the Ionian coast. There, their army suffered a rout at the hands of a local (mythical) warrior called Telephos, who, inspired by Herakles himself, fought like a berserker and drove the intruders ignominiously back to their ships. Archilochus' point is what is called paraenetic: he wishes to encourage his compatriots after their recent humiliation in battle by referring to 'higher powers'; it is no disgrace to retreat in the face of the *force majeure* of no less a figure than Herakles. Incidentally, it is quite interesting to follow the dispute that arose among scholars when this papyrus text from Oxyrhynchus was first identified and deciphered by

Dirk Obbink at Oxford (P.Oxy. vol. LXIX no. 4708). Immediately a scrum of scholars, one of them of Herculean scholarly stature himself, Martin L. West, entered the fray of decipherment and fought over every letter in the text like warriors reluctant to give an inch.

Although the battle to which Archilochus refers is mythical, thus having absolutely no documentary value at all, the details of the battle are graphic enough and no doubt reflect aspects of the defeat Archilochus' compatriots recently suffered. As said, the poet's purpose is to mitigate the bitterness of the defeat and offer a perspective to comfort bruised morale:

> If one [is forced to retreat] under the powerful compulsion of god, it is not appropriate to speak of weakness and cowardice. We [abruptly] turned to flight, but there is a time for flight. Once in the past Telephos, the descendant of Arkas, single-handedly put the fear of god into a large Argive force. They did not display courage – so strong was the fear instilled in them by divine fate – although they were stalwart fighters. The River Kaïkos was filled with the bodies of the fallen, as was the Mysian Plain. The armed force of the Achaeans ran in panic back to the shore of the sounding sea, as casualties were inflicted by the hands of the unrelenting warrior . . . Herakles confronted them, shouting encouragement to his brave son, an unflinching bulwark in the killing fields, Telephos, who on that day single-handedly inflicted a humiliating rout on the Danaans, doing his father proud.

The context of this salutary tale is purely Homeric: the Greek fleet suffered a setback on their way to Troy. Herakles is the *force majeure* here; like Athena or Apollo appearing on the Trojan battlefield in Homer to breathe courage or strength into warriors on their respective sides, here Herakles is said to have stood beside his son (in myth) Telephos and shouted exhortations to him as he fought. In this sense, a 'divine force of necessity' opposed the Greek force on that day, making their defeat excusable – and, a fortiori, that of Archilochus' countrymen. Likewise the filling of the River Kaïkos with corpses is purely Homeric, as Achilles similarly fills the Scamander with fallen Trojans. Like a football coach talking to his players in the changing room following a defeat, Archilochus here wants to take the edge off their despondency by placing the result in a bearable perspective: 'we were unlucky with that referee's decision'; 'we were weakened by two injuries'; 'their number eight had a particularly good game: that run was unstoppable.'

The same poet Archilochus comforts himself similarly in a well-known verse fragment in which he both laments the loss of his shield in battle and comforts himself that he can get another one just as good. To place such an incident in context: to drop one's shield and run from the hoplite formation called a phalanx was considered the epitome of cowardice and was punishable automatically by death in Sparta. Clearly such draconian conditions did not apply in Archilochus' state, the island of Paros.[2]

> A Saïan [Thracian] is crowing over my shield. I left it
>   by a bush.
> Nothing wrong with the shield: I was sorry to leave it.
> But I saved my own skin. Never mind. What's it to me?
> Let it go. Soon I'll get another just as good.
> (Archilochus fr. 5)

33 Hoplites engaging, accompanied by an *aulos* (flute) player, detail of the Chigi Vase, *c.* 640 BC.

One step further along the line from tragedy to comedy, and a world away from Homer, Theophrastus' Cowardly Man reacts to the noise and confusion of battle (around 317 BC) in a way that, I imagine, strikes a chord with many readers: how would we acquit ourselves if asked to fight hand-to-hand with spear and sword against an enemy whose lives depended on killing us first? At the same time, we notice how very different military service must have been in cities and armies other than those of Sparta. The Cowardly Man would not have lasted long there. Here is how he tries to avoid the danger (*Characters* no. 25, *Deilia*, Cowardice):

> And hearing the din of battle and seeing men falling, he says to his comrades that, in his haste, he forgot to pick up his sword and runs back to the tent. Telling his slave to keep a watch out for where the enemy are, he hides it under his pillow and then spends much time pretending to look for it.
>
> And, seeing one of his friends being brought back to camp wounded, he runs over and, telling him to be brave, says he'll take charge. Tending the man and sponging away the blood, he sits beside him, shooing away the flies, and doing anything but engage with the enemy.
>
> When the bugle call sounds the attack, sitting in his tent, he says 'To hell with him! Won't he allow a body to get some sleep with all his bugle-playing?'

One of the tenets of narratology is that 'immersion' – that is, the immersive experience of the reader when reading a narrative – works best when the reader is confronted not with a plethora of descriptive detail, which tends to blunt the attention rather than engaging it, but rather with actions performed by the agents in the narrative, which the reader can 'reperform' in their imagination. In this way, the reader of the above passage of Theophrastus can vividly imagine what it is like to hide in one's tent, pretending to look for the sword that one has just hidden oneself, while the battle rages outside. Likewise a reader's imagination falls into step with the Coward's attempt to avoid danger by attending to a casualty who has been brought back to camp, rather than sallying forth to fight. It is said that although one might be utterly sedentary on the living-room couch, watching a tennis match or a boxing match on TV causes one's own mental faculties and, to a degree, one's nerves and muscles to mimic those of the contestants on screen. In other words, these mini character sketches of Theophrastus are extremely immersive as they consist of a selection of behavioural traits exhibited by a certain character type. The reader has no difficulty putting themselves in the place of the type being characterized by Theophrastus. By analogy with the saying 'one picture is worth a thousand words,' a mental image evoked by immersive writing is worth a thousand words of description, however detailed and accurate.[3]

The Greek word for courage is *andreia*, which is clearly derived from *anēr*, man, with its genitive *andros*. Yet not all men are courageous, as the previous two passages show, and plenty of women are. Courage altogether seems to have been seen as an elusive quality. In Homer, courage, strength and success are 'breathed' into heroes by gods and goddesses standing beside their protégés like seconds in the boxing ring. The image is perhaps not a bad representation of what we now explain as a 'surge of adrenaline' kicking in to increase sporting performance. I suspect most of us have less idea what adrenaline is, or looks like, than the archaic Greeks had a mental image of Athena, Apollo, Artemis or Poseidon.

The dialogue that Plato devoted to courage, *Laches*, shows Socrates in conversation with two seasoned generals, Laches and Nikias. The men have met with two fathers to watch a display of 'fighting in arms' by a solo performer in order to see whether this would be a good discipline for the fathers' children to learn and practise in order to become brave men. Nikias and Laches take opposing positions on this question, with Nikias ready to accept that it might be a good partial training for military service, while Laches expresses scepticism. He says that this man whose performance they have been watching – appropriately called Stēsileōs, which means something like 'bulwark of the people' – is more show than true grit. He says he saw him in real action once, when Stēsileōs was an armed combatant on a warship that attacked a cargo vessel. Stēsileōs fought with an odd weapon, a sort of sickle attached to a spear-shaft. The curved blade of this weapon became entangled in the rigging of the cargo ship and, instead of inflicting any damage with his weapon, Stēsileōs was dragged along the length of the warship as it overtook the cargo vessel, as he clung on to the shaft of his weapon. Finally he was forced to let go of the spear handle and let the weapon dangle harmlessly from where it was caught in the rigging – to gales of laughter from his fellow crew members, according to Laches (*Laches* 183c ff.). Laches means that Stēsileōs may be a good solo performer or entertainer, but his skill and dexterity are no use to him in a real battle.

Laches suggests, on Socrates' prompting, that one might define 'courage' as the ability to stand one's ground on the battlefield. This, indeed, was the prime quality of the good hoplite fighter, as the phalanx depended on all men standing side by side, holding their shield so as to protect their neighbour. If one man 'threw in the towel' (his shield), he exposed the whole formation to danger. Socrates, however, is quick to point out that not all forms of fighting, all requiring bravery, depend on standing one's ground. The Scythian horsemen, for example, he says, shoot their arrows both when they ride into the attack and when they rapidly retreat: for them, courage has nothing to do with standing one's ground.

Laches' second try at a definition of courage is that it is steadfastness, resilience, resoluteness: Greek *karteria*. Perhaps, says Socrates, but there is also resoluteness in bad things such as spending money, or overeating: is this courage? Laches again has to concede that courage does not seem to be simply *karteria*. Now he adds 'sensible' to resoluteness: courage is resilience, backed by good sense or knowledge (of what's right or wrong). Socrates promptly punctures that by asking who is braver – the man who is an expert swordsman and stands his ground, or the man who is not expert in swordsmanship but who nevertheless stands his ground in a swordfight? Laches reluctantly concedes that the man who is not an expert is, in this case, braver. At this point Laches admits *aporia*, being at his wits' end, and hands the discussion to Nikias to see if he can do any better. We note that Socrates has chipped away at Laches' quite reasonable proposals by objecting, in sophistic manner, that the definitions are not always applicable, and are therefore flawed.

Nikias does not fare any better when he attempts to answer Socrates' question 'what is courage?' (the argument is a little diffuse to summarize here). The dialogue is of the type known as aporetic, meaning it ends in impasse. One notes that Socrates' style of debating is to pick logical holes in an interlocutor's position. He always claims that this is not to be annoying but in the hope of finding the truth in partnership with the interlocutor through a dialectic process. But the nagging style of intellectual nit-picking does grate on the reader. Can we define courage purely through words? Is it not more like a feeling, less like a move on a chess board? Socrates famously held that a person is 'good' insofar as he (or she) is 'wise' (*sophos*): a 'good' economist is the person who knows the subject inside out; a good doctor is an expert in medicine, and so on. But this is a purely intellectual, or cognitive, position. What is conspicuously absent are the emotions. For example, a very clever medical expert may be a not very good doctor through lacking other qualities such as communication, patience or empathy.

Xenophon in his *Memorabilia* also takes up the subject of courage and seems to be correcting Socrates' position in the *Laches* as he, too, refers to the Scythian style of fighting, and he, probably deliberately, adds the dimension of 'inborn' courage to the discussion, showing perhaps that he is aware that Plato's take on the subject is inadequate in that regard. Nor should we forget that Xenophon had considerable military experience, in particular on the Expedition of Kyros (*Kyrou Anabasis*), which involved leading Greek mercenaries back from the wilds of Asiē (Anatolia) to the Black Sea, then the Bosporus in 401 BC. He introduces the section by saying that Socrates was once asked whether courage was 'innate' or 'taught', to which he answered:

> I think that as one body is born stronger in labours than another, so one person [*psychē*, lit. 'soul'] is naturally more resilient than another when it comes to dangers. For I observe that people raised in the same customs and conventions differ widely from each other in valour [*tolmē*]. However, I also think that everybody's nature is improved with regard to bravery through learning and training. Clearly Scythians

> and Thracians would not dare to take up shields and spears and fight it out with Spartans. Nor would Spartans care to be pitted against Thracians with slings or with bows against Scythians. Similarly I observe that in all other areas people both differ widely from one another by nature and improve greatly by training. (*Memorabilia* 3.9.1–3)

That seems a sensible position with which we might readily concur. Even West Indians can compete in the Winter Olympics given the right preparation, even if their own country has no snow. One notes in this passage the Spartans' reputation for hoplite warfare, the Scythians' prowess as archers on horseback and the Thracians' use of 'slings'. Courage alone is not enough; a good horse must also be trained to clear the jumps through practice. Sport scientists talk nowadays of movements in sport becoming automated, or internalized, through repetition and practice. The brain learns to execute certain skilful movements automatically, and therefore more quickly and efficiently. One might add to Xenophon's account that confidence in any activity, fighting included, grows with practice and proficiency, so that natural bravery can be augmented by the confidence that comes from training. In Archilochus' narrative above, we saw how his poem was aimed at restoring the confidence of his side after it had suffered a blow through an unexpected occurrence (some *force majeure*, as we saw). One cannot train for the unexpected, Archilochus is saying.

War Is the Father

It is possible, and has often been claimed, that one war fought in Greece in the early fifth century BC was indeed the father of Greece's fate for the coming centuries until Greece became part of the Roman Empire, and possibly thereby the father of European history altogether. Some Greek city-states clubbed together in 480 BC and managed to fight off an invasion of some two million soldiers (as counted by Herodotus) led by the Persian king Xerxes.[4] Xerxes was told by his advisers that, if he defeated the Spartans, no other people would oppose him anywhere. We have already encountered some of the oracles cited by Herodotus during the Persian Wars and Xerxes' various dreams before taking the decision to invade in Chapter Four. A sequence of engagements saw off the Persians. First, a relative success in a naval battle at Cape Artemision, off the island of Euboea. Then the Spartan resistance to the Persian advance by land at Thermopylai. Then the resounding victory in a sea battle off the island of Salamis, close to Athens. After Salamis, Xerxes decided to withdraw. The Persian war effort continued under the leadership of Mardonios. His (still huge) army was then defeated at Plataia, just north of Athens, mainly by the Spartans and Athenians, while the remains of Xerxes' forces were defeated on the same day at Mykalē, across the Aegean Sea in Asia Minor (4 Boedromion (roughly September) 479 BC). That is the bald outline, which has been dealt with repeatedly and in minutest detail in the history books. It is as well to remember that we would have little idea of this momentous struggle without Herodotus' account, written in the second half of the fifth century. Herodotus' style is not particularly immersive; it is rambling, inclusive, almost chatty. The narrative momentum is constantly held up by excursuses and diversions, all interesting and informative in themselves (and invaluable for historians) but the opposite of gripping. His account is like a slow, stopping train, or a tourist bus meandering through a great capital city, with an excellently informed tour guide determined to tell the passengers everything he knows about the sights and stories encountered along the way. In this, his *Histories* (*Historiai*, whose literal meaning is Studies or Investigations) are the opposite of Thucydides, whose *History of the Peloponnesian War* is one of the most immersive works of history ever written. We will look at a section of that, too, below.

As throughout, my purpose here is not to write, or interpret, history but to try to convey an impression of what the experience must have been like. Let us start with the famous Three Hundred Spartans who held up the Persian advance in a narrow defile in Phokis called Thermopylai. As I said, Herodotus is not good on the individual experience of the people in his narrative, or what one might call psychological depth, but his narrative here is immersive enough and allows one to imagine what the Spartans (and some Thespians) must have experienced. His lack of focus on the fighting individuals,

34 Hoplite warriors, shown with naked bodies, fighting with spears, helmets and shields (the inscriptions are meaningless). Side A of an Attic black-figure Tyrrhenian neck amphora, *c.* 540 BC, by the Fallow Deer Painter.

or the pathos of war, is in strong contrast to what we have seen in Homer's *Iliad*. Herodotus himself may not be entirely to blame. Prose writing was a relatively new art form in his day; predecessors such as Hekataios may have been even less focused, less experienced in transferring the narrative art of epic poetry to the new medium. Prose was called in Greek *lexis eiromenē*, which means 'strung together speech'. The verb involved, *eirō*, string together, could be applied to beads on a necklace, for example. Herodotus' prose style is very like a long chain of beads, each gleaming and polished in its own right but somehow unable to cohere collectively into a larger, more majestic whole.

Thermopylai

It takes until near the end of Herodotus' seventh book (out of nine) finally to get round to describing the engagement at Thermopylai in Phokis between three hundred Spartiates (high-ranking Spartans), led by Leōnidas, a 'descendant of Herakles' (Heraclid) by birth, and the Persians. In chapters 175–87 of Book 7, the Greeks decide to make a stand against the advancing Persian hordes: by land at the narrow pass of Thermopylai and at sea at Cape Artemision. Other Greeks advocate retreating to the Isthmos (of Corinth) and defending that against a Persian invasion, but the Spartans insist on making a stand at this point. Preparations and preliminaries to battle are described by Herodotus in chapters 207–21. The actual battle and its aftermath occupy chapters 223–34. The main story is easily told. The Three Hundred under Leōnidas hold off the Persian advance valiantly for several days until a local, Ephialtes, tells the Persians there is a way round the pass of Thermopylai through the mountains so that a force taking this route could bypass the blockade and attack from the rear. Even when the Spartans notice the Persian force above them on this path and realize they are doomed, they continue to fight, knowing they will be attacked from the rear, too. Leōnidas falls; there is fighting over his corpse. The Three Hundred are wiped out. Poets get busy composing epigrams on the valour of the fallen. Tactically, the Spartans have achieved very little: they have held up the Persian invasion for days rather than months. In terms of morale and courage, however, their stand became legendary, and somehow symbolic of the Greek defiance in the face of Persia's vast numerical superiority. Leōnidas' stand came to represent Greece's stand against the invaders. We saw something similar in the Ukrainian war in the determined resistance of fighters in Mariupol on the Sea of Azov, outnumbered and outgunned by the Russian artillery. They fought on to the bitter end, too, until defeat was inevitable.

In the build-up to the battle itself, Herodotus dwells on some details that enable us to enter the minds of the Spartans, to a degree. A spy is sent by Xerxes to see how many Greeks are facing up to him at the pass, and what they are doing. The spy rides up to the defensive wall blocking the pass and observes the Spartan contingent who are posted outside the wall; the remaining force is invisible to him behind the wall. The Spartans, he observes, are either exercising or combing their hair, which they wore long, like the Homeric warriors before them who were described as 'long-haired Achaeans' (*karē komoōntes Achaioi*). Puzzled both by the small number of warriors and by their strangely nonchalant behaviour, the spy returns and reports to Xerxes, who is similarly nonplussed. He summons his Greek adviser, Dēmarātos, and asks him what it means. Dēmarātos says:

> You heard what I said earlier about these men, when we were planning the invasion of Greece. You mocked me then when I told you how our plans were likely to proceed. It is my highest priority, Your Highness, to tell you the truth. So listen now. These men are here to stop our invasion [of Greece] and they are preparing themselves for the fight. It is their custom when they are about to lay their lives on the line that they formally arrange their hair. (*Histories* 7.209.7–15)

Such limbering up and preening is more typical of the *palaistra*, sportsground, he feels, than the battlefield. Now Dēmarātos tells the Persian king that it is in fact the Spartan way of preparing themselves mentally and physically for death on the battlefield, a kind of meditative ritual to concentrate the mind. The previous occasion to which he refers, when he had told the king about the Spartan mindset, was earlier in Book 7 (101–4), just after Xerxes' army had crossed the pontoon bridges over the Hellespont and begun their march through Thrace towards Greece. There Xerxes had questioned Dēmarātos, himself an exiled Spartan king, about the Greeks. Dēmarātos had answered that the Spartans were the best among them and would resist subjugation by Xerxes regardless of the size of the army facing them, and regardless of whether they stood alone among the Greeks. A Spartan, Dēmarātos says, is willing to fight ten men. Xerxes scoffs, saying men might fight when outnumbered if they were whipped and coerced by their commander. But the Spartans, he says, enjoy freedom (*eleutheria*): why on earth would they risk their lives in an unequal contest? Dēmarātos explains:

> They may be free, but not in all respects. They have a master, ancestral custom [*nomos*], of which they stand in greater awe than your men of you. They do its bidding. Its order is always the same: not to run from any number of men in battle, but to hold the line and either win, or die. If you think these my words are nonsense, I will hold my tongue in future. (7.104.16–23)

Xerxes laughs indulgently, taking Dēmarātos' words, perhaps, as an expression of pride in his Spartan heritage, even though Dēmarātos had expressly denied this, as he had been humiliated and exiled by his own countrymen.[5] At Thermopylai his words turn out not to have been empty.

Following the exchange with Dēmarātos, Xerxes waits several days to see whether the enemy will abandon their position. They do not. First Xerxes sends Medes into the attack at the pass, but they are cut to pieces by the more experienced Greek fighters and fail. Of course, Xerxes' forces were vastly superior numerically, but they could not take advantage of that in the confined space at Thermopylai. On one side of the road along the coast were steep mountains; on the other, the sea, or better, swampland. It was said that the width of the pass was sufficient only for one horse-cart. Nowadays the coast is further seaward, through silting. On the following day, Xerxes sent his so-called 'immortal' Persians (rather like modern-day SEALS) into battle, but they too were inferior to the Spartans, who employed a tactic of appearing to retreat, then turning and, in perfect formation, facing the enemy chasing them and inflicting heavy casualties.

At that juncture, when Xerxes was becoming exasperated, Ephialtes, a local, told him about the hill path round the pass to the rear of the Greeks' defensive position. Here Herodotus inserts two short excursuses, which deflate any suspense beginning to build in the reader's mind (what happens next?). He relates Ephialtes' subsequent fate after betraying the Greeks at Thermopylai, how he met his end in exile, killed in fact for another reason! Herodotus also tells us of an alternative version of the betrayal of the Greek position – it was not Ephialtes but others who betrayed them – only to say that he does not believe this version (7.213–14). Clearly Herodotus is more interested in preserving the record than gripping future readers.

He picks up the narrative thread again in section 215. Xerxes is pleased by Ephialtes' promise and picks officers and men for the rear-guard action along the mountain path. They walk the whole night and reach the top at dawn. There the Greek force defending the path, consisting of men from Phokis, take to their heels when Persian arrows rain down on them. The Persians do not chase them but make their way down the mountain as quickly as possible, behind the Greek lines. These latter get wind of the Persian ambush, while it is still dark, both from defectors and their own watchmen. The seer Megistias is said to have consulted the omens (the liver of a sheep) and declared that death would come with the dawn. At that point the Greeks are divided whether to stay and fight or to flee to safety. Finally, most leave, leaving the Spartans accompanied only by Thespians (voluntarily) and Thebans (unwillingly). Herodotus suggests that Leōnidas sent the remainder of the Greeks home so as to magnify his own glory in staying, although – or rather, because – the Delphic oracle had said before the war that either Sparta would fall to the Persians, or their king, a descendant of Herakles, would die; the oracle seemed to be saying that if Leōnidas sacrificed himself, Sparta would emerge victorious. Leōnidas also gave permission for the seer Megistias to leave, as he was said to be descended from Melampous (a legendary seer); Megistias declined but sent his only son home to preserve the line. These details given by Herodotus go some way towards increasing narrative suspense before the showdown, rather as in the Western *The Magnificent Seven* (1960), when the Seven prepare for the final onslaught by Calvera's band, each performing individual preparatory rituals, expecting death.

Herodotus manages to blunt the drama of the battle itself by adding names and family trees to some of the Greeks and Persians who fall in the final engagement. He adds that he managed to establish the names of all the three hundred who fought and fell there, although he spares the reader the full list at this juncture.[6] First the Spartans face off against the Persians before the rearguard contingent with Ephialtes arrives. Leōnidas falls in the fierce fighting; the Spartans and the Persians fight over his body, and the Spartans manage to retrieve it. Then the contingent from the mountain path arrives and the fight swings. The Spartans withdraw to a small hill and continue to fight with knives, and literally tooth and claw. They are pelted with stones from all sides by the Persians until all are dead. This is the spot where the cenotaph in their honour, Herodotus says, stands.

When the narrative dust settles, so to speak, Herodotus, in a reprise of the battle, fills in some individual feats and fates among the Three Hundred. The description that follows is reminiscent of

Homer's description of the *aristeia*, moment of glory or pinnacle of achievement, of individual fighters.

> Of the Spartans and Thespians who acquitted themselves in this manner, one Spartan in particular called Diēnekēs excelled. They say he made the following remark before the battle against the Medes. On hearing one of the men of Trachis say that, when the enemy fired their bows, they eclipsed the sun with the sheer number of their arrows, he appeared untroubled, saying merely that he was not impressed by their numbers; what their friend from Trachis had said was very good news. If the Medes shut out the sun, they could fight them in the shade and not under the sun. This and a number of other such remarks the Spartan Diēnekēs is said to have left to posterity. (*Histories* 7.226.1–12)

The remark shows that Spartan valour was a question not only of deeds but of speech: short, pithy, memorable remarks – that was what was meant by 'laconic'. Herodotus names a few others who had distinguished themselves in various ways and cites the epigrams that were composed for the dead (and displayed on their cenotaph at the site), including the famous epigram composed by Simonides commemorating the Three Hundred, also laconic in its understated style:

> Passer-by, tell the Lakedaimonians that here
> we lie buried, obedient to their commands. (7.228)

and one for Megistias the seer, who had chosen to remain:

> This is the tomb of famous Megistias, whom the Medes
> killed after crossing the River Spercheios.
> A seer, he clearly foresaw Death approaching then,
> but chose not to leave his commander's side. (7.228)

He then launches into another, rather convoluted account of two among the Three Hundred, who had been discharged by Leōnidas because they were suffering from ophthalmia (and presumably could not see). The account opens a window both on the Spartan attitude to anything that could be construed as cowardice, and Herodotus' desire to scrutinize the stories he had collected and told. His attention to detail is commendable, but at the same time this very quality detracts from the immersive quality of his history. After the narrative *kairos* (key moment) of Thermopylai we find ourselves tied up in the intricacies of two men's illness and the effect that had on their participation in the battle. It is as if a modern historian were to describe D-Day and get tied up in the problems one landing craft had with its transmission.

Two of the Three Hundred, Eurytos and Aristodēmos, had been discharged by Leōnidas on the eve of battle as they were both suffering from a serious eye infection. Herodotus comments that all would have been well if they had only acted jointly: they could have both returned to Sparta, and nobody would have held it against them. Or they could have chosen together to remain and share in the fate of the others. However, they 'could not agree but were divided in their resolve' (7.229.7–8). Eurytos called for his armour and asked to be led to the battle (he could not see). The slave escorting him ran off, he entered the fray and was killed. Aristodēmos, on the other hand, had lost consciousness and was left behind. 'If they had both escaped together,' Herodotus comments, 'the Spartans would in my opinion have harboured no grudge against them at all. As it was, since one of them died while the other, who was in exactly the same situation, had not been prepared to die, it was inevitable that they were very angry with Aristodēmos' (7.229.15–19).

If this was not complicated enough – Eurytos' choice to fight (although he presumably was not fit to do so) made Aristodēmos look bad in Spartan eyes, as being less courageous than Eurytos – what follows muddies the waters altogether, as Herodotus relates an alternative version of Aristodēmos' survival, which also pivots on the question of cowardice and bravery. According to this, Aristodēmos and another man had been sent as messengers from the camp; Aristodēmos had lingered along the way and missed the battle, while his fellow messenger had returned in time for the battle and had been killed.

In either case. Aristodēmos faced social exclusion when he returned to Sparta, being dubbed 'Aristodēmos the Spineless' (7.230–31). Herodotus adds that Aristodēmos was rehabilitated in the subsequent Battle of Plataia (later in that campaigning season), when he fought valiantly. As a final touch, he narrates how yet another of the Three Hundred, one Pantitēs, had also been sent as a messenger to Thessaly and had survived. When *he* returned to Sparta, he was also vilified, and hanged himself (unlike Aristodēmos).

One's head is left somewhat spinning from this account of two individuals who had *not* shared the fate of the Three Hundred but who had been branded cowards, not, one feels, through any fault of their own. Instead of giving an immersive account of the battle itself, Herodotus has, as it were through the back door, conveyed the Spartan dedication to valour in battle to his readers. It is a very indirect method, and it was not his primary purpose: he could take it for granted that his contemporary readers were all familiar with Spartan military discipline. But for the modern reader his account gives useful glimpses of the ethical backdrop against which the suicidal bravery of the Three Hundred should be seen. Even a man dying of an eye infection (modern sepsis?) was not absolved from his duty to show courage at least equivalent to those fighting to the death.

Olpai, 426 BC

Fast-forward half a century and the cities of Greece are no longer fighting off an aggressor and standing (to some extent) together but are locked in an internecine war known as the Peloponnesian War. It was fought basically between Sparta and Athens and their respective allies in two phases between 431 and 404 BC. The war produced its own monumental work of history, written by an Athenian, Thucydides, who was himself an Athenian general at one stage but fell into disrepute by failing in one command and spent the time afterwards writing a history of the war down to 411 BC, at which point his work breaks off. He writes annalistically, that is, dealing with events year by year, and covers all the various theatres of the war from a lofty, almost Olympian stance. His work is much more intellectual than Herodotus' histories. He claims at the beginning that he wishes it to be a 'possession for all time', so that future generations can learn from it. He says that the 'truest reason' for the war was the Spartans' resentment of Athens' rise to greatness (1.23.6), and exploitation of its empire, known as the Delian League. Athens, it was said, was behaving like a tyrant towards the subject states. The Athenians were Ionians, the Spartans Dorians. The war had an ethnic axis as well as a political one. It was a fight between the two major groupings of Greeks, who both spoke Greek but with different vowel sounds and word forms and, to a degree, vocabulary.

A battle that took place in the northwest of Greece in 426 BC is a good example of the issues and aspects involved in the Peloponnesian War as a whole, and also of Thucydides' treatment of it. Although he was by no means partisan in his support of the Athenian cause, he was no impartial military historian reporting dryly on battles, logistics and strategies. On the contrary, his work has a tragic flavour. He involves the reader in the narrative in an almost uncanny way. While maintaining an analytic, intellectual stance, he nevertheless manages to expose the emotions involved in the fighting, the experiences of the participants.

The battle took place in a small region on the Bay of Ambrakia. In a way it was a battle between local peoples: the Ambrakiots on the north side of the bay, and the Akarnanians and Amphilochians (considered barbarians by the Ambrakiots) to the east. But what gave it greater than local significance was the involvement of the major powers of the Peloponnesians under the command of Eurylochos on the one hand, siding with the Ambrakiots, and on the other the Athenians siding with the Akarnanians under their commander Demosthenes. Thus this minor theatre of war illustrated the typical pattern of the Peloponnesian War: the Greek cities, great and small, took sides in the conflict between Athens and Sparta. They benefited in local conflicts and rivalries with their neighbours from support from the major powers, but the latter were not acting selflessly. On the contrary, they sought to extend their own power bases by enlisting, or rather coercing, regional powers to support them in the Panhellenic conflict. As said above, the basic axis for these divisions was between Ionians and Dorians. Thucydides' account is both complex and meticulously clear. The following summary is much simplified, in order to highlight certain aspects.

A contingent of Ambrakiots with the Peloponnesian force under Eurylochos (a Spartan) took a hill called Olpai at the eastern extremity of the Bay of Ambrakia, with a view to attacking a town just south of that along the coast, Amphilochian Argos. Against this the Akarnanians called on the Athenians under Demosthenes for assistance, as well as a small Athenian fleet stationed in the Ambrakiot Bay under one Aristoteles. Demosthenes stationed his combined force just south of Olpai. The Ambrakiots with Eurylochos, fearing they might be encircled, sent back to Ambrakia for reinforcements. On the sixth day, the first battle took place. Demosthenes positioned himself and the Athenians on the right wing of the phalanx, where he faced the Peloponnesians under Eurylochos. However, he feared that the Peloponnesians on their left wing would outflank his right wing, being more numerous. To forestall this, he sent an ambush party of four hundred hoplites and light-armoured soldiers to hide 'in a sunken track with much undergrowth', from which they could fall on the enemy from the rear when the time came (*History of the Peloponnesian War* 3.107.3). Demosthenes' ploy worked. The ambush fell on the enemy's left flank from the rear (the weak point of a phalanx of hoplites) and spread panic. The remaining Ambrakiot line, seeing their strongest part in disarray, likewise turned and fled. The right flank of the enemy, however, prevailed, routing the Akarnanian left and pursuing them back towards Argos. However, when they wished to return to camp in Olpai, the victorious Akarnanians fell on them and inflicted many more casualties (3.107–8). The battle went on until sundown.

Eurylochos and another commander fell in this battle. His place was taken by one Makarios. He feared, following this defeat, that the Peloponnesian force at Olpai would likely perish before the reinforcements from Ambrakia arrived. He negotiated terms of surrender with Demosthenes, who secretly agreed that the Peloponnesians would be allowed to withdraw, but not the Ambrakiots. 'He wanted', says Thucydides, 'to leave the Ambrakiots and their mercenary force defenceless, but principally to bring the Spartans and Peloponnesians

35 Detail of a map of ancient Greece, northern part (dated 1844), showing the Gulf of Ambrakia with Amphilochian Argos and Olpai.

into disrepute with the local Greeks for looking after their own interests first and foremost' (3.109). After the dead had been recovered from this battle (three hundred on the Athenian side, many more on the Ambrakiot), news reaches Demosthenes that the reinforcements were now on their way from Ambrakia, the entire fighting force of the city, who were unaware that their army in Olpai had been defeated. In response, Demosthenes sends a large skirmishing party north, to intercept these reinforcements and take up positions on the high ground at a place called Idomenē.

Back at Olpai, the Peloponnesians (who had secretly been promised safe passage by Demosthenes) say they are going out foraging for firewood and victuals (to deceive the Ambrakiots) but in fact abscond. When the Ambrakiots realize this, they set off in hot pursuit, not wanting to be left defenceless at Olpai. The Akarnanians, seeing this general exodus (which had not been agreed), stand in the way of the retreat and threaten force against them, Peloponnesians and all. Finally, the Akarnanians abide by the previous agreement (to let the Peloponnesians go), but lay into the rest: 'And there was considerable dispute and disagreement who was an Ambrakiot and who a Peloponnesian,' Thucydides says. One can well imagine. Some two hundred are killed, but the rest manage to escape over the border, where a local king, Salynthios, gives them shelter.

However, now the reinforcements from Ambrakia, still unaware of what has happened, are approaching Idomenē and the forces waiting to meet them there. Demosthenes allows his army at Olpai to eat dinner, then orders a forced march through the night to join up in Idomenē, where:

> At first light they fall upon the Ambrakiots, who are still in their beds and taken totally by surprise. They even thought the attackers were on their own side. Demosthenes had deliberately placed the Messenians [Messenia is in the Peloponnese] at the front and told them to call out in the Dorian dialect, thus gaining the confidence of the watchmen. Moreover, it was dark and their faces could not be seen. (3.112)

Thucydides' description of the rout that follows exemplifies how narrative details secure the reader's immersion in the fate of the unfortunate Ambrakiots:

> The Ambrakiots were immediately put to flight. Most were killed there and then, but some managed to escape to the mountains. There the mountain paths had already been secured by the Amphilochians, who were familiar with their own terrain and lightly armed while the Ambrakiot hoplites did not know which way to turn. They fell into the ravines and the ambushes along the paths and were killed. All manner of escape routes were tried. Some even turned towards the sea, which was not far away, and when they saw the Athenian ships sailing past there they tried to swim towards them, thinking

> in their state of panic that it would be preferable to die at their hands if necessary rather than at the hands of their hated arch-enemies the barbaric Amphilochians. (3.112)

Athenian tragedy knew the formal element of a messenger speech, which follows on after the disaster or death in the play. Perhaps Thucydides had this in mind when he closed his narrative of this section of the war with a messenger sent by the Ambrakiots, who have found refuge after the first battle at Olpai with King Salynthios. He has come to request permission to collect the bodies of the fallen with their armour following the retreat from Olpai. When he sees the huge pile of armour collected from the Ambrakiot reinforcements killed at Idomenē, he is surprised and taken aback, as he is unaware of this second battle. Extraordinarily, Thucydides records the interview between this messenger and an anonymous interlocutor:

> Someone asked him why he was surprised. How many casualties had he been expecting? The herald said around two hundred. The man who had asked the question replied: 'Well, these don't seem to be them, then. There are more than a thousand here.' 'No, they don't seem to belong to the men who were fighting with us.' The other said: 'They do if you are referring to the battle at Idomenē yesterday.' 'We did not fight at all yesterday,' said the herald, 'but the day before yesterday during our retreat.' 'We fought against these men', came the answer, 'yesterday when they came as reinforcements from the city of Ambrakia.' When the herald heard this, he understood that the reinforcements from the city had been wiped out. He groaned out loud and, distraught at the magnitude of the disaster, immediately left without accomplishing his mission or requesting the bodies of the fallen any longer. (3.113)

Thucydides adds that this was the 'largest disaster' to befall any one city in Greece in this war in an equivalent span of time:

> I have not recorded the number of casualties, as the number of men who are said to have died does not seem credible given the size of the city. But I know one thing. If the Akarnanians and Amphilochians had wanted to take Ambrakia under Demosthenes' command, they would have done so without so much as a fight. However, they did not want this, as they were afraid that the Athenians might be even more dangerous neighbours [than the Ambrakiots] if they took control of the town. (3.113)

That last sentence reveals so much. The Akarnanian side were happy enough to ally themselves with the mighty Athenians when it helped them defeat their neighbours the Ambrakiots. But the thought that Athens would then be sitting on their doorsteps in Ambrakia as their overlords – no thank you. The episode is of relatively minor significance for the course of the Peloponnesian War, but it encapsulates in a local theatre of war many of the defining elements of the larger struggle. Complexity and tragedy are the keynotes of Thucydides' vision.

Lady Luck

Now we skip approximately a century. Following the Macedonian conquest of Greece in the later fourth century BC, in combination with Alexander's conquest of large areas of Asia Minor and North Africa, the Greek world was subject to the Macedonian court based in Pella, and then to the so-called Successors (of Alexander), who established their capitals at Alexandria, Antioch and Pella and divided up the whole *oikoumenē*, or then 'inhabited world', into kingdoms. The Greek city-states lost their individual importance and influence and became subjects of their Macedonian rulers. These last fought with each other, with their eastern (India) and western neighbours (Carthage: Phoenicians), so that there was a big demand for mercenaries, that is, Greeks who were no longer fighting for their cities in a patriotic effort but for *merces*, pay. Leaving the wide field of history to others, let us look here at one curious interaction: that between

Menander's Athenian comedy, which was written around the turn of the fourth century BC, and the world of these mercenaries from once respectable and proud *poleis*. Menander is, on the face of it, completely oblivious to the historical and political issues involved in the wars of the Diadochoi (Successors), as we will be, but very interested in individual Athenian mercenaries who fought overseas for Macedonian masters and, in so doing, acquired the wealth with which to impress a pretty *hetaira* and win her affection. Lucian's *Dialogues of Hetairai* are also full of these show-off warriors (some more show than warrior); we met one earlier.

Kleostratos in Menander's play *Aspis* (The Shield) is one such mercenary fighting in Lycia, but for whom or against whom is not said. The play begins with his old *paidagōgos* (guardian, roughly), Daos, coming on stage carrying a shield and accompanied by a group of prisoners traipsing along behind him. He explains how his master Kleostratos had left home to fight abroad and make his fortune, partly to support his sister, whom he intended to marry to a high-status groom on his return. Now Daos is carrying only the shield while the owner, his master, has fallen. The opening scene is played between Daos, who laments his late master, and an uncle, Smikrines, who, as he listens to Daos' account of Kleostratos' fate, realizes there is a fortune to be had by marrying Kleostratos' sister, who has become his heiress (*epiklēros*). While Daos is focused on the pathos of war, Smikrines' greed, expressed in interjections throughout Daos' narrative, becomes apparent. Menander interweaves the two currents – of bereavement and greed – with typical artistry, striking a comic spark from the hard rock of war and death in battle. To Smikrines' question of how Kleostratos had died, Daos says: 'For a soldier, Smikrines, it's hard to find a way to survive, but all too easy a way to die' (ll. 20–21).

Daos explains how Kleostratos' company had won a number of battles against the 'barbarians' (non-Greek speakers, Lycians in this case) and had lowered their guard somewhat. The enemy had fled; the Greeks left camp rather too readily to plunder, take prisoners and cut the enemy crops. 'Perhaps it was not such a good thing to have been so successful,' comments Daos. 'Setbacks breed caution. With us, over-confidence led us to being unprepared for what was coming' (ll. 27–30). Daos says his master, in this spree of pillaging and plundering, accrued six hundred gold coins (of some sort), a huge number of drinking cups and a considerable number of prisoners (to be sold for profit): 'Jolly good!' is Smikrines' comment. Kleostratos then sent Daos off with this hoard to Rhodes to a friend – the word is *xenos*, denoting a particular kind of friend: a friendly contact in a foreign city. On the day that Daos left, the enemy covertly occupied a hill before the mercenary camp. In the evening when the mercenaries were back at camp, they indulged themselves with wine, women and song, as the land around 'had everything in abundance'. 'Most were drunk,' says Daos. 'Disgraceful!' Smikrines comments.

Some text in the Florentine parchment is missing here, but when Daos' narrative continues, he is relating the aftermath of what had clearly been a battle during the night when the Lycians launched a surprise attack on the Greek camp:

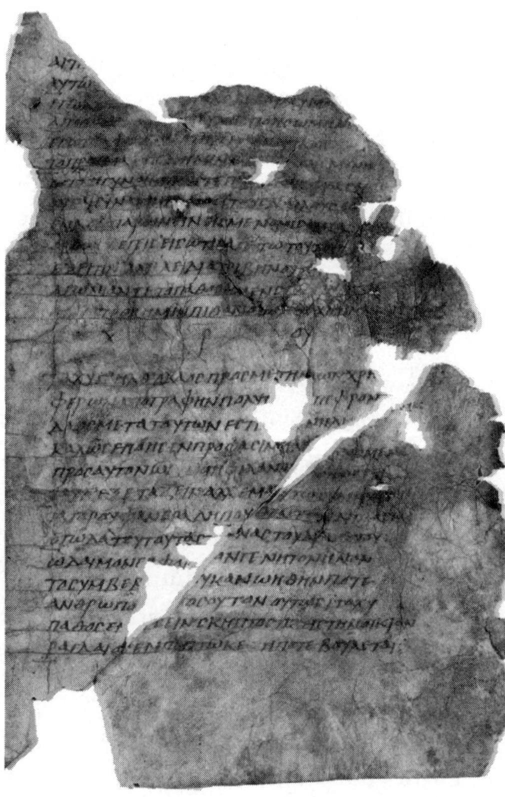

36 Section of the Florence parchment manuscript containing Menander's *Aspis*, or Shield.

> Around midnight it must have been, I was keeping watch over the money and the prisoners, walking in front of my tent, when I hear a commotion, groans, running, cries, men calling to each other by name – I heard what had happened from them. By luck there was a steep hill close by; we all gathered there on the top: cavalrymen, shield-bearers, soldiers – and the wounded – joined us. (*Aspis* 53–62)

Daos went on to tell how they stayed at this makeshift camp for three days, then proceeded back to the main camp where the night fight had taken place. Smikrines is interested in whether there were any witnesses to confirm Kleostratos' death:

> (*Smikrines:*) And you saw *his* body among the dead? (*Daos:*) He wasn't clearly recognizable. They'd been lying there three days already, and their faces were swollen up. (*Smikrines:*) So how do you know? (*Daos:*) He was lying there holding his shield. None of the enemy had taken it, it seems, because it was broken. Our trusty commander told us not to cremate the dead individually and collect up their bones as it would cause a delay. He told us to pile them all together and burn them. After burying them hastily, he ordered us to march. (ll. 68–79)

The communal cremation and burial is important as it prevented any close identification of those who had fallen. Smikrines goes on to question Daos further about the plunder he has managed to save from the debacle. Daos mentions drinking cups worth about forty *mnai* (a lot), clothes, riding coats and the company of prisoners he can see; the rest was lost in the night ambush by the Lycians. Daos shows he understands Smikrines is interested in the amount of booty Daos has brought home, as he taunts him with the address 'heir' (*klēronome*; l. 85). Smikrines huffily replies that he is not in the slightest interested in the material possessions: 'If only *he* [Kleostratos] had lived,' he sighs hypocritically.

Daos' account of the fate of Kleostratos' company of Greek mercenaries far away in Lycia is realistic enough, with vivid details conveying the nastiness of war. It emerges clearly that the Greeks were chiefly intent on personal enrichment rather than fighting for a cause. That is why Kleostratos had sent Daos off to Rhodes to bring his haul of treasure thus far to safety. Up to this point we might wonder where this comedy is going. There has been a tragic death in the family. An uncle has his beady eyes on the booty which has been left. Can that be all? How is Menander going to make a comedy of manners out of this unpromisingly stark beginning?

No sooner has Daos left the stage with all the extras (the prisoners) than a lone female figure enters to deliver the prologue of the play, which was a standard feature of the genre of New Comedy, used to fill the audience in on the background of the play. Typically, this puts the audience 'in the know', while the characters in the play muddle through the tangle of misunderstandings and false assumptions that arise from their being 'in the dark' about the true situation. In this case it is Lady Luck (Tychē) who speaks the prologue and explains what really happened on that occasion in Lycia. I have given, here and above, a prose translation of Menander's impeccable trimeters, in which the lines are written. The trimeter used in New Comedy (Menander's genre) consists basically of three iambic measures (see Note on Metre), but the metre was free enough to accommodate the patterns of conversational speech, with all its nuances.

> (*The Goddess Tychē:*) Now, if anything untoward had happened to these people, it would hardly beseem me, a goddess, to associate with them. As it is, they're wandering in the dark . . . [When someone] announced the enemy attack, they all rushed out in defence, each man picking up whatever armour came to hand. Thus it occurred that the man who was next to Kleostratos ran out carrying his shield and fell immediately. The shield was lying among the fallen and the youth underneath was swollen up and unrecognizable, so Daos made a mistake. Kleostratos, on the other hand, ran out with other arms and was taken prisoner. He's as alive and well as can be. You've [that is, the audience] heard enough now. (ll. 97–113)

Tychē goes on to explain about Smikrines, how he's a despicable character with only one thought in his head: how to enrich himself. Now the play can begin properly. The players all think Kleostratos is dead, so the wrangling over his estate can begin in earnest, while the audience know Kleostratos has been saved by Luck, so the 'unpleasantness' that Tychē wanted to avoid herself (death) is spared them, too, and they can sit back and enjoy the players' antics on stage.

The story is contrived, of course, but the social background is real enough, and Daos' account of the fighting is realistic. Menander's 'soldier plays' – there are several of them[7] – may be seen as offering some light relief to an audience grown weary of the endless wars between Alexander's Successors and their own political irrelevance. From being a state matter, war had become more of an individual adventure, a way, perhaps, of enriching oneself, if one was lucky. That luck plays an enormous role in individual fates in war is self-evident. They say one woman with her child was late arriving at the airport and missed flight MH17 from Amsterdam to Kuala Lumpur in 2014, when the war was beginning in eastern Ukraine. Her husband, when they telephoned, was cross with her and initially she cursed her bad luck.

8
Dress Code

Clothes are not only a way of keeping dry in rain, warm in winter, or otherwise protected from the elements, but, just as important, a form of non-verbal communication with other members of society. They make a statement, whether of gender (or rejection of it), taste, income bracket, status, affiliation, age and no doubt other things. We catch glimpses of Greek dress code in many authors and genres, but the evidence is scattered and unsystematic. This chapter can only offer a taste of some of the factors that may have been relevant to the ancient Greek dress code. Think of just one, simple piece of modern clothing, a pair of jeans, and all the nuances its variants can express. First it was only worn by working men; when women came to wear blue jeans in America, that was already a political statement. Now, decades later, there have been many different styles and cuts, all associated with social movements, groupings, lifestyles: flared, bell-bottom jeans; embroidered flower-power jeans; hipster jeans; hosepipe jeans; torn, cut or patched jeans; bleached or faded jeans; baggy jeans; jeans worn below the seat; jeans worn with suspenders; cut-off jeans, to mention only some. Probably readers of this page (if they are old enough) will remember some of the associations of these various cuts and styles. I doubt that ancient Greek dress was less nuanced. The comparison shows, I think, that it is a hopeless task attempting to retrieve all the signals sent out by ancient Greek garments and accessories, but at least one can try to scratch the surface, or sketch the broad outlines.

Women

First ladies

When Prometheus stole fire from heaven as a gift for mankind, Zeus conceived, according to the Greek myth retold by Hesiod, a curious act of revenge: primordial woman.[1] Instead of constituting a gift to men, the first woman, Pandora, was seen as the source of all evil. Beautiful on the outside, she harboured within her a malevolence and deceit that would make men's lives a living hell. This is how Hesiod tells the fashioning and couture of Pandora, whose name admits the interpretation of 'gift of all'; in other words, she consisted of gifts from all the (important) gods who contributed to her make-up. If a camel is a horse designed by a committee, Pandora was a life-size sex toy assembled by a company of trolls. The scene as envisaged by Hesiod is rather like the dressing of a mannequin in a shop window. Zeus speaking:

> 'I'll give them [humans] recompense for fire. Let them enjoy that, cherishing their own undoing.' So the father of gods and men spoke, and laughed out loud. He ordered renowned Hephaistos [the craftsman god] to set to it and mix some clay, put a human voice in it, and strength, and give it a girl's desirable body as pretty as the immortal goddesses. Athena he told to teach it a woman's works, to weave on a finely crafted loom. And Aphrodite to pour golden beauty over its head, and [give it] sheer sex appeal and knee-weakening desirability. He ordered Hermes to implant in it a foxy mind and tricky character . . .
>
> These were his orders, and they obeyed King Zeus, born of Kronos. Hephaistos shaped her from clay according to Zeus' instructions. Athena, blue-eyed goddess, dressed and decked her out. The immortal Graces and Lady Credibility [lit. 'Persuasion', *Peithō*] hung golden jewellery on her body. The fair-haired Seasons crowned her in the darling buds of May. Pallas Athena beautified every inch of her body. Hermes implanted falsehoods, deceitful speech and a tricky character

in her heart, according to the will of deep-thundering Zeus.
As herald of the gods he gave her a voice, and he named this
woman Pandora because all the gods who live on Olympus
gave her a gift, a bane for men who have to earn a living.
(Hesiod, *Works and Days* 57–81)

The key features of this description are the external beauty of Pandora combined with inner deceitfulness. Pandora is dressed by the gods so as to be irresistibly attractive, but then she proves a bane to men. Hesiod explains: before, men lived happily, untroubled by work and illnesses. Then woman joined him – and now suddenly a new element in the myth is introduced, which Zeus had not even mentioned in the above passage. The woman has a jar (a *pithos*) containing all the ills of the world. And she lifts the lid of this jar and lets them all out, like a virus leaking from an experimental laboratory, and out they fly to plague mankind with all the afflictions and illnesses with which we have become familiar. Only one thing remains at the bottom of the jar, like the lees of wine, and does not escape: hope. Man still has hope, however bad his situation, however desperate his circumstances.

The making of Pandora is retold (or perhaps it was the other way round) in Hesiod's other great epic, the *Theogony*, Birth of the Gods (ll. 571–84), in which greater attention to detail is given to the dressing up of the Pandora mannequin. Taken together, the myth has received a great deal of scholarly attention, which we must mainly leave aside here. It seems, however, that Hesiod's account conflates at least two strands of myth here: on the one hand a myth of the first woman, made in heaven and set beside man in a kind of Garden of Eden to tempt him. The germ of this myth is the labour that men endure when woman arrives, then children, requiring work in the fields to feed them. In this connection it is very important that, at the end of Zeus' instructions, men are described with their traditional epithet of *alphēstēs*, which, in accordance with the dominant interpretation, I have translated as 'who have to earn a living'. In other words, the advent of women necessitates the earning of a living: work, or *labor improbus* (wicked work), as Virgil put it. In the *Theogony* version, Hesiod compares women with drones in a hive, who do nothing but eat, while the workers go out and do all the hard work. But there is another strand of the myth: Pandora's jar, a vessel that she maliciously (or accidentally?) opens and lets out all the world's ills.

In all events, this is the prototype dressing-up episode in myth. Pandora is given a beautiful, irresistible appearance, which men love, while they suffer the consequences of falling for it in terms of work and the sweat of their brow.

By analogy with FLOTUS, one might coin the term FLOTET (First Lady Of The Epic Tradition) for Penelope, Odysseus' wife, who represents a kind of prototype wife of the heroic world in which Homer's *Odyssey* is set. Luckily, she is everything Pandora is not: beautiful but supremely faithful, true, dignified, devoted. She too is deceitful, but in a good way: she deceives the suitors with her endless weaving of a tapestry, which she undoes again by night, to avoid marrying one of them when she finishes it. Odysseus has been gone nearly twenty years by this time. There is also a deceitful dressing scene later

37 A maid helping her mistress to dress, Apulian amphora, 4th century BC. The maid is wearing a simple, monochrome *chitōn*; her mistress holds a mirror and looks at herself wearing a red *chitōn* and a light-coloured top (no *strophion* underneath). The maid holds in her right hand a *kistē* (box) holding clothes, and in her left (probably) a hairnet.

in the *Odyssey*, after Odysseus has returned to Ithaka but before he has revealed himself to Penelope, in which Penelope is beautified by Athena. Ostensibly, this is to make her presentable for the suitors, as she has finally agreed to choose one as husband; in reality, it is to inflame renewed desire in Odysseus, who is now present among the suitors, albeit disguised as a beggar.

Under the influence of Athena, Penelope complains to her maid Eurynomē that the years have taken a toll on her looks. The maid encourages her to take a bath and powder her face, as grief has disfigured it. Athena seizes her chance when Penelope is alone and casts a 'beauty sleep' over her:

> She [Athena] poured sweet sleep over the daughter of Ikaros [Penelope]. She lay back and slept. All her joints went slack there on her couch. While in that state the mighty goddess bestowed her immortal gifts on her, so the Achaeans would marvel at her. First she gave her face a deep cleansing with divine beauty, applying the same lotion Aphrodite uses when she joins the lovely choral dance of the Graces with a crown on her head. She also made her seem taller and shapelier in appearance and made her skin paler than freshly cut ivory. Having finished her work, the goddess made off.
>
> [*An interval in which Penelope laments the loss of Odysseus once more, but still agrees to go downstairs and show herself to the suitors, accompanied by two maids, who will veil her.*]
>
> When this queen among women presented herself to the suitors, she stood beside a pillar supporting the ornamental ceiling, holding a thin veil in front of her cheeks, a maid on either side of her. And the suitors' knees went weak, their eyes filled with desire. They all vowed to be the one to lie with her in bed. But she spoke rather to Telemachos, her dear son. (*Odyssey* 18.188–214)

In this description we note that no item of clothing or jewellery is mentioned in Athena's lifting of Penelope. We hear about pale skin, a magical lotion used by Aphrodite, embellishment of her stature and figure, and a veil to give her a nuptial look. We imagine her appearance through the eyes of the suitors, who swoon with desire, and vow to win her. However, what is lacking – we might think – in the description of her appearance is interestingly added indirectly later in the same scene. When one of the suitors, Eurymachos, challenges Penelope, saying if all the Argives (Greeks) could see her now, there would be many more suitors in her palace, such is her beauty, she launches into another long speech lamenting Odysseus' departure and absence. At its close she says the suitors are not behaving like proper suitors anyway; normally they should be bringing gifts, not eating the bride's family out of house and home. Overhearing this, Odysseus is pleased, partly no doubt to hear her loyalty to him confirmed, but partly because she has slyly challenged the suitors to bring her gifts. He assumes the thought in the back of her mind (*noös*; 283) is to trick the suitors into lavishing gifts on her, although she has no intention of remarrying.

Eurymachos accepts the challenge and tells the suitors to give what they see fit. Now follows a list of gifts, all articles of a woman's outfit, complementing perfectly the groundwork Athena has laid by cleansing and rejuvenating her face and body:

> Each [of the suitors] dispatched a man to fetch the gifts. Antinoös' man fetched a long, exceptionally beautiful embroidered *peplos* [long woman's gown]. It had twelve golden fastenings, all told, fitted with well-made clasps. Eurymachos' servant brought a wonderfully crafted necklace of gold; it was inset with amber and shone like the sun. Two attendants brought earrings on Eurydamas' behalf, with a triple cluster ornament positively radiating charm. And from Peisander's home the servant fetched a pendant, a beautiful piece of jewellery. The remaining suitors all brought beautiful gifts, too. (18.291–301)

One notes that Homer only lists a selection of the gifts brought by the company of suitors. This selection comprises a perfect set to complete the wardrobe of Penelope as bride: first, a long, dignified garment,

38 Women's gold jewellery (pendant, bracelets, earrings) from Colchis, Georgia, mid-5th century BC.

the *peplos* – an article of clothing favoured by Athena herself at her festivals – then pieces of jewellery, all of which she could put on without being overdressed: a necklace, earrings and a pendant. Although in fact Penelope goes back upstairs with the gifts at this point, we can imagine her appearance were she to put them on for a second marriage. Odysseus himself is watching all the time, impressed no doubt, like the suitors, by his wife's looks and pleased that she refused Eurymachos' advances so resolutely.

These two dressings, then – those of Pandora at the hands of the gods, and Penelope at the hands of Athena, and then human jewellers and dressmakers – serve both to beautify the woman concerned and make them attractive to men, but they are both deceptive. Pandora brings all the ills into the world – work, neediness and sickness – while Penelope tricks the suitors into thinking that she is preparing to choose one of them as her next partner, while in fact remaining true to Odysseus and trying to make good some of the financial losses his household has suffered as a result of the suitors' prolonged stay there. This interpretation of bridal dressing – a kind of deception of the male gaze – would appear to be the opposite of the worship of female fertility and matriarchy. Some have held that an earlier stratum of Aegean culture was indeed matriarchal, and attempts have been made to interpret Cycladic figurines of large-bellied women from the Bronze Age accordingly as goddesses of fertility.[2] These episodes from Greek epic poetry, both Hesiod's *Works and Days* and Homer's *Odyssey*, tell a different story, one that has often been called misogynist by scholars: Greek men were basically and fundamentally suspicious of women. However, Penelope is by no means a negative figure. While Pandora took the lid off the jar containing evils, Penelope did everything she could to preserve herself and Odysseus' estate from depletion by the suitors. As we saw in Chapter One, the women of the *Iliad*, in particular Hektor's wife Andromache but also even prizes of war such as Briseïs and Helen, are depicted as deserving of the love and devotion that lead men to fight over, and for, them. So: a mixed picture. What may be taken from these two stories from the epic tradition is the suspicion which a woman's couture can arouse – in men. What is behind the beautiful dress, the hairdo, the make-up and the *kosmos*, adornment? Is it a form of manipulation with ulterior – perhaps questionable – purpose?[3]

A true story?

In the fifth book of his *Histories*, Herodotus tells a strange story about the origin of the ethnic distinction between Doric women's attire and Athenian women (5.82–8). An Athenian army was defeated in its attempt to subjugate the nearby island of Aigina (sixth century BC). The war went back to a religious dispute over wooden idols between Aigina and Epidauros. The Delphic oracle had decreed that Attic wood should be used to replace the wooden *agalmata*, statues, of the gods, which had been removed. But the war itself was profane and bloody enough. It closed with a battle on Aigina in which all the Athenians but one were killed. This man made it back to Athens but was promptly set upon by the Attic women, who wanted to know what had happened to their men. According to the tradition, they stuck him with their *fibulae* (the Roman word for Greek *peronē*), the long pins used to fasten their dresses at the shoulder, to make him talk. Stuck by so many vindictive pins, the man died. The Athenians decreed that Athenian women should no longer wear Doric dress, which was fastened by these long pins, but should change to the Ionian *chitōn*, stemming from Caria in fact, which was more like a long gown sewn at the shoulders and sleeves and therefore not needing fastening pins or brooches. We saw above that the long *peplos* that Antinoös gave Penelope in *Odyssey* 18 was fastened by twelve gold *peronai*, making it exceptionally dangerous from the point of view of this story. Herodotus explains:

> The Athenians could think of no other way of punishing the women [for their collective murder of the man] than to change their style of dressing to the Ionian. Up to then Athenian women had worn a Doric style of clothing most akin to the Corinthian. So they changed now to the linen *chitōn*, so as not to need fastening pins. This style of dress is not in fact Ionian in origin but Carian, as all Greek women used to be clad in early times in the same manner, that which we call Doric. . . . Argive and Aiginetan women were still in my day wearing longer dress pins than before because of this bitter dispute with the Athenians. (*Histories* 5.87.14–88.13)

The story is what is called an *aition*, a 'reason why' something is as it is. Whether the story is strictly historical is difficult to say. Conceptually, however, it is clear that it marked a differentiation in identity through women's national dress between the Peloponnesian Dorians and the Athenians, who considered the Ionian Greeks in Asia Minor their relatives (descendants, actually). The *aition* derived the split between the ethnic groups from a war between the Aiginetans and the Athenians, but throughout we note the religious, or cultic, dimension: the dispute started originally over cult statues (wooden cult statues were known as *xoana*); after the battle, both sides altered their women's dress code. The Athenians stopped their women using *peronai*, because these had served as weapons in the *aition*, and changed to the Ionian *chitōn*, which was pinless, while the Aiginetans made them extra-long. Cult practice was also reformed on the Peloponnesian side: Attic ware (specifically drinking cups) was to be banned from Argive and Aiginetan sanctuaries.

This sounds like a historical account. In fact, however, one can easily imagine that the observed difference between Peloponnesian and Attic women's dress – the former wore a *peplos* with *peronai*, the latter a pinless *chitōn* – gave rise to the *aition*, which needed to focus on a particular use of dress pins (to kill a lone surviving Athenian in this case), which called for reform. In other words, it is perhaps more likely that the different dress of Dorian and Ionian women arose naturally as a result of ethnic divisions and tradition, and then the story was invented, or adapted, to explain it, than the other way round. But one cannot be completely sure. The Athenian–Aiginetan war was historical enough. Incidentally, many bronze *peronai* from the archaic period have turned up in excavations of the Argive Hēraion (temple of Hera at Argos), where they had clearly been placed as votive offerings.

The famous old commentary on Herodotus by 'How and Wells' says about the two respective dress styles:

> The Ionian *chitōn* was a long linen garment like a night-gown, with full sleeves to the elbow, requiring neither brooch nor pin. The Dorian was a square woollen cloth, with the upper edge folded down forming the *diploïs*. It was simply folded round the body and fastened at the shoulder. The right side was thus left unprotected, unless this opening was . . . sewn up. But in all cases a girdle was worn fastened round the loins, and under the girdle the dress could be so arranged as to overlap.[4]

Some of the language seems a little stilted here – 'night-gown', 'girdle', 'loins', 'right side unprotected', 'so as to overlap' – as if deliberately to avoid raised eyebrows at the High Table of an all-male Oxford college. Their note on women's clothing can be elaborated somewhat here. The *peplos* was fastened round the waist or under the bosom by a belt ('girdle'), which could be worn over or under the overhang of cloth (in effect, the outer layer of the dress). The *chitōn* did not have sleeves but rather quasi-sleeves, reaching approximately to the elbow, were formed by the overhang of material over the shoulders. Apart from the *chitōn* there was also a short version called a *chitōniskos*, or 'mini-*chitōn*', approximately knee-length. However, the general point made by Herodotus – the change from Doric *peplos* to Ionian *chitōn* in the early archaic period – is borne out by the archaeological record (statues, vase painting). The *himation* as third basic type was a wide wrap of material which could be worn in a variety of styles as an over-garment. Ancients did wear underwear of a sort: we hear of women's *strophion* as a kind of bra, and men and women could wear a loincloth (*perizōma*), particularly when exercising.

Apart from wool and linen (made from flax) as dress materials there is some evidence for the use of wild silk. Some dresses on statues and vases look diaphanous: perhaps these were of silk, or perhaps it was an artistic convention. The girl in Menander's *Epitrepontes* was wearing an extremely revealing *tarentīnon* (from Tarentum, Apulia) dress made of sea-silk for the nocturnal celebration of the Tauropolia (on which occasion she was raped and the dress was torn: ll. 488–90).[5] All material was woven on the loom. The resulting cloth could be dyed, whereas linen is difficult to dye; perhaps for that reason the linen *chitōn* was more like the white togas we imagine the ancients walking around in (although borders and other embellishments could be, and more often than not were, added). The heroine of Heliodorus' novel *Ethiopian Tale*, Charikleia, for example, puts on a white gown after a religious ceremony marking her return to 'normal' dress (3.6). Dyed colours frequently mentioned are saffron yellow, purple (from the murex shellfish), Sardian (Persian) red, blue, and black (squid ink) or grey (*phaios*; see for example Menander, *Misoumenos* 542). Patterns and motifs could be woven into the cloth or added later by embroidery (again, linen is difficult to embroider) or sewing on coloured bands. A possible reconstruction of Athena's *peplos* (illus. 39) shows both dyed material and woven mythical motifs. The chorus in Euripides' *Hecuba* mention Athena's coach-and-four and the Titanomachy as mythical motifs woven on her 'saffron-yellow' *peplos* (ll. 466–74).

It was assumed that women learned the basic skills of spinning, weaving and sewing in childhood. An anecdote in Xenophon's *Memorabilia* has Socrates tell one Aristarchos how to feed a large – and idle – family who has moved in with him as they had fallen on

39 Athena dressed in her *peplos*: reconstruction for the exhibition 'Bunte Götter', Glyptothek Munich, 2006.

hard times and are now eating him out of house and home. Socrates asks him whether the women can spin and weave. Yes, is the answer, of course. Well, says Socrates, let them employ themselves gainfully in making clothes for sale. Then you will all have enough to eat (2.7.1–12). The women in this family were reluctant to work because they had been rich (and idle), but Socrates says they must, now their family is penniless and dependent on Aristarchos' hospitality. In another work by Xenophon (*Oikonomikos*, Home Management), Socrates asks Ischomachos what his young wife has learned before marrying him.

Ischomachos replies: 'Doesn't she [my wife] seem adorable to you if she married me knowing only how to make a *himation* from wool, while the work of spinning was to be given to servants?' (7.5). Not all clothes worn were produced in the family, presumably. Aristarchos' women lodgers, for example, had clearly lost the habit of spinning and weaving and become accustomed to a life of ease. That meant buying clothes. Women's garments could be bought at certain stalls of the market. No doubt some families set up home businesses producing and selling clothes, as leatherworkers and helmet-makers had workshops and sales counters.

Social distinctions

An anecdote about the tyrant Peisistratos of Athens (sixth century BC) recorded by both Herodotus (*Histories* 1.60) and the *Constitution of Athens* (14.4, ascribed to Aristotle or his school) says that his political ally Megakles helped to get him reinstated in Athens after he had been banished by dressing a woman up 'as Athena' and pretending that the goddess herself was escorting Peisistratos back to Athens in a carriage. The *Constitution of Athens* says that the woman chosen was 'tall and handsome'. Some say she was an Athenian woman from a local deme, while others say she was a Thracian garland-maker called Phyē (that is to say, not a free woman). Clearly 'Athena', or rather her statues (*agalmata*), which formed people's picture of her, was recognizable by her traditional appearance (dress, hairstyle and, above all, weapons). The story is made more poignant if it was the market vendor Phyē who imitated her. Our sources say the people of Athens were taken in by the ploy and thought Athena was really sitting beside Peisistratos as he drove into Athens.

What did it mean to dress up like Athena? Athena's traditional dress was the *peplos:* see illus 39, which also shows a hypothetical reconstruction of the garment's traditional decoration (mythical motifs). This intricately decorated *peplos* was a cult object of Athena in itself. A new one was made for the goddess every four years by girls known as the Arrephoroi and given to her in the ceremonial procession called the Panathenaia; the procession is illustrated in the so-called Elgin Marbles, still, controversially, in the British Museum, despite Greece's requests to return them to Athens. Apart from this *peplos*, Athena was typically shown with the arms she was born with. Myth told how she emerged originally from Zeus' head, fully armed with shield and spear, and a thing called her *aegis* (see for example Aristophanes, *Birds* 830–31). The word basically means 'goatskin' (from *aix*, 'goat'), but it bore on it the image of the Gorgon, a mythical dragon-woman whose gaze could transfix. So, a human girl dressing as Athena would probably imitate this warrior-like outfit: *peplos*, *aegis*, shield and spear. Anyone looking at her would immediately see the resemblance to cult depictions of Athena.

Confirmation of this comes from an anecdote told by the writer Polyainos in connection with an event in 241 BC when the Aetolians attacked Pellēnē (in Achaia, Peloponnese). The defenders of Pellēnē formed up on high ground, from where their acropolis with its temple of Athena was clearly visible opposite. There they saw, before battle was joined, a figure dressed like Athena emerge from the temple. It was sufficient to convince them Athena was personally supporting them, and they routed the Aetolians that day. The figure is described by Polyainos as follows: 'The priestess of Athena, in accordance with ritual custom on that day, dressed in full battle-dress and wearing a triple-plumed helmet, looked down from the acropolis at the assembled army of the Pellenians; she was the tallest and most beautiful of the local girls' (*Stratēgēmata* 8.59 *Hiereia*, Priestess). Several points coincide with the story told about Peisistratos' reinstatement: the beauty and stature of the girl chosen, the wearing of Athena's 'full suit of armour' (*panoplia*), the fact that onlookers somehow took her as an embodiment of Athena herself.

In these cases, then, dressing as a goddess meant, for a girl or woman, putting on the goddess's typical cult attributes. It was not just a question of clothes, hairstyle or cosmetics. The iconography of Greek deities was the result of a combination of their mythical attributes (for example, that Athena was born fully armed) and artistic tradition. The gods acquired typical attributes – Apollo his lyre, Zeus his thunderbolt, Hekatē her torch – so that worshippers were familiar with their appearance from monumental sculpture down to small votive statuettes. In a novel of the imperial period by Xenophon of Ephesos we encounter another example of a human dressing up as a goddess, Artemis this time. Xenophon's novel treats the love affair between exceptionally handsome young people: Anthia (Flowery) is the girl (14), Habrokomēs (Soft-Hair) the boy (16). The couple first meet, by arrangement of Erōs himself, during a procession to Artemis Ephesia (Of Ephesos). The crowd *ooh* and *aah* profusely at their respective appearances in the procession. Xenophon describes Anthia first as a beautiful girl, finely dressed (her hair and eyes, purple-dyed *chitōn*), then adds attributes of a huntress: 'Her dress was knee-length, with open sleeves. Over it she wore a fawnskin, and was armed with bow and quiver . . . hounds followed' (*Anthia and Habrocomes* 1.2.6–9). The attributes immediately associate her with Artemis Huntress (Agrotera) in the spectators' eyes, who wonder whether they are seeing Artemis in person.

The divide here between humans and gods is clear: humans do not normally dress up as gods. Both stories we have just looked at involve ceremonial occasions (Athena escorting Peisistratos to her citadel; the procession to Artemis Ephesia), not daily life. However, 'godlike' was a standard poetic way of praising both men and women if they were looking their best or dressed in their finest; it was common hyperbolic praise. In the *Odyssey*, Helen appears looking 'like' Artemis (4.122); Nausikaa playing ball with her friends looks 'like' Artemis sporting with the Nymphs (6.102ff); and the king of the Phaeacians, Alkinoos, sits on his throne drinking wine, next to his wife (who is weaving) 'like a god' (6.309). The converse is also true: in Homeric epic the gods are constantly taking on the appearance of a named mortal in order to convey some message to their protégé. Athena appears in the likeness of Mentes (or Mentor) to Telemachos, as a friend of Nausikaa to her, and so on. In epic and myth at least, the divide between human and divine was permeable in two directions. If the Greeks made their gods in their own image, as the early philosopher Xenophanes said (B14 DK), they also aspired to raising themselves to the ideal images they had created.

For gods, then, to appear to humans, they put on a human appearance, and, conversely, a human had to dress up in the known apparel of cult to impersonate a specific deity. Were there such clear categories between the classes of women? Were wives, *hetairai*, slave-girls (perhaps working as prostitutes) immediately recognizable by their dress?[6] We have already seen in Chapter One that *hetairai* were dependent on their lovers for their material comfort. The richer the male lovers were, the more luxurious their lifestyle was likely to be. A story told by Herodotus in the aftermath of the Battle of Plataia (479 BC) concerns a Greek girl who had been enslaved by a Persian potentate and then dolled up like a queen:

> After the Persians [called 'barbarians'] had been defeated by the Greeks at Plataia, there came to them [the Spartans] a woman deserter. She had been the *pallakē* [long-term mistress] of Pharandatēs, a Persian man, son of Theaspēs. When she learned that the Persians had been defeated and the Greeks were victorious, she alighted from her carriage, decked out in much gold – she herself and her servants – and wearing the most beautiful dress of those present, and approached the Spartans, who were still gory from the battle. Seeing Pausanias [the Spartan general] . . . she clasped his knees in supplication and said: 'O King of Sparta, save me, your suppliant, from slavery and captivity. You have already helped by killing these men who had no regard for gods or divine powers. I am from Kōs by birth, the daughter of Hēgētoridēs, son of Antagoras. My Persian captor took me by force from Kōs.' (*Histories* 9.76)

This girl, then, had been abducted from her native island of Kōs and reduced from citizen daughter to war captive and sex slave. However, her captor Pharandatēs had clearly dressed his enslaved mistress in all possible finery: gold jewellery, beautiful dresses, even a coach-and-four with women servants to ride around in. This was true luxury, but, as soon as she got the chance, the girl preferred to throw herself on Pausanias' mercy rather than continue in this condition. Pausanias, Herodotus tells us, said that he happened to be guest-friends with Hēgētoridēs of Kōs, to whom he eventually repatriated the girl.

This is like the plot of a New Comedy by Menander, two hundred years before his day, and from real life rather than the comic stage.

In his 'soldier plays' we hear much of the efforts by Greek mercenaries to woo the girls they have taken as captives of war, or otherwise acquired, with fine clothes and jewellery. We have already seen that Kleostratos in the play *Aspis* was depicted as intent on plunder when he served as a mercenary in Lycia. Polemōn, another successful mercenary, in *Perikeiromenē* (The Shorn Head), shows off the beautiful clothes he had given to his *pallakē* Glykera to a neighbour, distraught that she has left him despite his generosity (ll. 519–21). Thrasōnidēs in *Misoumenos* (The Hated Man) complains similarly that he had heaped fine gifts on Krateia (whom he had bought on the slave market while he was abroad in Cyprus fighting), and now she is rejecting him (ll. 39–40). Such gifts have at least two purposes: on the one hand to please their recipient and possibly compensate for other, more humiliating aspects of their situation, such as slavery (!), but also to deck the woman out in finery as a kind of trophy. If the girls are admired by others, the admiration reflects well on their owners.

Menander's *Samia* shows the difference between the condition of a long-term partner (*pallakē*) maintained by a generous lover and a more downmarket *hetaira*. The play does not tell us how the girl came from Samos to Athens, whether by forced 'trafficking' or voluntarily, but she was taken up by a well-off older gentleman called Demeas (old enough to have a grown-up son, that is), who seems in the play to really love her (not an impossibility). However, he discovers at the beginning of the play (or thinks he does: it is not in fact true) that Chrysis (Goldie), the girl from Samos, has had a baby by his adoptive son Moschiōn while he was away on a business trip in Byzantium. Enraged, he decides to throw her out in the street, shouting at her in an impassioned scene: 'You didn't appreciate a life of luxury! . . . You came to me dressed in cheap linen!' (ll. 376–9) A little later in the tirade he contrasts the life of poverty to which she is now returning with the good life she enjoyed with him:

> Unlike you, other girls make a measly ten drachmae running off to men's drinking parties till their dying day – or die of hunger if they don't do so readily and promptly enough. You'll experience that no less than any other, for sure. You'll

see who you really are and what a mistake you've made!
(*Samia* 390–97)

In other words, Demeas is claiming that Chrysis has failed to appreciate the luxury he has provided for her and has thrown it all away by getting pregnant by his son, of all people. The fate to which he now condemns her is not essentially different – she will still technically be a sex worker – but it will be worlds apart from her present state in terms of material security and comfort. In other words, the generosity of a lover was decisive for a non-free woman's basic security and standard of living. The grandes dames among ancient Greek *hetairai*, like Perikles' Aspasia, Demosthenes' Lamia and Menander's Glykera, who were famous for their beauty, expensive dress, jewellery and sometimes their cultural or artistic achievements, were dependent financially on the prominence and wealth of their lover(s). And, as indicated, an ostentatious display of wealth by a woman was two-sided: it reflected well on the woman and her patron. One of the Mytilene mosaics (see illus. 16) shows Chrysis at the moment in Act Three when Demeas throws her out in the street. Although the medium is not given to fine detail, we can make out her elaborately coloured and patterned *chitōn* (blue, red, yellow), probably with a throw (*himation*) over it, and her elaborate hairdo with headdress (*krēdemnon*) and gold tassels is visible over the 'hetaira' mask she is wearing.

What, then, of wives? Were they kept cooped up at home without any of the finery lavished on *hetairai* and *pallakai*? Was the ideal for an Athenian woman really, as Perikles said in his Funeral Speech at Athens in 430 BC, 'to be least talked about by men either in a good sense, or a bad' (Thucydides 2.45.2)? The evidence of Aristophanes' plays is more nuanced. The wives of Athens feature large in three of his plays, *Lysistrata*, *Women at the Thesmophoria* and *The Assemblywomen*, and they do not well comply with the cliché of the down-at-heel wife compared to the bird-of-paradise *hetaira*. The plot of *Lysistrata* (411 BC) is that the (merry) wives of Athens, led by Lysistrata, plan a sex strike to force the menfolk to stop fighting the Spartans in the Peloponnesian War. 'Soon we will all be wiped out!' she says. Her interlocutor at the beginning of the play, Kleonikē, scoffs: 'What can we women do of weight or merit, stuck at home in our Laura Ashley dresses [lit. 'with flower motifs'] or in our saffron yellow one-pieces, our make-up, our high heels and fancy shoes?' (ll. 42–5). 'That's exactly what I think is going to save us!' Lysistrata replies. 'Our saffron-dyed dresses, our perfume, our fancy shoes, our rouge and our see-through nighties' (ll. 46–8). As becomes clear, she plans an enormous sex tease: the women of Athens will flaunt themselves before their men but refuse sex. Tongues hanging out, the men will agree to terms: no more war for sex. She explains to Kleonikē:

> (*Lysistrata:*) No one of the men will raise his spear against another. (*Kleonikē:*) By the twin goddesses (Demeter and Korē) I'll dye myself a saffron dress. (*Lysistrata:*) . . . nor pick up a shield. (*Kleonikē:*) I'll wear my heels! (*Lysistrata:*) . . . nor sword! (*Kleonikē:*) I'll buy party shoes! (ll. 49–53)

The plot of this play would not work if Athenian wives were to be imagined as grey mice waiting for their husbands to come home from their *hetairai* lovers. Clearly, wives (*gynaikes*) were quite capable of dressing up and seducing their husbands (compare ll. 219–20 of this play). A famous passage in pseudo-Demosthenes' *Against Neaira* (*c.* 340 BC) (122) divides women into three clear categories according to their function from a male point of view: 'We have *hetairai* for the sake of pleasure, *pallakai* for our bodily comfort day by day, and wives for producing legitimate children and to watch over family affairs.' But these are functional categories; they do not necessarily imply distinctive dress codes in each case. In Aristophanes' comedies things were not so simple. Dressing up attractively was not the sole prerogative of courtesans; wives could dress up, too, when they wanted to. On the other hand, it is risky to treat Aristophanes' comedy as documentary evidence. He was a man, writing for the entertainment of men, without women in the audience to cry out in indignation or boo if they felt they were being insulted or belittled. He might be teasing his male audience here with a message along the lines of: just imagine if our wives dressed and behaved like *hetairai*! It is difficult to judge. Are the women in illus. 40 preparing one of them for marriage, or *hetairai*? The Erōs flitting above the scene admits both interpretations. Art historians recognize that the visual record of women's dress in Greek vase painting and sculpture does not permit an easy distinction between wives and *hetairai*. We may think we recognize a streetwalker by costume and context, but would we recognize an 'escort' at a cocktail party?

What about the girls at the bottom of the pile, then, the enslaved prostitutes called *pornai* who were farmed out by pimps (*pornoboskoi*) in brothels (*porneion*)? How did they dress and prepare themselves for business? One thing is clear: they were absolutely distinct from *hetairai*, not by choice, of course, but by the luck of the draw, social deprivation, like nowadays. When a character in Menander wants to denigrate the heroine *hetaira* in *Epitrepontes*, he calls her a 'thrice-wretched little tart' (*pornidion trisathlion*; l. 667), while another passage of the play flatly denies that she is a cheap little whore (*to tychon (paignion)*; l. 985). A passage of Aristophanes' *Assemblywomen* gives a number of indications that may help us to triangulate the status of *pornai* in society. The first and most important point is that Praxagora, the leader of the women's uprising, is not sympathetic to

40 A group of *hetairai* with young Erōs, Hellenistic polychrome vase painting.

them. She only wants to abolish their trade because they siphon off the best young men, keeping them from decent women, not from philanthropy. She announces:

> Next I want to abolish prostitution completely and utterly. (*Blepyros:*) What for? (*Neighbour:*) Well that's obvious. So that these women here [*points to the chorus and their fellow revolutionaries*] can have their p(r)ick of the young men. (*Praxagora:*) And slaves won't be allowed to get tarted up to snatch sex [Kypris, that is Aphrodite] from the free. They'll only be allowed to sleep with other slaves, plucking their pubes like a workman's leather jacket. (*Assemblywomen* 718–24)

Quite an encoded statement. The word rendered here as 'p(r)ick' is *akmē*, literally meaning peak or pinnacle (indicating the best young men), but by innuendo their 'tips' (erections). 'Tarted up' is a form of *kosmeō*, dress up, adorn, beautify, with its noun *kosmos*, and can apply to clothes, hair and make-up. Praxagora is referring disparagingly – and class-consciously – to slaves' attempts to mask their status by dress and make-up so as to tempt free men. Praxagora wants to abolish slave prostitution in order to keep slave girls firmly in their place, only sleeping with other slaves. In a normal household that will have been the case. Hekabē in Euripides' play laments when she is about to be sold into slavery following the capture of Troy: 'The only person to defile my bed will be a slave bought somewhere – I, who in a previous life was thought worthy of kings' (*Hekabē* 365–6). Praxagora then refers disparagingly to another mark of the prostitute, the plucked pubic hair, which she compares to a working class item of clothing, *katōnakē*, leather jacket, perhaps again intended to put these whores in their place. Praxagora may have initiated an uprising of the women of Athens and the establishment of a communist state run by women, but she does not extend the new privileges of women to slave prostitutes.

An even more graphic picture of the lot of *pornai* comes from Theophrastus' Slanderer, who may say, when asked: 'These women pull in passers-by off the street . . . That house there [he means a brothel] has its legs in the air[7] . . . It's not a joke, you know, what they say: they really copulate in the streets like dogs. They're absolute predators. They answer their own front door [normally a slave opens a front door]' (*Characters* 28.3). The word used for 'pull in' (*synarpazō*) is nearly the same as that used by Aristophanes in the previous passage for 'snatch' (men: *hypharpazō*). Combining these accounts, we get a clear picture of the prostitute dressed provocatively in a doorway, addressing any passer-by and taking them in for sex, virtually on the street itself. Herodas' second *Mime*, *Pornoboskos* (The Pimp), is the tirade in court of one Battaros, who runs a brothel in Kōs, against the defendant Thales, who tried to take one of Battaros' slave prostitutes by force. We hear how Battaros himself is 'gay' (*kinaidos*), that he brought the girls from Tyre to the Greek island of Kōs and set up his brothel there. At one point he calls the girl herself, Myrtale (Myrtle), to the witness stand and points out her smooth 'plucked body, above and below', indicating she may be imagined as being naked. Foreign girls offering themselves to passers-by by standing naked or nearly naked in doorways of houses – that sounds like Amsterdam's red light district.

Some broad lines of conclusion may be permissible. *Hetairai* lived by making themselves attractive to men: there was no other way to survive, as the path to security through marriage was closed to them. That makes it intrinsically likely that they walked the streets in clothes and make-up which wives usually did not wear except for celebrations or religious festivals of some sort, and anyway they did not walk the streets of Athens freely at all. Among the *hetairai* there will have been degrees of finery and luxury dependent on the means of their patrons. *Hetairai* of rich men will have displayed that wealth through ostentatious dressing, hair styles, cosmetics and jewellery. That does not mean that wives, as we have seen in Aristophanes, could not dress up richly and attractively, merely that they will not normally have displayed themselves freely in that state around town. Prostitutes, on the other hand, will have been easily recognizable by the establishments to which they were bound and the conditions under which they sold themselves for sex. The *pornoboskos* will only have paid for their appearance to the extent that was necessary to make them saleable. Since all clothes in antiquity were hand-made, embroidery and patterning in women's clothes was likely to have been very individual in its fine detail. On the other hand, basic dress design and styles of ornamentation – as we see from literary as well as visual sources – was conservative and obeyed regional traditions; for that reason, the fundamentals of dress will have been relatively traditional compared to today's consumer-oriented and fashion-driven global mix.

Men

Basically, men wore the same garments as women: the *peplos* (see for example Euripides, *Herakles* 627), the *chitōn* (undergarment) and *himation* (overgarment). A simple coat or jacket, typically worn by slaves (and philosophers!), was called *tribōn* or *tribōnion*, contrasting with the fine *chlanis*, jacket. Farm workers wore plain skins, *diphthera*. A military cloak, or tunic, was called a *chlamys*. The horsemen in an extravagant parade in Delphi, for example, are described as being dressed in 'white tunics, drawn in at the waist by a golden clasp, with a dark border running round the lower edge' (Heliodorus, *Ethiopian Tale* 3.3). Men sometimes wore a loincloth as underwear, *perizōma*, and for athletics.

Dressing up and dressing down

The *Odyssey* is basically the story of Odysseus' *nostos*, return home, after the Trojan War. He wanders round the western Mediterranean, blown by storms, held up by fairy-tale adventures and lovers, for ten long years before reaching Ithaka, where Penelope, amazingly, has managed to hold off the suitors' pressure to remarry. The adventures at sea reduced Odysseus, once a king and warrior hero at Troy, to a shipwrecked sailor. Athena transformed him once already when he was washed up on Scheria and encountered Nausikaa. Now, when he arrives back in Ithaka in Book 13, he must first dress down radically so as not to be recognized prematurely by the suitors. Athena gives him not only a beggar's rags but physically ages him, too:

> She [Athena] shrivelled the fine skin on his limbs. She removed the fair hair on his head and spread over every limb of his body the skin of an old man. She dimmed the sparkle in

> his eyes, which had been so bright. Round his shoulders she cast rags, and a creased, soiled *chitōn* that had been blackened by soot. Then she dressed him in a large, hairless, deerskin, gave him a staff and a wretched bag all tattered with a cord for a grip. (*Odyssey* 13.430–38)

In this disguise he must infiltrate his old palace, in which the suitors have been squatting, living at his expense while they lay siege to Penelope's hand in remarriage. He must choose his moment to attack them, as he is vastly outnumbered. That moment comes when Penelope manoeuvres the suitors into an archery contest. Out comes the famous bow of Odysseus, which only he can string. Armed with his bow, Odysseus throws off his beggar's rags and starts picking off suitors with his arrows: 'Quick-witted Odysseus threw off his rags and, jumping to the great palace threshold with bow and quiver full of arrows, he tipped out the swift arrows before his feet . . . and shot one at Antinoös' (22.1–8; see illus. 49).

In the next book, Odysseus, still covered in gore, finally meets Penelope face to face, who refuses to believe it is really him. Odysseus comments to his son Telemachos: 'Now because I am bedraggled with only a poor covering over my body, she scorns me and does not yet see it's me' (23.115–16). Then Odysseus is bathed by Eurynomē and Athena lends him *charis* ('grace' or 'charm'). This is the reverse of the process of degradation he suffered on landing on Ithaka:

> The housemaid Eurynomē washed him and rubbed him down with olive oil. She dressed him in a fine coat over a *chitōn*. Athena covered him from the head down with great beauty to look taller and more muscular. She gave spring to the hair on his head, dark now as the flower of a violet. As when a skilled craftsman gilds silver with gold . . . so she spread beauty over his head and shoulders. He got out of the bathtub with the body of a god. (23.154–63)

The transformation in his appearance marks the hero's reinstatement in two senses: reunion with Penelope, and a resumption of his 'throne' (*thronos*; l. 164) in Ithaka. In their conversation he reveals intimate knowledge of the marriage bed he had made himself back in the day, uniquely built around a tree growing through the room. Penelope is finally convinced, and they are reunited. The transformation in Odysseus' appearance is partly of human origin – the bath, oil and clothes provided by Eurynomē – but significantly also by Athena's divine hand.

In Plato's *Phaedo*, it is agreed that philosophers should scorn material wealth, including showy clothes:

> (*Socrates:*) What about all the other adornments of the body? Does the philosopher value such things? Clothes, for example: does he value the possession of extra fine garments, or shoes, or other such things which are worn for show? Apart from the bare necessity to be dressed, of course. (*Simmias:*) No, the true philosopher scorns such things, in my opinion. (*Phaedo* 64d–e)

Socrates himself was well known for walking around Athens and engaging in philosophical disputes dressed shabbily. He demonstratively eschewed a conventionally respectable public persona. So it called for comment when he attended the celebration party for Agathon's victory in the theatre festival in 416 BC. Aristodēmos tells how he met Socrates once 'freshly bathed and wearing shoes, which was unusual for him. I asked him where he was going so well dressed.' Socrates answers that he is going to Agathon's dinner party: 'I dressed nicely so as to look good for a fine man' (Plato, *Symposion* 174a). Elsewhere we hear more of Socrates' down-dressing, which seems to have been his personal statement. When the notorious Athenian statesman Alkibiades was a boy, he tried to seduce Socrates one night in order to gain access – so he claimed – to the older man's wisdom. He describes how he placed his *himation* (expensive outer garment) over Socrates and climbed in under the other's 'shabby jacket' (*tribōn*) and put his arms round him (without success: Socrates did not take the bait; 219b). One might notice here that the men had no bedclothes; they slept under the clothes they wore, in Socrates' case a 'shabby jacket'.

Another incident told by Plato in the same work shows Socrates on military service, similarly scorning the appropriate clothes. It was winter in Poteidaia (in northern Greece) in 429 BC and the other men

> either did not leave their tents at all, or, if they did, dressed in many layers of clothes and with felt or sheepskins wrapped round their shoes, whereas Socrates left the tent wearing the *himation* which he was accustomed to wear normally, and walked *barefoot* through the snow with more ease than the others in shoes. The other soldiers looked at him askance, as if he was mocking them. (*Symposion* 220b)

It is hard to know whether there was an element of bravado in this behaviour of Socrates or whether he was physically hardier than average, perhaps by training (*askēsis*). Either way, it belonged to his philosophy, which viewed the lives of his contemporaries extremely critically, always probing whether a conventional view held water. It led to the later cliché of the 'miserable philosopher', embodied in Diogenes and the Cynics and mocked by Lucian in his *Ikaromenippos* (5), for example. Cynicism about life was expressed non-verbally by a cynical attitude to the conventional dress code. By dressing down and living frugally, the philosopher marked himself out from the crowd as someone who was not competing in the usual race for money and prestige. This was different from the man who simply did not care about his appearance and appeared 'gross' to others, like Theophrastus' Unkempt Man (*Characters* 19). The philosopher was rather the man driving at 40 miles an hour in the inside lane of the motorway in his beaten up old Morris Minor, scorning the BMWs and Mercedes flashing past at twice the speed and disregarding the fact that his car is the worse polluter.

In Aristophanes' play *Acharnians*, in which one Dikaiopolis makes a private peace treaty with the Spartans because he is sick and tired of the Peloponnesian War and wishes to live in peace, the hero has to defend his action against the chorus of men from Acharnia, the 'Marathon Generation' (like the 'war generation' in England), who despise the thought of peace with Sparta. To make his defence speech, Dikaiopolis decides that he must look as abject as possible (it was a common strategy of defendants in the law courts, to elicit sympathy from the jury). To do this he determines to visit the playwright Euripides, who has written many plays about fallen grandeur: mythical figures who were deposed or otherwise brought low and marked their new lowly station by wearing beggar's rags. Euripides, an associate and contemporary of Socrates on the intellectual front in later fifth-century BC Athens, favoured plots, it seems, in which the heroes of myth became the underdogs and wore rags instead of robes. Tradition had it that Euripides himself lived as a recluse in a cave on the island of Salamis, where he composed his tragedies. The cave, at least, is historical.

Dikaiopolis is shown visiting Euripides and asking for rags from one of his past tragedies, which appear to have been notorious. They run through a number of Euripides' past works – the *Oineus* (exiled king), *Phoinix* (blinded and exiled), *Philoktetes* (castaway beggar), *Bellerophon* (crippled by Zeus) – 'No, no,' says Dikaiopolis, 'someone even more abject.' '*I* know who you mean,' Euripides says, 'Telephos.' We have already met Telephos in Archilochos' poem about the Greeks' mistaken landing at Mysia when they were trying to find Troy to attack it. There was a sequel to that episode: Telephos, despite his bravery on that day, was wounded by Achilles in the battle. The wound refused to heal; Telephos received an oracle saying only the one who inflicted the wound could heal it. Accordingly, Telephos went to Argos, where Achilles was stationed, and down-dressed as a beggar to disguise himself. He took the young Orestes as hostage and sat on an altar, demanding asylum. The scene was famous; vase paintings showed the Mysian king as a supplicant on the altar, dressed in rags (illus. 41). In the present passage of Aristophanes, Dikaiopolis asks Euripides not only for Telephos' rags but also for his Mysian cap, so as to cement the visual allusion to Telephos.

This scene of Aristophanes' *Acharnians* is a skit on Euripides' penchant for writing tragedies in which the hero is reduced to rags. In broader terms, these plays by Euripides constitute a challenge to the social order of traditional myth: kings, princes, heroes and warriors are shown from the other side: as beggars, dependent on charity. His 'riches-to-rags' plays clearly became notorious enough at Athens to attract Aristophanes' parody. The prototype, however, was Homer's *Odyssey*, in which the hero falls low and rises high. In a state without welfare support schemes to speak of, poverty was an ever-present nightmare. Socrates' scorn for the dress code, Euripides' stage heroes dressed in rags, even the 'new men' who became prominent in politics reflect a key question raised by democracy and freedom of expression (*parrhēsia*, it was called): are the privileged, entitled class better than poor people? Do clothes make a man, or are they merely an outer dressing that easily comes off?

The question is handled amusingly by Menander in *Dyskolos*, The Bad-Tempered Man. Sostratos, a rich man from town, has fallen in love (at first sight) with the grouch Knēmōn's daughter; the latter, however, shuns contact with anyone, let alone a city slicker who is after his daughter, making it unlikely that he will be sympathetic to Sostratos' approaches. On the advice of the slave, Daos, of the 'good' farmer Gorgias, Sostratos takes off his fine jacket (*chlanis*) and exchanges it for a farmworker's goatskin (*diphthera*, leathern jerkin or goatskin; l. 415). Daos says that if Knēmōn sees Sostratos labouring like a peasant, he might listen to what he has to say:

> (*Daos:*) [*incredulously*] You'll stand beside us wearing *that* fine tweed [lit. 'fine woollen jacket'] while we till the soil? (*Sostratos:*) Why not? (*Daos:*) He'll [Knēmōn] throw clods of earth at you straightaway, curse you as a useless layabout. You need to dig with us. Then, perhaps, if he sees that, he might deign to listen to what you say, thinking your station in life is that of a poor workman. (*Dyskolos* 363–70)

Sostratos shoulders Daos' hoe, exclaiming at its weight, and they set off to Gorgias' plot. Sostratos has agreed to Daos' terms: he must dress the part of the labourer or Knēmōn won't even give him the time of day. In fact the plan misfires. Knēmōn does not come out to his field with his daughter on this day, as there is a (small) crowd of celebrants outside the Shrine of the Nymphs that day, and he shuns

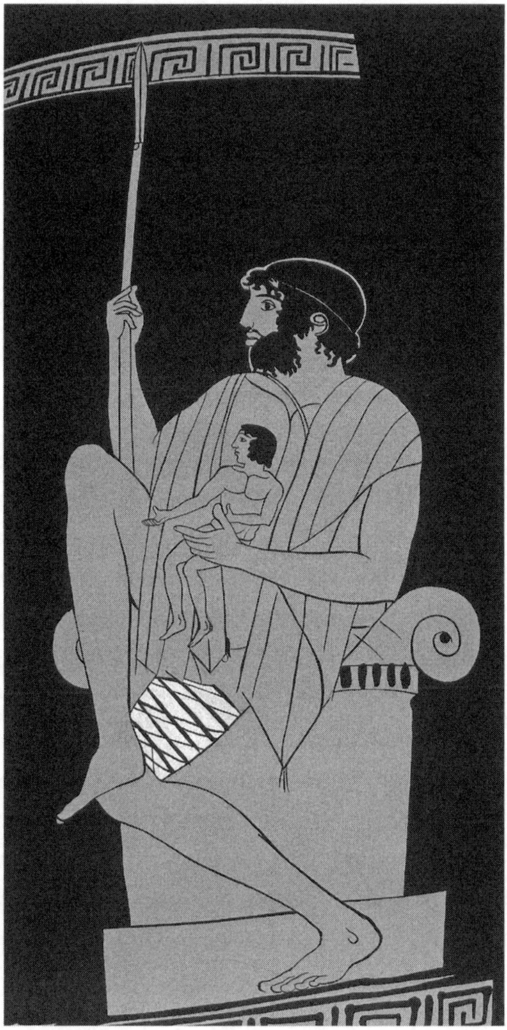

41 Telephos seeking asylum on the altar, with bandaged thigh, holding a spear and the infant Orestes. Ink drawing after a detail from an Athenian red-figure *pelike* (jug), *c.* 450 BC.

them, ducking back indoors. When Sostratos returns from his labours exhausted, he tells how he wasn't up to a farmhand's toil:

> If anyone's short of stress, let them come to Phylē to hunt [that is how Sostratos had first arrived at Knēmōn's home]. God dammit, how the small of my back hurts! My whole back! My neck! My whole body in fact! I set to work with a flourish to begin with, since I'm young, raising my hoe high in the air, like a true farmhand, and striking deep. I worked with a will

> – but not long. Then I made to turn and look behind me to see when the old man might come along with his daughter. That made me really clutch my back, covertly at first. Then when that went on for some time, I was bent double, stiff as a board. But still no one came. The sun burned down. Gorgias watched me arduously trying to straighten – like the beam of a pump – then slumping down with all my weight. 'I don't think he [Knēmōn] is coming any more today, my friend,' he said. (*Dyskolos* 522–39)

The tone is of course humorous, but there are serious underlying issues. Sostratos had to dress down before Knēmōn would even listen to what he had to say. Otherwise Knēmōn would simply dismiss him as a 'good-for-nothing layabout'. Here simple dress is the mark of the simple, honest farmer. However, when Sostratos did try to fit the bill, by dressing appropriately and wielding a hoe under the sun, he rapidly tired and ended up bent double, clutching his back in pain. In other words, his real substance was not up to the trial. The right country jerkin could not disguise the city-boy's untrained body. The opposition honest work versus lazy rich boy comes out clearly, as it does in the rescue scene of the play when it is Gorgias who does the real work in pulling Knēmōn from the well, while Sostratos is only interested in ogling the girl. Whether Knēmōn's daughter would object to marrying into an affluent town family, of whom Sostratos was the son, is another matter.

Cross-dressing

These plays mentioned – one Old and one New Comedy and a range of tragedies by Euripides – experiment with status as marked by contrasting suits of clothes: the rags of the beggar contrasted with the robes of a king. Literature – and real life – also played with the gender divide: men dressing as women, and vice versa. In myth, the tribe of women called Amazons were known for their masculine prowess as warriors despite their feminine bodies. Myth (the epic *Aithiopis*) even told of Achilles' tragic love for Penthesilea, an Amazon queen, whom he slew. This is not cross-dressing. Rather, a far-flung (Thracian)

42 Battle between the Greeks and the Amazons, marble relief on a sarcophagus from Cyprus, *c.* 320 BC. The Amazons are dressed in Persian style with trousers with attached shoes, under a *chitōn* with cap (*tiara*). The Greeks are shown naked (like athletes) with hoplite arms.

warrior tribe of women usually shown as bare-breasted. One would say that they were crossing 'gender stereotypes'. Ironically, myth also knew the story of Achilles' dressing up as a girl before the Trojan War to avoid military service.[8]

Another play of Aristophanes, the *Women at the Thesmophoria*, has a great deal to say about effeminate men and men dressing up as women.[9] It is another play about Euripides: Aristophanic comedy would not have chosen him as its butt, or Socrates (in *Clouds*), unless the men – and their foibles – were really well known in Athens: the satirical puppet show *Spitting Image* only targets the top politicians and public figures for its ridicule. In *Women at the Thesmophoria*, Euripides complains that the women of Athens are conspiring against him in a secret nocturnal conspiracy at the Thesmophoria, because he allegedly bad-mouths them in his plays (Phaidra, for example, in his first *Hippolytos* was wanton).[10] Now his plan is to go to the poet Agathon – well known for his effeminate voice and manners – and persuade him to speak in his defence before the women; the women will, hopefully, not register him as an intruder. When Euripides, together with a Relative, visits Agathon, he is busy composing an ode for a tragedy. He comes out of his house and sings a choral ode, imitating both the parts of the poet and the women's chorus who respond. Such an arrangement is called an *amoibaion*, or 'reply song'. The song is a hymn to Apollo, Artemis and Lēto, in very flowery language.

The Relative exclaims on hearing the song that it sent a shiver up his spine with its lascivious melody and words – like a tongue-kiss, he says. Then he questions Agathon about his identity, as he can't decide from the way he is dressed whether he is a man or a woman. He sees conflicting evidence:

> How does the lyre go with the yellow frock? The skin with the hairnet? Why the perfume and the bra? They're out of place. What's the mirror doing side by side with a sword? And you yourself, young fellow, are you a man? If so, where's the penis? The sports jacket? The Spartan shoes? Or are you a woman? In that case, where are your tits? (ll. 137–43)

Agathon explains that the poet must adapt to the person he is portraying: 'If I'm writing about women, I must change the look of my body accordingly. If one's writing about men, well, that's in one's nature anyway. But for what doesn't come naturally, an imitation must be sought for' (ll. 151–6). The Relative comments sardonically: 'Well, tell me when you're writing a satyr-play; I'll help from behind with a hard-on.'[11] Agathon seems to be preaching an extreme version of the 'method' school of acting. The playwright himself must dress up to match the kind of play he is writing: 'I dress according to what I have in mind: for the writer must adapt his behaviour to the plays he is writing' (ll. 148–50).

Euripides explains to Agathon why he has come. Can Agathon, please, infiltrate the women's gathering in the precinct of Demeter and Pherephatta (the goddesses of the Thesmophoria) and speak in his defence? Why don't you do it yourself? Agathon responds. I'm old and have a beard, says Euripides, whereas you're 'handsome, pale-skinned, clean-shaven, with an effeminate voice, soft-skinned, adorable to look at' (ll. 191–2). Agathon protests that the women will think he is spying on their clandestine rites and hoping to steal some 'female-style sex' (he means, as a woman); he refuses. Euripides is disappointed, but his Relative comforts him and offers to take on the part. At this point the play has a lot of fun with the transvestite theme. The Relative undresses, and dresses up as a woman on stage.

The humour is unsubtle, meant to amuse men, real *Carry On*-style farce with Kenneth Williams as Agathon, perhaps, and Sid James as the Relative.

However, the scene is more revealing of women's typical dress, as seen through male eyes, than representations in art. The Relative first drops his *himation* (perhaps the only garment he is wearing). Euripides borrows a razor from Agathon and begins to shave him. Then he gets him to bend over to singe off his pubic hair, having called for a torch or a lamp. The Relative squeals and protests; Euripides threatens to stick a pin in him (a woman's weapon) if he is not quiet. After the singeing, the Relative complains he is covered in soot. It should be explained that comic actors in Old Comedy (Aristophanes' genre) wore an artificial phallus as part of their costume, so this horseplay could be enacted without really baring the actor. Then comes the dressing:

> (*Euripides:*) Agathon, since you refuse to play the part yourself, lend him [the Relative] clothes and a bra. Don't tell me you don't have any. (*Agathon:*) Help yourselves. I don't mind. (*Relative:*) What should I put on? (*Euripides:*) Take the yellow frock first and put it on. (*Relative:*) By Aphrodite, I will. It has the sweet smell of sex. Help me fasten the belt. Now hand me the bra. (*Euripides:*) There. (*Relative:*) Now arrange the pleats nicely round my legs. (*Euripides:*) We need a hair net and a hairband. (*Agathon:*) Here's a wig, which I wear at night. (*Euripides:*) Perfect. (*Relative:*) Will it fit? (*Euripides:*) Like a dream! Now for a suitable top. (*Agathon:*) Take one from the couch. (*Euripides:*) And we'll need shoes. (*Agathon:*) Take mine here. (*Thesmophoriazousai* 249–62)

This quick-fire three-way exchange between Euripides, Agathon and the Relative shows how all three stage characters were involved in the dressing up of the Relative in women's clothes provided by Agathon. Euripides comments on the result: 'Well, here's our man who looks like a woman. If you say anything, be sure to use a woman's voice, and make it convincing' (ll. 266–8). Even without seeing the stage action, we can imagine the 'man's' appearance quite well. After the clowning removal of facial and body hair, we have heard mentioned his dress, his underwear (only a bra), belt, hair arrangement, top and shoes. Presumably the stage props used were quite realistic and the end result convincing, to draw laughs. The disguise shows that men expected women to be smooth-skinned, dressed in pretty clothes, with their hair nicely done up, wearing women's shoes (remember, the Relative had commented on Agathon's effeminate shoes when he first appeared, and Agathon had lent these to the Relative). The other important thing, of course, is that the dressing of a man as a woman spy is meant to draw ribald laughter. This is not a Love Parade or Pride march, but more men's locker-room fun, not exactly at the expense of women but certainly not in sympathy with women or cross-dressing men, either.

There is a little more to the Agathon skit than meets the eye, however. It is of course a comic exaggeration to say that a poet or playwright must dress like a woman to write from a woman's point of view. However, it *is* necessary for that poet to assimilate mentally with the person he is (re)creating in fiction. Agathon is saying, in effect, that his appearance is a reflection of his empathy with the figures he is creating for the stage. He names other writers who have cultivated a well-groomed appearance in harmony, as it were, with their polished writing:

> Besides, one can recognize a bad poet as someone who is unkempt and uncombed. Look at Ibykos and Anakreon of Teos and Alkaios – they cultivated harmony; they wore hairbands, they dressed in the polished, Ionian style. And Phrynichos – you've heard of him – he was naturally good-looking and dressed accordingly. For that reason his plays were attractive, too. One necessarily writes what suits one's nature. (*Relative:*) So that's why ugly Philokleēs writes ugly plays, and Xenokleēs, who's bad, writes badly. And Theognis, being a cold fish, writes cold poetry. (*Agathon:*) It's inevitable. That's why I look after my appearance. (ll. 159–72)

43 Bust of Demetrios of Phaleron, pro-Macedonian governor of Athens (317–307 BC), Roman copy of Greek original, 1st century BC–1st century AD.

Now we are getting a slightly different picture of Agathon. Instead of 'effeminate' Agathon, we get a glimpse of a poet who cultivates his image, as we say now, as a reflection of his poetry. He is not expressing any kind of sexual preference or orientation, but rather takes care about his appearance as he takes care about his verses. A disreputable exterior might reflect a disreputable interior, and vice versa.

It is a message that emerges clearly in an anecdote about another dramatic poet, Menander, a hundred years later. In 317 BC, Demetrios of Phaleron took control of Athens in cahoots with the Macedonian conquerors of Greece. A poem by the Latin author of fables Phaedrus (1st century AD) describes how even the leaders of Athens sucked up to him, while inwardly lamenting their loss of freedom. Even the retiring, who cultivated the pursuits of leisure,[12] followed suit:

> Among them was Menander, well known for his comedies. Demetrios had read his works but didn't know the man personally. He was a great admirer of his genius. So Menander showed himself, anointed with perfumed oil, dressed extravagantly, mincing along with dainty step. When the tyrant saw him at the end of the line, he said: 'Who's this poof [*kinaidos*] who dares to come before my eyes?' His entourage replied: 'It's the writer Menander.' Demetrios immediately changed his tune: 'No man', he said, 'has ever looked more comely!' (Phaedrus V.1; PCG *Testimonia* 10)

So Menander seems to be bearing out what Agathon had said: the good poet dresses well, takes care about his image. The anecdote shows how Demetrios' perception immediately changed when he knew who it was he was looking at. His first impression was that the man passing in the procession belonged to the class of male prostitute (*kinaidos*); but when he knew who he was dealing with, he revised his opinion and admired Menander's flamboyant look. It seems that (some) artists cultivated a distinctive dress code in Athens: the dandy look, one could perhaps call it. One might add that a shaved face, as Menander had, has been interpreted as pro-Macedonian, as opposed to the Greek norm before, which was full-bearded.

9
Celebration

The music of the phorminx
and clear-voiced choral songs
do not suit grief-laden war
any more than the battle-clash
of bronze suits celebrations.
There is a right moment
for all men's activities.
Bacchylides, *Ode* 14.12–18

Myth

Silver City

As we saw earlier, Hephaistos' depiction of humanity on the Shield of Achilles juxtaposed a city at war with a city at peace. The war scene was a vignette of the war itself – two armies, one besieging, one defending, a city – while the city at peace, which is described at greater length and detail, is, in context, like the mirage of an oasis seen shimmering and inviting on the horizon. In the context of the *Iliad* it feels like a depiction of everything life isn't in the ten-year-long battle for Troy. It represents, one feels, a deliberate counterfoil to the epic story itself: what the participants in the war have left behind and what, at this juncture, seems unattainable. Its chief characteristic is celebration, as if the whole city is on holiday, flags and bunting flying, everyone dancing in the streets.

> On it [the shield] he fashioned two fine cities of human beings. In one there were weddings and celebrations, brides were being led from their childhood bedrooms through the town by the light of torches, and strains of the wedding song rang out. Young male dancers danced around them, while flutes and lyres played loudly. The womenfolk stood in their doorways marvelling at the sight, and crowds were gathered in the market square. (*Iliad* 18.490–97)

Interestingly, the other conspicuous feature of the city at peace hammered out by Hephaistos is a law court: a civil dispute is being resolved by peaceful, fair means rather than by force. Although the divine craftsman Hephaistos was capable of making drinks trolleys move by themselves through the halls of Olympus (18.375–7), he could never in fact have depicted the action and speeches of this legal dispute in the static medium of metal. Clearly it was important to Homer that he spelled out this aspect of his allegory: law and justice stand in direct opposition to arms and warfare, which immediately follow in his creation. Then Hephaistos passes on to further peaceful scenes, as if the war scene had been a sudden twister on an otherwise fine day, raising the dust and causing havoc but subsiding relatively quickly to make way once more for the celebrations of peacetime:

> Then the famous lame craftsman-god added a dancing place like the one Daidalos made once for Ariadne of the beautiful hair in wide Knossos. There young men and desirable girls were dancing holding their partners' wrists in their hands. The girls were dressed in light linen dresses, whilst the youths wore *chitōns* of fine material, gleaming slightly with oil. The girls wore fine diadems, the boys held golden knives with silver sheaths. Now they danced light-footedly in a circle, like a potter who twirls his wheel between his palms where he is seated, to see if it spins smoothly. Now again they danced in lines facing each other, surrounded by a crowd of spectators all enjoying themselves. And in their midst, two acrobats whirled and tumbled in time to the music. And when the

> divine craftsman had completed the set of arms . . . Achilles' mother took them from Hephaistos . . . and dived down from Olympus like a hawk. (18.590–617)

It is interesting that Homer compares Hephaistos' dance floor with that made by Daidalos for Ariadne, as the verb he used before for silver relief work was *daidallō*, embellish, decorate. Daidalos was the master craftsman of myth – once even making wings for himself and his son Ikaros to fly – and either his name derives from the verb, or perhaps vice versa. Similar silver relief work from Mycenaean times has been discovered by archaeology, but the wealth of detail and illusion of lively movement created by Hephaistos are, of course, superhuman. The key elements of both scenes of celebration are music, song and dance. At the wedding celebration, the wedding hymn (*hymenaios*, or Song of Hymen) rings out with accompaniment by wind (*aulos*) and string (*phorminx*; *lyra*) instruments. There is dancing in the street, and the townsfolk look on as the bridal procession passes. The second celebration seems to be more a harvest festival, as, between the city at war and this, there is a long description of working the fields and bringing in the harvest. In this second scene, two chorus lines are mentioned: the boys in one and the girls in the other, but they dance together, holding hands in the formation called 'wrist on wrist' in ancient dance terminology. They dance either in circular formation (*kyklios choros*), as shown by the simile of the potter's wheel, or in line formation. Their festive clothes are named, as are some accessories: garlands of flowers for the girls, ceremonial knives for the men (some folk dances in Georgia today involve men twirling knives in their hands). We also hear of acrobats or tumblers, in the crowd, livening up the atmosphere still further. Homer has focused on two reasons for celebration: weddings and the harvest, two essentials for the survival of the community, both the antithesis of war.

Delia

The Shield of Achilles is a kind of mirror of the world as it was known to the epic. The celebrations depicted on it have their corollary in the real world, that is, the world known to Homer and his audience.

The most famous public celebrations from the earliest period were the Panhellenic festivals held at famous sites of common worship: Delphi, the seat of the Delphic oracle; the Isthmos of Corinth, where Poseidon was worshipped; and then, and above all for the Ionian Greeks, Delos, where Apollo's birth was celebrated in a gathering of all Ionian peoples. That included the Greek towns along the seaboard of Asia Minor, the Aegean islands with Ionian communities, and Athens itself as the homeland of the Ionians. Delos in myth was the birthplace of Apollo and Artemis; Letō was the mother and Zeus the father. Another poem in the epic style but probably somewhat later than the *Odyssey*, the *Homeric Hymn to Apollo*, narrates the birth of Apollo and Artemis on Delos; then it describes the calendrical festival called Delia, celebrating the birth, before moving on to Apollo's other great triumph, his takeover of the Delphic oracle, which before in myth had previous occupants. The Ionian peoples sent delegations to Delos

44 The gods of the Delia: Apollo (with *phorminx*) and Artemis, accompanied by Hermes heralding them. Attic black-figure amphora, *c.* 530 BC, found in Caere, Cerveteri, Italy.

to sacrifice, take part in choral dances celebrating the cult of Apollo (and Artemis), and participate in other competitions. Delos itself was the 'dance floor' of the Aegean. The Cyclades islands were so called because they were arranged in a circle round Delos, as a chorus dances in ring formation (*kyklios choros*, we have already met) round a god's altar (Callimachus, *Hymn* 4.300–303).

The *Homeric Hymn to Apollo* contains a vivid description of the ships putting into Delos to celebrate the festival, and the dances, songs and athletic competitions performed there. The hymns called 'Homeric' are so-called because the metre and diction are just like Homer's epics *Iliad* and *Odyssey*. Probably the long hymns are somewhat later than the epics, but they belong to the same world and cultural orbit. In fact they were probably composed for recitation at precisely the Panhellenic festivals that they mention: the *Hymn to Apollo* for the Delia, the *Hymn to Demeter* for her major festival at Eleusis in Attica, for example. On the other hand, it is very unlikely that they were composed by the same poet as the major epics.[1] The hymn describes the celebrations at the Delia as follows:

> But you, Phoibos Apollo, delight most in Delos [of all the places you frequent], there, where the Ionians in their ankle-length *chitōns* gather together with their children and their demure wives. They celebrate memorial games in your honour: boxing, dancing, singing in a joyful competitive spirit. Anyone watching the Ionian meeting might think them immortal and ageless for all time to come. He would see the beauty of it all, the heart-warming sight of the men and their elegantly dressed women, the swift ships and their rich possessions. In addition there is this special attraction, whose fame will never die: the girls of Delos who serve in Apollo's cult. First they sing a hymn for Apollo, then one for Lēto and Artemis, who loves archery, then they sing a hymn celebrating men and women of old, and their song delights the audience. They have the knack of imitating the vocals and intonation of all possible peoples. Each one would say it was themselves speaking, the beautiful song is so well matched. But come, may Apollo be

45 The circular dance of the Deliades, 'wrist on wrist'. Lyre player second from left (Apollo!). Drawing after a *lebes gamikos* (nuptial vase) from Delos, 470–460 BC.

> gracious and Artemis, too, and you all enjoy the celebration!
> (*Homeric Hymn to Apollo* 146–66)

The keynote of this description is *charis*, delight, gratitude, enthusiasm – all these things applying to the human celebrants rejoicing in their worship of Apollo and Artemis through performative arts. It is also the word used for the *charis*, grace or blessing, which the god is thought to grant people who celebrate him/her in this way. In other words, the celebration is a reciprocal festival of display and enthusiasm. It has little to do with inner contemplation of a transcendent god. Rather, it is a feast of the senses, aspiring to the beauty and bliss of the gods. And they could see Apollo and Artemis were among them as their cult statues were on view for the festival. One of the human achievements is also, unashamedly, wealth. We note the 'many possessions' (*ktēmata polla*) the people bring with them: these are the sacrifices and votive offerings for the gods, and the rich costumes and accessories which the people have brought with them for the display. In the previous chapter we met the 'ankle-length *chitōns*' for which the Ionians were famous.

Athens, the Ionian islanders and the Ionian cities in Asia Minor sent annual choruses to Delos to celebrate the Delia. The *paians* (roughly, hymns to Apollo) of Pindar (first half of the fifth century BC) have been partially recovered from a tattered papyrus from Oxyrhynchus. A number of them are written for choruses from Ionian cities to be sung at the Delia – unfortunately, most of them are only partially legible. One, *Paian* 5, probably written for the

Athenians themselves, gives a good impression of the chauvinistic (or, more politely, patriotic) tenor of this gathering of Ionians on 'their' island, Delos, sacred to Apollo. Incidentally, this angle on Delos was a deliberate challenge to 'Doric' Apollo, whose cult centre was Delphi. Thus the ideology of the Delia in the *Homeric Hymn to Apollo* was perpetuated and strengthened in the following centuries. It is a phenomenon comparable to Christmas celebrating the birth of Jesus in Bethlehem or the Islamic festival at Mecca celebrating the birth of the prophet Muhammad. Scholarship on this text suggests that 'they' at the beginning of this fragment are the Ionian Greeks coming from Athens, colonizing Euboea first, then moving through the Cyclades encircling Delos:

> . . . they
> conquered and settled Euboea
> – hail, Apollo of Delos! –
> and they settled the scattered
> sheep-rearing islands and took over
> famous Delos once golden-haired
> Apollo granted them the right
> to dwell on Asteria's body
> – hail, Apollo of Delos! –
> where Lēto's children may, please,
> receive me [Pindar] kindly in their hearts,
> your minister with the resonant
> and melodious strains
> of the widely famed *paian*! (*Paian* 5.35–47)

No coincidence, then, that after the Persian Wars when Athens gathered allies (and subjects) around her, purportedly as a bulwark against future aggression from Persia, the alliance was called the Delian League. Subjects and member states paid an annual levy into a war coffer (*phoros*), which was first stored in the sanctuary of Delos, then transferred – to Athens. From being a champion of freedom and democracy, the grumbles among subject states grew louder until Athens' hegemony began to be called a *tyrannis*, tyranny, which led indirectly some fifty years after Plataia to the Peloponnesian War. Delos, in this time before things began to turn sour, became a beacon of freedom for the Ionian Greeks. Time and time again, choruses in Euripides' plays (last three decades of the fifth century BC) sing longingly of the ideal beauty of Delian celebration. The situation in *Iphigeneia in Tauris*, for example, is this. Iphigeneia was going to be sacrificed to Artemis so the Greeks could sail against Troy; headwinds (or a calm) were holding them up at Aulis, where the fleet had assembled. Kalchas (see illus. 15) read the signs to indicate that Artemis was offended, and must be placated by the sacrifice of first-fruits. According to (one version of the) myth, Artemis herself whisked her from her own altar to safety in the Tauric Chersonese (Crimea). There she was instated as priestess of Artemis' barbaric cult, involving the human sacrifice of any unfortunate sailors who happened to be cast up there – like Orestes, Iphigeneia's own brother. Before Orestes' 'great escape' with his sister from Tauris back to Greece, the chorus of captive Greek women sing:

> I long for the public spaces of Greece,
> I long for Artemis, goddess of childbed,
> whose home is the Delian shore
> and the soft-leaved palm,
> the flourishing laurel
> and the sacred trunk of grey-green
> olive, friend to Lēto in travail,
> and the lake with its circular,
> eddying water where the swan
> celebrates the Muses with its song.
> (*Iphigeneia in Tauris* 1096–105)

Their longing for escape from bonds in a barbaric land takes the form of nostalgic recall of the Delia festival in honour of Lēto's delivery of Apollo and Artemis. Here further details of the cult topography of Delos are mentioned: the laurel and olive as well as the palm tree. Here it is the olive that is said to have supported Lēto's labour and delivery – this in deference to an Atheno-centric audience, devotees of the sacred olive of Athena. Also the lake on Delos called Kynthos, on which Apollo's bird, the swan, was thought to, well, swan around. There was a connection between the swan's reputation for song and Apollo as the leader of the Muses. It is an ideal topography: a sacred grove of trees, a sacred bird, on the spot where the sacred birth of Lēto's twins – Zeus' progeny – was celebrated.

Another triumph was celebrated annually on Delos by the Athenians, again deriving from myth. Theseus was said to have ended the gory tyranny of King Minōs of Knossos, who demanded a tithe of Athenian girls and youths each year, by killing the Minotaur. The story is famous: the hybrid monster of Crete (half man, half bull) in his labyrinth; his hunger for young human flesh; Ariadne's famous thread, which helped Theseus to retrace his steps out of the labyrinth after killing the Minotaur; Theseus' triumphant return with Ariadne to Athens; Ariadne's abandonment on Naxos (saved by Dionysos). Despite this unchivalrous turn at the end of the story, the Athenians celebrated Theseus' heroic act by sending each year a *theōria*, or 'sacred embassy', to Delos. Theseus was a legendary king of Athens. The annual ritual was an expression of national pride in their hero, his ending of an annual sacrifice of Athenian youth, Athens' connection to the sacred isle of Delos. A song of the lyric poet Bacchylides (early fifth century BC) tells part of the story in a *paian*-hymn intended to be sung on Delos by a chorus from Kēos (probably at the Delia). King Minōs is escorting the 'twice-seven' girls and youths to Knossos as the fatal tithe. On board ship, he conceives a desire for one of the girls and makes to rape her. Theseus (the *architheōros*, leader of the young men) challenges him. Minōs boasts of his descent from Zeus and challenges Theseus to dive to the bottom of the sea to fetch Minōs' ring as proof that he is descended from Poseidon. Theseus dives in after the ring, is conveyed to Nēreus' palace under the sea by friendly dolphins, receives divine gifts from the Nereids and Amphitritē (Nēreus' wife) and swims up to the surface again, emerging beside the ship. All are astounded:

> How he shattered the King of Knossos' expectations when he emerged not even wet from the sea, a wonder to all! The divine gifts shone on his body, the seven girls cried out in

> sudden jubilation and the sea rang out. Next to them, the youths struck up a joyful paian. Delian [Apollo], may your heart be warmed by the choral dance of the Keïans and grant a divine share of good fortune! (Bacchylides 17; Dithyramb 3, *Youths or: Theseus* 120–32)

The poem itself is a choral song meant for performance by a chorus of youths from Kēos in honour of Delian Apollo. The mythical story it narrates involves choral song both on the seabed, by the Nereïds, and again when Theseus rejoins the ship by the twice-seven Athenians. Their mood on seeing Theseus saved from what they took to be certain death is spontaneous joy and celebration. Minōs, on the other hand, is stunned to see his rival reappear after the ordeal. In other words, the myth told by the song mirrors the anticipated performance on Delos. A celebration of Theseus' heroism and triumph over the brutish Minōs will be performed for Delian Apollo in tune with ritual celebration. One notes how Bacchylides has selected a preliminary episode in the Theseus and the Minotaur myth: before even reaching Crete, he has won a moral victory over the tormentor of Athens' youth, Minōs, as a foretaste of his major victory over the Minotaur. One feels that the job is already half done, morally at least, on board ship: now all that remains is to finish off Minōs' pet monster. At the same time, the poem gives a full impression of what choral celebration at the Delia may have entailed: girls and youths formed the chorus dancing wrist-on-wrist after the precedent of the Delian Maidens themselves. What they sang and celebrated in dance was an episode of myth in tune with the god's cult. All we are missing is the music.

The Athenian *theōria* to Delos to thank Apollo for Theseus' deliverance was a public festival during which the wheels of state were put on hold. Socrates owed a stay of execution in 399 BC to this cult regulation, as Plato explains in the *Phaedo*, the dialogue describing Socrates' last hours. One of those present, Echekrates, has asked Phaidōn why Socrates' execution followed so long after the trial. Phaidōn replies:

> It so happened that on the day before his trial the stern of the ship which the Athenians send to Delos was crowned.

46 Theseus slays the Minotaur in his Labyrinth, with a girl and youth on either side representing the 'twice-seven' Athenian youths saved by Theseus' heroic act. Attic black-figure neck amphora, *c.* 550 BC, workshop of Exekias.

(*Echekrates:*) What is the meaning of that? (*Phaidōn:*) This is the ship, according to Athenian lore, in which Theseus once took the 'twice seven' to Crete. He saved them and was saved himself. They had vowed to Apollo on that occasion, so legend goes, that, if they were saved, they would send an annual *theōria* to Delos. They still do this to this day once a year. When they commence the ceremony, it is sacred law at Athens at this time to purify the city and not to conduct public executions, before the ship sails to Delos and back again. Sometimes this takes a good while, when the winds happen to be contrary. (*Phaedo* 58a6–c1)

It seems we have the Delian *theōria* of 399 BC to thank for Plato's *Phaedo*, a dramatic and moving dialogue set in prison, in which Socrates expounds reasons for not fearing death. The Roman Stoic Cato the Younger, it is said, read the *Phaedo* (twice) as consolation before his (politically imposed) suicide in 46 BC (Plutarch, *Cato Minor*, 68–70). Plato writes that he personally was absent from these final hours with Socrates owing to illness. The Aristotelian *Constitution of Athens* adds a little detail on the ceremony: '[The Governor of Athens] appoints the chorus-masters for Delos and a commander of the thirty-oared ship carrying the youths' (56.3.14–16). This confirms that choruses were sent on the occasion, and that the youths taking part (male and female) were still called *ēïtheoi*, youths, which was the official designation of the 'twice seven' sent as tithe to Minōs in Knossos. It was a relatively small ship at thirty oars. It is very unlikely that the voyage to Delos included any kind of diving contest en route! Interestingly, it seems from a long hymn to Delos written by the Alexandrian poet-scholar Callimachus in the third century BC, that Theseus thanked *Aphrodite* on Delos when he returned triumphant from killing the Minotaur. It would seem that the focus on Aphrodite initially – she had an altar on Delos – reflected Ariadne's love for Theseus, when his life was hanging by a thread, so to speak (even if he did forgetfully leave her behind on Naxos!).[2]

> And then the sacred and far-famed image of ancient Kypris [Aphrodite] which Theseus dedicated when he returned from Crete with the youths [of Athens], is decked out in garlands. They [the 'twice-seven' youths] fled the dire bellowing of Pasiphaē's ferocious child [Minotaur] and its hidden lair in the twisting labyrinth. Lady [Aphrodite], around your altar they danced the ring-dance to the stirring music of the kithara [lyre], and Theseus led the dance. From then on in perpetuity the children of Kekrops [Athenians] send the theoric ship with its sacred tackle to Phoibos [Apollo]. (*Hymn IV to Delos* 307–15)

Although Theseus, according to tradition, dedicated the image and altar of Aphrodite at the inaugural celebration of salvation, the annual

Athenian theoric mission was to Apollo. Curiously, it seems that the tackle of the ship was offered to Phoibos each year: a votive offering in kind, memorializing Theseus' ship. The dance is to lyre music, so not a dithyramb, more likely a *paian*, victory song, to Apollo. The ode of Bacchylides above was a contribution to the Delia festival by the islanders of Kēos, not an Athenian song commemorating Theseus' salvation, although the myth it sets to music – Theseus' dive for Minōs' ring – is pure Athenian national tradition.

A wedding made in heaven

As we have seen in other areas of life (love, status, war, for example), Homeric themes pass into other, later genres as effortlessly and naturally as water flowing through an irrigation system. The conjugal love of Hektor and Andromache, Hektor's tragic death and Andromache's disconsolate mourning form a leitmotif of the *Iliad*. The lyric poet Sappho, who reflects epic in other ways, too, wrote a poem in celebration of their marriage, thus inverting the emphasis in the *Iliad*, just as she had inverted her priorities in poem number 16. It focuses, perhaps deliberately, on one of Hephaistos' scenes of celebration on the Shield of Achilles, a wedding. It is transmitted on two papyri dug up in the late nineteenth century by Bernard Pyne Grenfell and Arthur Surridge Hunt: P.Oxy. 1232 (first half of the third century AD) and P.Oxy. 2076 (first/second century AD). Both are fragmentary, preventing full or seamless translation, but still it is another miraculous acquisition from the rubbish dump of used papyri in a village called Oxyrhynchus on the Nile in Egypt. The poem describes how Andromache was fetched from Hypoplakian Thebes (in Cilicia) and brought to Troy for her wedding to Hektor. The major features of a wedding procession illustrated by Hephaistos on the shield recur in Sappho's poem:

> Idaios the swift messenger [announced] the following: '... Hektor and his comrades are bringing from Thebes and the waters of River Plakia in their ships soft, bright-eyed, Andromache over the salt sea. And with her, many gold twists of jewellery, perfumed, purple garments, a rich variety of accessories, countless silver drinking cups and ivory.'

> . . . they move . . . to holy Ilion [Troy] and the sweet-tongued flute . . . accompanies [the bridal procession], and the sound of castanets . . . while the girls sang the ceremonial song whose strains rose high into the air. And everywhere along the streets mixing bowls [of wine] were placed, and cups . . . and myrrh, cassia and incense smells wafted . . . older women let out the ritual yodelling while all the men sang the ritual paean, an invocation of Paōn Apollo, lord of the lyre, and they sang the praises of Hektor and Andromache, like unto the gods. (Sappho fr. 44 Voigt)

Sappho's poem may have been intended as accompaniment for an actual wedding in Mytilene (in Lesbos). In other words, there would have been a comparison intended between the splendour of a real couple's wedding and a mythical precedent, one as famous as any: Hektor and Andromache. If that is true, one assumes the congregation concentrated on the fame of Hektor's wedding without thinking too far forward to his tragic death in the *Iliad*, orphaning his small son Astyanax and condemning Andromache to a future as slave of a Greek. Incidentally, one notes a certain structural similarity between the two types of celebration we have focused on: the various occasions of *theōria* to Delos and the wedding of Andromache: both involve movement towards a cult centre by the participants, accompanied by lavish display, song and dance. The ritual delegations to Delos arrived by ship; they sang their choruses both as they approached Apollo's sanctuary (*prosodia*) and around his altar (*paian*). When Andromache arrived in Troy from overseas in Thebes, her progress up towards Priam's palace on the citadel of Troy was also accompanied by ritual chants, communion in wine, a paean to Apollo, the bridal couple resplendent as gods on their day. Celebration in these two cases aims to join the human with the divine spheres, even if only briefly for the occasion. The typical means for this assimilation are song, dance, wine and play. They allow the participants to enter into a mood of thanksgiving, of heightened receptiveness, in which they can feel the presence of the gods.

History

Festival of Freedom

The Battle of Plataia in 479 BC marked the end of the Persian invasion of Greece led by Xerxes the year before. The commander, Mardonios, was killed. Only a fraction of the initially enormous army of Mardonios made it out of Thebes once the battle was lost. The day was celebrated as Freedom Day that year, with honours paid to Zeus Eleutherios ('Of Freedom'), and every four years a festival of freedom, the Eleutheria, was held from then on for centuries afterwards. The magnitude of the event, and the scale of the celebrations marking it, can be compared to VE Day in Europe, for example, which is also celebrated every year.

The inaugural celebration went anything but smoothly, however. Plutarch in his *Life of Aristides* gives us a detailed account, based on Herodotus' narrative of the battle mainly, but with details supplemented from other historians. So far, we touched on the defeat of the Persian army under Mardonios when hearing the story of a girl from Kōs, who had been enslaved by the Persian aristocrat Pharandatēs but regained her freedom through the Spartan general Pausanias before the smoke of battle, so to speak, had cleared. Below, we hear of a grim *symposion* held in Thebes just before the battle. From Plutarch's account, we gain a good impression of the dynamics of such an interstate celebration, involving as it did vying states, celebration and mourning (for the fallen) and, above all, divine sanction.

He tells how the Spartan force defeated the Persians, while the Athenians routed the Thebans, who had sided with the Persians. The word for this 'siding with the Persians' is *mēdizō*, literally 'medize', or 'be like the Medes'. One Aeimnēstos managed to kill Mardonios himself by hitting him with a stone: this was said to be in accordance with an oracle from Amphiaraōs. The remaining Persians retreated inside their defensive palisade at Thebes; there the Athenians came to support the Spartans, who had little experience with siege warfare. Plutarch records that of the 30,000-strong Persians some 4,000 survived, including those who fled Thebes with Artabazos. Of the entire Greek army 1,360 fell; 52 Athenians fell, all of these from one tribe (*phylē*) called Aiantis. For this reason, this tribe sacrificed to the Sphragitid Nymphs (deities of Mount Kithairōn in Attica) according to instructions from Delphi, and charged the Athenian state for the celebration.

Ninety-one Spartans, eleven Tegeans. That was the entire death toll of this momentous battle on the Greek side. Immediately the quarrels began. The Athenians did not agree that the Spartans should get the prize of honour (*aristeion*), nor that they should erect the victory marker (*tropaion*). Since both sides were still armed for battle, it was a dangerous stand-off; the 'Hellenic cause', says Plutarch, 'was very nearly sunk.' However, the Athenian Aristides ('The Wise') used all his diplomatic skills to calm tempers and avert a crisis. Finally, both sides agreed to give pride of place to a third party, the Corinthians, and to formulate the victory epigram, attributed to Simonides, as follows:

> This altar, on the strength of their victory, a deed of Ares,
> the Greeks who freed Greece by driving out the Persians
> dedicated jointly to Zeus the god of Freedom.

Nota bene, says Plutarch, 'jointly', even though Herodotus only mentioned casualties among three city-states, Athens, Sparta and Tegea. At the council at which this was decided, one Kleokritos of Corinth eulogized the Plataians themselves, where the battle was fought. The sides agreed to raise eighty talents (a large sum) for the Plataians' commemorative acts. The following things were done, Plutarch says:

> They rebuilt the temple of Athena complete with a seated cult image. They decorated the temple with artworks, which still remain in perfect condition [second century AD]. The Spartans erected their own victory monument and the Athenians likewise. When they consulted the Delphic oracle about the appropriate sacrifice, it stipulated that they should dedicate an altar of Zeus Eleutherios ['Of Freedom'], but should not sacrifice on it before the fires in the country were extinguished, as being polluted by the Persians, and

> fresh fire fetched from Delphi from the communal hearth . . . A man from Plataia, Euchidas, promised to fetch fire from the god [Apollo] in the minimum possible time. He arrived there, washed his body with appropriate ablutions, put on a crown of laurel [Apollo's plant], took fire from the altar, and ran off back to Plataia, managing to arrive before sunset. On that one day he covered a thousand stades [about 180 kilometres/112 mi.]. He managed to greet his people and hand over the fire, but then immediately collapsed and died. The Plataians buried him in the precinct of Artemis Eukleia ('Of Fame') as an honour, with the following inscription: 'Euchidas ran to Pytho (Delphi) and back in one day.' (*Life of Aristides* 20.3–6)

The temple of Athena (Areia, Warlike) in Plataia was refurbished; it had been built, apparently, after the Battle of Marathon (490 BC; Pausanias 9.4.1–2), so was intimately connected with victory over the Persians. A pair of victory markers were diplomatically erected. Note how Delphi, consulted about the appropriate sacrifice – no celebration without sacrifice – stipulated that the fire used should be ritually cleansed, as a living thing that had been polluted by the enemy presence. The incredible feat of Euchidas as a runner reflects the heroism of the hour: it seems he felt that the fire from Apollo should not be sullied even by an intervening night, but should arrive pristine, as it were, at Plataia.

There followed another post-war council, at which Aristides proposed the following motion. Delegations from Greece should be sent to Plataia annually, and a festival called Eleutheria be celebrated every four years. There should be a confederate Greek task force raised to pursue the war against the Persians consisting of foot soldiers, cavalry and navy. The Plataians should be granted inviolable and sacred status to sacrifice on behalf of Greece to Zeus.[3] Once the proposal was passed, a separate commemoration was inaugurated in honour of the fallen at Plataia. Here a special sort of sacrifice, known as chthonian ('for the dead': *enagizein*), distinct from the normal type on a raised altar followed by a banquet (*thyein*) was to be conducted. The ritual was to be annual, on the sixteenth of the month Maimaktērion (winter), and Plutarch records that it was maintained until his day:

> They conduct a procession at dawn led by a bugle player who plays the rallying call to war. Carts follow filled with myrtle [a plant of mourning] and wreaths. There is a black bull, and young free men carry libations of wine and milk in jars, and vessels full of oil and myrrh. It is not permitted for anyone of slave status to be involved in these rites as the men had given their lives for freedom. On behalf of all the Plataians, the governor, who the rest of the time is not permitted to touch steel or wear any garb except white, on this occasion dresses in a red *chitōn*. He carries a water jug and walks, armed with a sword, from the town hall through the middle of the town to the graves [of the war dead]. Then he fills the water jug at the fountain and washes the tombstones [of the fallen] and anoints them with myrrh. He sacrifices the black bull into the fire-pit and prays to Zeus and Hermes Chthonios ['Of the Underworld']. He calls on the heroes who had died for Greece to feast upon the blood offerings. Then, having mixed a krater of wine, he pours a libation accompanied by the words: 'I toast the men who died for the freedom of Greece.' The Plataians observe this tradition to my day. (*Life of Aristides* 21.3–6)

Plutarch's account gives us a vivid and detailed picture of the rites following Plataia in their twin aspect: on the one hand the sacrifice for Zeus Eleutherios to celebrate the victory, and on the other the solemn procession and sacrifice of a black bull for the fallen. The tombstones mentioned in the latter (*stēlai*) will have borne a sepulchral epigram, although Plutarch does not record it. The libations of wine and milk are typical offerings for the dead; the black bull sacrificed into a fire-pit, into which its blood ran, likewise. Already in the *Odyssey*, Odysseus lets sheep blood flow into a trench to attract the souls of the dead, who, like hungry bats, gather round the trench, squeaking. In both rites the keynote of 'freedom' is apparent, from Zeus' epithet to the ban on slaves participating in the procession for the war dead. It is perhaps also worth noting that two councils of war decided democratically on the manner in which the freedom festival was to be celebrated then, and into the future: this in itself was a fist shaken in the face of the retreating enemy ruled by a tyrant king. Plutarch even records the friction involved in the democratic process and mentions the amounts of money that had to be approved to enact the rites. The governor of Plataia walked from the town hall (called the 'civic archive', *grammatophylakion*) to the cemetery, thus linking the administration with the commemorative event.

Historical Delia

To return to the Delia festival. So far we have considered it in an ideal context. A pure purpose: to re-enact myth in ritual. A pure procedure: choruses hymning the god(s) in a show of ethnic solidarity. In 417 BC, just before the second phase of the Peloponnesian War, the Athenian general Nikias – the one who died ignominiously in Sicily just four years later – conducted an ostentatious celebration of the Delia in order to enhance his political status and, of course, to honour the god. Plutarch in his *Life of Nikias* gives a detailed account of the affair. The episode shows how devotion to god is one thing; it can, however, have ulterior motives directed more to one's fellow citizens than to the divine. Partly Nikias was known for his devotion to the public cults of Athens, and partly, Plutarch tells us, he was competing with Kleon at the time for popularity and influence over the Athenian assembly.

> Perikles led the people by genuine excellence and eloquence and had no need of cultivating an image before the people, or of gimmicks. Nikias lacked these qualities but was super-rich, and used this to influence the people. He could not plausibly mimic Kleon's so-called charm or clowning to sway the Athenians, so he turned to public celebrations and games and other such competitions to win over the people [*dēmos*], outdoing all rivals past and present with his lavish expenditure and splendour . . . It is told that at one choral display [for Dionysos] his own slave, a very handsome and tall man

> and still unbearded, walked past dressed up as Dionysos. The spectators were delighted by the spectacle and applauded profusely. Nikias stood up and declared that it was not right for anybody devoted to the god to be a slave, and freed the man on the spot. (*Life of Nikias* 3.1–4)

According to this account, Nikias used religious display in particular to enhance his public persona, where Perikles could rely on natural political skills and Kleon on an easy-going manner and clowning in public. Nikias spent lavishly on festivals, games and such like, and donated eye-catching *sacra*, votives. Interesting, too, is his democratic gesture in first providing a handsome slave from his retinue as model for Dionysos (a popular god), then liberating him in public. Plutarch goes on to describe his extravagant outlay as *chorēgos*, master of ceremonies, on the Athenian *theōria* to Delos in 417 BC. In terms of prestige, this was like staging the Olympic Games or hosting a global climate conference.

> There is also a story told about the brilliant and ambitious show he put on for the Delian celebration. The choruses sent by the individual cities to sing hymns for the god [Apollo] were accustomed to put into Delos in a disorderly fashion . . . When Nikias led the sacred delegation [*theōria*], however, he landed on the adjacent island of Rheneia together with the chorus, sacrificial animals and all the paraphernalia. He also brought a pontoon bridge constructed back at Athens of the right dimensions, lavishly embellished with gold and enamel, and festooned in garlands and banners. By night he bridged the narrow strait between Rheneia and Delos. Then, at daybreak, he led the procession for the god across the bridge while the extravagantly attired chorus sang its hymn. Following the sacrifice, the games and the feasting, he dedicated the bronze palm tree as a votive offering for the god. (3.5–7)

What was being celebrated here? A complex of things. First and foremost, Apollo and Artemis, of course. Then Athens, then Nikias himself and his generosity. Clearly he wished everyone to know about his charitable donation, which, we are told, was to be literally set in stone with a memorial stele. The entire display, from procession over a garlanded bridge from Rheneia to Delos, to the choral hymn, sacrifices and banqueting (on meat from the sacrificial animals), served to celebrate Nikias in the entirely honourable duty of serving Apollo. The cause went horribly wrong later, however, when Nikias fell, with an entire Athenian army, in Sicily in 413 BC. Apart from the self-aggrandisement of Nikias, however, the description is valuable for the light it sheds on the nature of such public celebrations. All the basic aspects of cult – the processional hymn for the god known as *prosodion*, or approach-song; the sacrifices, games, banqueting and prayers – are there. What is special on this occasion is the splendour of everything. The *prosodion* is performed in an entirely new and improved way, the performers are dressed and equipped magnificently, a special *temenos*, sacred area, is set aside for post-sacrifice banqueting, a lavish votive offering – the bronze palm tree – is dedicated. Incidentally, the species of tree here is significant. The same *Homeric Hymn to Apollo* relates how Lēto leant against a palm tree when she gave birth to Apollo and Artemis in a crouching position. Odysseus even mentions the palm tree he had seen on Delos when he is spinning a yarn about his identity to Nausikaa (*Odyssey* 6.162–5). Plutarch adds that this votive offering also came to grief: winds blew it over, and it fell onto the giant cult statue of Apollo dedicated by the Naxians and knocked it over: our heroes' feet are made of clay.

Deus imperator

The first women in myth were descended from the gods. Likewise the heroes of Greek mythology were descended directly from the gods. In the Hellenistic age, following the conquests of the Macedonians and the establishment of the kingdoms of the Successors, the reverse process is observable: the kings became gods (see illus. 47). Alexander identified with Dionysos and wished to be respected as a god. The Ptolemies and their wives, who ruled in Alexandria, set themselves up as divine rulers. Another Demetrios, this one called Poliorkētēs, 'City-Sacker', son of Antigonos, was given the titles of 'King' (*Basileus*) and

'Saviour God', along with his father Antigonos (*theoi sōtēres*, Saviour Gods), when he defeated the Macedonian garrison stationed at Athens to impose the rule of Kasandros (Lat. Cassander, one of the Successors, who ruled over Greece). He relieved the proxy governor of Athens, Demetrios of Phaleron, who had been instated by Kasandros, in 317 BC and proclaimed that Athens should be ruled according to its ancestral constitution and laws. For this he was welcomed and celebrated as a god. Plutarch, in his *Life of Demetrios*, describes the excessive adulation that was given to Demetrios. Plutarch says it went to Demetrios' head, corrupting him.

Plutarch mentions at one point that, among the tributes paid to Demetrios, a motion was passed that, whenever Demetrios should enter Athens, he should be received with the divine honours and reception normally given to the gods Demeter and Dionysos. Interestingly, a poem by one Hermoklēs of Kyzikēnos (otherwise unknown) has been transmitted celebrating this very triumphal entry of Demetrios into Athens as a kind of Dionysos in the company of Demeter. He is celebrated as a god; his divine regalia are not spelled out in the poem; it is only said that he shone like the sun among the stars in his train. We must imagine the crowns and royal robes of everyone in this procession. The poem is in an interesting metre: a combination of iambics and the verse unit called ithyphallic. This indicates that the rhythm was used in processions for Dionysos in which a giant puppet phallus was carried along, an accoutrement of this god. It is a further indication that Demetrios was being assimilated into the cult of Dionysos (like Alexander himself). I translate it in prose:

> For the greatest and most beloved gods of our city are assembled. The occasion has brought here together Demeter and Demetrios. She comes to celebrate the sacred mysteries of Korē [Persephone/Pherephatta], whilst He is among us, resplendent as befits a god, handsome and merry. It is a splendid sight: all his friends around him in a circle, with him in the middle. It is as if his friends are the stars, and he the Sun in their midst. O child of Poseidon, greatest god, and Aphrodite, we salute you. The other gods are either miles away or they're deaf, or

> don't exist, or don't care about us one bit: but we see YOU among us! Not of wood, or stone, but in the flesh. (ll. 1–19)

Then the song continues with an appeal to Demetrios to liberate Athens' from tyranny:

> We bow down to you. Please, dear god, first make peace: it's within your power. The Sphinx who tyrannizes, not Thebes, but all Greece . . . sits on its rock, like the original one, snatching up our people and carrying them off, and I cannot fight it off . . . Best of all: punish it yourself! If not, find some Oedipus, who'll either dash this Sphinx on the rocks – or turn it to ash! (ll. 20–34)[4]

The Sphinx here – an allusion to the original Sphinx, which carried off the children of Thebes and whose riddle was finally solved by Oedipus – is probably Kasandros, the Macedonian regent ruling over Athens and the rest of Greece. As said, Demetrios was welcomed as the liberator of Athens from his dominion in 307 BC. While Demetrios' royal dress in this procession is not mentioned (but self-evident), an interesting connection with Athena's ceremonial *peplos* is mentioned by Plutarch in his *Life of Demetrios*. Another of the adulatory motions introduced by the Athenians to pay homage to Demetrios and his father Antigonos was to weave images of these two Macedonian generals onto Athena's ceremonial *peplos* at the Panathenaia, which normally bore only mythical motifs. Her cult image was dressed in this *peplos* during the festival, thus giving her a change of sacred clothing. However, the decision to include Demetrios among the gods shown as woven motifs on the *peplos* appeared to rile the gods themselves, as it was torn into pieces in the course of the Panathenaic procession by a violent storm wind as it was passing through the Kerameikos on its way to the Acropolis. This was – naturally – taken as a sign of divine displeasure.

The Greeks had, to put it mildly, an ambivalent relationship with their gods: they attributed in myth the origin of all their human woes to a woman, Pandora (or Anesidora, as she was also called), given them by Zeus. They also aspired to the condition of the gods, and the Hellenistic rulers obviously wished to put that aspiration into practice by having themselves worshipped as gods. A story such as the rent *peplos* with Demetrios' image shown on it next to Zeus and Athena herself showed that the Athenians were not happy with the equation of a human general with the gods. But they had little choice: their Macedonian overlords had more direct autocratic power over them than the Olympians ever had. As Hermoklēs' poem says, Demetrios was present among them not as a statue of wood or stone, but in the flesh.

Private Celebration

Symposion

Dionysos is naturally linked to celebration as he was the wine god, or rather, he was the god associated with drinking wine collectively.[5] He is conspicuously absent from epic works, not because the Homeric heroes do not drink wine. For some time scholars wondered whether perhaps Dionysos came to Greece after the Homeric period of poetry; this idea was laid to rest when a Mycenaean writing tablet (Bronze Age Greece) turned up his name in a recognizable form. Demeter, too, hardly features in epics; perhaps both country gods – Demeter associated with field crops, Dionysos with wine – are simply alien to the heroic world. Another *Homeric Hymn*, this one devoted to Dionysos (no. 7 in the collection), describes how the young god was captured by pirates and carried off in their ship. He 'appeared' to them (*epiphany*) and their ship's tackle sprouted vine and ivy shoots, wine flowed in the ship, the young prisoner himself turned into a lion roaring at the pirates; he set a bear in their midst. They fled to the stern, then jumped into the sea and were turned into dolphins. Only the helmsman was spared and exalted, because he alone had recognized the young man as a god. The pirates had literally experienced a bad trip; the narrative can be read partly at face value and partly as an allegory of the experience of drinking wine: reality and identity changes. The god reveals himself. Crazy things can happen. The hymn might be seen as an early precursor of Arthur Rimbaud's

47 Deified rulers: Ptolemy II Philadelphos and his sister-bride Arsinoē II, monarchs of Alexandria. Onyx cameo, *c.* 275 BC.

poem 'Le Bateau ivre' (The Drunken Boat, 1870).[6] Any *symposion* indulging in Dionysos can turn into a drunken ship where all orientation is lost. At its most superficial level, drunkenness leads to a loss of balance, a feeling of rocking and reeling; but taken further, drunkenness strips off inhibitions and unlocks behaviour that convention normally keeps in check.

Still in epic territory, the suitors at the end of the *Odyssey* experience something similar in their never-ending carousing, when Odysseus appears and puts paid to them. Eurykleia, Odysseus' housekeeper, gives orders in the morning for the preparation of the banqueting hall:

> Jump to it! Sweep out the hall and wipe it down. Place purple coverings over the well-made chairs. Others, wipe down all the tables, wash out the mixing bowls and the two-handled drinking cups. One party, fetch water from the fountain and bring

> it quickly home, for the suitors will not be long in coming but will show up very early, as today is a holy day [*heortē*, festival]. (*Odyssey* 20.149–57)

All preparations are made; the suitors arrive; the animals are slaughtered (with a conspicuous omission of due portion given to the gods); the wine is mixed and served. All the while Odysseus, dressed as a beggar still, is in their midst, awaiting his moment. After eating and drinking, Athena clouds the minds of the suitors and sends a vision to Theoklymenos, the seer, of impending doom. This is epic's way of saying that the atmosphere at this day's carousing was full of foreboding:

> Pallas Athene stirred wild laughter among the suitors, and sent them out of their minds. They laughed with a strange look in their faces. The meat they ate dripped with blood. Their eyes filled with tears, their minds sensed doom. Theoklymenos the seer spoke in their midst. 'Wretches, what is this ill that you suffer? Your heads and faces are veiled in night, and your knees below. A groan goes up, your cheeks are tear-stained. The walls and timbers are dripping with blood. The hall and yard are filled with spirits all bound for the nether darkness of Erebos. The sun has gone from the sky, an ill mist has descended.' These were his words but all those around him erupted in hysterical laughter. (20.345–58)

The *symposion* ship on which these men were sailing was headed for the rocks. Their behaviour became abnormal, their expressions changed. The seer, sensing disaster, predicted what they were destined for: impending death. The actual killing of the suitors (*mnēstērophonia*) takes place two books later, after Odysseus has strung the bow in Book 21. There, one of the suitors, Antinoös, says to Odysseus, when he calls for the bow, that the wine has gone to his head. He preaches on the possible adverse effects of drink, without realizing that it is his and the other suitors' undoing:

> Wretched stranger, your judgement is clouded. Are you not content to dine with us, your superiors, at your ease and not to miss out on the feast, but to listen to our conversation? No other foreign beggar enjoys that privilege. It is the good wine that deludes you, as it leads others astray if they guzzle it greedily and do not drink moderately. Wine destroyed the Centaur, famous Eurytiōn, in the hall of great-hearted Peirithoös, when he was among the Lapiths. When the wine had gone to his head, in his madness he trashed the palace of Peirithoös . . . So, too, I predict a bad end for you [Odysseus], if you string your bow now. (21.288–306)

In fact it is the other way round: wine (and dining) has gone to the heads of the suitors; *they* are more like the unruly Centaurs running amok among the Lapiths, and they will be killed shortly by Odysseus' arrows (illus. 49), and their departed souls escorted by Hermes to the underworld. The battle of the Centaurs and the Lapiths was one of the mythical themes of the frieze of the temple of Apollo Epikourios at Bassai, on show at the British Museum. It remains, as mentioned above, a puzzle why Dionysos is not mentioned anywhere in this final *symposion* of the suitors, only Athena and, in connection with the public festival taking place that day on Ithaka, Apollo.

48 Dionysos (right) beside a reclining guest at the *symposion*. Note the wine krater at left. Part of a temple pediment, *c.* 500 BC.

49 Odysseus picks off the suitors with his bow while they are feasting. One hides behind a table. Behind him are two maids, shocked by the scene. Drawing after *skyphos* (cup) by the Penelope Painter, *c.* 440 BC.

A similar doomed *symposion* is recorded by Herodotus in connection with the decisive Battle of Plataia (479 BC). Mardonios' Persian army is stationed at Thebes, still vastly outnumbering the combined army of the Greek states who dare to oppose it, the Spartans and Athenians chiefly. Before the battle, a Theban called Attaginos invited the Persian commanders, including Mardonios himself, to a lavish banquet, and invited Greek guests too, from those cities which, like Thebes, had thrown in their lot with the Persians. Herodotus records that he heard the details from one Thersandros of Orchomenos, who had been present. The *symposion* was remarkable in deliberately mixing Greeks with Persians:

> Thersandros said that he had received a personal invitation from Attaginos to this banquet, along with fifty Thebans. They had not lain on separate couches but rather one Persian and one Theban lay on each lounger. When they had finished eating and turned to the drinking, the Persian who had been his couch-mate asked him in Greek where he came from, and he had answered that he was from Orchomenos. The other had said: 'Since you are my table-mate now and we have shared our libation vows, I wish to share my assessment of the situation with you so that, forewarned, you can deliberate on the best course for yourself. You see these Persians dining here and the army which we left encamped by the river?

> Of all these men you will see within a short time only a few survivors.' The Persian man said this while the tears rolled down his face. Amazed by what he had said, Thersandros asked: 'Shouldn't you tell this to Mardonios and the other high-ranking Persians directly under him?' And the other replied: 'Friend, what has been decided by god cannot be averted by man.' (*Histories* 9.16)

The wine had loosened the Persian's tongue, and he told his foreboding about the forthcoming battle to Thersandros, who seems to have survived to tell Herodotus the tale. The incident bears some similarity to the last supper of the suitors in the *Odyssey*. There, too, had been the sense of foreboding when the wine flowed after dinner, which had come true. The Battle of Plataia, which was won mainly by the Spartans, Athenians and Tegeans, finished the Persian invasion of Greece and literally turned the course of history. Recording this conversation is partly Herodotus' way of indicating that the defeat of the Persians was god-ordained; on the other hand, it is unlikely that he invented Thersandros and his account of the dinner in Thebes.

Drinking has its inherent dangers: when even slightly drunk, one's guard is lowered; and again, one doesn't always know what one is drinking. There are endless possibilities for a malevolent person to spike one's drink with some noxious substance. Precisely that happened in the Piraeus (Athens' harbour town) one day, according to a speech written by Antiphon entitled *Against the Stepmother*. The plaintiff is accusing his stepmother of poisoning his father. He recounts how his father had a friend, Philoneōs, who stayed with them in an upstairs room whenever he was in Athens. Philoneōs kept a *pallakē* whom he had clearly lost interest in, as he intended to send her (back?) to a brothel. The speaker's stepmother made friends with this woman and told her she, too, was being 'treated unfairly' by her husband (the speaker's father): she means, presumably, that the man was cheating on her, or possibly wished to be rid of her. She suggests to her friend that, if she helps, she has a means of winning both men back. The friend agrees to help. What she doesn't know is that the drug she is supposed to administer to both men when they are 'in their cups', is a deadly poison, not a love philtre. The men walk down to Piraeus, a few kilometres distant from Athens. Philoneōs wants to make an offering to Zeus Ktēsios ('Of Property') there; the father intends to sail on to Naxos. He will combine the celebration of Zeus Ktēsios with a prayer for a safe voyage. Philoneōs makes his sacrificial offering; the *pallakē* ponders whether to give them the love potion (as she thinks) before the meal, or after. She decides on the latter. The speaker continues:

> When they had finished dining, as was normal . . . they poured their libations (of wine) and placed some incense on the fire on their own behalf. As Philoneōs' mistress was pouring out the libation for them while they prayed – prayers which were fated not to be heard, gentlemen of the jury – she tipped in the poison. Thinking she was doing the right thing, she gave more to Philoneōs, hoping presumably that he would love her even more if she did. She did not realize that she had been tricked by my stepmother until the harm had already been done. She gave less to my father. And when they had poured their libations, they drained their last drink even while they petted and fondled their own killer. Philoneōs died on the spot, my father fell ill and died nineteen days later. (Antiphon 1.18–20)

There were no forensics in antiquity, but courts employed a method that Western courts do not: slaves could be tortured to obtain evidence. The poor *pallakē*, having slave status (otherwise Philoneōs could not have dumped her in a brothel), was tortured and gave her evidence. Whether or not the stepmother was convicted or not, we do not know. What had started as a private dinner party shared by friends, who each had a reason for a festive meal – the one honouring Zeus Ktēsios, the other praying for a safe voyage (probably to Poseidon, but there are other possibilities) – ended in their demise. Would they have had any reason to be on their guard? Philoneōs might possibly have suspected that his *pallakē* would not be so well-intentioned, given that he intended being rid of her, but it is a faint possibility. Some readers may feel that the two men had it coming to them, not only for the way they were (allegedly) treating their women, but also for the blasé way in which they treated the girl serving them their wine as a sex slave. We do not have to believe that she was not aware of what she was serving them, however. Nowadays different drugs are used in clubs and bars to achieve whatever (nefarious) purpose someone has, but the principle seems to be the same: when celebrating, people's guards are down. At the same time this vignette of a private dinner party for two (or three) shows the multiple dimensions involved: the joint purpose, the family tensions, gender conflict, even the amounts of poison administered is differentiated.

We should not leave the institution of the Greek *symposion* under an unlucky star, as it were. It was a central, enduring, ubiquitous institution for men (and their entertainers) to gather and celebrate together (illus. 50). True, the above incidents illustrate what could go wrong in various ways, but this is the counterfoil to the ideal: a happy indulgence in Dionysos, a socially approved occasion for licentiousness, camaraderie, singing, talking and joking. After the party there was a recognized outlet for exuberant spirits, too: the *kōmos*, or street

50 Garlanded men at the *symposion*, Attic red-figure krater (detail) by the Nikias Painter, *c.* 420 BC. An *aulētris* plays her *aulos* while they play the *kottabos* game with their cups. Food is laid out on the table.

revel, at which drunken young men roved the streets at night with greater or lesser incidence of violence; this was singing, shouting and brawling after pub closing time on an institutional scale. The *symposion* featuring in Plato's *Symposion*, a party held among Athenian intellectuals on the day after Agathon's celebration of his victory in the tragic competition that year (417 BC), deliberately avoided excessive drinking. The guests agree that the party on the previous day had been boozy enough; now was the time for more serious conversation – on Erōs, Love – and less drinking. Xenophon also wrote a *Symposion*, no doubt in competition with Plato's, and that too is a fairly respectable affair with good conversation among intellectuals and few excesses. It ends in a sex show, but with the declared purpose of sending the guests home to their wives in a good mood. Xenophon has this to say about the moderate consumption of wine, as opposed to excesses (Socrates speaking):

> Yes, I absolutely believe we should drink wine, too. Wine really eases the pain in men's souls on the one hand, just as mandrake sedates people, and on the other awakens merriment just as olive oil feeds a flame. However, it seems to me that men's bodies react like plants growing in the earth. For when the god [Zeus] waters them excessively, they too can't stand straight or withstand buffeting by the wind. But when they get just the right amount of water they grow straight and tall and, when ripe, produce a good harvest. So it is with us. When we down too much wine, our bodies and minds rapidly fail us. We can hardly breathe, let alone talk. But if the servants ration our drinking by serving us only thimblefuls – to speak in Gorgias' style[7] – then we are not made drunk by the wine but rather we are revived by it and reach a merrier state. (*Symposion* 2.24–6)

So: *mēden agān*, nothing in excess, as the famous Delphic motto instructed. As with courage, where we noted that Xenophon's common sense was sometimes an improvement on Plato's strict dialectic – which can lead to impasse – so here Socrates' advice on wine sounds eminently reasonable. At its best, the Greek *symposion* was an occasion to let Dionysos stimulate and excite the spirits: an analgesic to banish worries (Dionysos *lathikēdēs*, 'banishing care', as he was known). The sixth-century BC philosopher-poet Xenophanes of Kolophōn wrote a famous verse description – or prescription – of how a *symposion* was supposed to be:

> Now the floor is nicely swept, everyone's hands are washed, as are the drinking cups. One servant hands out woven garlands, another offers sweet-smelling myrrh in a flask. A mixing bowl stands ready, full of good cheer. More wine stands at the ready, promising an unfailing supply. It's sweet to taste, with a bouquet like the scent of a flower. A servant places odoriferous frankincense in the middle. There is chilled water, too, sweet and pure. White bread stands on side tables; there is a table of honour laden with cheese and rich honey. An altar in the middle is decorated with flowers on all sides, song resounds through the rooms, and a party mood.
>
> The first duty for honourable men is to hymn the god [Dionysos] with songs of praise and untainted words. One should pour libations and pray to be able to act properly. For that is preferable to acts of violence. One should drink only so much as to be able to get home without the assistance of a servant, unless one is old, that is. That man is to be praised who utters noble thoughts when he's drinking, such that the choice of subject, and his tone, accords with virtue. (Xenophanes fr. 1)

Sound advice!

Family celebrations

The reader will have noticed that celebrations in Greece, including religious festivals, were called by neuter plural words ending in *-ia* (agreeing with an omitted noun *hiera*, rites): Thesmophoria (women's festival in honour of Demeter and Persephone), Dionysia (Dionysos), Delia (festival of Delian Apollo) and so on. There were literally hundreds of other public rituals and festivals throughout Greece and over the centuries, all obeying this principle of nomenclature. To mention only a few better-known ones: the Mysteria (Mysteries) of Demeter and Korē at Eleusis; the Panathenaia ('All-Athens') of Athena at Athens; the Anthesteria (Flower Festival) of Dionysos; the Karneia (probably 'Ram Festival') of Apollo at Sparta. There are books upon books on the festivals of Athens and other Greek cities; the evidence they draw upon is literary, epigraphic, archaeological. In focusing on the Delia above I have singled out a representative and internationally important example.

The same naming principle holds true for a myriad of smaller, private celebrations, mainly relating to small circles of people or families. The following is a sample rather than a complete list. Celebrations were always what we would call religious; in other words, sacrifice, or prayer or libation, is offered to the god(s) in acknowledgement of the good fortune that they have granted, or not withheld.

Epinikia were celebrations of victory (*nikē*, victory) of all sorts: athletic, military, artistic. Plato's *Symposion* took place on the day after Agathon's *epinikia* celebration of his victory at the Dionysia (theatre festival) in 417 BC (174a). A whole poetic genre of *epinikia* grew up around the victory celebrations for athletes at the Panhellenic Games. Pindar and Bacchylides are the most famous names associated with the genre.

Genethlia were celebrations of birth and of birthdays, on which offerings were made. When Xouthos in Euripides' *Ion* discovers his long-lost son Ion working at the Delphic oracle, he pronounces: 'I want to celebrate (literally 'sacrifice') your *genethlia* which I omitted previously' (*Ion* 653). A god could also have *genethlia*, for example Aphrodite in Plato (*Symposion* 203c3). Further instances are Plato's *Alcibiades* 1.121c and Lucian's *Hermotimos* 11.

Amphidromia was a 'christening' rite on the fifth (that is, fourth, by our counting) day after a child's birth, so called because the parents' friends carried it round (*amphi-dromos*) the hearth: see Aristophanes, *Lysistrata* 757; Lysias fr. 22.

Euangelia was any celebration of good news (*eu-*, good + *angelia*, news). One 'sacrificed' *euangelia*, that is, offered a sacrifice to an appropriate god(s), or 'crowned' (*stephanoun*) the god's image, as thank-offering for the welcome news. At the end of Menander's *Perikeiromenē*, for example, when all the obstacles in the plot are overcome, the maid says to Polemōn, who has got his girl back: 'You'd better celebrate the good news immediately. Everything – somehow – has turned out right and *her* [Glykera's] position has been set to rights again' (ll. 992–4).

Sōtēria was a thank-offering for deliverance. When Xenophon in the *Anabasis* (Return of the Greek army supporting Kyros in Persia) makes a speech saying that with 'god on our side' the Greeks will succeed (in returning home to Greece), someone sneezes – and all the soldiers take that as a good omen from Zeus Sōtēr ('Saviour'). Xenophon suggests they vow to sacrifice *sōtēria* to this god as soon as they reach a safe country (3.2.9). Another (tongue-in-cheek) example: Hermotimos in Lucian's *Hermotimos*, disabused of his illusions about philosophers, vows to sacrifice *sōtēria*, like a sailor saved from shipwreck (86.18–20).

One man's peace treaty

In the previous chapter we saw how Dikaiopolis in Aristophanes' *Acharnians* dressed in rags to make his defence speech before the chorus of rough Acharnians. He had made a private peace treaty with the Spartans to put an end to the Peloponnesian War, at least for himself and his family, and the bellicose Acharnians (a suburb of Athens) were having none of it. When he pulls off the impossible and secures peace with the Spartans for himself, he celebrates riotously with the rest of his household (family and slaves, that is). In honour of which god? As with Demetrios' triumphal entry into Athens after 'liberating' it from Kasandros in 307 BC, it is Dionysos, and here, too, Dikaiopolis conducts a mini march with Dionysos' symbol, the carnival phallus. We have to imagine Dikaiopolis coming on stage with his wife, daughter and servants, each carrying something for the procession. The chorus of Acharnians hear his call for ritual silence and stand by, ready to pounce on him for breaking ranks with Athens.

> (*Dikaiopolis:*) Silence! Silence! Basket-bearer, move forward a bit. Xanthias [a slave], stand the phallus upright. Put down the basket, daughter, so that we may begin. (*Daughter:*) Mother, pass me the soup ladle so I can spoon some pea soup over the holy cake. (*Dikaiopolis:*) Perfect! O Lord Dionysos, may it please you that I am organizing this procession and sacrificing with my servants. May I conduct Dionysos' country rites with your blessing, free from military service, and may my thirty-year peace treaty serve me in good stead . . . I'll follow on and sing the phallos-song. Wife, you watch from the roof. Come on now!
>
> [*He starts singing*] Phallus, friend of Bacchus, drinking mate, night wanderer, adulterer and paedophile, six years now since I last addressed you, happily walking abroad. I've made a peace treaty for myself, cast off hassle and battle and generals like Lamachos. How much more pleasant is it, Phalēs, O Phalēs, to come upon that Thracian girl . . . out stealing wood in the scrubland, grab her by the waist, lift her up, plonk her down and pit her cherry. Phalēs, Phalēs, if you join in our carousing, at dawn you'll drink the cup of peace. I'll hang my shield beside the fire. (*Acharnians* 241–79)

Dikaiopolis' words 'six years now' refer to the war years, in which it was not safe to conduct Dionysos' rural festival in Attica as the Spartans marched in and razed the country. His name can be interpreted as 'set-the-city-to-rights' if it is formed from *dikaioō*, set to rights, rather than simply *dikaios*, just, and *polis*, city. Dikaiopolis' solitary action would be his personal crusade to correct the course of the city, which was locked in war with Sparta. Not that Dikaiopolis is following an altruistic agenda; rather, he is fed up with military service and fighting as opposed to the pleasures of the countryside, exemplified by the Dionysiac revel. We may frown on his cheerful reference to raping the Thracian girl if he catches her stealing firewood, but Old Comedy (Aristophanes' genre) was a ribald, no-holds-barred genre written for all male classes. Dikaiopolis is meant to be the lovable rogue rather than the despicable macho.[8] This is several registers below

Hephaistos' city of peace set in silver relief on Achilles' shield, but the mood of jubilation is still recognizable.

A reluctant guest

It became de rigueur, first in New Comedy, then in the novel genre, that a convoluted plot should end in a wedding. There is something about a wedding as a form of celebration that concludes fictional matters on a happy note, as many Hollywood films also testify. All sorts of difficulties stand in the way of a couple's love or union, which by the end of the story are resolved and everyone can join in their wedding celebration. It is a bit like a tangle of string that, when untangled, produces a straight length of string with two ends.

We already met Menander's Knēmōn figure in his play *The Bad-Tempered Man*. The young couple in the play are Sostratos, son of a rich townsman, Kallippides, and Knēmōn's daughter, a country girl. The main obstacle to their love is Knēmōn's disgruntlement: he is disenchanted with his fellow man and is basically against everything and everyone. However, by the end, having fallen down his own well and been pulled out by Gorgias and Sostratos, thus proving that 'no man is an island' but is dependent on others, he agrees to the wedding, although he refuses to join the celebration.[9] Two slaves, Getas and the cook Sikōn, decide to get their own back on the injured Knēmōn, who had refused to lend them a pot for their sacrifice. At the same time, they intend to force Knēmōn to join the wedding party. They call on Knēmōn, who is languishing in bed, injured by his fall. They manhandle him outside (in ancient theatre only outdoor action can be shown) and then demand a string of furnishings and utensils to mock him for his refusal to lend the pot earlier. Then they insist on him joining the wedding party, which they describe as follows:

> (*Sikōn:*) It was time for the libation. A bed of straw [for the guests to sit/lie on] had already been made. I [arranged] the tables – that's my job – are you listening? I'm a cook, don't forget . . . Someone else tipped a flask of the good stuff [lit. 'old grey wine-god'] into a bowl, added water from the Nymphs, and handed it round to the men in a circle, while

> another served the women. It went down like water on sand. You get me? Then a good-looking serving girl became tipsy and, with a garland of flowers, began a sexy, rhythmic dance, suggestive and coy at the same time. Then another girl joined hands with her and danced along. (*Dyskolos* 943–53)

In what follows, the two manage to coerce Knēmōn into agreeing to allow himself to be pushed to the wedding party. 'Take me,' he sighs. 'Probably better to endure what's going on there' (ll. 957–8). Interestingly, this point in the action is marked by a change of metre. Sikōn had used longer, more excited, tetrameters for the description of the goings on at the party; now we revert to comedy's normal pace of trimeters. The two carry Knēmōn towards the other stage door, where the party is taking place. At that point Menander combines celebration over Knēmōn's acceptance of defeat with an appeal to the audience to clap for his play. Getas addresses first Sikōn, then turns to the audience (*apostrophē*):

> The victory is ours! Donax, Sikōn [two slaves], lift him up, carry him in . . . [*Then, turning to address the spectators*] If you've enjoyed our beating the troublesome old man [Knēmōn] into submission, boys, men and children, then kindly put your hands together now! May Victory [in the dramatic competition], that true-blue, laughter-loving girl, be always on our side and helping us to win! (ll. 959–69)

Menander has not just defeated the grouch Knēmōn in this piece. In a light-hearted manner he has also struck a blow for class equality – not only does Sostratos get his girl, but her poor brother Gorgias marries the rich man Kallippides' daughter – and enacted in the last scene a triumph of slaves over a free landowner. One can say this is all make-believe, a carnivalesque inversion of roles, and once the play is over everyone will return to the status quo, but still: make-believe has a way of spilling over into reality.

Town and Country

The happy ending of Longos' novel *Daphnis and Chloē* also involves interesting inversions around the axis town–country or urban–rustic. We already met Daphnis and Chloē in winter on Lesbos when Daphnis cast around for ways to meet up with Chloē now winter was keeping all the pastoral folk at home. The ancient genre of the Greek novel contains ludicrous elements. The plot is often impossibly convoluted, involving absurd adventures for the young couple until the final page. There are long passages of excruciatingly boring *ekphrasis*, description, of some thing or place. Psychological depth is nil. The ending is entirely predictable. Undoubtedly, the novel as a genre has come a long way since then. However, Longos – whoever he was, no one knows – manages much better than most. His rural idyll of the young goatherd and his shepherdess girlfriend tending their flocks in the fields and falling in very chaste love right up to the end has real charm; the style is naive, but not off-puttingly faux-naive. One really gets a sense of the innocence of country life compared to the corrupt goings-on in town.

The conventions of the ancient genre of love story, which derive more or less directly from New Comedy, Menander's genre, dictate that young love will win through difficulties to marriage or reconciliation at the end.[10] Disenfranchised slaves will discover their true identities and become free citizens again. Recognition, reconciliation, celebration – as the gateway to procreation – are the hallmarks of the ancient novel. In Daphnis' case, it is the discovery that he is not in fact a country goatherd but the son of a Mytilenean dignitary, Dionysophanes, who had exposed him as a baby, thinking that, at three, he already had enough descendants and did not need a fourth. Daphnis was saved and brought up by foster parents, Lamōn and Myrtalē, and lived as a goatherd. When his father recognizes the handsome young Daphnis as his son by means of the standard recognition tokens placed with the exposed child, there is great celebration among the countryfolk and the visiting dignitaries. A problem presents itself, however: now Daphnis is alienated from his low-born love, Chloē. Chloē laments:

> Daphnis has forgotten me. He's dreaming of a grand marriage. Why did I make him swear [to be true to her] by the goats and not the Nymphs? He's abandoned them like his Chloē. Even when he sacrificed to the Nymphs and to Pan [giving thanks for finding his father], he did not express the wish to see Chloē. No doubt he's found girls in the service of his mother who are better than me. Forget him! I will not continue living! (*Daphnis and Chloē* 4.27.1–2.)

A rival suitor of Chloē, Lampis, sees his chance and snatches the girl away to her howls of protest. Daphnis hears about it. He is distraught:

> O wretched recognition! How much better it was for me to herd goats! How much happier I was as a slave! Then I could be with Chloē, then . . . Now Lampis has carried her off. When night comes he'll sleep with her [Daphnis hasn't yet]. And I'm drinking and living it up! In vain did we swear by Pan, the goats and the Nymphs [to be true to each other]. (4.28.2–3)

Again, however, the rules of genre step in. Chloē discovers in turn that she, too, is a citizen of Mytilene by birth, from one Megakles, who had exposed her as a baby in the Cave of the Nymphs because he was destitute and could not afford a child (now he's not!). She had been brought up in the country by foster parents, Dryas and Napē. So the couple can marry after all. Daphnis and Chloē dedicate items (pipes, milking pails, goatskins and so on) from their pastoral lives to Pan and the Nymphs (illus. 51) as a way of signing off, as it were, from their past. All these exposed babies, by the way, in Greek literature do reflect a social reality – unwanted children really were exposed on occasion – but are probably more literary convention than reflection of reality, much as modern genres such as crime thrillers inevitably start with the discovery of a corpse in the woods, although that is not common in reality.

There is a twist in the obligatory end-wedding of *Daphnis and Chloē*, however, as I said. Daphnis and Chloē, now high-status citizens

51 Rustic gods: Mildenhall Bacchic silver plate with Pan and Nymph, 4th century AD.

of Mytilene, tire rapidly of city life and decide to marry in the countryside they know so well. When children are born to them in the future (the narratologists' *prolepsis*), they give them to goats and sheep to suckle, as they themselves had as children. They finally get around to sleeping with each other, Daphnis employing a technique for that which he had learnt once from an obliging neighbour's hetaira, Lykainion (Little She-Wolf). When one considers that Longos was writing in Roman imperial times (as far as we know), when Rome, Alexandria and Antioch were teeming *metropoleis*, and that Longos' readers were almost certainly the educated classes in cities, the appeal to a pastoral way of life may seem phoney. However, as I said, the rural idyll of Daphnis and Chloē does not cloy and probably answers to a genuine wish – then as now – to get back to a greater innocence in nature (illus. 52).

52 Camille-Félix Bellanger, *Daphnis and Chloē*, 1893, oil on canvas.

At daybreak, however, they all travelled back to the country [from Mytilene] by agreement, as Daphnis and Chloē requested, as they could not stand city life. They decided to celebrate their wedding in country style. Arriving at Lamōn's house [Daphnis' foster-father] they introduced Dryas [Chloē's foster-father] to Megakles [her birth father] and likewise Napē to Rhodē [her birth mother], and prepared the wedding feast on a grand scale . . . Dionysophanes prepared the couches out of fresh leaves in front of the Cave [of the Nymphs], as the weather was fine, and, placing all the guests on them, feasted them opulently. [*The guest list*] Given the background of the company, all was rustic and country-style. One man sang harvest songs, one joked in the manner of joking round the wine presses. Philētas played the panpipes, Lampis played the flute, Dryas and Lampon danced, Chloē and Daphnis exchanged kisses.

Some goats were grazing nearby as if they too were joining in the celebrations. This was not completely to the taste of the guests from town. But Daphnis called some of them by name, gave them fresh leaves to eat and, grasping them by the horns, kissed them.

And they continued in this manner not only then but as long as they lived, leading a pastoral life most of their time, honouring the Nymphs and Pan and Erōs, owning a great many herds of sheep and goats, and enjoying their favourite food of fruit and milk.

When later they had a boy, they let it drink from a goat, and a second child, a girl, they let suck at the teat of a sheep. The boy they called Philopoimēn [Shepherd-Friend] and the girl Agelē [Herd] . . . They decorated the Cave, and dedicated statues and an altar of Erōs Herdsman. To Pan they gave a shrine of Pan Combatant to live in instead of the pine.[11]

But that came later. When the wedding night came, all the guests escorted the couple to the bridal chamber, some playing panpipes, others flutes, some holding up large torches. When they approached the doors, the company sang in a rough, gravelly manner, like labourers breaking the soil with pitchforks, instead of the Hymenal.[12] Daphnis and Chloē undressed and lay down together. They embraced and kissed each other, and slept that night less than owls. Daphnis did to Chloē what Lykainion [the *hetaira*] had taught him, and then Chloē first learned that what they did in the woods had just been shepherds' play (4.37–40).

Notes on Ancient Authors and Sources

Author translations of Greek and Latin texts are throughout from standard editions of the works cited.

Achilles Tatius (Achilleus Tatios, second century AD) Author of the Greek romance *Leukippē and Kleitophon*, an adventure story set mainly in Lebanon and Egypt.

Adespota The word used for literary works by unknown authors. These include poetry, prose works and documentary texts. The number of anonymous texts has grown enormously through epigraphy (inscriptions) and papyrology (papyri dug up mainly in Egypt).

Aeschylus of Athens (*c.* 525/4–*c.* 456/5 BC) The earliest of the three great tragic poets, famous in particular for his *Oresteia*, a trilogy of plays about Agamemnon's family history.

Alkaios of Mytilene (*c.* 625–*c.* 580 BC) Lyric poet of Aeolic (literary 'dialect') verse, involved in the factional fighting in Lesbos. Inspired, and imitated by, the Roman poet Horace. Contemporary of Sappho. Mainly fragments remain.

Andokides of Athens (*c.* 440–*c.* 390 BC) Athenian orator banished for participation in a religious scandal in 415 BC, but rehabilitated later.

Antiphon of Rhamnous (Attica, 480–411 BC) Earliest of the canonical ten Attic Orators. He wrote lawcourt speeches for clients, and model speeches, and sided with the oligarchs in the revolution of 411 BC in Athens. Praised by Thucydides for his keen intelligence.

Apollonius of Rhodes (first half of the third century BC) Active in Ptolemaic Alexandria, author of the *Argonautica*, an epic poem about the quest of Jason and the Argonauts to fetch the Golden Fleece from Kolchis (Georgia) on the Black Sea.

Archilochus of Paros (*c.* 680–*c.* 645 BC) Lyric poet, famous for iambic verse (*iambus*, 'blame poetry') with polemical, *ad hominem* content.

Aristophanes of Athens (*c.* 446–*c.* 386 BC) Leading playwright of Old Comedy. His plays were political, fantastic, rumbunctious. He also features in Plato's *Symposion*.

Aristotle of Stagira (384–322 BC) Based in Athens; with Plato, the most famous ancient philosopher, founder of the Peripatetic school of philosophy at the Lyceum in Athens. Wide interests, from the theory of drama to ethics and biology. Tutor of Alexander the Great.

Bacchylides of Kēos (*c.* 518–*c.* 451 BC) Choral lyric poet, contemporary of Pindar. Works only extant on papyrus. Author of festive poetry – victory odes, dithyrambs and paeans – among others.

Callimachus of Cyrene (*c.* 310–*c.* 240 BC) Based in Alexandria, Hellenistic poet and scholar, favouring small-scale, recondite themes as opposed to lengthy epics. His *Hymns* transmitted in manuscript, otherwise fragments. Compiled a catalogue of the great Library at Alexandria.

Catullus of Rome (*c.* 84–*c.* 54 BC) Roman lyric poet, famous for love poems for his 'Lesbia', imitator of Sappho.

Constitution of the Athenians (fourth–third century BC) A work surviving on papyrus ascribed to Aristotle's school, as one of the synopses of the constitutions of the main Greek cities (*poleis*).

defixiones Latin term for curse tablets, *katadesmata*, or 'binding spells'. Usually of thin, folded, sheets of lead, these were inscribed with a curse against one or more people and buried in graves or wells.

Demosthenes of Athens (384–12 October 322 BC) Most distinguished of the Attic orators, siding with the Greek resistance against Philip II of Macedon's conquest of Greece. Admired and emulated by Roman Cicero.

Dio Chrysostom of Prusa (Bithynia. *c.* AD 40–*c.* AD 115) Travelling orator and sophist, representative of the Second Sophistic, the Greek revival under the Roman Empire.

Epicurus of Athens (341–270 BC) Philosopher, founder of the Epicurean School at Athens, called the Garden. Prolific writer, most of whose works are lost, some preserved in a carbonized state in a library of Herculaneum.

Euripides of Athens (*c.* 480–*c.* 406 BC) The last of the three great Athenian tragedians. He modernized Greek myth to reflect issues of the day and experimented with tragedies with 'happy' endings.

Greek Anthology A collection of epigrams from two medieval manuscripts (tenth and fourteenth centuries AD) but based on Hellenistic anthologies, written by various authors in elegiac couplets. Epigrams were short, occasional poems, originally for historical inscriptions, then becoming a literary genre.

Greek Magical Papyri A collection of anonymous compendia of magical practices (*praxeis*) and recipes. They stem mainly from Roman imperial Egypt and contain a mix of Greek, Egyptian and Near Eastern *arcana* (secret knowledge).

Heliodorus of Emesa (Homs, Syria, third–fourth century AD) Author of the romance *Ethiopian Tale* (*Aithiopika*), of Charikleia, princess of Ethiopia, and Theagenes, descendant of Achilles. The novel is set mainly in Egypt (under Persian dominion), Athens and Delphi.

Hephaistion of Thebes (early fifth century AD) Author of an astrological treatise called *Apotelesmatika* (Astrological Signs).

Heraclitus of Ephesus (early fifth century BC) Presocratic philosopher whose work only survives as short, pithy sayings. Famous for his (simplified) saying 'everything flows' (*panta rhei*).

Herodotus of Halikarnassos (*c.* 484–*c.* 425 BC) Has the nickname 'Father of History'. His *Histories* in Ionic prose dialect narrate the Persian Wars (490–479 BC), but they include much ethnography, local history, mythology and geography.

Hero(n)das (third century BC) Alexandrian writer of burlesque *mimes* (dramatizations of scenes from life) in Ionic dialect and limping iambic metre.

Hesiod of Boeotia (seventh–sixth century BC) Author of didactic and heroic epic poems, chiefly *Theogony*, on the genealogy of the Greek gods, and *Works and Days*, on farming.

Homer (probably eighth century BC) The famous legendary author of epic poetry. His life is utterly unknown, although many legends circulated. His famous surviving works are the *Iliad* (Trojan War) and the *Odyssey* (return home of Odysseus).

Homeric Hymns (seventh century BC onwards) A collection of post-Homeric epic poems on the Olympian gods. Some are as long as a 'book' of Homer, others short.

Ibykos of Rhegium (second half of the sixth century BC) Lyric poet, active in Samos. Only fragments survive.

Longos Probably of Lesbos (second century AD?), author of *Daphnis and Chloē*, a charming bucolic romance in the style of the Greek novel, set in Lesbos. The name may simply be a corruption of *log[g]ou*, genitive of *logos*, word.

Lucian of Samosata (*c.* AD 125–after AD 180) Writer of satirical prose in the style of the Second Sophistic (revival of Attic letters).

Lysias (orig. from Syracuse, *c.* 445–*c.* 380 BC) Athenian metic (migrant); was an advocate, that is, a writer of courtroom speeches. One of the canon of ten Attic Orators. He fell foul of the Thirty Tyrants in 404–3, survived and was briefly awarded citizenship.

Menander of Athens (342/1–291/90 BC) Leading playwright of New Comedy, the genre based on contemporary family life. A friend of the governor of Athens from 317 to 307, Demetrios of Phaleron, it is debated whether he was pro- or anti-Macedonian.

Orpheus Legendary poet, eponymous figurehead of the Orphic religious sect. Alternative mythologies and theogonic poetry are ascribed to Orpheus.

Orphic Lamellae A collection of (mainly) gold leaves inscribed with Orphic underworld texts and buried with deceased initiates.

Ovid of Rome (20 March 43 BC–AD 17/18) Roman poet, famously exiled by Augustus to Tomis on the Black Sea. Famous for his mythical epic *Metamorphoses* (Transformations) and poetry on love.

Oxyrhynchus Papyri Collection of papyrus fragments excavated in the late nineteenth century in Egypt by Grenfell and Hunt. A vast hoard of fragmentary texts now kept mainly in the Sackler Library (now renamed Bodleian Art, Archaeology and Ancient World Library), Oxford.

Phaedrus (first century AD) Roman verse compiler of Greek fables, particular those of Aesop.

Pindar of Thebes (*c.* 518–*c.* 438 BC) Choral lyric poet whose *epinikia*, victory odes, written on commission from rich patrons, survive. A papyrus containing his religious poetry was discovered at Oxyrhynchus.

Plato of Athens (*c.* 426–348/7 BC) Athens' most famous philosopher, founder of the Academy, writer of mainly dialogues led by Socrates. Famous for his theory of Forms, metaphysical blueprints of being.

Plutarch of Boeotia (*c.* AD 46–after AD 119) Philosopher (Platonic school), biographer, essayist, polymath, priest at Delphi. Famous for his *Parallel Lives* and *Moralia*.

Polyainos of Bithynia (second century AD) Author of the military treatise *Stratēgēmata* (Stratagems in War) and orator.

Sappho of Lesbos (*c.* 630–*c.* 570 BC) Lyric poet, with Alkaios, famous author of Aeolic verse. Only one complete poem survives, the *Hymn to Aphrodite*; many fragments in various metres.

Socrates of Athens (*c*. 470–399 BC) Famous oral philosopher and focus of Plato's dialogues. Convicted, and executed, in 399 BC for, allegedly, 'corrupting the youth and not honouring the gods of state religion'. A captivating character, given to irony.

Sophists A collective term for the travelling philosophers and teachers who emerged in the later fifth century BC, gathering in Athens. They taught mainly rhetoric and became famous for 'clever' (but not necessarily valid) arguments (sophistry). Famous names are Gorgias, Protagoras, Hippias, perhaps Socrates himself. A revival of their linguistic skills and their mode of living as travelling lecturers from the first century AD is referred to as the Second Sophistic.

Theocritus of Sicily (third century BC) Active in Alexandria, writer of shorter hexameter poems (*Idylls*), many on bucolic (rustic) themes, in Doric dialect.

Theophrastus (*c*. 371–*c*. 287 BC) From Lesbos but based in Athens, successor to Aristotle in the Peripatetic school of philosophy (Lyceum), author of many philosophical and scientific works and an amusing series of character sketches (*Characters*, (?)317 BC).

Thucydides of Athens (*c*. 460–*c*. (?)404 BC) Wrote the *History of the Peloponnesian War* (unfinished: 431–411 BC). His style is austere, intellectual, but also passionate.

Xenophanes of Kolophōn (*c*. 570–*c*. 478 BC) Presocratic philosopher, author of philosophical and moral/critical hexameter and elegiac verse.

Xenophon of Athens (*c*. 430–355/4 BC) A pupil of Socrates who wrote philosophy, history and biography. Famous among his works are the *Expedition of Kyros*, describing the hazardous return to Greece of the Greek mercenaries who served under Kyros, aspirant to the Persian throne, and *Memorabilia*, a memoir of Socrates.

Xenophon of Ephesos (second–third century AD) Author of the Greek novel *The Ephesian Tale of Anthia and Habrocomes* (*Ephesiaka*).

Glossary of Ancient Terms

aegis Goatskin, Athena's aegis
***agalma* (pl. *-ata*)** Pleasing gift (to a god), cult image
agorā Marketplace, meeting place
agos Religious pollution, curse
aition (Story explaining) reason why (something is)
andrapodistēs Slave-trader, kidnapper
andreia Courage
andrōn Men's living/dining room
aphrodisia, ta ('Things of Aphrodite') Sexual intercourse
aporia Embarrassment, bafflement
aretē Manliness, virtue
ariston Meal taken early in the day
askēsis Practice, training
asty Town
ataraxia Untroubledness, tranquillity
ātē Blindness, error
aulētris Girl flautist and entertainer
aulos Wind instrument (double flute)
***bakchai* (pl.)** Female worshippers of Dionysos
***barbaroi* (pl.)** Non-Greek speaker, barbarians
barbitos Stringed instrument
basileia Kingdom, monarchy
basileus King
biblion Book (scroll)
boulē Council
bouleutērion Council chamber
boustrophēdon Writing in alternate directions
***casus belli* (Lat.)** Reason for war
charis Gratitude, grace
chitōn Ionian dress
choros Dance troupe, song-dance
***chous* (pl. *-oes*)** Jug
***chrēmata* (pl.)** Money
chrēsmologos Oracle-monger
***codex* (Lat.)** Manuscript in book form
defixiones Curse tablets or 'binding spells'
deipnon Evening meal
dekatē Tythe of a tenth

***deltos* (pl. *-oi*)** Writing tablet
dēmos People
diathetēs Organizer
diēgēsis Narrative
diosēmia Sin from Zeus
diphthera Skin (jerkin)
drachmē Drachma
***eidos* (also *ideā*)** Form
eikōn Image
ekklēsia Assembly (of the people)
ekphrasis Description in prose
eleutheria Freedom
emporos Merchant
enargeia Vividness
epinikion Victory song
epos Epic poem (word)
erastēs Lover
ergasia Business
ergon Work, deed
erōs Love
***eupatrides* (pl.)** Noblemen
***fibula* (Gr. *peronē*)** Dress-pin
gamos Marriage, wedding
gē earth, land
***genos* (pl. *genē*)** Type, family, genre
gnōmōn Ruler, measure
gorgōneion Head of Gorgon
***grammata* (pl.)** Letters, writing
grammatikē Reading and writing
***gynē* (pl. *gynaikes*)** Woman, wife
***haruspex* (Lat.)** Inspector of entrails
hēdonē Pleasure
heortē Festival
***hestia* (Ion. *histiē*)** Hearth
***hēsychazontes* (pl.)** Peaceful citizens
***hetaira* (Lat. *amica*)** Courtesan
hiereus Priest
himation Outer (wrapped) garment
***hippeis* (pl.)** Cavalry
***historia* (Ion. *-iē*)** Inquiry, history
holkas Cargo ship
***hoplitēs* (pl. *-ai*)** Armed foot-soldier
hybris (Excessive) pride, aggression, offence
hymenaios Wedding song
iynx Magical top
kairos Decisive moment, opportunity
kaloi kāgathoi 'The great and the good'
kapēlos Shopkeeper

karteria Endurance
katabasis Descent (to the underworld)
kēpos Garden
kerdos Profit, gain
kinaidos Male prostitute
kleos Fame, glory
klepsydra Water-clock
klinē Bed, couch
koinē Common (Greek) language
kōmos Street revel
kosmos World, finery, jewellery
kottabos Game played at *symposion* with wine cups
kratēr Mixing bowl for wine
kūdos Glory
Lēthē (River of) forgetfulness
lexis eiromenē ('Strung-together speech') Prose
lōpodytēs (Clothes-) thief
mageiros Cook, butcher
***manteion* (Lat. *oraculum*)** Oracle
mantis Prophet
mēdismos Medizing (siding with Persians)
mēnis Anger, wrath
metempsychōsis Rebirth, reincarnation
metoikos Immigrant, resident alien
metron Metre
mīmēsis Imitation, make-believe
***mnā* (pl. *mnai*)** Mina (hundred drachmae)
***mystēria* (pl.)** Mystery rites
***mystēs* (pl. *-ai*)** Initiate in mystery rites
***mythos* (pl. *mythoi*)** Story, myth
nikē Victory
nomisma Currency, coinage
nomos Law, custom, convention
nostos Return (home)
nous Mind, intelligence
***novus homo* (Lat.)** Self-made man (not born into nobles)
ōdē Song
ōdeion Concert hall
oikoumenē The inhabited world
oinochoē Wine jug
oiōnopolos, -skopos Reader of bird flight
oligoi (Rich and powerful) few, oligarchs
oneirokritēs, -polos Dream reader
paian Cult hymn for Apollo
paidagōgos Slave guardian of boy, tutor
paideia Education, learning
paidion Small child
palaistra Wrestling place, gym

pallakē Long-term (unmarried) female partner
panoplia Full suit of armour
paraklausithyron Love song performed on doorstep
parodos Entry-song of chorus
parrhēsia Freedom of speech, outspokenness
penia Poverty
peplos Long (Doric) dress
peripeteia Turning point (in drama)
philia Friendship, love
***philtron* (pl. *philtra*)** Love charm, potion
phorminx Stringed instrument
physis Nature
***pithos* (pl. *-oi*)** Wine jar
ploion Boat, ship
poikilia Variety
polis City (as political entity)
politeia Constitution
pornē Prostitute
porneion Brothel
pornoboskos Pimp, brothel-keeper
pōros (Stone) Marble
***praxis* (pl. *praxeis*)** Act, deed, rite (in magic)
promantis Mouthpiece of oracle
***psiloi* (pl.)** Light-armed troops
psychē Soul, psyche
Pythia Apollo's priestess at Delphi
rhētorikē Rhetoric, the art of public speaking
***seirai* (pl.)** Chains (in neo-Platonic cosmology)
skazōn Limping iamb (a metre)
skēnē Painted backdrop of theatre, scene
skolion Drinking song
sophistēs Expert, teacher (in adult education)
stasis Civil discord, faction
stēlē Pillar, monument
stoā Roofed colonnade
sympatheia Sympathy, affinity (philosophy)
symposion Drinking party
sōphrosynē Modesty, chastity, dignity
***sōtēr* (pl. *-ēres*)** Saviour
***tabella defixionis* (Lat.)** Curse-tablet
technē Skill, art, technique
***teletai* (pl.)** Religious rites
***telōnai* (pl.)** Tax collectors
theōria Religious embassy, mission
thronos Seat
thysia Sacrifice
timē Honour
***toxotai* (pl.)** Archers, policemen (at Athens)

trapeza Table, bank
tribōn Shabby coat
***triērēs* (sc. *naus*)** Warship
tropaion Victory marker
trophos Nurse (fem.)
tychē Chance, fate, luck
tyrannis Tyranny
***tyrannos* (pl. *-oi*)** Tyrant, autocrat
***volumen* (pl. *volumina*) (Lat.)** Book, volume
xenos Friend, foreigner, friend abroad

NOTE ON METRE

Greek metre measured long ('closed') and short ('open') syllables rather than stresses in a line of poetry. There was an amazing variety of metres used by ancient Greek poets, and their study is an academic discipline in itself. Here are a few notes to point readers in the right direction.

Hexameter: a line consisting of six dactylic *metra* (Homer, Hesiod, Apollonius, Theocritus). A dactylic *metron* consists of long-short-short (dactyl), or long-long (spondee): —⏕

Pentameter: a line consisting of five dactylic *metra* with a break (diaeresis) in the middle

Elegiac couplet: a combination of the two above (elegy, epigram)

Iambic trimeter: line consisting of three iambic *metra* (spoken verses of Attic tragedy and comedy). An iambic *metron* consists of: ⏓—⏑— (anceps-long-short-long; where anceps indicates either short or long)

Limping iamb: iambic line with the penultimate syllable long (Herodas)

Aeolic lyric: the metres used first by Aeolic (Lesbos) poets Sappho and Alkaios. Many are built around the choriambic *metron*: —⏑⏑— (long-double-short-long)

References

Introduction

1 And including the northwest Mediterranean littoral (Nice, Marseilles, Antibes, Monaco).

2 Here and elsewhere Greek names are given in a transliterated form with correct vowel quantities added for the sake of authenticity. Only in the case of 'household names' such as Socrates and Plato are the latinized forms in common usage retained.

1 Love

1 Madeline Miller's novel *The Song of Achilles* (London, 2011) is a reimagining of Homer's story in terms of the love between Achilles and Patroklos.

2 Unexplained: we expect 'tenth'.

3 He is the stage character known as *parasītos*, lit. one who 'eats with', in return, as we see here, for certain services.

4 The song bears comparison with Carole King's song 'I Feel the Earth Move' (1971).

5 In Aristophanes' *Women at the Thesmophoria* (443ff.), a woman wreath-maker explains how it became necessary for her to work when her husband was killed in Cyprus, and she was left with five children to support.

6 The poem known as *Fragmentum Grenfellianum* is the lament of an abandoned *hetaira*, as is Simaitha in Theocritus' second *Idyll*.

7 This is another passage of Greek that has only recently been restored. See William Furley, *New Fragments of Menander's Epitrepontes* (London, 2021; freely available online).

8 P. Lond. Lit. 50. With Arthur Hunt, Bernard Grenfell was one of the famous Victorian excavators of Oxyrhynchus in Egypt (1907), where innumerable papyri were found. Their dig was turned into a play by Tony Harrison: *The Trackers of Oxyrhynchus* (1990).

9 B. P. Grenfell, *An Alexandrian Erotic Fragment* (Oxford, 1896).

10 A good example is in Aristophanes' *Wealth* (1041), where a young man arrives on stage, dressed for a *kōmos* (symposion), with a wreath on his head and carrying a torch.

11 Audollent, *Defixionum tabellae* no. 68 (Paris, 1904); Wünsch, *Fluchtafeln* no. 16 (Bonn, 1912).

12 Lucian's fourth dialogue in *Conversations of Courtesans* is the story of one Melitta, who is on the lookout for a Syrian sorceress who might conduct rites on her behalf to recover the amour of Charinos.

13 Audollent, *Defixionum tabellae* no. 68.

2 Status

1 This is because he swallowed his children as they were born to prevent them rising up against him, then regurgitated them in reverse order.
2 The story is told in a poem attributed to Hesiod in antiquity called the *Catalogue of Women*. It survives only in fragments.
3 He names the three (l. 145), including one called Iphianassa. Has he forgotten he sacrificed Iphigeneia at Aulis before the fleet sailed, or were there two originally, Iphigeneia and Iphianassa?
4 Think Charlie Chaplin in *The Great Dictator* (1940).
5 These slaves were identified already in ancient manuscripts with the prominent Athenian politicians Nikias and Demosthenes.
6 The Aristotelian *Constitution of the Athenians* (28.3) notes that Kleon's dress while addressing the assembly was also demonstratively provocative.

3 Sail and Oar

1 Another flight (in thought): Kerdōn in Herodas' seventh *Mime* (108–9) says a woman's foot is so fetching it could lend him wings to fly up to the gods.
2 By contrast, the storm and shipwreck in Heliodorus' *Aethiopika* (1.22) is abridged and almost formulaic.
3 The idea of lovers being united even in death is found already in Plato, *Symposion* (192e).
4 Herodotus, *Histories* 4.42.

5 The Daily Round

1 In Aristophanes' *Assemblywomen* (718), for example, it is suggested as a revolutionary step that slaves in future will sleep together, instead of women slaves having to dress up 'to snatch love from free men'.
2 Aristophanes knows of more comic indignities inflicted on adulterers caught in flagrante, such as having a radish pushed up their anus, or having their pubic hair forcibly plucked out or singed with hot ash.
3 Russell Meiggs and David Lewis, eds, *A Selection of Greek Historical Inscriptions to the End of the Fifth Century BC* (Oxford, 1969), no. 79.
4 In Demosthenes' speech *Against Meidias* (48) it is said explicitly that the Greeks obtain their slaves 'from barbarian peoples'.
5 *Kanēphoros*, basket-bearer, was a role of honour for Athenian girls in Athena's procession.
6 With a pun on 'bags', presumably: sacks of flour and, by innuendo, the speaker's trousers.
7 Old Comedy made jokes *ad hominem*, here one directed at a public figure who dyed his hair.
8 Probably referring to his cockerel.
9 For another list of household goods passed down through the generations, see Aristophanes, *Thesmophoriazousai* 819–23.
10 For example at Herodotus 9.76.
11 Theophrastus, *Aischrokerdeia* 30.15 seems to refer to the same change from copper to silver coins.

12 This remark might contain a clue to 'solving' the murder mystery in Antiphon's speech *On the Murder of Herodes*. Herodes seems to have been a slave trader, an *andrapodistēs*.
13 This links up with the 'Property of the Hermokopids' listed in the inscription discussed earlier.
14 D. R. Jordan, 'A Survey of Greek *defixiones* Not Included in the Special Corpora', *Greek, Roman and Byzantine Studies*, XXVI/2 (1985), pp. 151–97 (SGD).
15 R. Wünsch, *Defixionum Tabellae Atticae*, Inscriptiones Graecae, vol. III, pt 3 (Berlin, 1897) (DTA).
16 In Demosthenes 21, *Against Meidias* (16), we hear of a goldsmith's shop that was engaged in preparing the golden crowns and costumes for a religious celebration. Meidias broke and entered the shop by night in order to destroy Demosthenes' preparations for the event.
17 John K. Davies, 'Athenian Citizenship: The Descent Group and the Alternatives', *Classical Journal*, LXXIII (1977–8), p. 120.
18 Ion of Chios (fifth century BC) humorously attributed three sets of gnashing teeth to Herakles to serve his voracious appetite: *TRGF* 19 F*30; Pollux 2.95.
19 Both pairs of parents are, in fact, foster-parents.

6 A Better World

1 In the 1933 novel *Lost Horizon* by the English author James Hilton.
2 Tourists in Corfu are shown the place where the encounter, so locals claim, took place: Palaiokastritsa, as good a spot as any.
3 One very important papyrus found early in the excavations of Oxyrhynchus by Grenfell and Hunt preserves long passages of Pindar's *Paians*, which are a type of hymn, for Apollo.
4 Interestingly, Pindar reverses this situation; in this victory ode Achilles is said to have attained paradise on the Isle of the Blessed after his mother Thetis succeeded in persuading Zeus to allow this (ll. 78–9). Plato in the *Symposion* (179, Phaidros' speech) also says Achilles earned a place in the Isles of the Blessed for making the ultimate sacrifice (of dying young to avenge Patroklos).
5 Further relevant sources are *Odyssey* 4.563–9; Hesiod, *Works and Days* 169–73, Plato, *Gorgias* 523A–E.
6 Actually, this was the second play Euripides wrote on the theme; in the first we are told that Phaidra was more the wanton woman acting upon her passion. In the second Euripides seems to have revised his portrayal of her to that of an unhappy woman suffering from an unfortunate – god-given – *erōs*.
7 A statue, or bust, of Aphrodite was clearly a stage prop here.
8 This is text 1, from Hipponion (toe of Italy), in Fritz Graf and Sarah Iles Johnston, *Ritual Texts for the Afterlife*, 2nd edn (London and New York, 2013).

7 Warfare

1 Count by N. S. Gill (2019); see 'Deaths in The Iliad', https://ancthisttangents.wordpress.com, accessed 23 November 2023.

2 Plutarch, *Institutions of Sparta* 34.239b, reports that Archilochus was prosecuted when he arrived once in Sparta for having composed these lines, saying it was better to survive than to hold on to one's shield, cost it what it may.

3 The original saying of Henrik Ibsen seems to have been: 'A thousand words leaves not the same deep impression as does a single deed.'

4 Modern scholars estimate the number as far lower than that given by Herodotus, more in the hundreds of thousands. Xerxes himself gives a rough estimate of five million (Herodotus, *Histories* 7.103.16–18), but that is very likely to be wishful thinking.

5 His story is told by Herodotus earlier, in books five and six.

6 Prose had clearly not learned at that stage of the usefulness of footnotes, or endnotes, for adding information that would otherwise interrupt the flow of the argument!

7 In particular, *Perikeiromenē* (The Shorn Head) and *Misoumenos* (The Hated Man).

8 Dress Code

1 Why it was necessary for Prometheus to steal fire from the gods for humankind is another story, told in Hesiod's other great epic *Theogony* (535ff).

2 The so-called 'Goddess Trilogy' (1974, 1989, 1991) of Marija Gimbutas (UCLA, among others), for example.

3 One of the most misogynist texts of Greek literature is a poem by Semonides (seventh century BC) on the types of women. He depicts Zeus creating these women 'from' various animals such as pigs, dogs, foxes and others, with correspondingly distasteful character traits. However, their bad character is attributed to the *noös*, mind, which Zeus implants in them and has nothing to do with tarty dressing or seductive make-up.

4 W. W. How and J. Wells, *A Commentary on Herodotus*, vol. II (Oxford, 1912), pp. 48–9.

5 Sea silk was an extremely fine fabric made from the long silky filaments (*byssus*) of pen shells (*Pinna nobilis*).

6 The material in this section is, by necessity, more than usually Atheno-centric.

7 In Aristophanes' *Lysistrata* (229) the same image is used.

8 T. S. Eliot in *The Waste Land* (1922) picked up the story of the Theban seer Teiresias who experienced life as a man and as a woman.

9 This was a women's festival of Demeter and her daughter Korē, celebrated in autumn.

10 The so-called 'Shrouded Hippolytos', as distinct from the surviving play *Hippolytos Crown-Bearer*.

11 With a play on satyrs' typical lascivious antics. Tragedians wrote three tragedies and a satyr-play for their entry into the theatre competition called Dionysia.

12 Greek had a word for the apolitical, peace-loving citizens: *hēsychazontes*, lit. 'quietists'.

9 Celebration

1 One possibility is that the *Homeric Hymn to Apollo* was composed by one Kinaithos.

2 Ovid wrote a wonderful fictive letter by Ariadne to Theseus, after he had left her behind on Naxos: *Heroides* (Letters of Heroines), no. 10.

3 This was only violated by the Spartan general Archidamos when he razed the town during the Peloponnesian War in 427 BC.

4 J. E. Powell, *Collectanea Alexandrina* (Oxford, 1925, reprinted 1970), pp. 173–5.

5 Euripides, *Herakles* 682, calls Dionysos *Bromion oinodotān*, wine-giving Bromios.

6 A similar episode of drunken sailors having hallucinations occurs in Longos' *Daphnis and Chloē*, Book 2, no doubt inspired by the *Homeric Hymn*.

7 A famous rhetorician from Sicily who impressed the Athenians in 427 BC with his elaborate style.

8 Note also how his wife is supposed to watch from their rooftop (that is, the roof of the stage building): the phallus-fun is strictly not for her.

9 In this he is like Theophrastus' 'Churl' (*Characters* 15, *Authadeia*), who similarly refuses to take part in religious celebrations or join in hymn-singing.

10 Its authors have traditionally been known as *scriptores erotici*, erotic writers, but erotic only in the sense of focusing on Erōs, the god of love. Nothing (or very little) titillating about them, although the whole thing turns on the consummation of a couple's relationship.

11 Because of his role in the brief war between Mytilene and Mēthymna in Book 2.

12 This is presumably a reflection of the Greek marriage formula, that a girl was given to a man 'for the ploughing of legitimate children'.

Further Reading

Introduction

Cartledge, Paul, *Ancient Greece: A Very Short Introduction* (Oxford, 2011)
Garland, Robert, *The Greek Way of Life: From Conception to Old Age* (London, 1990)
Osborne, Robin, *Greek History: Classical Foundations* (London and New York, 2004)

1 Love

Balme, Maurice, *Menander, The Plays and Fragments. Edited with Translation and Commentary. Introduction by Peter Brown* (Oxford, 2002)
Bassett, Samuel Eliot, and Bruce A. Heiden, *The Poetry of Homer: Greek Studies*, 2nd edn (Lanham, MD, 2003)
Faraone, Christopher A., *Ancient Greek Love Magic* (Cambridge, MA, 1999)
Konstan, David, *In the Orbit of Love: Affection in Ancient Greece and Rome* (Oxford, 2018)
Latacz, Joachim, *Troy and Homer: Towards a Solution of an Old Mystery* (Oxford, 2005)
McClure, Laura K., *Women in Classical Antiquity: From Birth to Death* (Oxford, 2019)
Pomeroy, Sarah B., *Goddesses, Whores, Wives and Slaves: Women in Classical Antiquity* (New York, 1975)
Powell, Barry B., *Homer: Blackwell Introductions to the Classical World* (Malden, MA, 2007)
Zagagi, Netta, *The Comedy of Menander: Convention, Variation and Originality* (London, 1994)

2 Status

Adkins, Arthur W. H., *Merit and Responsibility: A Study in Greek Values* (Oxford, 1960)
Clay, Jenny Strauss, *The Politics of Olympus* (Princeton, NJ, 1989)
Connor, W. Robert, *The New Politicians of Fifth-Century Athens*, 2nd edn (Princeton, NJ, 1992)
Kamen, Deborah, *Status in Classical Athens* (Princeton, NJ, 2013)
Torrance, Isabelle, *Euripides: Understanding Classics* (London and New York, 2019)

3 Sail and Oar

Casson, Lionel, *Ships and Seamanship in the Ancient World* (Princeton, NJ, 1971)

—, *Travel in the Ancient World* (Baltimore, MD, 1974)
Clay, Diskin, *Lucian, 'True History': Introduction, Text, Translation and Commentary* (Oxford and New York, 2021)
Hall, Edith, *Introducing the Ancient Greeks: From Bronze Age Seafarers to Navigators of the Western Mind* (New York and London, 2015)
López-Ruiz, Carolina, *Phoenicians and the Making of the Mediterranean* (Cambridge, MA, 2021)
Whitmarsh, Tim, *Greek Literature and the Roman Empire: The Politics of Imitation* (Oxford, 2001)

4 Signs

Bowden, Hugh, *Classical Athens and the Delphic Oracle: Divination and Democracy* (Cambridge, 2005)
Burkert, Walter, *Greek Religion*, trans. John Raffan (Cambridge, MA, 1987)
Johnston, Sarah Iles, *Ancient Greek Divination* (Oxford, 2008)
Woodard, Roger D., *Divination and Prophecy in the Ancient Greek World* (Cambridge, 2023)

5 The Daily Round

American School of Classical Studies at Athens, *The Athenian Agora Site Guide*, 5th edn (Princeton, NJ, 2010)
Diggle, James, *Theophrastus: Characters*, Cambridge Greek and Latin Classics (Cambridge, 2022)
Dover, Sir Kenneth J., *Greek Homosexuality* (London, 1978)
Eidinow, Esther, *Oracles, Curses, and Risk among the Ancient Greeks* (Oxford, 2007)
Kurke, Leslie, *Coins, Bodies, Games, and Gold: The Politics of Meaning in Archaic Greece* (Princeton, NJ, 1999)
Oakley, John Howard, *A Guide to Scenes of Daily Life on Athenian Vases* (Madison, WI, 2020)
Parsons, Peter J., *The City of the Sharp-Nosed Fish: The Lives of the Greeks in Roman Egypt* (London, 2007)
Robson, James, *Aristophanes: An Introduction* (London, 2009)
Rotroff. Susan I., and Robert D. Lamberton, *Women in the Athenian Agora* (Agora Picture Book), American School of Classical Studies at Athens (Princeton, NJ, 2006)
Seaford, Richard, *Money and the Early Greek Mind: Homer, Philosophy, Tragedy* (Cambridge, 2004)
Sparkes, Brian A., and Lucy Talcott, *Pots and Pans of Classical Athens* (Princeton, NJ, 1977)
Thompson, Dorothy B., *An Ancient Shopping Center: The Athenian Agora* (Princeton, NJ, 1993)

6 A Better World

Garland, Robert, *The Greek Way of Death* (Ithaca, NY, 1985)
Graf, Fritz, and Sarah Iles Johnston, *Ritual Texts for the Afterlife*, 2nd edn (London and New York, 2013)
Sayers, Sean, *Plato's Republic: An Introduction* (Edinburgh, 1999)

Sellars, John, *The Fourfold Remedy: Epicurus and the Art of Happiness* (London, 2022)
Stoneman, Richard, *An Introduction to Pindar* (London and New York, 2014)

7 Warfare

Finley, Moses I., *The Portable Greek Historians* (New York, 1959; 1975)
Lendon, Jon E., *Soldiers and Ghosts: A History of Battle in Classical Antiquity* (Ithaca, NY, 2006)
Van Wees, Hans, *Greek Warfare: Myths and Realities* (London, 2004)
Willekes, Carolyn, *Greek Warriors: Hoplites and Heroes* (Casemate Short History) (Oxford, 2017)

8 Dress Code

Figueira, Thomas, 'Herodotus on the Early Hostilities between Aegina and Athens', *American Journal of Philology*, CVI/1 (1985), pp. 49–74
LaBeaux, David, gives a good demonstration on YouTube of draping a *peplos*, *chitōn*, *himation*. See 'Draping Classical Greek Clothing | Peplos, Chiton, Himation', 29 April 2021, www.youtube.com, accessed 21 November 2023
Lee, Mireille M., *Body, Dress, and Identity in Ancient Greece* (Cambridge, 2018)

9 Celebration

Murray, Oswyn, *Sympotica: A Symposium on the 'Symposion'* (Oxford, 1990)
Parke, H. W., *Festivals of the Athenians* (London, 1977)
Parker, Robert, *Athenian Religion: A History* (Oxford, 1996)
Robertson, Noel, *Festivals and Legends: The Formation of Greek Cities in the Light of Public Ritual* (Toronto, 1992)

Photo Acknowledgements

The author and publishers wish to express their thanks to the sources listed below for illustrative material and/or permission to reproduce it. Some locations of artworks are also given below, in the interest of brevity:

Allard Pierson Museum, Amsterdam: 6, 12, 13, 26 (photo William Furley), 40 (photo William Furley); Antikensammlung, Staatliche Museen zu Berlin (photo Johannes Laurentius, CC BY-SA 4.0): 23; Archaeological Museum of Corfu (photos William Furley): 4, 8, 11, 20, 48; Biblioteca Medicea Laurenziana, Florence: 36; The British Museum, London: 19 (photo Michel wal/Wikimedia Commons, CC BY-SA 3.0), 51 (photo William Furley); Cornell University Library Map Collection, Ithaca, NY: 1; İstanbul Arkeoloji Müzeleri (photo Giovanni Dall'Orto/Wikimedia Commons, public domain): 39; The J. Paul Getty Museum, Los Angeles: 27, 46; Kunsthistorisches Museum, Vienna (photos William Furley): 24, 42, 43, 44, 47; Kunsthistorisches Museum, Vienna (photo Carole Raddato/Flickr, CC BY-SA 2.0): 7; Lugdunum Musée et théâtres romains, Lyon (photo William Furley): 14; The Metropolitan Museum of Art, New York: 3; Musée d'archéologie d'Antibes (photos William Furley): 21, 37; Musei Vaticani, Vatican City: 15, 30; Museo di antichità, Turin (photo William Furley): 31; Museo Arqueológico Nacional, Madrid (photo Marie-Lan Nguyen/Wikimedia Commons, CC BY 2.5): 50; Museo archeologico regionale Paolo Orsi, Syracuse (photo Zde/Wikimedia Commons, CC BY-SA 4.0): 25; Museo Civico Archeologico di Marciana (photo Wolfgang Sauber/Wikimedia Commons, CC BY-SA 3.0): 10; Museo Nazionale etrusco di Villa Giulia, Rome: 33; Museum of London (photos William Furley): 29; National Archaeological Museum of Athens (photo George E. Koronaios/Wikimedia Commons, CC BY-SA 4.0): 32; New Archaeological Museum of Mytilene: 16; The New York Public Library: 35; private collection (photo Heritage Auctions, HA.com): 52; Simon Janashia Museum of Georgia, Tbilisi (photos William Furley): 38; Staatliche Antikensammlungen, Munich: 5 (photo ArchaiOptix/Wikimedia Commons, CC BY-SA 4.0), 28 (photo Carole Raddato/Flickr, CC BY-SA 2.0), 34 (photo Bibi Saint-Pol/Wikimedia Commons, public domain); map Tomisti/Wikimedia Commons, CC BY-SA 4.0: 17; Universitätsbibliothek Heidelberg: 2 (Cod. Pal. graec. 88, fol. 138v), 49 (from A. Genick and Adolf Furtwängler, *Griechische Keramik* (Berlin, 1883)); The Walters Art Museum, Baltimore, MD: 9, 18; Wellcome Collection, London: 41; from Richard Wünsch, *Defixionum tabellae Atticae* (Berlin, 1897): 22.

INDEX

Illustration numbers are indicated by *italics*